China
and the World

Third Edition

China and the World

Chinese Foreign Relations in the Post–Cold War Era

EDITED BY

Samuel S. Kim
COLUMBIA UNIVERSITY

Westview Press
BOULDER • SAN FRANCISCO • OXFORD

Copyright © 1984, 1989, 1994 by Westview Press, Inc.

Published in 1994 in the United States of America by Westview Press, Inc., 5500 Central Avenue, Boulder, Colorado 80301-2877, and in the United Kingdom by Westview Press, 36 Lonsdale Road, Summertown, Oxford OX2 7EW

Library of Congress Cataloging-in-Publication Data
China and the world : Chinese foreign relations in the post–cold war
   era / edited by Samuel S. Kim. — 3rd ed.
     p.   cm.
   Includes bibliographical references and index.
   ISBN 0-8133-1595-6 — ISBN 0-8133-1596-4 (pbk.)
     1. China—Foreign relations—1976–   . I. Kim, Samuel S., 1935–   .
DS779.27.C4873   1994
327.51—dc20   93-39204
                                                                              CIP

Printed and bound in the United States of America

The paper used in this publication meets the requirements
of the American National Standard for Permanence of Paper
for Printed Library Materials Z39.48-1984.

10   9   8   7   6   5   4   3   2   1

Contents

Preface to the Third Edition

The relationship between China and the international system should be reassessed periodically, partly because of its importance and partly because of its changing nature. The student of Chinese foreign policy needs to understand the forces that shape this evolving and complex relationship. Indeed, the phenomenal growth and intensification of Sino-global linkages in the post-Mao era challenge Chinese foreign policy makers as well as Western analysts. Examination of these reciprocal impacts is an essential part of the study of Chinese foreign relations and as such the main concern and focus of this volume. The interplay between China and the world—how external systemic factors shape China's international conduct, on the one hand, and how the China factor shapes international structures and the actions of other states toward China, on the other—is exceedingly complex, the more so because both China and the international system are experiencing profound transformations. The contributors to this volume proceed from the premise that the way in which the outside world responds to China is closely connected to the way in which China itself responds to the outside world, but the extent and nature of this interaction and its domestic and global consequences remain a genuine puzzle. It is this puzzle that the present volume seeks to address, with particular emphasis on the most recent post-Tiananmen and post–Cold War years.

In this third edition, the main issues and organizational outlines of the previous editions have been largely retained. In subjecting this edition to a thorough revision, we have given primacy to making it reflect our most recent thinking on Chinese foreign relations in the post–Cold War era; two new chapters, one on global interdependence and the other on human rights, have therefore been added. Without prematurely privileging any particular theory or methodology, we have asked each contributor, within the framework of a specific assigned topic, to address some of the essential and enduring questions in the study of Chinese foreign policy: How does China relate to the outside world in the post–Cold War era? To what extent, and in what specific ways, has the nexus between China and the world remained constant or changed? What are the reasons for these changes or continuities? What are the implications and prospects for both China and the world at large?

For better or worse, this volume is not designed to cover the entire spectrum of Chinese foreign relations. It has been and remains a set of analytical essays on selected issues in the field—on the problems and progress, the limitations and possibilities, of China's shifting role in an increasingly interdependent and interactive world. Adopting a variety of theoretical and analytical frames of reference and combining a broad theoretical framework with issue-specific or interaction-specific case studies, the contributors assess the relative weight of domestic and external factors reflecting and affecting Beijing's policy goals and behaviors in different contexts, toward different reference groups, and across time. In doing so, they seek to identify the changes and continuities that have characterized Chinese foreign relations over the years and the reasons for the persistence of features that inhibit fundamental learning in Chinese foreign policy behavior—especially the discrepancies between rhetoric and reality, policy pronouncements and policy performance, and intent and outcome.

All the chapters were completed recently enough, I believe, to display a firm grasp of the changes and continuities underlying the foreign policy of the post-Tiananmen years (from early 1989 to early 1993). More than the second edition, this volume has been subject to restructuring to take into account the issues raised by China's increasingly complex encounter with "postinternational" politics in the post–Cold War era. Reference to "China" or to "China's foreign policy" is not meant to connote a single-minded set of decision makers in Beijing, much less a single, coherent, and unified China. Of particular concern to the Beijing government as a multinational state is the emergence of local and regional ethnonational conflicts previously overshadowed and repressed by the global superpower contention. Indeed, there is now broad scholarly consensus that the Chinese party-state is no longer the almighty Leviathan of yore. The term *China* is used throughout the volume merely for analytical and semantic convenience.

This volume is the continuation, not the culmination, of a collaborative effort that was started a decade ago in the hope of remedying the dialogue of the deaf between China specialists and world politics analysts. From the inception of our effort, it was the intention, in keeping with China's enduring *ti-yong* dilemma, to combine looking backward with going forward—and to link theory with practice. It seemed as if the iron cage of Sinocentrism had stymied the theoretical imagination of the field. This book represents a joint venture into the seemingly forbidden territory of interdisciplinary inquiry in the study of Chinese foreign policy. In spite of diverse intellectual backgrounds, methodological inclinations, and theoretical orientations, the contributors are united in the conviction that we can and must study Chinese foreign policy as if international relations really mattered—or, conversely, that we must study international relations as if China really mattered. This volume, the offspring of an invisible college of bridge builders, has, more than most, been the work of many. Throughout the preparation of the first, second, and third editions, I have received invaluable support from Allen S. Whiting, who, along with contributing the final chapter, has always offered wise counsel. For various reasons, a number of scholars in the field could not contribute to the first and second editions, and several contributors to the previous editions could not be persuaded to shift gears in the midst of other projects to do the necessary revisions for this volume. I thank June T. Dreyer, Melvin Gurtov, Harry Harding, James C. Hsiung, Alastair Johnston, Andrew Nathan, Jonathan Pollack, Robert Sutter, Peter Van Ness—and David Bobrow, Steven Chan, Michael Ng-

Quinn, Susan Shirk, Chi Su, Denis Fred Simon (previous-edition contributors regrettably absent here)—for their contributions in the various stages of the project. At the same time, three outstanding scholars in the field—Lowell Dittmer, Thomas W. Robinson, and James D. Seymour—have come aboard as new contributors. Susan McEachern of Westview Press has been, as always, an invaluable collaborator and invisible contributor to the volume. Without her coaxing diplomacy, the book would not have been possible. Special thanks are also due to Alison Auch, Shena Redmond, and Barbara Metzger for their efficient steering of the manuscript through the various stages of the production process. The usual disclaimer still holds: that the editor and contributors alone are responsible for the views and interpretations—and the errors that may persist—in the book.

Samuel S. Kim

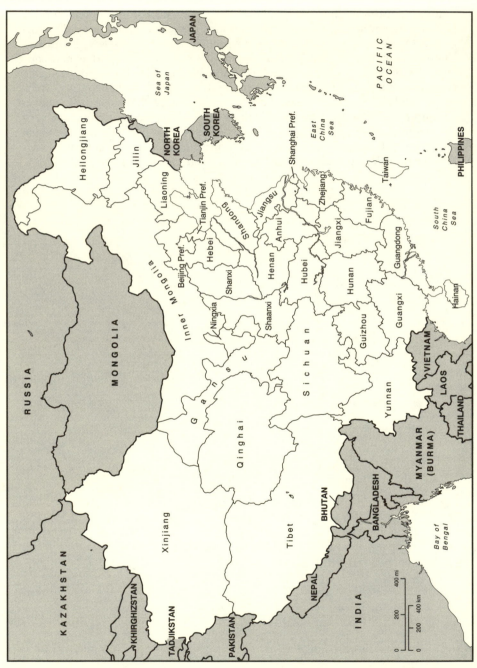

China and Its Neighbors

PART ONE

Theory and Practice

1

China and the World in Theory and Practice

SAMUEL S. KIM

China in a Post–Cold War World

Chinese foreign policy today is complex, variegated, flexible, and refractory, defying any neat characterization or confident prognostication. Even in the long Cold War years, Chinese international comportment often seemed in such a constant state of ambiguity that no full understanding was possible. Ever since the collapse of the traditional Sinocentric world order in the late nineteenth century, this proud and frustrated Asian giant has had enormous difficulty finding a comfortable niche qua nation-state in the modern international system. The People's Republic, for example, has succumbed to wild swings of national identity projection over the years, mutating through a series of varying global roles.

The study of Chinese foreign policy at this critical juncture in world history is all the more complicated by the profound domestic social, economic, and ecological transformation that China is experiencing even as the global system in which it is now anchored undergoes a structural and political metamorphosis as well. At the same time, problems of internal and external legitimacy—underscored by the Tiananmen carnage and the collapse of international communism—are conflated as never before in the history of the People's Republic. It is precisely this intensification of Sino-global linkages that challenges Chinese foreign policy makers as well as outside analysts. For all its cultural uniqueness and political self-sufficiency, post-Mao China has been subject to all the external pressures and dynamics that are characteristic of an increasingly interdependent and interactive world.

What roles does China play in the transition from a bipolar to a multipolar world and in the collective quest for a more peaceful, equitable, democratic, and ecological world order? By dint of what it *is* and what it *does*, China is inescapably part of both the world-order problem and the world-order solution. As one of the Permanent Five, its voice cannot be ignored in the conflict-management process of the UN Security Council. No major military, social, demographic, or environmental conflict, especially in the Asia-Pacific region, can be managed without at least tacit Chinese cooperation. As the world's third-largest nuclear weapons power and one of its top five arms exporters, China must be a party to any meaningful global and regional arms control and disarmament. It has been suggested that if recent growth rates persist China could overtake the United States as the world's largest economy in a decade or two (between 2003 and 2020), with almost incalculable consequences for the political economy of China and the world.[1] Inevitably, the government's treatment of nearly one-fourth of humanity within its porous borders has become a continuing global human-rights issue and one of the many problems taxing Beijing's precious global time and diplomatic resources. There can be little hope of stabilizing world demographic pressure unless the Chinese—and the Indians—improve their family-planning programs and services. Some scholars and policy analysts believe that China has already crossed critical thresholds of environmental sustainability, presaging new conflicts of seriousness unprecedented in recent times.[2]

Yet the interplay between China and the world—how external factors shape Chinese conduct at home and abroad, on the one hand, and how domestic factors shape international structures and the actions of other states toward China, on the other—is complex and even confusing. We may proceed from the premise that the way in which the outside world responds to China is closely keyed to the way in which China responds to the outside world, but the nature of this interaction remains a genuine puzzle.

At no time since the Korean War has Beijing encountered a more daunting challenge in coping with the global political system in turbulent change than it has since 1989. The acceleration of global transformation warns against any premature prognostication about the shape and substance of the new world order or about the complex and evolving relationship between China and the world at large. Already the euphoria engendered by the sundering of the Berlin Wall and the demise of global communism has been overshadowed, if not completely belied, by the emergence of new regional dangers and conflicts. While the dangerous pattern of ideological and military confrontation between the two superpowers has withered away with the disintegration of the socialist one, other, more deeply embedded social, economic, ecological, and ethnonational conflicts have come to the fore.

Paradoxically, Beijing points to what it considers the best external security environment and the deepest peace since the founding of the People's Republic while at the same time increasing its real military spending at double-digit rates in the 1989–1992 period.[3] Given the acceleration of world history and the uncertainties of post-Tiananmen Chinese politics, it is not easy to determine whether these policy pronouncements indicate rising confidence in China's position in a multipolarizing world or are merely whistling in the dark. In some respects China has never been more at peace with its neighbors (especially Russia, Japan, and India) than in 1991–1992, and it has established or normalized official diplomatic relations with Indonesia, Singapore, Saudi Arabia, Israel, India, Vietnam, South Korea, and 15 states newly minted from the ruins of the former Soviet Union (partly out of fear that they would otherwise recognize Taiwan). There is at the same time a sense in which such pro forma diplomatic networking (including 154 countries by the end of 1992) is making a virtue of necessity, bespeaking a deep anxiety about the viability of one sovereign, unified, multinational Chinese state amidst turbulent global politics.

Given the centrality of sovereignty issues in Chinese foreign policy, the greatest of all challenges is to cope with the postinternational phenomenon of perforated sovereignty. The ending of the Cold War has merely highlighted the extent to which state sovereignty has been compromised by technology, demography, the global integration of economic life, and substate fragmentation—ethnonationalist, religious, social, and cultural strife. This is not to suggest the demise of sovereignty and its external corollary, the state system. The collapse of the Soviet Union and Yugoslavia alone gave birth to 20 new "sovereign" states in 1991–1992, increasing UN membership from 159 to 179. What is suggested instead is that sovereignty as a fact and as the dominant organizing principle of world affairs no longer goes unchallenged. The traditional realist view of the state's positive role in "anarchical" international society is being called into question on both empirical and normative grounds by a growing number of international relations scholars. All the contending approaches to world order and competing international relations theories—whether system maintaining, system reforming, or system transforming—take state sovereignty as a point of departure, even if on the basis of different notions of the nature and viability of statism in a changing world.[4] Given the unfolding contest between the centripetal pressure of global integration and the centrifugal pressure of substate fragmentation, exploring sovereignty-bound Chinese international relations in a comparative theoretical framework seems crucial to their study.

The Relevance of Theory

Despite the quantitative explosion of the Chinese international relations literature and the Marxist proclivity to theorize on almost every subject, the Deng era has produced no officially sanctioned Chinese theory of international relations comparable to Mao's now-defunct three-worlds theory. The plethora of publications in international relations in the 1980s obscures the paucity of theoretical work that constrains—or perhaps challenges—the study of Chinese foreign policy.[5] There is growing consensus that post-Tiananmen China in a post-Marxist world desperately needs a new theory of international relations as a guide to preparing for the twenty-first century, but there is little to fill this lacuna.

Chinese international relations scholars have, of course, been under constant pressure to come up with a Marxist theory of international relations with "Chinese characteristics." Even Chinese international legal scholars, specializing in the normative domain of international relations, are constrained by the imperative to pose all inquiry in these terms. At the inaugural meeting of the Chinese Society of International Law held in Beijing in February 1980, for instance, Huan Xiang, president of the society, formulated the challenge in a politically safe and methodologically elusive way: as a progressive development of New China's own theory and system of international law, guided by Marxism-Leninism and Mao Zedong Thought and integrating and justifying China's international practice.[6] As a socialist country under the leadership of the Chinese Communist Party, according to *Dangdai Zhongguo waijiao* [Contemporary Chinese Foreign Relations], an official history of Chinese foreign relations covering the period 1949–1986, China "takes the scientific theories of Marxism, Leninism, and Mao Zedong Thought as a guide to its analysis of the international situation and the formulation of its foreign policies."[7] In short, Chinese international relations scholars are confronted with the task of formulating an integrated theory that meets the multiple requirements of Marxism, Leninism, and Mao Zedong Thought, national identity (Chinese characteristics), and utility and molding them to fit the realities of the changing world situation.

Mao's essay "On Practice" is generally regarded as one of his most theoretical, though not one of his most original, works. Here we find a clear expression of his preference for practical (revolutionary) theory over abstract (academic) theory—a theory of praxis. As in the Western tradition of political philosophy, theory is considered a guide for action, and what is significant or trivial is defined in terms of what will help practice: "From the Marxist viewpoint, theory is important … but *Marxism emphasizes the importance of theory precisely and only because it can guide action.*"[8] Viewed in this light, theory and ideology are not all that different. The easy and safe way to meet this Marxist/Maoist challenge is simply to consider it a synonym for the current "party line." In fact, this is one of the things Chinese "theoretical workers" have done in the wake of the Fourteenth Party Congress of October 1992. The Chinese media treated the new party line (Deng's *theory* of building socialism with Chinese characteristics) as the most significant *theoretical* breakthrough of the congress. Thanks to its systematic expositions and scientific appraisal of Dengist theory, according to Zheng Bijian in a two-part excursive essay in the *People's Daily*, this congress has had a far-reaching impact ideologically and theoretically—to wit, Deng's theory is nothing less than "Marxism in present-day China, in which only this set of theories, and no other, can solve the issue [problem] of the country's future and destiny. Only by clinging to this set of theories, persisting in taking economic construction as the key link, persevering in reform and opening up, adhering to the four cardinal principles, combating the bourgeois liberalization, and guarding against right but mainly [against] 'left' tendencies can we really uphold Marxism." This basic theory "should remain firm for 100 years."[9]

Rhapsodizing about Deng's theory in fact became part and parcel of the revival of a cult of the personality for paramount leader Deng Xiaoping, now referred to as "helmsman of the country" and the formulator of "an original theory" that has enriched and integrated "the universal principles of Marxism-Leninism with the practice of the Chinese Second Revolution—economic construction, reform and opening to the outside world."[10] As the originator of a theory of praxis, Deng is said to have succeeded where Mao had failed: "In short, Deng's theory has answered the fundamental question of how to build a modern socialist country in China, the biggest developing nation in the world. This was the problem to which Mao, the leading founder of the People's Republic, failed to find an answer."[11] And yet, in a remarkably cautious and contradictory way, Zheng Bijian warns that the quest for a theory of praxis as a guide for developing and perfecting a socialist market economy has just begun: "A title has just been chosen for the long article, and the magnificent piece of writing has yet to follow."[12]

The basic theoretical dilemma of post-Mao China has a lot to do with an apparent inability and unwillingness either to embrace or to reject socialism as a unifying ideology. A post-Tiananmen editorial in the *People's Daily* charged that, at an internal party meeting in early 1987, Zhao Ziyang had actually proposed abandoning adherence to socialism on the grounds that nobody knew any longer what socialism or the socialist road really meant and that the new Dengist/party line was that only socialism could save China.[13] In the first major speech delivered at the Fifth Plenum of the Thirteenth Chinese Communist Party Central Committee on November 9, 1989, General Secretary Jiang Zemin put "special emphasis on studying and researching basic theories of Marxism-Leninism and Mao Zedong Thought," at the same time acknowledging that "the Party as a whole has not yet established a proper atmosphere or a perfect system for studying and researching the basic theories of Marxism." Blaming rampant ideological trend "favouring bourgeois liberalization for a period in the recent past" for confusion about many theoretical issues, Jiang issued a new directive: "It should be made clear to comrades that whether they study Marxist theory seriously or not, and whether they raise their Marxist theoretical level or not through study and work, are important indications of the intensity of their Party spirit. This should also be a basic standard for assessing and appointing of [*sic*] leading cadres."[14]

The contents of the new party line emerging from the 1992 Party Congress are remarkably vague even though the outlines of the new theoretical quest have been revised and reformulated: "In the past, we said that only socialism can make China develop. Now, we should say more accurately that China will develop only if it takes the road of building socialism with Chinese characteristics."[15] The old instrumental conception of theory remains constant; Chinese still seek a theory to rationalize and legitimate the basic party line at a given point in time and ultimately to serve as intellectual glue to hold the communist multinational empire together. More recently, Chinese international relations theorists and publicists have been entrusted with the task of repudiating the "China threat theory" (*Zhongguo weixie lun*) that some Western scholars and statesmen are accused of espousing.

It seems that at least one of the major causes of the poverty of Chinese international relations theorizing is conceptual. Although Marxism-Leninism has clearly had a major impact on the shaping and legitimation of a PRC political identity, it has provided no pervasive and long-lasting operational guide for seeking China's proper role in a state-centric world. Marx himself made little contribution to international relations theory; the motor of human progress was class struggle, not interstate conflict. Nor has Marxism—or, for that matter, Western liberalism—ever paid much attention to the question of ethnicity or national identity in international relations. Marxism is therefore a poor fit to a state-centered quest for national identity, for it argues that the state is the instrument of exploitation of man by man and therefore a transitory phenomenon destined to wither away. Lenin, in contrast, updated and rescued Marxism by fusing it with the concept of the nation-state. States replaced classes as the leading protagonists in the revolutionary struggle and world politics. Imperialism as the twilight of advanced Western capitalism now provided the ways and means for national movements to link up in an emerging global united front of the proletarian underdogs against the imperialists. Marxism, as reformulated by Lenin in his *Imperialism: The Highest Stage of Capitalism*, resting on economic determinism, posits that imperialism is the natural expression of contradictions in the capitalist economic system, and imperialist wars are inevitable as long as capitalism persists.[16] Lenin in effect globalized Marxism through a subtle but significant reformulation of a critique of the capitalist world system in which the principal actors were no longer contending classes but competing mercantilistic nation-states driven by the laws of contradiction (e.g., concentration, disproportionality, uneven development, self-destructive irrationality). As thus reformulated by Lenin, Marxism in both theory and practice has become increasingly indistinguishable from the theory of political realism. There is a sense in which Lenin's *Imperialism* can be read as straightforwardly realpolitik in its analysis of state competition for land and resources.[17]

It is hardly surprising, then, that after World War I and the Bolshevik Revolution Lenin had much greater appeal in China than Marx, although the differences between the two were blurred in the Marxism-Leninism that eventually merged with Mao Zedong Thought in the official ideology of the People's Republic. Nor is it surprising that post-Mao China had to abandon the Leninist/Stalinist inevitability-of-war theory as a conceptual and practical liability in its strategy of piggybacking on the capitalist world system to achieve modernity. Yet entirely abandoning the legitimating prop of socialism would be ideological suicide akin to that of the "self-strengthening" reformers of the nineteenth century. Herein lies the logic of China's advocacy of a sovereignty-centered international order. The Westphalian principle of state sovereignty is believed to serve as a kind of legal shield behind which to resolve the enduring *ti-yong* antinomy—the essential pursuit of integration of Chinese learning for national identity with Western learning for state empowerment. Sovereignty is also—the usual assertion to the contrary notwithstanding—a sword with which, in a quite un-Marxist fashion, to carve domestic and foreign policies into two separate and independent domains. The separation of domestic and foreign policies may appear advantageous because it allows external criticism to be labeled interference in internal affairs and therefore illegitimate.

As in the Western realist image of world order, sovereignty in mainstream Chinese international relations scholarship seems to serve as a theory of limits, dismissing any claim for a transculturally valid world order given the putative tenacity of multicultural systems of public order throughout the world.[18] Citing Hedley Bull's work with approval, one prominent Chinese international relations scholar argues that human rights cannot be recognized if to do so would negate state sovereignty and therefore to make human rights the basis of international relations is to reject the essence of the international order.[19] This pronouncement underscores but does not resolve the abiding antinomies between the traditional obsession with autonomy and self-reliance and the normative pressures generated by China's growing dependence on the foreign aid, foreign direct investment, foreign trade, and foreign science and technology needed to fuel the modernization/status drive. In addition, the tyranny of patriotism narrowly defines the outer limits of the possible and the permissible in Chinese international relations theorizing. As a result, scholarship in the field is a pervasive mixture of normative and empirical analysis, with little if any "is-ought" distinction.

Even in the West, theory about any country's foreign policy and international relations is easier to promise than to produce. In a recent thoroughgoing review and analysis of "theoretical" activities in international relations research, Yale Ferguson and Richard Mansbach argue that, despite the "scientific revolution" that has dominated the field for the past several decades, we now face theoretical gridlock. The main reason for this is a fundamental misunderstanding of theory in the social sciences. Every theoretical debate or controversy "is colored by hidden normative and policy preferences, an absence of conceptual clarity, and the repeated intrusion of policymakers' concerns and slogans into intellectual discourse."[20] At the same time, the radical changes in the socialist world in recent years, largely unexplained, let alone predicted, by international relations theories,[21] should serve as a reminder of how primitive the "science" of international relations remains; we should be wary of paradigmatic pretensions.

In the Chinese case, the problem is magnified by the nature of the beast. Theory requires not only conceptual clarity in the observer but also behavioral consistency over time in the actor, and Chinese dialectical steering of the ship of state between the Scylla of dogmatic foreign policy and the Charybdis of unprincipled foreign policy has set a highly unpredictable and variegated course. The chronic gap between principles and policies can be accounted for by China's pronounced tendency to espouse principles beyond its capability and willingness to implement them. The imbalance between principle and power—theory and praxis—is often compensated for by excessive moralizing, as if repeated claims to be taking a "principled stand" would somehow magically produce closer theory/praxis concordance. The greater the rhetoric/reality disjuncture, apparently, the stronger the need to square the circle of deviant behavior.

As a country supersensitive to the rise and fall of the legitimating "Mandate of Heaven," China remains haunted by the decay of its moral regime.[22] The challenge of "remaking" the hard facts of its international behavior validates its professed self-image and leads to a constant reformulation, renumbering, and redramatization of China's basic foreign policy principles (e.g., the Five Principles of Peaceful Coexistence, Mao's three-worlds theory, Hu Yaobang's eight basic principles of foreign policy, Zhao Ziyang's ten basic principles of foreign policy, Deng's four cardinal principles, Deng's theory of building Chinese-style socialism). Such multiprincipled posturing—and multiple role playing—allows China to be all things to all nations on all global issues. At the same time it helps Chinese foreign policy elites to create out of inconsistent and contradictory policies a consonant normative and cognitive self-perception, a convenient and all-enveloping legitimating cocoon.

Under the circumstances, perhaps we should refrain from theoretical pursuits altogether. In practice, however, the term "theory" has been used for a variety of disparate analyses and orientations. In the strict philosophy-of-science sense, theory calls for a logically interrelated set of propositions that specify a causal relationship between one or more antecedent (independent) variables and a consequent (dependent) variable capable of explaining and predicting specified classes of phenomena. International relations can seldom come close to meeting these rigorous criteria, and there is no reason that the study of Chinese foreign policy should be cast in so rigid a framework. There is an alternative, middle-range instrumental conception of theory as a way of bridging the gap between academic theory and practical policy making. Although policy makers may shy away from theorizing, they do in fact make use of various theoretical perspectives.[23] An instrumental theory is judged, of course, in terms of its richness and rigor but, more important, in terms of its usefulness in performing this bridging function. An instrumental theory, then, serves as a conceptual map that helps us make sense of a great mélange of confusing and contradictory information. If practical/instrumental theory provided the official "guiding principle for knowing and changing the world" in Mao's politics of transformation,[24] it should provide the criteria, based on policy relevance, for separating the significant from the trivial and for selecting, categorizing, ordering, simplifying, and integrating the "significant" issues and data in a more orderly, systematic, cumulative study of Chinese foreign policy. The instrumental conception of theory is suggested as one way of escaping the atheoretical Sinocentric cul-de-sac and linking the study of Chinese foreign policy with the parent discipline of international relations.[25] What Jack Snyder has identified as the triple requirements for the advancement of Soviet foreign policy—richness, rigor, and relevance—seem equally compelling for the advancement of the study of Chinese foreign policy.[26] Empirical richness through case studies, theoretical rigor through hypothesis testing, and policy relevance through the selection of significant issues and problems of common concern to all state actors in world politics should be conceptualized as complementary rather than mutually exclusive.

Contending Approaches

Chinese foreign policy seems so multifarious and multiprincipled as to transcend prima facie almost any theoretical framework. Still, it is safe to say that no single theory is accepted as the dominant "paradigm"—in the Kuhnian sense—and has cornered the truth on Chinese foreign policy. Thus, we have no choice but to draw on various contending theoretical models and approaches in comparative foreign policy and international relations to bring order out of enormous complexity and contradiction. Despite the highly convoluted sense of state secrets and the inaccessibility of documentary materials, China has interacted with sufficiently large numbers and types of international actors over a sufficiently long period of time that the usual complaint about the lack of relevant source materials is no longer as compelling as it used to be. The widening engagement in world politics made possible by its open-door policy has created myriad new linkages, new opportunities, and new payoffs and penalties for its international relations, providing a broader empirical basis for testing various theoretical propositions and perspectives.

Although the 1980s witnessed a dramatic increase in Chinese and Western scholarly monographs, there is as yet no widely accepted metatheory that explains the wellsprings of Chinese behavior in any succinct and persuasive fashion. If anything, the June 1989 massacre not only shattered bipartisan consensus in American politics but also greatly sharpened divergent scholarly views on the "whither China" question. There is a need for more integrated and synthetic theoretical approaches to the study of Chinese foreign policy behaviors in various issue areas, toward major international actors, and across time. There is also a need for more imaginative interdisciplinary approaches that will cross-fertilize and invigorate the field with advances made in international relations and other related social science disciplines. There is, in short, a strong case for moving the field toward new issue areas and theoretical approaches that will relate disparate variables in a more comprehensive picture of the dynamics of Chinese international conduct. To be theoretical, as James Rosenau reminds us, is to avoid taking the fundamentals of foreign policy and international relations for granted, on the one hand, and to be tasked with probing how diverse sources of behavior might give rise to diverse outcomes, on the other.[27]

Let us proceed, then, from the premise that what we see and read is not necessarily what we get in Chinese foreign policy. Let us also assume that there is no single magic formula, grand theory, or master road map for the study of Chinese foreign policy. We live in an age of rapid and unpredictable change and disruption in world history. Our normative assumptions, methodological tools, and theoretical approaches therefore require periodic reassessment and restructuring. To establish a measure of richness, rigor, and relevance, we need to identify first of all some key questions: (1) How constant or changeable is Chinese foreign policy over time, and why? (2) How particularistic or general is Chinese foreign policy behavior compared with that of other countries, and why? (3) How wide is the gap between ideals and reality, between policy pronouncements (principles) and policy performance (behavior), and between intent and outcome in Chinese foreign policy, and why? (4) What is the relative weight of domestic (societal) and external (systemic) factors in the shaping of Chinese foreign policy, and with what domestic and international consequences?

In the interest of developing more orderly, cumulative, and contextual knowledge about Chinese foreign policy, this chapter explores the possibilities and limitations of various contending approaches, proceeding from the following assumptions:

- The epistemological principle of "seeking truth from facts" (*qiushi*) serves as a useful point of departure in any theoretical undertaking. Truth is the prime criterion in the sense that a set of linked propositions in any theory must be accepted or rejected solely on the basis of their demonstrated consistency with the evidence of Chinese international behavior in various issue areas and across time.
- The empirical/evidential reality of Chinese foreign policy need not be limited to the category of idiographic inquiry; a more rigorous comparative and contextual approach can be taken without sacrificing empirical richness and policy relevance.
- Given the complex, involved, and multidimensional nature of post-Mao Chinese foreign policy, no single concept, method, or perspective is sufficient to describe and explain Chinese foreign policy as a whole.

Changes Versus Continuities

The legacies of the past shape the international relations of all nation-states. We make our own history not, as Marx once reminded us, just as we please, but only "under circumstances directly encountered, given, and transmitted from the past."[28] But in no country does history seem to be playing as omnipotent and omnipresent a role as in China. A genuine puzzle for many contemporary Sinologists is comparable to that which has both fascinated and frustrated Western Sinologists since the early Jesuits began to write about the Middle Kingdom.[29] What was the glue that held Chinese society together and sustained Chinese civilization for so many centuries? Indeed, no issue of Chinese foreign relations has received as much scholarly attention or generated as much controversy, albeit more among historians than political scientists, than the contemporary impact of the traditional Chinese world view and world order. For years debate on the weight of the past has been divided into two schools of thought: the *exotica sinica* "continuity" school, which stresses the essential uniqueness and inscrutability of historically rooted Chinese behavior ("a single Chinese nebula in the western world's firmament"), and the revolutionary "discontinuity" school, which argues that the lines of continuity with traditional China have been broken.[30] Arguing the need to recognize differences in world view of state actors in international relations, the continuity school asserts that the traditional Chinese world view has not been altered in its fundamentals. The notion of different "worlds," not different powers, is a point of departure in the study of both traditional and contemporary foreign policy. As Mark Mancall writes, "Policy is made and executed by people who define the world and themselves in terms provided to them by the world view within which they lead their daily lives. The intellectual assumptions, emotional predispositions, cognitive maps, and perceptual structures of the foreign policy-makers are all rooted in the prevailing world view of his [*sic*] society."[31] C. P. Fitzgerald agrees: "The Chinese view of the world has not fundamentally changed; it has been adjusted to take account of the modern world, but only so far as to permit China to occupy, still, the central place in the picture."[32]

The continuity school is challenged by many scholars on various grounds. Even among diplomatic historians, who generally stress the weight of the past, there is disagreement between the "great (single) tradition" school and the "multiple traditions" school, ranging from the Middle Kingdom approach to participation in an amoral interstate system characterized by Machiavellian realpolitik.[33] The discontinuities with tradition are far more important than the stylistic similarities. The cosmology on the basis of which Maoist China projected its image of world order is far removed from the cosmology of the traditional tribute system, because the history that influenced Chinese Communist leaders' foreign policy thinking was modern history, the century of national humiliation.[34] The foreign policy tradition of imperial China is, according to recent studies, not as Sinocentric, unvarying, and monolithic as the continuity school of thought has contended.[35]

Reform and opening to the outside world in the 1980s generated a series of debates as Chinese intellectuals began to probe their country's political problems as stemming from elements of China's culture and tradition. While the state was encouraging a revival of scholarship on Confucianism and Sun Zi, many Chinese intellectuals were attracted to a bewildering array of Western concepts and isms ranging from modernism, futurism, and poststructuralism to democracy, neoauthoritarianism, socialist alienation, and convergence theory. It seemed as if post-Mao China had one foot mired in the past while the other foot was trying desperately to leap into the future of the promised land. As was dramatized in the 1988 television documentary *He Shang* (River Elegy), which came close, *faute de mieux*, to being the functional equivalent of a national referendum on the traditional symbol system of Chinese identity and as such generated a great stir among Chinese at every level of society everywhere, there is no longer any popular or intellectual consensus on the proper cultural foundation for nation building and modernization in China.

For the study of contemporary Chinese foreign policy, however, assessing the weight of the past poses a serious methodological problem. Given the vast scale of Chinese history, we must ask *which* period or tradition "the weight of the past" refers to and *how* it affects the various dimensions of Chinese foreign policy. The continuity school skates over this problem by assuming a relatively unbroken causal chain of the Great Tradition in Chinese international relations thinking and conduct. A ubiquitous Chinese aphorism—"Qianshi bu wang, houshi zhi shi" (Past experience, if not forgotten, is a guide for the future)—serves merely to highlight the question "Which past experience?": (1) periods of *neiluan* (internal disorder) and *waihuan* (external calamity) in the long cycles of China's imperial history? (2) periods when China lived at peace with its neighbors, whom it recognized as equal morally and in terms of realpolitik (e.g., the Tang vis-à-vis the Uygurs and Tibetans, whom the Chinese did not then insist belonged to the Chinese Empire)? (3) the tribute system of high Qing? (4) the memories of Western and Japanese imperialism during the century of national humiliation (1839–1945)? (5) the final phase of the civil war (1945–1949)? (6) the alliance and war experiences with Moscow and Washington since 1949? (7) the ten lost years of the Cultural Revolution (1966–1976)? or (8) the most recent reform and opening decade of 1977–1987, during which post-Mao China established an all-time global record by doubling per capita output in the shortest time period in the history of the global political economy?[36] Ernest May and Richard Neustadt, among others, have called our attention to the dangers of international conflict escalation when policy makers resort almost instinctively to the use of a particular historical analogy or a particular war experience to cope with new conflicts in a new setting.[37]

There seems little doubt that the revolutionary experience of the 1921–1949 period—the so-called Yan'an complex—exerted considerable pull in the formulation, experimentation, and application of the Party's basic lines during the Maoist period, especially the translation of the Maoist strategy for revolutionary success into China's Third World policy in the 1960s and the early 1970s (e.g., Lin Biao's 1965 programmatic essay on "people's war" and the power transformation theory implicit in Mao's three-worlds theory). In the context of China's Japan policy, there can be no doubt that it is the historical burden of the half-century from 1894 to 1945, not the more ancient Confucian legacy of teacher-student relations, that weighs heavily upon contemporary Sino-Japanese relations.[38] The historical experience of Western and Japanese imperialism during the century of national humiliation, far from being forgotten, seems to have endowed the Chinese with the nineteenth-century conception of absolute state sovereignty and taught the lesson of the importance of power politics in international relations and its corollary—that China could not be respected without power. The driving force for Beijing's current military expansion has little to do with any sense of an imminent military threat; it merely reflects a "strategic culture" stemming from the century of national humiliation and the drive to become a great power in world politics. Military power, as the most important component of the so-called comprehensive national strength, is viewed as indispensable if China is to regain its status as a leading world power and to defend Chinese sovereignty and integrity against all threats, actual or imagined. The same experiential logic of the Korean War seemed to be on Mao's mind when he said in 1956: "If we are not to be bullied in the present-day world, we cannot do without the [atomic] bomb."[39] As a result of its experience in the global power politics of the 1970s and 1980s, China is also a firm believer in and a skilled practitioner of national security as a function not only of pure muscle power but, more important, of the impression it conveys of having both the capability and the will to play the pivotal role of mediator in the central strategic contest between the two superpowers.

Still, a properly cultural approach to the change/continuity puzzle can open up a potentially promising way of understanding the deep structure, particularly the long-standing *ti-yong* antinomies, of Chinese international relations thinking. The feasibility of resolving the richness/rigor dilemma via the feedback between history and theory need not be prematurely ruled out. More rigorous uses of cultural theory are not unrelated to learning theory, as "culture" is now of increasing interest to international relations theorists and strategic analysts. By rejecting the acultural and ahistorical biases of mainstream structural realism, cultural theory seeks to delineate consistent and persistent historical patterns in the way particular state elites think about the outside world.

Applying a psychocultural approach to the study of both traditional and contemporary Chinese foreign policy, Chih-yu Shih adopts the notion of "face" in describing and explaining Chinese international conduct over the centuries. Face-saving foreign policy behavior not only reflects the national self-image of Chinese statesmen but also serves to maintain the integrity of that self-image in a fast-changing environment. In explaining Chinese international behavior across time and on all issues in these terms, however, there is a risk of forcing it into a predetermined mold wherein even the use of force may be viewed as a way of dramatizing "the sincerity of the Chinese leadership toward the fulfillment of its world view."[40] The psychocultural approach seems to assume an absence of variation in behavior that leaves nothing to be explained. Moreover, as cultural analyses of religion and ideology show, coherent, integrated, and consistent sets of normative assumptions, ideas, and axioms may have only a tenuous linkage to observable behavioral choices.[41]

A synthetic theory of national identity attempts to resolve this problem by examining the interplay between deeply rooted, primordial cultural and ever-changing situational factors. Although it postulates that a national identity, once congealed, may be expected to provide a basis for reasonable expectations concerning state behavior under various contingencies or at least to set the outer limits for such behavior, the theory does not presuppose specific behavioral choices, modalities, or outcomes of the nation-state identity dynamic. This is because national identity projection is situation-specific (Frank Borman, looking at the planet Earth from 240,000 miles away, could confidently and fleetingly project a global human identity). National identity mobilization and enactment are postulated as subject to leadership styles, particularly those of the "founding fathers," as a crucial intervening variable. Given such intervening variables, responses to such situational factors as an identity threat and/or an identity opportunity may be expected to vary from inertial absorption to fundamental transformation of national identity, with a slight shift in policy options and strategies being the most likely response.[42]

In a pioneering work, Alastair I. Johnston takes a past-as-prologue approach to China's "strategic culture" as symbolized and structured in a particular period of Chinese history—the Ming (1368–1644). Acknowledging that cultural norms and behavioral patterns are not the same, Johnston nonetheless takes strategic culture—an integrated system of symbols that serves as a framework for enduring strategic preferences—as a point of departure. Thus, he seeks to establish the historical and cultural baseline for a macrohistorical inquiry into Chinese thinking on war and peace to meet the criterion of relevance in the study of contemporary Chinese foreign policy. This carefully conceived, historically delimited, and well-documented study demonstrates that Chinese strategic culture—contrary to the conventional wisdom of uncritically accepting Sun Zi's famous *Art of War* (e.g., "subduing the enemy without fighting," "disesteem of violence," "defensiveness," "limited war") as its only tradition—shares many assumptions with what in the West is known as the *para bellum* or realpolitik world view. Warfare is viewed as a relatively constant element in international relations, stakes in conflicts with the adversary are viewed in zero-sum terms, and pure violence is considered highly efficacious for dealing with the threats that the enemy is predisposed to make. The Chinese *para bellum* strategic culture has two other elements: an explicit doctrine of "absolute flexibility" (*quan bian*) and an explicit sensitivity to relative material capabilities.[43]

In a massive compilation of internal and external historical wars from the Western Zhou (ca. 1100 B.C.) to the end of the Qing dynasty (1911), scholars at the Chinese Academy of Military Sciences have uncovered a total of 3,790 recorded wars. From the Northern Song dynasty (A.D. 960) to the late Qing they list a total of 1,765, or an average of almost 2 per year. In the Ming era alone there was an average of 1.13 external wars per year through the 270-plus years of the dynasty.[44] China stands out, according to a major cross-national empirical study of foreign policy crisis behaviors, as one of the ten most "crisis-active states" in the international system during the 50-year period 1929–1979, with all but one of its foreign policy crises deriving from the core issue of national security and occurring along the peripheries of what it regards as "sacred home territory," whether or not so recognized by others. In contrast with the Guomindang period of 1929–1949, the overwhelming choice of conflict-coping and crisis management techniques during the post-1949 era was violence.[45] If Chinese analyses of their own concepts of military strategy and operations are any indication, Chinese military planners are deeply wedded to the *para bellum* doctrine that preparing for war is still the only way to keep peace.[46]

Despite the apparent remoteness of the subject, Johnston succeeds to a remarkable extent in meeting Snyder's call for establishing richness, rigor, and relevance as mutually complementary. At the very least, his study provides an alternative interpretation of traditional Chinese strategic culture with which to assess the weight of the past upon contemporary Chinese thinking on war and peace.

Elite Perceptions Versus Foreign Policy Behavior

For analytical convenience, we may conceptualize the Chinese foreign policy system as a pyramid-shaped structure with the most visible and flexible domains at the top and the most invisible and invariant ones at the base. This foreign policy pyramid has four levels: *policies* (most variable), *principles* (most vocal), "*basic line*" (*jiben luxian*, reaffirmed or revised every five years at the Party Congress), and *world view* (*shijie guan*) and *national identity* (most constant). All four levels represent inputs to the foreign policy decision-making process. Outputs (behaviors) too can be divided into interconnected, interacting, sequential phases of implementation and discrete functional behaviors in issue areas and relational behaviors toward other international actors.

The recent books of Gilbert Rozman, Allen S. Whiting, and David Shambaugh are remarkably alike in terms of level of analysis, extensive use of *neibu* (internal) materials and/or field interviews, and cognitive mapping framework.[47] Each applies perception theory to Chinese foreign policy on the assumption that human behavior cannot be understood, let alone judged, without first knowing the actor's self-image and image of the outside world. Rozman starts from the premise that Chinese debates about Soviet socialism as manifest in scholarly writings permit us to penetrate the inner dynamics of the foreign policy decision-making process. His study offers a year-by-year analysis beginning in 1978 of changes in Chinese perceptions of Soviet socialism in the period 1978–1985. It seeks to capture the sociology of Chinese international relations by focusing on the deepest or fourth level of the Chinese foreign policy pyramid, arguing that "we learn from this [debate] literature about the Chinese worldview on sensitive matters critical to domestic and international affairs."[48]

Shambaugh, largely taking Rozman's book as a model, probes beneath the surface of state-to-state relations to capture the changing perceptions of the United States articulated by China's "America Watchers" (numbering between six hundred and seven hundred), whose occupation is interpreting the "beautiful imperialist" for Beijing's elite and attentive public. As does Rozman, Shambaugh moves away from the behavioral toward the perceptual dimensions of China's U.S. policy, methodically delineating internal scholarly debates on American imperialism. Even more self-consciously than Rozman, he seeks to bridge the chasm between Chinese foreign policy and international relations through perception theory. His main conclusion is that "the depth of understanding of the United States among these America Watchers remains very shallow," apparently owing to "the sustenance of the Marxist-Leninist worldview in China and its application to analyzing specific countries such as the United States."[49]

Drawing on field interviews in China and Japan and on Chinese media coverage, Whiting attempts to move beyond official state-to-state relations to capture

Chinese elite and popular perceptions of Japan. Central to his argument is the enduring tension between two contradictory sets of images: one consisting of widely prevailing negative perceptions of Japan as a ruthless historical enemy and predator and the real assumption that a past enemy remains an enemy, the other consisting of positive perceptions of Japan as a developmental model and rising expectations of what Japan as an economic superpower could do for China's modernization. The antinomies between hostile imagery and pragmatic self-interest, never fully or satisfactorily resolved, exacerbated tensions in Sino-Japanese relations between 1982 and 1987. Whiting challenges the realist conventional wisdom that post-Mao Chinese foreign policy is driven by the rational pursuit of national economic and strategic interests. Instead, he persuasively argues that Chinese ignorance, misunderstanding, misperception, and mistrust, widespread among the elite and students and abetted by provocative remarks by Japanese officials, all stand in the way of stable, cooperative Sino-Japanese relations. For the first time, public opinion—or, more accurately, "attentive public opinion," such as that articulated by university students in major Chinese cities—has been factored into the study of Chinese foreign policy. As Whiting demonstrates, attentive public opinion has become an important factor in the shaping of Chinese foreign policy, at least policy toward Japan. To a far greater extent than Rozman and Shambaugh, Whiting links perception and policy in the two countries in a sustained manner.

Perception theory is plagued by the attitude/behavior problem. It is true that human behavior, including state behavior, tends to be patterned on a few core values and dominant perceptions. But it is equally true that a word/deed or perception/policy dichotomy exists in all state behavior—an inevitable corollary of the differential capabilities of human thought and rhetoric (which can easily transcend temporal and spatial bounds) and human behavior (which cannot). More significant, human behavior is often time- and situation-specific. One of the most important findings to emerge from a collaborative project on "learning" in Soviet and American foreign policy is that a change in beliefs and perceptions does not necessarily result in a change of foreign policy; rather, policy change often takes place in the absence of a prior change in beliefs and perceptions when governments pragmatically redefine their self-interest with little or no reassessment of basic beliefs and goals.[50] Perception theory has yet to solve the problem of explaining the disjuncture between internally articulated perceptions (manifest in internal documents) and public policy pronouncements, on the one hand, and the disjuncture between policy pronouncements and policy implementation, on the other. What all of this suggests is that it is generally easier to specify when policies changed than it is to establish a direct causal relationship between changes in beliefs and changes in policy behavior.

Chinese foreign policy may be viewed as an aggregate of purposeful external actions and activities designed to affect the international situation or the behavior of other international actors in the pursuit of certain values, interests, or goals. The behavior-centered approach is a way of minimizing the vagueness and mystique of "state behavior" by focusing on discrete, observable, empirical units—the foreign policy actions of political leaders in various contexts and issue areas. This approach is suited to deal with three key puzzles. The first puzzle, continuity versus change, can be addressed by comparative/diachronic analysis. Human behavior has both spatial and temporal dimensions amenable to comparisons across time. A diachronic analysis should ask: What discrete, manifest behavior at what level or in what domain has changed over what time interval, at what rate, with what outcomes or consequences? Foreign policy continuity (or stability) can be assessed by the consistency with which behavior toward a particular actor, issue, or problem recurs with the same mix of instruments over a given period of time. To the extent that policy behavior demonstrates a consistent pattern across historical periods, there is a sound basis for inferring a stable determinant for it. Specifically, we may compare and focus on (1) the general Chinese foreign policy line, (2) specific issue-oriented or functional Chinese foreign policy behavior, and (3) Chinese behavior oriented toward international actors. Such comparisons over time may reveal the extent to which the basic line has been maintained, revised, or transformed, and the degree of constancy can be confidently inferred from repeated behaviors. By analyzing recurring patterns of policy behavior over time and across issue areas, this approach transcends the artificial division of domestic and external, systemic and nonsystemic factors. In sum, the behavior-centered approach seeks to minimize the common methodological problem of taking Chinese foreign policy rhetoric too seriously as evidence of how policy makers actually believe or think.

The concept of "learning" can be applied in the study of Chinese foreign policy, as it has so imaginatively and fruitfully been employed in Breslauer and Tetlock's study of Soviet and American foreign policy, to address the enduring change/continuity puzzle:[51] Are Chinese foreign policy makers capable of learning about the complex and rapidly changing global situation they must deal with? To what extent and in what ways do they recognize and adapt to multiple transnational forces for change in preparing themselves for the twenty-first century? Is policy not the source of its own change in a process of learning? Although the notion of learning in foreign policy is vague and subject to multiple interpretations, it does open up promising avenues for exploring the change/continuity puzzle as well as for examining the relationship between changes in perceptions, beliefs, and values and changes in policy behavior. If learning is defined too broadly, subsuming any governmental attempt to cope with the changing domestic and external situation, or if any change is accepted and explained as evidence of learning, the concept loses its explanatory power. To deal with this problem of overdetermination, some scholars insist on a distinction between "adaptation" and "learning," the former referring to tactical adjustments in a mechanistic or cybernetic fashion and the latter to fundamental change in the basic values and objectives undergirding foreign policy behavior.[52]

Despite its ambiguity, the concept of national identity presents both the challenge and the opportunity to construct general propositions about changes and continuities in China's enactment of its national essence. At the very least, national identity is an important factor in explaining otherwise inexplicable twists and turns in Chinese international comportment. As a bridging concept, identity suggests a cross-cultural comparative framework through which Sinological richness can be combined with social science theoretical rigor by linking the symbolic and behavioral dynamics of a nation-state in its interaction with the world at large. In short, national identity can be conceptualized as a critical link for integrating the study of relevant aspects of political culture, role theory, realpolitik and idealpolitik perspectives on national interest and purpose, and long-term continuities amid historical flux.[53]

In addressing the second puzzle—the uniqueness/generality of China's foreign policy behavior—the Comparative Research on the Events of Nations (CREON) project, based on foreign policy events in thirty-eight nations for thirty months over a ten-year period (1959–1968), has produced a comprehensive body of cross-national data analyzed in terms of substantive problem areas, target scope of action, goal properties, instruments, commitment, specificity, independence/interdependence of action, acceptance/rejection, and effect (cooperation/conflict).[54] A major cross-national empirical study of foreign policy crisis behavior during the fifty-year period 1929–1979 by Michael Brecher, Jonathan Wilkenfeld, and Sheila Moser also goes a long way toward addressing this puzzle.[55] A major collaborative project on patterns of cooperative behavior in the foreign relations of modern China challenges some of our most familiar ways of thinking about China's foreign policy in terms of its *conflict behavior in bilateral contexts*.[56] International crises were seen during the Maoist period as intensifications of existing contradictions rather than deviations from the norm of international life.[57] To what extent and in what ways such Maoist dialectics have been retained or repudiated in the post-Mao era remains to be more fully explored.

The third puzzle—word/deed disjuncture—can be approached by drawing a conceptual distinction between the ideals, principles, and orientations expressed in policy pronouncements and policy implementation. As if to accentuate the word/deed disparity of their adversaries, the Chinese habitually assert that deeds are the critical test of Soviet conduct—and, more recently, U.S. conduct—while insisting that they themselves always mean what they say and are resolute and unyielding on their major principles. At the level of policy pronouncements, China's projected self-image of domestic policy is in sharp contrast to that of foreign policy. The post hoc verdicts of recent Party Congresses, especially the Twelfth and Fourteenth, suggest that at times not even *past* Chinese domestic policies, often characterized by turmoil and discontinuity, can be authoritatively interpreted. At the same time, the projected self-image of Chinese foreign policy is one of unvarying constancy marked by the habitual use of "always" (for the Five Principles of Peaceful Coexistence, independence, world peace) and "never" (hegemonic ambition or behavior). Can this be accepted as the continuing influence of the past, proper behavior rather than power remaining the bedrock of Chinese civilization? Analysis of the word/deed dichotomy also needs to focus on the role of words and their effect on behavior.

Of course, these pronouncements should not be accepted at face value. The real task here is to compare the extent of incongruity between professed values and actual conduct in different issue areas, toward various actors, and over time.[58] Like any other dimension, the word/deed dichotomy needs to be assessed in comparative and contextual terms. In international relations as in law, what really matters for statesmen, if not for scholars, is the behavior of other state actors, not the underlying elite perceptions and motivations. Foreign policy makers seldom have the time or even the inclination to probe the attitudes and motivations that might have produced such behavior. Herein lies another comparative advantage of the behavior-centered approach in meeting the policy relevance test.

Studies of Chinese conflict behavior over the years have revealed a relatively coherent strategy for conflict management. To a significant extent, this behavior manifested a purposeful orchestration of maneuvers characterized by five distinct and sequential phases: probing, warning, demonstrating, attacking, and deescalating. It is therefore said to have reflected the "coercive diplomacy" model of limited and controlled use of force in the pursuit of specific political objectives in a given situation. When China has gone to war, it has done so in response to perceived threats to its national security.[59] Gerald Segal disputes this thesis, arguing that Chinese behavior during foreign policy crises is anything but consistent. Every instance of crisis management is highly context-specific and context-dependent: "The notion that crises inevitably pass through a common and in this case an especially Chinese method of crisis management is patently untrue."[60]

As for cooperative behavior, over the years China has formed cooperative relationships with stronger states as well as weaker ones. Yet many of these cooperative relationships have been troubled, and many of them (e.g., with the Soviet Union, India, Albania, Vietnam, and the United States) have degenerated into open conflict. Paradoxical as it may seem, many of China's most intense international conflicts have been the product of the degeneration of what had once seemed to be close cooperative relations.[61]

In the course of its international life, China has participated in various bilateral and multilateral conflict management processes. The picture that emerges from various studies is that it has proved a difficult partner in these diplomatic and commercial situations.[62] Closely connected to the dialectics of Chinese conflict/cooperative behavior is a deductive approach in diplomatic and commercial negotiations; Chinese officials constantly try to evaluate the wider implications of the issues in question and prod the other party to agree on the "basic principles" underpinning their position while showing willingness to yield ground on concrete details. "Seeking common ground while preserving differences" (*qiutong cunyi*) is advocated as the code of conduct for multilateral negotiations that other states should emulate.[63] This deductive approach has enabled Beijing to insinuate its own ground rules of "agreed common principles" as a way of improving its bargaining position. These principles are later unilaterally interpreted and constantly invoked as ways of testing the counterpart government's "sincerity" and commitment to a friendly relationship with China. In multilateral diplomacy China has shown a pronounced discrepancy between symbolic activism in the public espousal of general principles, especially the Five Principles of Peaceful Coexistence and the UN Charter, and passivity bordering on indifference in the translation of general declaratory principles into norm-specific multilateral conventions.

The behavior-centered approach is not a theoretical cure-all—no single approach is. It has several weaknesses. First, covert foreign policy activities tend to slip through the conceptual and empirical net. It seems safe to assume, however, that China's covert activities constitute a relatively small (albeit not insignificant) portion of the total repertory of external activities. Because of the global communication and transparency revolutions, Chinese foreign policy behavior is far more visible today. More serious is the inability of the behavior-centered approach to *explain* foreign policy actions and their absence; it is best suited to generating empirical findings as a first step toward theory construction. Beyond this is the problem of aggregating individual behavior to the level of the policy-making unit as a whole. Nor is the approach generally applicable to the cognitive mapping of the belief systems of individual political leaders and their impact on the decision-making process;[64] it can only infer decision makers' belief systems from their behavior. That behavior-centered analyses can only provide inferences about belief systems is good reason for linking the two in any empirical analysis. Finally, the behavior-centered approach is plagued by interactions between the status and image of the actor and the values and perspective of the analyst.[65]

Domestic Versus External Sources

Exploring the causal relationships of independent variables located in the policy input phase with the dependent variables made manifest in the policy implementation phase clarifies the linked processes that produce foreign policy behavior. A 1980 critique of the literature identified seven explanatory approaches to Chinese foreign policy: historical legacy, Mao's domination, factional politics, national interest, ideology, capability, and multicausal analysis.[66] All of the possible explanations embodied in these approaches can be reclassified into three broad categories: domestic/societal, external/systemic, and domestic/external.

Domestic/Societal Factors

The search for domestic factors to explain foreign policy action or change assumes that such policy is an extension of domestic politics. "The foreign policy is," as Foreign Minister Qian Qichen announced in 1990, "the extension of China's domestic policies."[67] Even a cursory review of the literature suggests that the overwhelming majority of Chinese foreign policy specialists focus on a variety of domestic factors in the search for an explanatory model. Not surprisingly, there was also growing consensus in the related field of Soviet foreign policy not only that "domestic sources" had become more important but also that linkages between domestic and foreign policy issues had intensified in the post-Stalin era.[68] A 1982 cross-national study of the foreign policy "restructuring" of Bhutan, Tanzania, Canada, Burma, China, and Chile concluded that domestic factors, defined in terms of the perceptions, values, preferences, and objectives of key decision makers, have assumed critical importance in all cases except Canada.[69]

Of the domestic factors, the historical/cultural approach, as already discussed, is generally resistant to causal linkage with contemporary foreign policy behavior. Although its proponents insist that there is no better way to comprehend and explain the present-day international conduct of the People's Republic than by reference to the tradition of imperial China, this approach, with a few exceptions, suffers from undifferentiation and overdetermination. The various historical and strategic traditions of the pre-1949 period do not all point in the same direction. Moreover, this approach, more a theory of continuity than of change, tends to ignore one crucial determinant of foreign policy development: experiential and learning effects. It is better suited to delineating certain recurring ideas and values that seemed made to order for Chinese leaders interpreting the outside world and even delimiting the range of legitimate foreign policy goals than to establishing a one-to-one linkage between the legacy of the past and any specific foreign policy behavior.

Closely related to the historical/cultural approach is the so-called second-image explanation that a state's war-prone behavior depends more on its particular type of national government or social system than on the nature of the global system. Proceeding from sharply divergent premises, Kant, Wilson, and Lenin have all situated the cause of war and the condition for peace in the nature of the social and political system of the state. Recently, the Kantian second-image theory that liberal democracies simply do not fight against each other has gained wide, if not paradigmatic, acceptance in international relations scholarship. As Levy writes with exaggeration, "This absence of war between democratic states comes as close as anything we have to an empirical law in international relations."[70]

In the post-Mao era, the Leninist/Stalinist theory of imperialism and the inevitability theory of war had to be jettisoned as normative and practical obstacles to China's integration into the capitalist world system. How else could China cope with Lenin's belief that the slicing of the Chinese melon would be the final drama of imperialism as the highest stage of capitalism? Despite all the conceptual and policy changes and shifts in international conduct over the years, the PRC remains a repressive, autocratic state that has resorted to the use of military force more often than any other regional or middle-ranking power in the world—validation, perhaps, of the Kantian peace-loving-democracies theory. Yet there is at best only minimal evidence that Chinese leaders have used military force to promote their domestic political agenda abroad or that the outcome of factional strife has been the key determinant in China's decisions to go to war. The broader point is that China has yet to resort to military force purely on behalf of the communist revolutionary cause or to apply the doctrine of "people's war" in any of its armed conflicts, from the Korean War to the most recent gunboat diplomacy in the disputed Spratly Islands.

An important part of the literature links domestic politics with Chinese superpower policy, arguing that the outcomes of intraelite factional strife shape China's choices in the strategic triangle. Early studies by Melvin Gurtov and Harry Harding, Uri Ra'anan, and Donald Zagoria all focused on intraelite conflict over the appropriate response to escalating American involvement in the Vietnam War and the ensuing purge of Marshal Luo Ruiqing. While differing over the degree of Sino-Soviet unity and the extent of China's support for Vietnam in the 1960s, these scholars all seemed to agree on the primacy of domestic politics in shaping China's foreign policy response.[71] Kuang-Sheng Liao has demonstrated through multivariate analysis a close relationship between internal crisis and external hostility, especially at a time of authority crisis such as that in 1967–1969.[72] However, the principal findings of Andres Onate's empirical study of Chinese conflict behavior during the period 1950–1970 do not jibe with Liao's; although there is a moderate relationship between domestic strife and external conflict behavior, the causal relationship is from the latter to the former.[73]

The limitations of the factional model derive primarily from the methodological challenge of identifying the membership of specific factions and assessing the shifting and indeterminate factional roles in policy making. Given the paucity of relevant *neibu* materials on the internal debate over national security issues and choices, most work utilizing this approach tends to be based upon allegorical articles framed in obscure Aesopian language rather than on any reliable direct evidence. Thus, different conclusions about the putative relationship between policies and factions can be reached by different analysts depending on which individuals are assigned to which faction and what policy or power purposes are imputed to each faction. By stressing the pursuit of power and privilege as the motive force in national security decision making, this factional approach greatly underestimates the filtering effect of Chinese nationalism. Taking issue with most studies of great-power behavior for focusing exclusively on the two superpowers and overlooking China's role in world politics, Joshua Goldstein and John Freeman conducted a cross-national comparative study of U.S.-Soviet-Chinese relations with results that contradict the notion that great-power behavior is purely self-driven by bureaucratic routine and related internal factors. This rigorous study demonstrates that the behaviors of the three powers are driven by a relatively stable mix of internal bureaucratic and external reciprocity factors consistent with the notion of a strategic triangle. It shows that in its engagement in the world of great-power politics—a world that comes close to approximating the premises of realist theory—China has indeed enjoyed reciprocity.[74]

The "Mao-in-command" model—that between 1949 and 1976 all important ideological developments, policy shifts, redefinitions of the international system, and the basic line were authorized, if not personally dictated, by Mao —has been suggested as a more appropriate "domestic" explanation for the redefinition and restructuring of China's foreign policy.[75] Research has yet to unearth any new evidence to repudiate this thesis. To the contrary, A. Doak Barnett discovered in his field interviews in Beijing in 1984—including one with then-premier Zhao Ziyang—that "some Chinese who were involved in or close to the process at that time now say that Mao was totally dominant and made almost all of the 'big decisions.'"[76] Robert Ross argues that the unique authority exercised by paramount leaders in Chinese politics, both Mao and Deng, in foreign policy decision making has made factional strife and debates among their lieutenants marginal and tangential. It is in the absence of such a paramount leader, for example, at the height of a succession crisis, that foreign policy can be held hostage to intraelite factional strife.[77] As David Bachman argues,[78] China's next-generation leaders will not be able to dominate the political system and foreign policy decision making as Mao did and, to a lesser extent, Deng has done. Lacking the most crucial power resources, authority and legitimacy, the new leadership will not be in a position to manage the tension between nationalism and internationalism or to make the necessary compromises on issues of state sovereignty relating to Hong Kong, Taiwan, and Tibet and the remaining irredentist claims to territory held by neighboring countries. Given another round of succession crisis in the current passage into a post-Deng era, both the leadership structure and foreign policy making will remain vulnerable to the logic of shifting factional coalitions in domestic politics.

With the growing globalization of the Chinese political economy, the devolution of power at home, and the fragmentation of authority and decision-making structures at the apex during the post-Mao era, the Mao-in-command or paramount-leadership approach becomes increasingly problematic. The existence of multiple power centers within the Chinese government places the Ministry of Foreign Affairs in the uncomfortable position of making international pledges and commitments that it has no power or authority to implement at home.[79] As a consequence of the Tiananmen tragedy, the People's Liberation Army (PLA) has emerged to play a pivotal role in the implementation of domestic and external policies. Although recent developments do not necessarily invalidate the domestic-factors approach, they do tend to weaken the paramount-leadership model.

There is also disagreement on the impact of domestic politics on the shaping of China's international economic policy. In contrast to the limited evidence available for documenting intraelite conflict over China's security policy, in the course of the 1975–1976 campaign against Vice Premier Deng Xiaoping the Chinese media revealed a number of divisive issues including the role of foreign trade, the meaning of self-reliance, and proper developmental strategy.[80] As China's integration in the global economy has expanded and deepened in the 1980s, scholars have begun to explore domestic/societal sources of China's foreign economic policy.[81]

To the extent that the paramount-leader thesis holds, it can be argued that the primacy of domestic factors (ideology, factional coalitions, elite beliefs and perceptions, revolutionary experience) in the shaping of Chinese foreign policy was largely coterminous with the Mao era. There is broad consensus in the literature that during much of the Maoist period three factors—ideology, national interest, and tradition and experience—were always at work. Of the three factors, however, the ideological factor can be said to have played the dominant role.

The paramount-leader thesis seems to have suffered substantial slippage in the post-Mao era. A growing body of empirical and theoretical literature in comparative foreign policy and international relations in recent years has shown that foreign policy leaders generally engage in "satisficing" behavior rather than "rational" behavior. Lieberthal and Oksenberg's recent study of domestic policy-making structures and processes combines "rationality" (policy) and factional "power" models in examining the bureaucratic structure in which the policy process and elite struggles over power and principle are embedded. What their study reveals is a fragmented bureaucratic structure of authority and a decision-making process that is protracted, disjointed, and incremental.[82] Although not focused on foreign policy decision structure and process and hence without clear-cut implications for the foreign policy decision-making process, this study nonetheless surpasses Barnett's slim book in scope, conceptualization, and execution[83] Moreover, it challenges the rationality model implicit in Barnett's study in that its fragmented-bureaucratic model comes close to the "garbage can model," in which policy outputs (final decisions) depend more on chance conjunctions of factions, interests, issues, and events than on causal logic.[84] As Zhao Quansheng argues, foreign policy making in post-Mao China has already shifted from vertical toward horizontal authoritarianism, as key decisions are made from several discrete power bases coordinated at the center but with multiple command channels reflecting different interests and policies.[85]

External/Systemic Factors

Until recently, the comparative foreign policy literature has been primarily concerned with the linkages between domestic/societal sources and resultant external behavior. As we have seen, this bias is even more pronounced in the study of Chinese foreign policy. If the breakdown of consensus politics in the United States and China's self-imposed isolationism provided a rationale for the domestic/societal approach in the 1960s,[86] the globalization of economic life and the perforated sovereignty of the 1970s and 1980s have highlighted the importance of external/systemic factors. Against this backdrop, various contending macrostructural systemic approaches have emerged as alternative models for explaining what shapes state behavior in international relations. In search of the "lost paradigm," scholars in comparative foreign policy have begun to incorporate a world-system perspective, moving in the direction of "a more judicious balance between quantitative and qualitative, historical and current, case-study, comparative, and statistical research designs."[87]

Practically all systemic/structural approaches proceed from the premise that the external behavior of states is shaped in varying degrees by external/systemic factors. No state is an island; every state is part of a larger world environment that provides opportunities as well as constraints on its behavior. The system itself defines the role, position, status ranking, and norms of its interacting units (states). The behaviors of states similarly situated with regard to the international system are similar and thus predictable.[88] To paraphrase Rousseau: The state is born independent and equal but everywhere is in systemic chains. The systemic approach is a theory of environmental determinism.

Two leading system theorists of sharply divergent normative orientations see the linkage between systemic variables and foreign policy behavior differently. The "world-system" approach, a variant of dependency theory, as exemplified in Immanuel Wallerstein's macrostructural and macrohistorical investigation of the emergence of world capitalism, views the international system as essentially based upon a global division of labor in which an exchange of unequal values takes place among core, peripheral, and semiperipheral areas. Even the "so-called socialist states," argues Wallerstein, "are in fact socialist movements in power in states that are still part of a single capitalist world-economy."[89] That is, the one and only capitalist world system makes it impossible to develop socialism through self-reliance.

For Kenneth Waltz, a system theorist of the more traditional realpolitik variety and a prominent proponent of bipolarity as a system stabilizer, the international system is composed of a structure and interacting parts. The structure of this system acts as a "constraining and disposing force," producing systemwide similarity in foreign policy behavior or what he calls "process and performance." State behavior is believed to be constrained, almost predetermined, by the structure of the international system (i.e., the international distribution of state power) and the given state's place in that structure. As a result, the behavior of states as interacting units and the outcomes of their behavior become both explainable and predictable.[90] In both cases, however, the impact of systemic variables is conceptualized in deterministic rather than probabilistic terms. Waltzian theory is a static theory of structural determinism, Wallersteinian theory a neo-Marxist macrohistorical one.

Modified structural realism, or "neorealism," as articulated with clarity by Stephen Krasner, accepts the basic assumptions of realism about states as the dominant international actors in world politics and the primacy of national interest defined in terms of national capabilities but argues that this conception does not give adequate attention to the independent importance of international regimes in affecting state behavior. Special emphasis is placed on politics rather than on economics for the demands for international restructuring. Thus, the Third World's call for a New International Economic Order (NIEO) is not part of a strategy to increase economic well-being but a strategy for changing the rules of the game in various international regimes in order to make nationalistic values and interests more secure.[91] A variant on neorealist theory explains why cooperation is still possible in an "anarchical" international society. Specifically, although the creation of an international regime reflects a given international power distribution, the maintenance of such a regime reflects other factors and can influence international behavior in ways contrary to what we would expect from realist theory. For instance, despite the decline of U.S. power—which under realist theory would indicate the decline of U.S.-sponsored regimes—the international trade and monetary regimes have continued to function in somewhat modified form. The dominant industrial states have cooperated to maintain these regimes because they reduce transaction costs and facilitate mutually beneficial behavior under anarchy.[92]

Structural approaches share in varying degrees with cultural theory the shortcomings of lack of differentiation and overdetermination in stressing the continuity of a single pattern of world politics. System continuity remains the underlying normative and methodological assumption of structural approaches. Their inability to explain recent systemic changes and differentiated behaviors of similarly situated Third World countries or even East Asian and Latin American newly industrializing countries (NICs) operating within the same international system stands out as their major weakness.[93] Even in times of stability, the international system only provides the context within which a member state may act; how each state responds depends on a host of other factors, such as its own definition of the international situation (which may not correspond with reality), its perceptions of national interests (which seem to change more rapidly than the configuration of power), and its political system and national role conceptions.

In the study of Chinese foreign policy, the question needs to be reformulated: What kinds of external/systemic factors *condition* (rather than *determine*) Chinese foreign policy behavior? International values and norms within the existing international structure can be singled out as the principal systemic factors, on the assumption that human behavior, including the behavior of the state, is conditioned by the values, norms, and structure of a given society and those of the larger international milieu. At the level of individual state behavior, whether or not international rules are at work raises the question whether evidence of normative restraint is tactical adaptation or real "learning." One needs evidence that a state clearly eschews behavior that would have been consistent with its interests defined as power.[94]

International values provide standards of desirable and preferable state behavior. But how and where do we find empirical evidence of values in a multicultural international society? A careful, systematic analysis of the policy pronouncements and policy performance of state actors in various global international intergovernmental organizations (IGOs) provides preliminary clues. International norms are specific prescriptive or proscriptive rules of state behavior appropriate to a particular role or situation, elaborated or codified in accordance with the value system of the global society. They vary greatly in scope and degree of precision or effectiveness. International norms may appear in the form of written bilateral and multilateral treaties and conventions, unwritten international customs and usage, hortatory resolutions and declarations of international organizations and conferences, and even unilateral self-restraint. A number of studies have addressed the influence of international values and norms upon the conduct of Chinese foreign policy during the Maoist era.[95] Yet China's "great legal leap outward" since 1979 has occurred in tandem with a rapid acceptance of international law that became part of China's effort to catch up with the rest of the world and to seek a stable and predictable external environment. With China's growing participation in a multitude of multilateral conventions and regimes, international law seems to be playing an important role in the input, output, and feedback processes of the Chinese foreign policy system.[96] We may take Chinese behavior in international institutions as a point of departure for this type of empirical and normative analysis.[97]

International structure reflects the composition and stratification of the interacting units. The nature and scope of interaction—a function of the number and type of actors participating in the social process—suggest an empirical image of international structure. The distribution of certain rights and responsibilities conveys a normative image of international structure. International structure defines the role, position, and status of each interacting member. Small states, given their size and dependency, are especially vulnerable to external/systemic pressures. Yet the restructuring power of the international system is such that China too lies within reach of systemic penetration.[98]

The core assumption of realist and neorealist theory is that states as the dominant international actors are functionally undifferentiated units in their unrelenting struggle for power. The problem with this realist line of inquiry lies in the elusive and multifaceted nature of power in contemporary international relations. First, focusing on traditional power resources ignores the rapidly shifting context of the changing world order. A situation-specific contextual analysis of power would suggest the existence of multiple power centers representing a wide variety of material and nonmaterial resources and keyed to an increasing number of new global problem areas.[99] Second, the statecentric treatment of power greatly exaggerates not only the fungibility of traditional power resources, especially military resources as the ultimate power base, but also "state power" in world politics. Different conceptions of power and legitimacy and different types of actors have emerged on a global scale in response to the multiple challenges of the nuclear-ecological age. And third, today more than ever before, military power ("violence power") is not as useful and fungible as it used to be. The life expectancy of a political regime sustained by pure violence is getting shorter every day. "Soft," nonmilitary "competence power" and "normative power" (e.g., trading power, patent power, knowledge power, ideological power) are becoming increasingly important. Indeed, the very notion of "power" or "great power" is subject to continuing reassessment.

With some risk of oversimplification, one can identify two basic kinds of power in contemporary international relations: *material power* and *normative power*. Material power is conventional national capability based on measurable economic, military, demographic, and technological factors; normative power is the ability to define, control, and transform the agenda of world politics and to legitimate a new dominant social paradigm. Demonstrated competence in the conduct of bilateral and multilateral diplomacy is an integral part of normative power.

This dual conception of power reveals a paradox in Chinese foreign policy. In both traditional and Maoist China the realist notion of equating "national interest" and "national power" was problematic not only because different Chinese leaders have often had different conceptions of national interest depending upon the given circumstances but also because Confucian thought holds that seeking power is a sign of moral decay.[100] This may well explain China's compulsive assaults on power politics.

In practice Beijing over the years has used a mix of force and diplomacy, negative and positive sanctions, in the service of its foreign policy objectives. The challenge has been to select the proper mix of instruments to balance the competing claims of Marxist ideology and Sinocentric concern for independence and great-power status. During much of the Maoist era, when the notion of normative power was still in its infancy in world politics, China made a virtue out of weakness by defining "national power" as material and normative power combined.[101] Mao repeatedly stressed justice (normative power) as a critical component of national and international power.[102] In the post-Mao era, however, as the notion of normative power has become an integral part of global idealpolitik, the Chinese concept of power has shifted significantly from normative to material.[103] Reacting to the debate on American decline and "imperial overextension" in 1988, the goal of nations is said to be a multidimensional but still largely military/materialist comprehensive national strength (*zonghe guoli*).[104] There is no escape from the all-out Darwinian struggle for comprehensive national strength if China is ever to recapture its proper place—"global citizenship" (*qiuji*)—in a multipolar world. It has to be competitive with more powerful military/industrial powers if it is to beat them at their own game. There is a strong proclivity to rely on the high priests of science and technology to facilitate China's attainment of great-power status. Against this backdrop, the concept of global interdependence seems to have replaced the Leninist/Stalinist theory of imperialism and the inevitability theory of war as the only theoretical justification for Beijing's growing dependence upon the capitalist world system. At the level of policy pronouncements, the concept of global economic interdependence has survived even the Tiananmen tragedy and the Western sanctions that followed, as the world economy is still said to be an "alienable whole" and the "global division of labor in industrial production" is viewed as "becoming a more and more important part of international coopera-tion."[105]

Contrary to the conventional wisdom prevalent in the West (particularly in conservative geopolitical and business circles in the United States) that post-Mao China's opening to the world capitalist system is inexorably moving the country toward greater economic and political liberalization, the post-Mao leadership has adopted neither a classical Marxist nor a neo-Marxist dependency nor a liberal global-interdependence model. Rather, its development strategy reflects a neomer-cantilist, state-centered, and state-empowering model. The acceptance of the con-cept of interdependence in the domain of the global political economy reflects and affects China's strategy of managing asymmetrical interdependence. In actu-ality, post-Mao China seems to have turned dependency theory on its head, view-ing interdependence—as Thomas Robinson puts it—as a one-way street, with the West supposed to provide the benefits without imposing the political, economic, military, and cultural costs.[106]

Starting from the widely accepted premise that the distribution of "power" in the international system is the most critical variable in foreign policy behavior, a number of writers have attempted to capture the quintessence of that policy by combining the national-interest (power) approach with the response-to-external-stimulus (reciprocity) approach.[107] The resulting amalgam has made a significant contribution to our understanding of the impact of the superpowers upon Chi-nese foreign policy. Yet an external/systemic model based on national-interest considerations has several problems. First, it is more relevant to crisis and strate-gic behavior than to routine political behavior. Second, the motives for Mao's re-structuring of Chinese foreign policy cannot be reduced to a predictable reaction based solely on the national interest or on realpolitik considerations, as is amply attested by China's dual-adversary strategy in the 1960s. Third, the response-to-external-stimulus model is a poor fit for the Sino-Soviet arms race, which showed neither the exponential nor the S-shaped logistic curve of the action-reaction model, obviously because of the nonsystemic intervening variables. The problem with this type of external/systemic approach is its inability to account for the dif-ferent reactions of states to the same systemic variables caused by the intervention of nonsystemic variables during the policy-making process. Finally, realpolitik re-alist theory cannot explain either the growing institutionalization of multilateral cooperation through international regimes or post-Mao China's growing involve-ment in such global issue regimes. Neorealist or institutional theory may, how-ever, explain China's international organizational behavior to the extent that China is using these international organizations to maximize its global status and access to multilateral aid, information, and technology while minimizing sover-eignty-restricting conditionalities.[108]

Domestic/External Linkages

Most of the above theoretical models demand an either-or (internal or exter-nal) causality choice. Yet the most salient impact on the state of the globalization of economic life is the intensification of domestic/external linkages. With the growing interaction between internal and external functions and an increasing associated interaction between security and economic policies, the factors that influence Chinese foreign policy behavior no longer fall neatly into the dichotomous categories of domestic/societal and external/systemic variables. Both sets of variables involve structural as well as cognitive elements, and they interact during the decision-making process. There is now a growing acceptance in the study of comparative foreign policy and international relations that in an increasingly complex and interdependent world domestic and foreign policies and objectives are interwoven in terms of cause and effect, constituting mutually essential parts of any theoretical (explanatory) approach. Whereas virtually all of the theoretical approaches to the study of Chinese foreign policy have sought to explain state behavior by analyzing the sources of policy, the domestic/external-linkage approach focuses more on consequences than on causes.

Which factors in the linkage between domestic and external variables are more relevant to decision making is a matter of considerable disagreement among scholars. The global system, with its various constraints or opportunities, cannot have any significant influence on Chinese foreign policy unless it is perceived and acted upon by Chinese policy makers through their own decision-making system. Chinese foreign policy is seen here as the outcome of an ongoing interplay between decision makers' perceptions of needs, interests, and beliefs and their perceptions of and responses to international pressures. While recognizing the restructuring impact of external pressures and shocks on foreign policy decision making, this approach also stresses the importance of domestic political institutions and policies in the timing and framing of specific responses to such external shocks.

There is some evidence that post-Mao Chinese leaders view domestic and external variables as interactive. In announcing the open-door policy as "another turning point in Chinese history," Deng Xiaoping said: "To accelerate China's modernization we must not only make use of other countries' experience. We must also avail ourselves of foreign funding. *In past years international conditions worked against us. Later, when the international climate was favourable, we did not take advantage of it. It is now time to use our opportunities.*"[109] In the Mao period, especially in the 1960s, because it defined the international situation in terms of exploitative constraints, China could procure foreign funds only at the expense of its sovereignty and independence. In the post-Mao era, especially since 1984, the international situation has been redefined as a complex, interdependent whole with payoffs for the open-door pragmatist and penalties for the closed-door dogmatist. The belief persists that China, because of its unique status as a "poor global power," commands a wide range of specific policy options to extract maximal benefits without at the same time suffering overwhelming constraints.

To note the substantial interaction between domestic and external variables is not to explain how and why the two intermix under certain circumstances and not under others. An understanding of the pattern of linkages between domestic/societal and external/systemic factors calls for closer attention to mediating intervening variables during the decision-making phase. The virtually unexplored notion of circular feedback may be crucial in determining whether the Chinese foreign policy system is adaptive or maladaptive. How does the system handle criticism from both domestic and foreign audiences? Is there a homeostatic self-critical and self-correcting control system, or does each input prompt a more intense recurrence of earlier behavior?

Conceptually, the epistemological principle of seeking truth from the facts represents the homeostatic feedback best suited to adaptive foreign policy behavior. Insofar as that process concerned Sino-Soviet relations, Wang Youping, the Chinese ambassador to Moscow during much of the 1970s, provided the revealing post hoc admission that, for a variety of reasons, his embassy always reported what the home audience wanted to hear. The Soviet Union was caught in a double bind of domestic and external difficulties from which there was no exit. Wang proposed in 1980 a more "realistic" approach, exposing and evaluating all the facts and reaching a consensus through a step-by-step incremental process.[110]

The second image reversed offers another promising way of exploring the domestic/external linkage process. As formulated by Peter Gourevitch, the second-image-reversed thesis argues that international factors can shape the structures and processes of domestic politics: "instead of being a cause of international politics, domestic structure may be a consequence of it. International systems, too, become causes instead of consequences."[111] A caveat is in order: the second-image-reversed thesis is contingent on a long season of peace at home and abroad. It is merely suggested as one relatively unexplored way of identifying and explaining the domestic/external linkage process in the shaping of Chinese international conduct. For our purposes, it can be reformulated as a circular feedback process in which external influences become part of the conceptual, definitional, policy-making, and institution-building processes of Chinese foreign policy making. In the post-Mao era, especially in the period 1978–1989, the *shishi qiushi* principle shifted the dominant influence in Chinese foreign policy from ideological to cognitive and experiential factors.[112]

At times, the domestic/external linkage process has constituted a preemptive strike against and a restructuring impact upon domestic politics. As Roderick MacFarquhar has shown, the principal reason for Mao's lack of attention to domestic affairs in 1959–1960 was the preemption of the Chinese political agenda by the worsening Sino-Soviet conflict. The resulting Sino-Soviet split restructured domestic politics, becoming one of the major causes of the Cultural Revolution. As Mao's ideological analysis extended from "the *nature* of the Soviet foreign policy mistakes to the *origins* of those mistakes," the Cultural Revolution became his response.[113]

The second-image-reversed process is also evident in the globalization of China's political economy in the 1980s. To varying degrees, some of the international organizations that China has joined during the post-Mao era have already begun to alter China's modernizing process and payoff structures. What is not widely recognized is that the key managers of world capitalism, especially the International Monetary Fund (IMF) and the World Bank, have entered Chinese domestic politics. Their material and normative power and influence have been wired into its conceptual, definitional, policy-making, and institution-building processes, supporting and reinforcing certain reform tendencies while opposing and discouraging others. "Zhao Ziyang and his advisers in effect elicited external views," according to Harold Jacobson and Michel Oksenberg, "that were compatible with their thinking. The external advice has drawn upon and reinforced the predilections of the reformers and provided them with additional valuable evidence and argumentation to rebut their internal critics."[114] China's application for "readmission" into the General Agreement on Tariffs and Trade (GATT) in mid-1986 and subsequent attempts to meet GATT's rigorous entry requirements have generated extensive public discussion about the restructuring impacts of international trading norms and standards upon China's domestic and foreign economic policies, processes, and institutions. The broader point here is not China's sudden normative conversion to the functional approach to world order (à la David Mitrany) but its discovery in the post-Mao era of the new self-serving truth that international organizations can be transformed into positive enabling and empowering instruments in the service of Chinese national interests—that they can help bridge the information, knowledge, capital, and technology gaps without imposing political control. Hence, external systemic factors are best thought of as defining the context for state action as well as offering incentives for one set of policies as opposed to another.[115]

The concept of national identity suggests another promising way of assessing the domestic/external linkage process in the enactment of China's national role conceptions on the world stage. National identity theory postulates that domestic/societal factors are generally more important than external/systemic ones in the formation of national identity, whereas external/systemic factors generally take precedence in determining the outcomes of national identity role enactments. Just as the domestic culture defines the identity options open to an individual at a given time, the international system can condition, if not actually determine, the national identity role options open to a nation-state at any point in its international life. National identity theory helps us to move beyond the dichotomous conceptualization of domestic and external factors to explore how domestic and external factors are interwoven in terms of cause and effect, constituting mutually complementary parts of any theoretical approach in the study of Chinese foreign policy.

In short, the globalization of post-Mao international relations provides a more solid empirical basis for formulating and testing a variety of domestic/external-linkage hypotheses for both qualitative and quantitative analyses. Each source, whether domestic or external, should be viewed in a relative and probabilistic rather than an absolute and deterministic manner to delineate the range of permissible and possible foreign policy choices that can be made in a given period.

Whither Chinese Foreign Policy?

Predicting the future of international relations, always hazardous, has never been more so than today, when the international system itself is undergoing profound and long-term transformation. Recent momentous global changes are unprecedented in their nature, scope, and rapidity. As Robert Jervis reminds us, past generalizations can no longer provide a sure guide for the future if they are themselves no longer valid. To a significant degree, the flow of world politics has become contingent or path-dependent, since particular unexpected events can easily force world politics along quite different trajectories.[116] As in any model, the accuracy of international predictions also depends upon the reliability of the data being employed.

The difficulties of predicting the future shape of world politics are directly connected to the challenge of prognosticating on the future of Chinese foreign policy, since any country's foreign policy will be significantly affected by the structures of world politics that prevail. Whether the future of world politics is dominated by state actors (realism), by a multiplicity of diverse actors (pluralism), by a single, integrated global system (globalism), or by sovereignty-bound and sovereignty-free actors in a multicentric two-worlds system (bifurcationism) will greatly influence the possible scenarios for the future of Chinese foreign relations. Each of these competing theoretical perspectives starts from different sets of premises and suggests different sets of opportunities and constraints, with different degrees of pressure upon China for change and continuity.

At the same time, we should be wary of any social science paradigmatic search for "general laws" of the political/human world. As Gabriel Almond and Stephen Genco have argued, the dynamics of political reality can better be described as "clouds" or "soft regularity" than as a the more mechanical "clock."[117] Given the unmanageably large number of variables that any international prediction has to take into account,[118] the study of foreign policy is unlikely to profit from prediction. The method that should be stressed in considering the future of Chinese foreign policy is *forecasting*. As Nazli Choucri has put it, "A prediction is generally made in terms of a point or event; a forecast is made in terms of alternatives. A prediction focuses upon one outcome, a forecast involves contingencies."[119] The recent history of foreign-policy/international-relations research is replete with examples of erroneous predictions and glaring failures to anticipate major events. In contrast, a forecast can help to foster a better understanding of the dynamics of Chinese foreign policy by identifying the range of plausible foreign policy options in a specific problem area or in relation to a specific target. A forecast based on a knowledge of recurring patterns in the history of Chinese foreign policy and the relationships between known variables can also help in developing contingency plans (in policy making and in research design) for alternative future events.

Thus, we have little choice but to project a spectrum of plausible scenarios, if only to learn from possible egregious errors and then return to the drawing board to ascertain where and why they were made. It is to be hoped that the concepts, methods, and theories scanned in this chapter for describing, explaining, and projecting Chinese international conduct will provide a more useful and reliable base for the study of Chinese foreign policy in the post–Cold War era.

Notes

I thank Thomas Bernstein, William R. Feeney, Alastair I. Johnston, Andrew J. Nathan, and James D. Seymour for their helpful comments on an earlier version of this chapter.

1. See Lawrence H. Summers, "The Rise of China," *International Economic Insights*, May-June 1992, p. 17; "When China Wakes," *The Economist* (London), November 28, 1992, inset, pp. 1–18; Nicholas D. Kristof, "Entrepreneurial Energy Sets Off a Chinese Boom," *New York Times* (hereafter cited as *NYT*), February 14, 1993, pp. 1, 12; Sheryl WuDunn, "Booming China Is Dream Market

for West," *NYT*, February 15, 1993, pp. A1, A6; and Steven Greenhouse, "New Tally of World's Economies Catapults China into Third Place," *NYT*, May 20, 1993, pp. A1, A8. See also International Monetary Fund, *World Economic Outlook* (Washington, D.C.: IMF, 1993), pp. 8, 116–119.

2. He Bochuan, *China on the Edge: The Crisis of Ecology and Development* (San Francisco: China Books and Periodicals, 1991); Vaclav Smil, *China's Environmental Crisis: An Inquiry into the Limits of National Development* (Armonk, N.Y.: M. E. Sharpe, 1993); idem, "Environmental Change as a Source of Conflict and Economic Losses in China," and Jack A. Goldstone, "Imminent Political Conflict Arising from China's Environmental Crises," in *Occasional Paper Series of the Project on Environmental Change and Acute Conflict* No. 2 (December 1992) (International Security Studies Program, American Academy of Arts and Sciences, Cambridge, Mass.); and Shanti R. Conly and Sharon L. Camp, *China's Family Planning Program: Challenging the Myths*, Country Study Series No. 1 (Washington, D.C.: Population Crisis Committee, 1992).

3. In his political report to the Fourteenth Party Congress, Jiang Zemin offers an assessment of the external security environment as having "never been more satisfactory since the founding of the Republic" coupled with a rationale for strengthening the military. See Foreign Broadcast Information Service, *Daily Report—China* (hereafter cited as FBIS-China), October 21, 1992, pp. 1–21, esp. pp. 15–16 (hereafter cited as Jiang's Political Report).

4. For further discussion on sovereignty and world order, see Richard A. Falk, Samuel S. Kim, and Saul H. Mendlovitz, eds., *Toward a Just World Order*, Studies on a Just World Order Vol. 1 (Boulder, Colo.: Westview Press, 1982), pp. 55–216; Joseph Camilleri and Jim Falk, *The End of Sovereignty? The Politics of a Shrinking and Fragmenting World* (Aldershot: Edward Elgar, 1992); James N. Rosenau, *Turbulence in World Politics: A Theory of Change and Continuity* (Princeton, N.J.: Princeton University Press, 1990); and R.B.J. Walker and Saul H. Mendlovitz, eds., *Contending Sovereignties: Redefining Political Community* (Boulder, Colo.: Lynne Rienner, 1990).

5. See Samuel S. Kim, "Advancing the American Study of Chinese Foreign Policy," *China Exchange News* 20:3–4 (Fall-Winter 1992):18–23, and Ni Shixiong, "IR Theory Studies in China" (Paper presented at the international conference "Facing the Challenges of the 21st Century: International Relations Studies in China," Institute of International Relations, Peking University, June 17–19, 1991).

6. See *Zhongguo guojifa niankan 1982* [Chinese Yearbook of International Law 1982) (Beijing: Zhongguo duiwai fanyi chuban gongsi, 1982), p. 306.

7. Xue Mouhong and Pei Jianzhang, eds., *Dangdai Zhongguo waijiao* [Contemporary Chinese Foreign Relations] (Beijing: Zhongguo shehui kexue chubanshe, 1987), pp. 2–3.

8. Mao, "On Practice," in *Selected Works of Mao Tse-Tung* (Peking: Foreign Languages Press, 1965), Vol. 1, p. 304, emphasis added.

9. Zheng Bijian, "Pen Talk on Arming the Whole Party with Comrade Deng Xiaoping's Theory of Building Socialism with Chinese Characteristics," *Renmin ribao* [People's Daily, hereafter cited as *RMRB*], December 11, 1992, and December 12, 1992, in FBIS-China, December 31, 1992, pp. 14–26; quote on p. 25.

10. "The Man Who Makes History," *Beijing Review* (hereafter cited as *BR*) 35:41 (October 12–18, 1992):17.

11. Ibid.

12. Zheng, "Pen Talk," p. 21.

13. See "Zhiyou shehuizhuyi caineng fazhan Zhongguo" [Only Socialism Can Develop China], *RMRB*, editorial, July 22, 1989, p. 1.

14. *BR* 32:49 (December 4–10, 1989):17–22, esp. 22.

15. Fang Xuangchu, "Pen Talk on Arming the Whole Party with Comrade Deng Xiaoping's Theory of Building Socialism with Chinese Characteristics: New Revolution, New Theory," *RMRB*, January 8, 1993, p. 5, in FBIS-China, January 15, 1993, pp. 22-23, quote on p. 22.

16. V. I. Lenin, *Imperialism: The Highest Stage of Capitalism* (Moscow: Foreign Languages Publishing House, 1974), originally published in 1917.

17. See Robert Gilpin, *The Political Economy of International Relations* (Princeton, N.J.: Princeton University Press, 1987), pp. 34–43; and Robert O. Keohane, *After Hegemony: Cooperation and Discord in the World Political Economy* (Princeton, N.J.: Princeton University Press, 1984), pp. 41–46.

18. For the Chinese mainstream realist view, see Zi Zongyun, "The Confluence of Interests: The Basis of State Relations," *Meiguo yanjiu* [American Studies] 2 (1989). A condensed version of this article was also published in *RMRB*, December 30, 1988, p. 7. For more discussion about the prevalence of Western realist and neorealist theories in Chinese international relations scholarship, see Samuel S. Kim, *China In and Out of the Changing World Order* (Princeton, N.J.: Center of International Studies, Princeton University, 1991).

19. Yi Ding, "Upholding the Five Principles of Peaceful Coexistence," *BR* 33:9 (February 26–March 4, 1990):13–16; quote on p. 16, emphasis added. Bull is cited twice in this article on p. 16. "When it comes to issues involving national interests and state sovereignty," according to the party line as articulated by Jiang Zemin's political report to the Fourteenth Party Congress, "China will never concede to outside pressure." Jiang's Political Report, p. 16.

20. *The Elusive Quest: Theory and International Politics* (Columbia: University of South Carolina Press, 1988), p. 211.

21. Daniel Deudney and G. John Ikenberry, "Soviet Reform and the End of the Cold War: Explaining Large-Scale Historical Change," *Review of International Studies* 17 (Summer 1991):225–250.

22. See Chih-Yu Shih, *China's Just World: The Morality of Chinese Foreign Policy* (Boulder, Colo.: Lynne Rienner, 1993).

23. See Alexander L. George, *Bridging the Gap: Theory and Practice in Foreign Policy* (Arlington, Va.: U.S. Institute of Peace Press, 1993).

24. See "Guiding Principle for Knowing and Changing the World—A Study of 'On Practice,'" *Peking Review* 14:25 (June 18, 1971):6–10.

25. James Rosenau, a leading theorist in the fields of comparative foreign policy and international relations, argues the inescapable relevance of theory based on instrumental reasoning. See "China in a Bifurcated World: Competing Theoretical Perspectives," in Thomas Robinson and David Shambaugh, eds., *Chinese Foreign Policy: Theory and Practice* (New York: Oxford University Press, 1993, in press), chap. 1.

26. See Jack Snyder, "Richness, Rigor, and Relevance in the Study of Soviet Foreign Policy," *International Security* 9:3 (Winter 1984–85):89–108.

27. Rosenau, "China in a Bifurcated World."

28. Karl Marx, *The 18th Brumaire of Louis Napoleon*, in Lewis Feuer, ed., *Basic Writings on Politics and Philosophy: Karl Marx and Friedrich Engels* (New York: Doubleday, 1959), p. 320.

29. For contending interpretations, see W.J.F. Jenner, *The Tyranny of History: The Roots of China's Crisis* (New York: Penguin Books, 1992); Ping-Ti Ho, "The Chinese Civilization: A Search for the Roots of Longevity," *Journal of Asian Studies* 35 (August 1976):547–554; Michael Ng-Quinn, "National Identity in Premodern China: Formation and Enactment," in Lowell Dittmer and Samuel S. Kim, eds., *China's Quest for National Identity* (Ithaca, N.Y.: Cornell University Press, 1993), pp. 32–61; and James L. Watson, "Rites or Beliefs? The Construction of a Unified Culture in Late Imperial China," in Dittmer and Kim, *China's Quest for National Identity*, pp. 80–103.

30. For further discussion on the two schools, see Robert Boardman, "Themes and Explanation in Sinology," in Roger L. Dial, ed., *Advancing and Contending Approaches to the Study of Chinese Foreign Policy* (Halifax, Nova Scotia: Centre for Foreign Policy Studies, Dalhousie University, 1974), pp. 3–50; John K. Fairbank, ed., *The Chinese World Order* (Cambridge, Mass.: Harvard University Press, 1968); Samuel S. Kim, *China, the United Nations, and World Order* (Princeton, N.J.: Princeton University Press, 1979), pp. 90–93; Mark Mancall, "The Persistence of Tradition in Chinese Foreign Policy," *Annals of the American Academy of Political and Social Science* 349 (September 1963):14–26; quote in the text is taken from John K. Fairbank, "The State That Mao Built," *World Politics* 19:4 (July 1967):665–666.

31. Mark Mancall, *China at the Center: 300 Years of Foreign Policy* (New York: Free Press, 1984), p. xvii.

32. *The Chinese View of Their Place in the World* (Cambridge, Mass.: Harvard University Press, 1964), p. 71.

33. Mark Mancall is the most vigorous proponent of the great-tradition school and Michael Hunt of the multiple-tradition school. See Mancall, *China at the Center,* and Hunt, "Chinese Foreign Relations in Historical Perspective," in Harry Harding, ed., *China's Foreign Relations in the 1980s* (New Haven: Yale University Press, 1984), pp. 1–42.

34. Benjamin I. Schwartz, "The Maoist Image of World Order," *Journal of International Affairs* 21:1 (1967):92–102; Albert Feuerwerker, "Relating to the International Community," in Michel Oksenberg, ed., *China's Development Experience* (New York: Praeger, 1972), pp. 42–54; Ishwer C. Ojha, *Chinese Foreign Policy in an Age of Transition: The Diplomacy of Cultural Despair* (Boston: Beacon Press, 1969), pp. 1–25; Kim, *China, the United Nations, and World Order,* pp. 49–93.

35. See R. Randle Edwards, "Imperial China's Border Control Law," *Journal of Chinese Law* 1:1 (Spring 1987):33-62; Hunt, "Chinese Foreign Relations in Historical Perspective"; Michael Ng-Quinn, "China and International Systems: History, Structures, Processes" (Ph.D. diss., Harvard University, 1978); and Morris Rossabi, ed., *China Among Equals: The Middle Kingdom and Its Neighbors* (Berkeley: University of California Press, 1983).

36. See World Bank, *World Development Report 1991: The Challenge of Development* (New York: Oxford University Press, 1991), Figure 1.1, p. 12.

37. Richard E. Neustadt and Ernest R. May, *Thinking in Time: The Uses of History for Decision-Makers* (New York: Free Press, 1986); John A. Vasquez, "Foreign Policy, Learning, and War," in Charles F. Hermann, Charles W. Kegley, Jr., and James N. Rosenau, eds., *New Directions in the Study of Foreign Policy* (Boston: Allen & Unwin, 1987), pp. 366–383; Yuen Foong Khong, "'The Lessons of Korea and the Vietnam Decisions of 1965," in George W. Breslauer and Philip E. Tetlock, eds., *Learning in U.S. and Soviet Foreign Policy* (Boulder, Colo.: Westview Press, 1991), pp. 302–349; idem, *Analogies at War: Korea, Munich, Dien Bien Phu, and the Vietnam Decisions of 1965* (Princeton, N.J.: Princeton University Press, 1992).

38. On the twentieth anniversary of the restoration of Sino-Japanese diplomatic relations, Fu Hao, the PRC's first ambassador to Japan, pondered this contradictory historical legacy: "The traditional friendship and cultural bonds between the two peoples, which go back to ancient times, can never be severed by force. ... [But] the history of friendly exchanges between China and Japan for more than two thousand years, also includes an unfortunate period of more than half a century." See *RMRB,* overseas ed., September 29, 1992, p. 1.

39. "On the Ten Major Relationships, April 25, 1956," in *Selected Works of Mao Tsetung,* Vol. 5 (Beijing: Foreign Languages Press, 1977), p. 288.

40. Chih-yu Shih, *The Spirit of Chinese Foreign Policy: A Psychocultural View* (London: Macmillan, 1990), p. 191. Despite the attempts to "reorganize the historical facts reported by others" (p. 2) in terms of the notion of "face," Shih has not made use as Johnston has of the vast literature on Chinese diplomatic and military history (e.g., memoirs, scholarly writings, and various declassified documents) that has become available in the 1980s.

41. See Edmund S. Glenn et al., "A Cognitive Interaction Model to Analyze Culture Conflict in International Relations," *Journal of Conflict Resolution* 14:1 (1970):35–50; and David Laitin, "Political Culture and Political Preferences," *American Political Science Review* 82:2 (1988):589–593.

42. For elaboration of such a synthetic national identity theory, see Lowell Dittmer and Samuel S. Kim, "In Search of a Theory of National Identity," in Dittmer and Kim, *China's Quest for National Identity,* chap. 1, pp. 1–31.

43. Alastair I. Johnston, "An Inquiry into Strategic Culture: Chinese Strategic Thought, the Parabellum Paradigm, and Grand Strategic Choice in Ming China" (Ph.D. diss., Department of Political Science, University of Michigan, 1993).

44. Ibid., chap. 1, p. 36.

45. A crisis-active state or a crisis actor is defined as "a state whose decision-makers perceive a threat to one or more basic values, finite time for response and a high probability of involvement in military hostilities." See Michael Brecher, Jonathan Wilkenfeld, and Sheila Moser, *Crises in the Twentieth Century*, Vol. 2, *Handbook of Foreign Policy Crises* (Oxford: Pergamon Press, 1988), pp. 2, 51, 160–164.

46. Gerald Segal and William T. Tow, eds., *Chinese Defense Policy* (Urbana and Chicago: University of Illinois Press, 1984).

47. Gilbert Rozman, *The Chinese Debate About Soviet Socialism, 1978–1985* (Princeton, N.J.: Princeton University Press, 1987); Allen S. Whiting, *China Eyes Japan* (Berkeley: University of California Press, 1989); and David Shambaugh, *Beautiful Imperialist: China Perceives America, 1972–1990* (Princeton, N.J.: Princeton University Press, 1991).

48. Rozman, *The Chinese Debate About Soviet Socialism*, p. ix.

49. Shambaugh, *Beautiful Imperialist*, pp. 279, 283.

50. Several essays in the Breslauer and Tetlock volume, especially Ernst Haas, "Collective Learning: Some Theoretical Speculations," in Breslauer and Tetlock, *Learning in U.S. and Soviet Foreign Policy*, pp. 62–99.

51. Breslauer and Tetlock, *Learning in U.S. and Soviet Foreign Policy*.

52. Several contributors to the Breslauer and Tetlock volume, especially Haas, insist upon this distinction between adaptation and learning. See Haas, "Collective Learning: Some Theoretical Speculations," in ibid., pp. 62–99.

53. For more detailed case studies demonstrating this point in various issue areas and across time, see Dittmer and Kim, *China's Quest for National Identity*.

54. For details, see Patrick Callahan, "The CREON Project," in Patrick Callahan, Linda P. Brady, and Margaret G. Hermann, eds., *Describing Foreign Policy Behavior* (Beverly Hills, Calif.: Sage Publications, 1982), pp. 31–51.

55. *Handbook of Foreign Policy Crises*.

56. Harry Harding, ed., *China's Cooperative Relationships: Partnerships and Alignments in Chinese Foreign Policy* (forthcoming).

57. See Davis Bobrow, Steven Chan, and John A. Kringen, *Understanding Foreign Policy Decisions: The Chinese Case* (New York: Free Press, 1979), and Samuel S. Kim, *The Maoist Image of World Order* (Princeton, N.J.: Center of International Studies, Princeton University, 1977).

58. Peter Van Ness's systematic analysis of the theory/practice discrepancy in 1965–1967 is still exemplary in this respect. See *Revolution and Chinese Foreign Policy: Peking's Support for Wars of National Liberation* (Berkeley: University of California Press, 1971).

59. See Steve Chan, "Chinese Conflict Calculus and Behavior: Assessment from a Perspective of Conflict Management," *World Politics* 30:3 (April 1978):391–410; Bobrow, Chan, and Kringen, *Understanding Foreign Policy Decisions*; Melvin Gurtov and Byong-Moo Hwang, *China Under Threat: The Politics of Strategy and Diplomacy* (Baltimore, Md.: Johns Hopkins University Press, 1980); Thomas Robinson, "The Sino-Soviet Border Dispute: Background, Development, and the March 1969 Clashes," *American Political Science Review* 66 (1972):1175–1202; Thomas Stolper, *China, Taiwan, and the Offshore Islands* (Armonk, N.Y.: M. E. Sharpe, 1985); Allen S. Whiting, *The Chinese Calculus of Deterrence: India and Indochina* (Ann Arbor: University of Michigan Press, 1975).

60. Gerald Segal, *Defending China* (New York: Oxford University Press, 1985), p. 242.

61. This is one of the major conclusions emerging from the collaborative project on the patterns of cooperation in modern China's international relations sponsored by the Social Science Research Council. See Harry Harding and David Shambaugh, "Patterns of Cooperation in the Foreign Relations of Modern China," in Harding, *China's Cooperative Relationships*.

62. For Chinese negotiating styles and strategies in various settings over the years, see Jaw-ling Joanne Chang, "Negotiation of the 17 August 1982 U.S.-PRC Arms Communiqué: Beijing's Negotiating Tactics, "*China Quarterly* No. 125 (March 1991):33–54; Robert A. Kapp, ed., *Communicating with China* (Chicago: Intercultural Press, 1983); Samuel S. Kim, "Behavioural Dimensions of Chi-

nese Multilateral Diplomacy," *China Quarterly* No. 72 (December 1977):713–742; idem, "Reviving International Law in China's Foreign Relations," in June T. Dreyer, ed., *Chinese Defense and Foreign Policy* (New York: Paragon House, 1989); Henry Kissinger, *White House Years* (Boston: Little, Brown, 1979), chaps. 6, 18–19, 24, pp. 163–194, 684–787, 1049–1096; idem, *Years of Upheaval* (Boston: Little, Brown, 1982), chaps. 3, 15, pp. 44–71, 678–699; Arthur Lall, *How Communist China Negotiates* (New York: Columbia University Press, 1968); Lucian Pye, *Chinese Commercial Negotiating Style* (Cambridge, Mass.: Oelgeschlager, Gunn & Hain, 1982); Richard H. Solomon, *Chinese Negotiating Behavior: A Briefing Analysis* (Santa Monica, Calif.: RAND Corporation, 1985); Shih-Chung Tung, *The Policy of China in the Third United Nations Conference on the Law of the Sea* (Geneva: Graduate Institute of International Studies, 1981); Kenneth T. Young, *Negotiating with the Chinese Communists: The United States Experience, 1953–1967* (New York: McGraw-Hill, 1968); and Zhai Qiang, "China and the Geneva Conference of 1954," *China Quarterly* No. 129 (March 1992):103–122.

63. For further elaboration of this deductive approach in both bilateral and multilateral settings, see Pye, *Chinese Commercial Negotiating Style*, p. 40, and Kim, "Behavioural Dimensions of Chinese Multilateral Diplomacy," pp. 741–742.

64. For further elaboration of this approach, see Robert Axelrod, ed., *Structure of Decision: The Cognitive Maps of Political Elites* (Princeton, N.J.: Princeton University Press, 1976).

65. See James T. Tedeschi et al., "A Reinterpretation of Research on Aggression," *Psychological Bulletin* 81 (September 1974):557–558, and R. T. Green and G. Santori, "A Cross-Cultural Study of Hostility and Aggression," *Journal of Peace Research* 6:1(1969):13–22.

66. Friedrich W. Wu, "Explanatory Approaches to Chinese Foreign Policy: A Critique of the Western Literature," *Studies in Comparative Communism* 13 (Spring 1980):41–62.

67. "Qian Qichen on the World Situation," *BR* 33:3 (January 15–21, 1990): 16.

68. See Seweryn Bialer, ed., *The Domestic Context of Soviet Foreign Policy* (Boulder, Colo.: Westview Press, 1981).

69. K.J. Holsti et al., *Why Nations Realign: Foreign Policy Restructuring in the Postwar World* (London: Allen & Unwin, 1982), p. 208.

70. Jack S. Levy, "The Causes of War: A Review of Theories and Evidence," in *Behavior, Society, and Nuclear War*, Vol. 1, Philip E. Tetlock, Jo L. Husbands, Robert Jervis, Paul C. Stern, and Charles Tilly, eds. (New York: Oxford University Press, 1989), p. 270. There is general, if not universal, consensus on the Kantian proposition that democracies do not fight each other. Disagreement lies in how to explain this seeming empirical regularity. See Michael Doyle, "Kant, Liberal Legacies, and Foreign Affairs," *Philosophy and Public Affairs* 12 (1983):205–235; idem, "Kant, Liberal Legacies, and Foreign Affairs, Part 2," *Philosophy and Public Affairs* 12 (1983):323–353; idem, "Liberalism and World Politics," *American Political Science Review* 80 (1986):1151–1169; Zeev Maoz and Nasrin Abdolali, "Regime Types and International Conflict," *Journal of Conflict Resolution* 33 (1989):3–35; Carol R. Ember, Melvin Ember, and Bruce Russett, "Peace Between Participatory Polities: A Cross-Cultural Test of the 'Democracies Rarely Fight Each Other' Hypothesis," *World Politics* 44:4 (July 1992):573–599; and David A. Lake, "Powerful Pacifists: Democratic States and War," *American Political Science Review* 86:1 (March 1992):24–37.

71. Melvin Gurtov and Harry Harding, *The Purge of Lo Jui-Ch'ing: The Politics of Chinese Strategic Planning*, R-548-PR (Santa Monica, Calif.: RAND Corporation, 1971); Uri Ra'anan, "Peking's Foreign Policy 'Debate,' 1965–1966," in Tang Tsou, ed., *China in Crisis*, Vol. 2, *China's Policies in Asia and America's Alternatives* (Chicago: University of Chicago Press, 1968); Donald S. Zagoria, *Vietnam Triangle: Moscow/Peking/Hanoi* (New York: Pegasus, 1967).

72. Kuang-Sheng Liao, "Linkage Politics in China: Internal Mobilization and Articulated External Hostility in the Cultural Revolution, 1967–1969," *World Politics* 28:4 (July 1976):590–610.

73. Andres D. Onate, "The Conflict Interactions of the People's Republic of China, 1950–1970," *Journal of Conflict Resolution* 18:4 (December 1974):578–594.

74. Joshua S. Goldstein and John R. Freeman, "U.S.-Soviet-Chinese Relations: Routine, Reciprocity, or Rational Expectations?" *American Political Science Review* 85:1 (March 1991):17–35;

idem, *Three-Way Street: Strategic Reciprocity in World Politics* (Chicago: University of Chicago Press, 1990), esp. chap. 3; see also Lowell Dittmer, *Sino-Soviet Normalization and Its International Implications, 1945–1990* (Seattle: University of Washington Press, 1992), esp. chaps. 9–16.

75. For the Mao-domination thesis, see Holsti et al., *Why Nations Realign*, pp. 204, 208–209; John Gittings, *The World and China, 1922–1972* (New York: Harper & Row, 1974); Kim, *The Maoist Image of World Order*; Michel Oksenberg, "Mao's Policy Commitments, 1921–1976," *Problems of Communism* 25 (November-December 1976):1–26.

76. A. Doak Barnett, *The Making of Foreign Policy in China* (Boulder, Colo.: Westview Press, 1984), p. 7.

77. Robert S. Ross, "From Lin Biao to Deng Xiaoping: Elite Instability and China's U.S. Policy," *China Quarterly* No. 118 (June 1989):265–299, and "China Learns to Compromise: Change in U.S.-China Relations, 1982 –1984," *China Quarterly* No. 128 (December 1991):742–773.

78. See chap. 2, "Domestic Sources of Chinese Foreign Policy," in this volume.

79. See John W. Lewis, Hua Di, and Xue Litai, "Beijing's Defense Establishment: Solving the Arms-Export Enigma," *International Security* 15:4 (Spring 1991):87–109.

80. For an excellent study of domestic/foreign policy linkage pivoting around the role of foreign trade in Chinese development strategy, see Ann Fenwick, "Chinese Foreign Trade Policy and the Campaign Against Deng Xiaoping," in Thomas Fingar, ed., *China's Quest for Independence: Policy Evolution in the 1970s* (Boulder, Colo.: Westview Press, 1980), pp. 199–224.

81. See Kenneth Lieberthal, "Domestic Politics and Foreign Policy," in Harry Harding, ed., *China's Foreign Relations in the 1980s* (New Haven: Yale University Press, 1984), pp. 43–70, and Susan Shirk, "The Domestic Political Dimensions of China's Foreign Economic Relations," in Samuel S. Kim, ed., *China and the World: Chinese Foreign Policy in the Post-Mao Era* (Boulder, Colo.: Westview Press, 1984), pp. 57 –81.

82. Kenneth Lieberthal and Michel Oksenberg, *Policy Making in China: Leaders, Structures, and Processes* (Princeton, N.J.: Princeton University Press, 1988).

83. Barnett, *The Making of Foreign Policy in China.*

84. For a pioneering work on the "garbage can model," see J. G. March, *Decisions and Organizations* (Oxford: Basil Blackwell, 1988).

85. Zhao Quansheng, "Domestic Factors of Chinese Foreign Policy: From Vertical to Horizontal Authoritarianism," *Annals of the American Academy of Political and Social Science* 519 (January 1992):158–175.

86. For an early elaboration of this point as the operational premise of a major interdisciplinary study of the domestic sources of foreign policy, see Rosenau's introduction in James N. Rosenau, ed., *Domestic Sources of Foreign Policy* (New York: Free Press, 1967), pp. 1–10.

87. Pat McGowan and Charles W. Kegley, Jr., eds., *Foreign Policy and the Modern World-System*, Sage International Yearbook of Foreign Policy Studies, Vol. 8 (Beverly Hills, Calif.: Sage Publications, 1983), p. 9.

88. This line of argument is most fully developed in Evan Luard's study of seven historical international systems. See Evan Luard, *Types of International Society* (New York: Free Press, 1976).

89. Immanuel Wallerstein, *The Capitalist World-Economy* (New York: Cambridge University Press, 1979), p. 280.

90. Kenneth N. Waltz, *Theory of International Politics* (Reading, Mass.: Addison-Wesley, 1979), pp. 79 –96.

91. Stephen D. Krasner, *Structural Conflict: The Third World Against Global Liberalism* (Berkeley: University of California Press, 1985).

92. Keohane, *After Hegemony* and *International Institutions and State Power* (Boulder, Colo.: Westview Press, 1989); see also Kenneth A. Oye, ed., *Cooperation Under Anarchy* (Princeton, N.J.: Princeton University Press, 1986).

93. For a superb study of differentiated responses of similarly situated states to the structure of the global political system, see Stephan Haggard, *Pathways from the Periphery: The Politics of Growth in the Newly Industrializing Countries* (Ithaca, N.Y.: Cornell University Press, 1990).

94. In addressing the puzzle of why powerful states obey powerless rules in international relations, Thomas Franck suggests that legitimacy, the normative potency of a rule or rule-making institution, exerts influence toward compliance even among powerful states largely because its functions accord with generally accepted principles of "right process." See Thomas M. Franck, *The Power of Legitimacy Among Nations* (New York: Oxford University Press, 1990).

95. See James C. Hsiung, *Law and Policy in China's Foreign Relations: A Study of Attitudes and Practice* (New York: Columbia University Press, 1972); Jerome Alan Cohen and Hungdah Chiu, *People's China and International Law: A Documentary Study*, 2 vols. (Princeton, N.J.: Princeton University Press, 1974); and Samuel S. Kim, "The People's Republic of China and the Charter-Based International Legal Order," *American Journal of International Law* 62 (April 1978):317–349.

96. Hungdah Chiu, "Chinese Attitudes Toward International Law in the Post-Mao Era, 1978–1987," *The International Lawyer* 21:4 (Fall 1987):1127–1166; Kim, "The Development of International Law in Post-Mao China"; idem, "Reviving International Law in China's Foreign Relations," in June T. Dreyer, ed., *Chinese Defense and Foreign Policy* (New York: Paragon House, 1989), pp. 87–131; and John R. Oldham, ed., *China's Legal Development* (Armonk, N.Y.: M. E. Sharpe, 1986); Byron N. Tzou, *China and International Law: The Boundary Disputes* (New York: Praeger, 1990).

97. For recent studies assessing the functional spillovers and feedbacks of China's growing enmeshment with global IGOs, see Harold K. Jacobson and Michel Oksenberg, *China's Participation in the IMF, the World Bank, and GATT* (Ann Arbor: University of Michigan Press, 1990); Samuel S. Kim, "International Organizations in Chinese Foreign Policy," *Annals of the American Academy of Political and Social Science* 519 (January 1992):140–157; "China's International Organizational Behaviour," in Robinson and Shambaugh, *Chinese Foreign Policy: Theory and Practice*, pp. 407–440; William R. Feeney, "China and the Multilateral Economic Institutions" (chap. 11 in this volume).

98. For the restructuring impact of external/systemic variables on Chinese foreign policy, see Joseph Camilleri, *Chinese Foreign Policy: The Maoist Era and Its Aftermath* (Seattle: University of Washington Press, 1980); Bruce Cumings, "The Political Economy of Chinese Foreign Policy," *Modern China* 5 (October 1979):450–452; Kim, "Post-Mao China, International Organizations, and Multilateral Cooperation"; Ng-Quinn, "The Analytic Study of Chinese Foreign Policy"; idem, "Effects of Bipolarity on Chinese Foreign Policy," *Survey* 26 (Spring 1982):102–130; and Edward Friedman, "Anti-Imperialism in Chinese Foreign Policy" (chap. 3 in this volume).

99. See David A. Baldwin, "Power Analysis and World Politics: New Trends Versus Old Tendencies," *World Politics* 31 (January 1979); Joseph S. Nye, *Bound to Lead: The Changing Nature of American Power* (New York: Basic Books, 1990); and Kim, *China In and Out of the Changing World Order*, pp. 49–66.

100. "If we want to restore our race's standing, besides uniting all into a great national body," according to Sun Yat-sen, the founder of the modern Chinese nation-state, "we must first recover our ancient morality—then and only then can we plan how to attain again the national position we once held." Sun Yat-sen, *San Min Chu I: The Three Principles of the People* (Taipei: China Publishing Company, n.d.), p. 37.

101. See, for example, "On Protracted War, May 1938," in *Selected Military Writings of Mao Tsetung* (Peking: Foreign Languages Press, 1966), p. 198; *RMRB*, editorial, November 25, 1957, p. 1; and Mao's statement on the occasion of the U.S.–South Vietnamese invasion of Cambodia, "Peoples of the World, Unite and Defeat the U.S. Aggressors and All Their Running Dogs," in *Peking Review*, special issue, May 23, 1970, p. 9.

102. See, for example, *RMRB*, editorial, November 25, 1957, p. 1.

103. For elaboration, see Kim, "The Political Economy of Post-Mao China in Global Perspective."

104. See *RMRB*, February 26, 1990, p. 2, based on an interview with Huang Shoufeng, China's leading military expert on the subject; and Li Tianran, "Guanyu zhonghe guoli wenti" [On the Question of Comprehensive National Strength], *Guoji wenti yanjiu* No. 2 (April 1990):52–58.

105. See Foreign Minister Qian Qichen's "state of the world report," delivered at the 1990 General Assembly plenary session, *RMRB*, overseas ed., September 29, 1990, p. 4.

106. See George T. Crane, *The Political Economy of China's Special Economic Zones* (Armonk, N.Y.: M. E. Sharpe, 1990); Robert Kleinberg, *China's "Opening" to the Outside World: The Experiment with Foreign Capitalism* (Boulder, Colo.: Westview Press, 1990); and Thomas Robinson, "Interdependence in China's Foreign Relations" (chap. 9 in this volume).

107. See Lowell Dittmer, "The Strategic Triangle: An Elementary Game-Theoretical Analysis," *World Politics* 33:4 (July 1981):485–515; Banning Garrett and Bonnie Glaser, *War and Peace: The Views from Moscow and Beijing* (Berkeley: Institute of International Studies, University of California, 1984); Harold C. Hinton, *China's Turbulent Quest*, rev. ed. (Bloomington: Indiana University Press, 1972); Ng-Quinn, "Effects of Bipolarity" and "The Analytic Study of Chinese Foreign Policy"; James Reardon-Anderson, *Yenan and the Great Powers: The Origins of Chinese Communist Foreign Policy, 1944–1946* (New York: Columbia University Press, 1980); Jonathan Pollack, *The Lessons of Coalition Politics: Sino-American Security Relations*, R-3133-AF (Santa Monica, Calif.: RAND Corporation, 1984); Franz Schurmann, *The Logic of World Power* (New York: Pantheon Books, 1974); Robert Sutter, *Chinese Foreign Policy: Developments After Mao* (New York: Praeger, 1986); and Allen S. Whiting, "The Use of Force in Foreign Policy by the People's Republic of China," *Annals of Academy of Political and Social Science* 402 (July 1972):55–66; and Donald S. Zagoria, "Ideology and Chinese Foreign Policy," in George Schwab, ed., *Ideology and Foreign Policy* (New York: Cyrco Press, 1978), pp. 103–116.

108. For analysis along this line, see Kim, "China's International Organizational Behaviour."

109. Deng Xiaoping, "Why China Has Opened Its Door," in FBIS-China, February 12, 1980, p. L3, emphasis added. For the same point stressing this conjunction of favorable domestic and external conditions, see Deng Xiaoping, *Deng Xioaping wenxuan 1975–82* [Selected Works of Deng Xiaoping 1975–82] (Beijing: Renmin chubanshe, 1983), p. 122, and Commentator, "Youli yu shijie heping de zhongda shijian" [A Significant Event Favorable to World Peace], *Hongqi* No. 1 (January 1979):6.

110. Wang Youping, "A Talk at Meeting of Chinese Ambassadors," *Guang jiaojing* [Wide-Angle Lens] (Hong Kong) No. 91 (April 1980):30–31.

111. Peter Gourevitch, "The Second Image Reversed: The International Sources of Domestic Politics," *International Organization* 32:4 (Autumn 1978):882.

112. See Kim, *The Third World in Chinese World Policy*, pp. 43–55.

113. Roderick MacFarquhar, *The Origins of the Cultural Revolution*, Vol. 2, *The Great Leap Forward, 1958–1960* (New York: Columbia University Press, 1983), chap. 11, pp. 255–292; quote on p. 292.

114. Jacobson and Oksenberg, *China's Participation in the IMF, the World Bank, and GATT*, p. 141.

115. In a thoroughgoing empirical/theoretical work, Thomas Moore takes up the second-image-reversed thesis to address one of the most conceptually important yet inadequately studied issues in the field of Chinese foreign relations: the restructuring impact of the global political economy on the process of change within China. See Thomas G. Moore, "China in the World Market: International Sources of Reform and Modernization in Chinese Industry" (Ph.D. diss., Department of Politics, Princeton University, 1994).

116. Robert Jervis, "The Future of World Politics: Will It Resemble the Past?" *International Security* 16:3 (Winter 1991–1992):39–45.

117. Gabriel A. Almond and Stephen J. Genco, "Clouds, Clocks, and the Study of Politics," *World Politics* 29:4 (July 1977):489–522.

118. For further analysis and elaboration, see Samuel S. Kim, *The Quest for a Just World Order* (Boulder, Colo.: Westview Press, 1984), chap. 8, pp. 301–342.

119. Nazli Choucri, "Key Issues in International Relations Forecasting," in Nazli Choucri and Thomas W. Robinson, eds., *Forecasting in International Relations: Theory, Methods, Problems, Prospects* (San Francisco: W. H. Freeman, 1978), p. 4.

2

Domestic Sources
of Chinese Foreign Policy

DAVID BACHMAN

The interplay of domestic and international factors in China's external behavior is profound and confusing. For example, the Tiananmen Massacre of June 1989 made China's leadership a pariah, and its apparent isolation was only compounded by the collapse of communism in Eastern Europe, the Soviet Union, and Mongolia from 1989 to 1991. The ending of the Cold War and with it the loss of the so-called China card further eroded China's international position. The decisive defeat of one of its principal arms clients, Iraq, in early 1991 was yet another blow. Finally, there was a widespread perception that its business environment was extremely difficult, corrupt, and unprofitable. Instead of being marginalized by these and other circumstances, however, since June 1989 China has established or reestablished formal relations with Indonesia, Singapore, Israel, and South Korea and made dramatic progress in trade and investment with Taiwan. Despite what remains a problematic investment climate, China was the largest low-income-economy recipient of foreign investment in 1989 and 1990, receiving 11 percent of all investment in developing countries, and investment totals have risen dramatically since 1989. According to the General Agreement on Tariffs and Trade (GATT), China in 1991 was the world's thirteenth-largest exporter, surpassing South Korea, and the leading Third World exporter. Foreign trade continues to grow by about 20 percent per year. Of all exporters to the United States in 1991, China had the second-largest trade surplus, and its overall trade surplus in 1991 was about $13 billion.[1] Industrial growth, particularly in coastal China, is surging despite the paucity of major reform initiatives.[2] And despite the end of the Cold War and the collapse of the Soviet Union, through the United Nations Security Council and other multilateral fora China's voice is being heard.

What explains the paradox of an international environment that has turned much more difficult, if not hostile to Chinese interests, and increasingly successful Chinese external involvement without fundamental internal change? Part of the answer is a matter of misunderstanding and misperception. Americans were repulsed by the brutality of June 4, but they overestimated the degree to which China was isolated internationally and the degree to which U.S. policy could alter

Chinese internal policies. Moreover, not even the United States, where human-rights concerns were expressed most loudly, employed the full range of sanctions available to it to try to change or punish China. Thus, in some ways, the situation China faced internationally was not as negative as was thought, and there were perhaps more opportunities for it to profit from the dramatic changes in the international system than outsiders recognized. But misperception and misunderstanding cannot entirely explain the paradox. China's domestic political economy is a key element in any effort to resolve it.

The International System and China

All states are influenced to varying degrees by the workings of the international system. Defining the international system in a precise way is often difficult. For the purposes of this chapter, the international system might usefully be conceptualized as having four components: structure, institutions, processes, and actions. Anarchy, the absence of authoritative superordinate actors enforcing law and order, is assumed.[3] *Structure* refers to the distribution of capabilities within the international system. The two principal structures in the history of international politics have been the bipolar one characteristic of the Cold War period and the multipolar one characteristic of Europe, for the most part, from 1648 to 1914. The capabilities in question have traditionally referred to military and economic power. Increasingly today, however, they include scientific, technical, and educational levels and societal entrepreneurial abilities. *Institutions* are to organizations, agreements, and norms established to try to regulate various processes of international interaction, specifically to overcome limitations on cooperation by reducing transaction costs and other barriers that inhibit mutual benefit in international politics and economics.[4] Major international institutions include the United Nations, the World Bank, and the International Monetary Fund (IMF). *Processes* are cross-national patterns of resource and other flows of goods, people, or ideas. Major processes include international investment, migration, trade, and pollution. *Actions* are behaviors of states or institutions designed to influence the behavior of other states or international institutions. Diplomatic visits, use of force, and the establishment of new international or multilateral institutions are types of actions.

Various schools of thought exist within the disciplines of international relations and international political economy about how large a role the international system plays in shaping the foreign and domestic policies of states. Some see the nature of the international system as almost totally determining state internal and external behavior. Others recognize the impact of the international system but argue that it cannot be predicted.[5] Still others argue that the nature of the state itself, particularly whether it is a democracy, determines fundamental aspects of its external behavior. One finding in this context is that democracies do not initiate wars against other democracies.[6]

Instead of offering simply another tendentious contribution about the relative weight of national and international factors in Chinese foreign policy, this chapter will briefly survey China's unique strengths in the international system and go on to discuss attributes of its political and economic system that affect its external behavior. I will try to show that Chinese "foreign policy is the extension of China's domestic policies."[7] This is not to say that the international system does not affect Chinese foreign or domestic policy. Rather, I will concentrate on the domestic origins of some Chinese foreign policy behavior and leave the weighing of domestic and foreign impacts to further, more extensive studies.[8] Finally, I will suggest an alternative way to conceptualize and evaluate state capacity in systemic perspective.

China's new leaders have limited power and authority. Bold policy initiatives require consensus, which is close to impossible. Prior commitments, particularly on issues related to Chinese nationalism, limit their flexibility. Their ability to enforce their policies is further limited by the highly articulated nature of the Chinese state. Incentives within the political economy encourage units at all levels to seek resources from the international environment, even if this means undermining the position of other units and the central decision-making apparatus. The leaders are largely cut off from organized societal and international interests and receive biased information. Because foreign policy is likely to be the product of many of the same decision-making structures as domestic policy, Chinese foreign policy is an extension of Chinese domestic politics.

China's International Strengths

With the collapse of the Soviet Union, the closing of U.S. bases in the Philippines, and gradual U.S. defense cuts, China's security situation is arguably the best it has been since the onset of the Opium War of 1839–1842. Put simply, no power stronger than China threatens core areas of China. Its limited nuclear forces are sufficient to deter other nuclear powers. In most cases, relations with states on its borders have improved or are reasonably stable. Realistically, the workings of the international system in the realm of security have limited impact on Chinese foreign or domestic politics. Although this has been true of most states since the end of the Cold War, it is especially significant in the Chinese case because of the repeated threats to China over the 1840–1980 period and because, in contrast to other major powers, China has increased its defense spending despite its secure position. The lessening of international security concerns appears to have created a window of opportunity for China to try to narrow the gap between the technical level of its forces and those of more advanced militaries.[9] Thus, in the security realm, China is in an enviable position, especially in light of the repeated perceived threats to the People's Republic of China since its founding in 1949.

But not all threats are military. Because the Chinese Communist Party (CCP) regime equates itself with the Chinese state, threats to the CCP's continuation in power are seen by the leadership as threats to China. In light of the collapse of communism in Europe and the Soviet Union, many in China and abroad believe that the CCP's time in power is limited. Certainly the official propaganda of the regime sees the CCP as under the serious threat of "peaceful evolution"—its gradual undermining by interactions with the outside world, particularly the most advanced bourgeois economies and democracies, as the Chinese political and economic systems increasingly move toward capitalism and democracy. That China's

Party leaders say this and believe this is beyond doubt. What they can do about it is unclear. In late 1992 the prevailing answer to this supposed threat was to encourage the economic system to grow more rapidly and expand on reform and the opening to the outside world while at the same time maintaining strict political controls. No CCP leader appeared to disagree with the need for tight political control and Party dictatorship, but since June 4, 1989, some leaders may also have advocated less involvement with major capitalist states, particularly the United States.[10] In the area of threats from international processes such as the spread of consumerism and materialism, the CCP appears fatally vulnerable in the long run.

In the economic realm, China's sensitivity and vulnerability to international actions, processes, and institutional arrangements are mixed and perhaps unique in international perspective. To state the obvious, China is a very large, populous country with a huge economy. That economy is technically backward and inefficient, but it is reasonably comprehensive. Indeed, several recent sources speculate that if current growth rates continue, by 2003–2020 it will be the world's largest.[11] China is not crucially dependent on any particular import or sets of imports for its economic health. It has become a leading exporting nation without developing all the industrial and trade promotion institutions characteristic of Japan and the newly industrializing countries and before beginning to export high-value (or high-value-added) industrial goods such as automobiles.

China does require outside assistance to modernize, particularly in the areas of technology and management skills. It is also much more cost-effective for it to absorb foreign investment to hasten its modernization than to try to pursue largely autarkic development. Thus, the degree to which international institutions and processes facilitate or hinder Chinese modernization has a major impact on Chinese behavior. China needs a continued relatively open international economy and most-favored-nation status with all major trading partners to continue to grow rapidly (at a minimum). Moreover, access to private and public international capital, high technology, and knowledge is essential for the rapid accomplishment of its economic goals. To facilitate these exchanges and processes it needs to modify its internal institutions to become attractive to foreign partners. Thus, in the area of international processes, it is susceptible to significant external influence.[12] This is also true to some extent in terms of international institutions as well. China must comply with basic trade, economic, and legal requirements before it can accede to full membership in the GATT.[13] Under external pressure, it is modifying its practices and institutions, but what is remarkable is how little institutional change has taken place. Despite the lack of legal transparency, a nonconvertible currency, corruption, low levels of management skills and technology, low labor productivity, and difficulties in freely hiring and firing workers, China arguably has since 1978 been the most successful Third World economy in terms of international involvement.[14]

China is already a member of many of the most important international and political institutions, the GATT being the major exception. It is not a member of a less formal but perhaps more important "international" grouping, the Group of Seven (G-7—the United States, Canada, Japan, England, Germany, France, and Italy), or the Organization of Economic Cooperation and Development. China's continued economic growth will force these organizations to confront the issue of Chinese relations with them. Entrance into these remaining international institutions will require China to satisfy various membership criteria. Again, it will be subject to international pressures to alter its internal and external arrangements and policies. But this influence should not be overstated. China is already a UN Security Council veto power and can use its international position and the extent of its international involvement to extract concessions from the international environment. It can force its own inclusion in international meetings and organizations by its ability to undermine almost any agreement to which it is not a party—arms sales, nuclear proliferation, Middle East peace talks, and pollution control all require some Chinese involvement. Its threat to renege on international agreements to which it is a party may deter the imposition of sanctions on China.[15]

Finally, the structure of the international system is improved if murky. China's security situation is perhaps unprecedentedly positive. The collapse of the Soviet Union meant the end of the bipolar world, but it is not clear how to characterize the present international situation. In the security realm, the world is unipolar, with the United States as the dominant military power, but with the end of the Cold War military power may be a less important indicator of international capabilities than before. Instead, economic power and international competitiveness, functions of the level of development of science, technology, and education, are increasingly becoming the measure of power in the international system. While China is making rapid economic progress, its educated manpower base remains very small, and its scientific and technological level is generally decades behind world standards. The consequences of its backwardness are hard to discern. If it wishes to become a major power, a goal to which all its leaders aspire, it must continue to expand education and do what is necessary to raise technical and scientific levels. Thus, again the international structure encourages China to pursue certain policies and discourages others, such as more egalitarian measures.

The result of this inventory is that there can be no denying that the international system in various ways provides a set of incentives that encourage China's continuation of economic reform and opening to the outside world. These policies have various functional linkages to areas such as higher education that have profound social and political implications. In most cases, however, the impact of the international system on China's behavior is not direct and sharply focused. Instead, the international system acts as a conditioning factor, rewarding some types of behavior and discouraging others. Within this broad pattern of incentives, China has a very significant range of options.

Domestic Politics and Foreign Policy

The domestic sources of foreign policy in any country include geography, size and ethnic composition of the population, resource base, and other factors. Instead of addressing these sources, this chapter will focus on the influence of three overarching political categories: political leadership, the structure of the political system, and the nature of the political economy.

Leadership

Individual political leaders bring many diverse concerns and attributes with them in making policy decisions of any sort. These include the conceptual equipment that enables them to perceive and comprehend developments (perceptual processes and ideological predispositions), their previous experience, the role requirements of top leadership positions and the nature of the political game at the elite level, their personal goals (power, prestige, material reward, political and sometimes physical survival), and their goals for China. This section will concentrate on the issues of power, authority, and the rules of the political game and how these issues affect Chinese foreign policy.[16]

China's leadership is in transition. The old powerful revolutionaries will soon die, and China will be led by men generally in their late fifties and sixties whose political skills, personal attributes, and other key variables are largely unknown. For years they have labored in the shadow of Deng Xiaoping and others. Outside observers, the Chinese people, and, indeed, the successors themselves are unclear as to how they will exercise power when the old revolutionary leaders are gone.

Arguably, the successors will have much less power than Mao Zedong and Deng Xiaoping. Although they will have higher education in technical fields and will likely be more physically vigorous than Deng was when he became China's preeminent leader in 1978, their power resources will be significantly more limited than Deng's, whose resources paled in the light of Mao's.[17] China's new leaders will have had less time at the top of the political system and the CCP than did Mao or Deng. Their political careers will have been relatively narrow—they will have served in only a relatively small number of China's administrative hierarchies. They will therefore have a narrower range of connections and contacts than did earlier generations of leaders. In particular, with some limited individual exceptions, they will have limited contacts with the military and public-security systems. All this means that these leaders will not dominate the political system as Mao and, to a lesser extent, Deng did. In particular, they will be deficient in the most crucial power resource, authority (or legitimacy).

China's next leaders will have an "authority deficiency" for several reasons. The first is that China is not a democracy, and its new leaders will not have been selected by the population. When these leaders adopt policies that the populace (and the bureaucratic systems) might oppose, the lack of a legitimating link between leaders and society will limit their ability to elicit voluntary obedience. A second factor limiting their authority is the Tiananmen Massacre and the general collapse of communism. A number of the candidates for succession to Deng Xiaoping were personally implicated in the bloodshed of June 4 or rose to positions of power by replacing other leaders more sympathetic to the people. Urban Chinese in particular are hardly predisposed to sacrifice their interests and obey politicians involved in suppressing the people in a system with an uncertain future. These politicians have little traditional authority and no charismatic legitimacy.

China's new leaders can gain authority and obedience from society only by two paths. They must continue to generate widespread economic benefits for society at large, linking economic expansion with Chinese nationalism. In short, they must prove through their actions that they are deserving of obedience and respect; a successful claim to authority will require them to produce significant and continuing benefits. The other route to obedience is through fear and coercion. Purge, terror, and threat are not a way to establish authority, but at least for a while they can induce outward conformity and submission. However, whether the new leaders will be willing to use state coercion and capable of insuring that the public-security and military forces will obey orders to use force is one of the key unanswerable questions determining the future of CCP rule. Widespread use of terror to stay in power will undermine the ability of the economy to produce benefits.

The rules of the political game after the deaths of the octogenarians will probably include a consensual basis for decisions, risk aversion, and an extended period of consolidation. All leaders have an interest in not losing out in a power struggle. All know that the system lacks legitimacy and authority and that soon they personally will no longer have the elders around to provide them with support if they get into trouble or a crisis emerges. These characteristics argue for incrementalism in policy making, no bold new initiatives unless a leadership consensus is achieved, and great care to prevent one leader from obtaining more power than others.[18]

The pursuit of power will require allies and coalitions within the leadership and major interests within the Chinese state, such as the military, many of the central economic ministries, and major regions of the country. Favors will be traded and promises made. In part, this is because some of these interests are now so entrenched that the new leaders will lack the power to enforce their will over them in the short run. In part it is because some of these interests, such as Guangdong province, are serving state economic interests so well that the center has little incentive to change.[19] Coalition building and alliances will require tangible payoffs to the key interests, and this also argues for a largely resource-based politics. Ideological appeals (with the exception of nationalistic ones) will attract few followers or allies. Politics will focus on questions of investment and budgetary shares, relative autonomy, and promotions.[20]

The implications of these leadership variables for China's foreign policy behavior include the following: First, because it lacks authority, the new leadership will not be in a position to make major compromises on issues of national sovereignty with regard to Taiwan, Tibet, Hong Kong, and the South China Sea (though there appears to be slightly more flexibility on the latter issue than on the others).[21] These issues have such a long and established history in Chinese nationalism and politics that the new leadership will be unable to move in new directions, and apparent compromises or tolerance for independence in areas over which China claims sovereignty will seriously weaken their already limited power.

Second, since the new leaders will be trying to secure alliances with major power centers in China, they will either overtly or covertly acquiesce in or promote behaviors that the United States and other major international actors find distasteful. The military budget will continue to grow, as will attempts to sell and purchase arms. Chinese arms and related material sales may still include missiles and nuclear materials.[22] Despite recent agreements on prison labor exports and other issues, abuses may continue.[23]

Third, because of its lack of power and the dynamics of succession politics, the leadership may be unwilling or unable to control foreign trade policy very well. Chinese units may be competing against each other on the international market without central coordination and control. Lower-level Chinese entities may violate export quotas with relative impunity. The relative lack of power at the center may mean that Hong Kong and Macao will be allowed a high degree of autonomy after they revert to Chinese control (after the current Sino-British row over Hong Kong is resolved, probably in China's favor), in 1997 and 1999, respectively. No competitor for power can be allowed to gain control of Hong Kong resources, and Hong Kong is providing so many benefits that their loss would be a devastating blow for China and for the leader(s) responsible for it.[24]

Finally, the position of the new leaders will force them to try to demand autonomy. Because they are weak, they cannot allow outside influences, whether they come from Chinese society or from external actors, to have direct input into the decision-making system. This is not to say that foreign or societal factors will not influence (or try to influence) China. The leadership has responded and will continue to respond to pressure in the areas of release of political prisoners and trade practices.[25] But foreign, especially American, pressure is not sufficient to modify China's internal structure. Demands for fundamental political change from external sources will only make such change more difficult politically; anyone who argues for such change can be charged with being a lackey of foreign interests. Foreigners may have the ability to modify specific policies and fundamentally alter the Chinese economy and Chinese society over the long term, but the leadership and the state apparatus will be unwilling to allow direct foreign pressure to restructure the Chinese state. This implies that if there are repeats of societal protests against CCP rule, the Chinese state will be unwilling to compromise with society, and the leadership will attempt another crackdown. Moreover, the limited costs imposed on China by the world after June 1989 may suggest to its leaders that China could survive any sanctions that future crackdowns might elicit.

Political Structure

The characteristics of China's political structure also importantly shape Chinese external behavior. The most important aspects of that structure in this regard are its authoritarianism, its highly articulated nature, its fragmentation, and the bargaining relations within the state.[26]

Obviously, China is not a democratic political system. There are few if any formal institutions that allow social forces to articulate and mobilize for their interests if the state is opposed to them. Foreigners also have relatively few regularized channels for articulating their interests. This is not to say that society or foreigners do not influence Chinese politics; rather, it is to suggest that in a formal sense the Chinese state is quite autonomous from direct pressure from non-CCP sources in China or abroad. This lack of formal institutions to mediate between state and society or state and foreign institutions implies that the state will be cut off from information sources that are critical of its policies. Subordinates tell their superiors what they want to hear because superiors control many of the keys to personal advancement. Few safe alternative channels exist for challenges to the established beliefs and policies of the leadership and state organizations.

It used to be said that the goal of Communist rulership in China was for every Chinese citizen to be a member of a Party-controlled secondary association.[27] Although this goal has faded with the reforms, China remains a highly organized and bureaucratized system at the formal level. Politics revolves around political organizations. Few political systems have as many organizations as China, and the necessity of organization for effective politics is recognized by all. During the Beijing Spring of 1989, the fundamental issue of contention between the state and students was the students' demand that the state officially recognize autonomous student organizations. To grant such recognition would have fundamentally undermined state control, and the refusal of the CCP and the state to do so led to the massacre.

The centrality of political organization has both advantages and disadvantages. The highly articulated nature of the Chinese state enhances state capacity by creating redundancy within the polity. Redundancy is a key component of state strength, and there are few states with as much formal redundancy as China.[28] If one organization fails in its mission, others may replace it. Other things being equal, China's high degree of formal organization and bureaucratic proliferation increases its ability to get things done.

This does not mean that its bureaucracy and organization perform efficiently or impartially. Gross overstaffing, corruption, faulty information flows, compartmentalization, and other defects are endemic to the system.[29] There are so many organizations that leaders cannot easily monitor their behavior. Upper levels simply cannot closely supervise the activities of any but the most important organizations, giving rise to bureaucratic fragmentation.

This fragmentation makes coordination difficult, encouraging organizations to be as self-reliant as possible and thus creating further redundancy and waste in the system. There are too many units to be supervised, and upward information flows are distorted either consciously or unconsciously. The system discourages specialization and comparative advantage.[30] With economic reform, this fragmentation enhances bureaucratic competition for markets and resources, but true competition is undermined by attempts by political authorities in the provinces, for example, to protect their industries from competition from other provinces.[31] In addition, the proliferation of bureaucracies is expensive and exacerbates state budgetary problems. Tight financial circumstances only encourage entrepreneurial activities by state organizations.

The state attempts to overcome the extremes of fragmentation by organizing bureaucracies into systems (*xitong*) or groups.[32] There are also fairly stable patterns of cooperation and alliance among systems.[33] Despite attempts to build self-sufficient units, organizations remain interdependent to varying degrees. The political system has not been immobilized by the organizational fragmentation, but fragmentation and compartmentalization do require leaders and bureaucracies to spend a great deal of time trying to strike bargains that will be binding on all players. The nature of the issue and project under discussion determines the difficulty of striking such bargains—the central government is able to agree on about two hundred high-priority large construction projects per year.[34] Logrolling and pork-barrel politics are extensive in China, with bargaining representing the cost of achieving consensus. Units and leaders seek to extract as many resources as possible in exchange for their consent. These payoffs may have nothing to do with the issue at hand and may take the form of IOUs to be cashed in at a later date.

Bureaucratic redundancy, fragmentation and compartmentalization, and bargaining affect foreign policy behavior via coordination and control problems and competition among Chinese entities, but they also enable the state to pursue a largely mercantilist international policy. The sale of intermediate-range ballistic missiles to Saudi Arabia is a fine example. The Ministry of Foreign Affairs was apparently not even aware that China was about to sell missiles capable of carrying nuclear warheads (and reaching Israel from Saudi Arabia) until after the fact. Indeed, it is not even clear how well-informed the top leadership was. Deng Xiaoping had to ask one of the military trading corporations how much money it made in the Saudi missile sale, and his response to the $2 billion figure was "Bu shao" (literally, "not a little").[35] This response suggests that, although he may have approved of the deal in advance, he certainly was not informed of (or had forgotten) key details of it, and a response of this kind would encourage trading corporations to strike what deals they could despite outside pressure on the Ministry of Foreign Affairs.[36] Recurring reports of Chinese exports of missiles and their technologies and nuclear technology transfers suggest that the military and its trading corporations continue to operate without input from the Foreign Affairs bureaucracy. The leadership's promise since late 1991 to abide by the Missile Technology Control Regime and the Nuclear Non-Proliferation Treaty may be an empty one.[37]

Missile sales provide another insight into the functionings of the Chinese state. At least one type of missile was developed solely for export because one of the units in the Ministry of Space Industry saw its budget and responsibilities drastically reduced. Other elements of the space industry turned to exports (and competition with subunits of the ministry) to tide themselves over current lean budgetary times.[38]

Within the Chinese state, it is clear that the military is in many ways a system unto itself, not subject to the same amount of supervision as others and given much more autonomy.[39] It is possible that the Ministry of Public Security and its prison-labor products are also not well controlled by the foreign trade bureaucracy.[40] Thus, the Ministry of Foreign Economic Relations and Trade is denying prison exports while at the same time the Ministry of Public Security is bragging about them. It would be unlikely that an economic ministry could give binding commands to the Public Security bureaucracy.

Other manifestations of the effects of the nature of the Chinese state on external behavior include the apparent requirement for important ministries and organizations to have their own joint-venture hotels. Some of Beijing's finest hotels have the Ministry of State Security and the Army's General Staff Department as their partners.[41] But not all manifestations of China's state structure must necessarily hurt foreign interests. Various Chinese entities compete against each other by offering better investment incentives or trade terms, thus undercutting the gains a more unified strategy might have achieved.[42] Provinces are so anxious to obtain foreign investments that they get into bidding wars in efforts to make their investment environments more attractive, but once the investment is secured they often renege on or undercut the original concessions to make good the financial losses they may have sustained in the original contract.[43] The influences of the nature of the state structure on external behavior are only reinforced by the operations of China's political economy.

Political Economy

China's economy is often called overcentralized, with strong socialist and planned elements. There is no denying that state ownership exists and that there is an economic plan, but there is hardly compelling evidence that the economy is overcentralized.[44] Some five thousand employees of the central planning organs in Beijing are charged with planning one of the world's largest economies, with millions of economic actors.[45] Even large and medium-sized state-owned industrial enterprises exist in the thousands. With primitive techniques and limited use of computers and advanced econometric models, Chinese planning has more often than not been reduced to "last year's output plus 5–10 percent."

Indeed, especially since reform began, the Chinese political economy has been significantly decentralized. Demand for investment materials, funds, and foreign exchange consistently exceeds supply. Given the limited ability of the center to meet demands for funds and other resources, units often pursue predatory strategies to obtain the materials they need or buy what they need on the market. Enterprises and units are increasingly encouraged or required to be self-financing and responsible for their own profits and losses. Significant segments of the economy are largely governed by market relations. Nonetheless, administrative and other forms of political intervention in the economy—the real basis for claims of overcentralization—remain widespread.[46]

The center is not powerless in the areas of finance and large-scale investment, but over the past twenty-five years, and especially since 1978, the autonomy of enterprises and local governments has increased tremendously, local governments being perhaps the most important economic actors in China today.[47] Their expanded role in the political economy, coupled with inherited elements of the old planned economy, has led to behaviors that have foreign policy implications.

The first of these is the overall shortage of capital for investment. Capital investment has greatly expanded, but the effectiveness of its use has continuously declined. Tax revenue has not kept pace with the rapidly growing economy. Foreign exchange reserves, although substantial, are especially valued and scarce, with the result that economic actors at all levels are continually searching for funds. This search is mostly confined to domestic actors, but it can also include attempts to use foreign actors to serve local needs. World Bank and Japanese governmental assistance to help build China's infrastructure is one example, and Hong Kong investment in building highway networks in South China is another. Use of international capital markets, sale of stock abroad, and other aspects of international finance will likely increase. Alongside these standard practices are predatory strategies and corrupt practices. Chinese officials extract bribes and gifts for doing business. The Chinese attempt to have Chinese managers paid at international rates (of which the managers receive a minimal percentage in domestic currency). These practices make the business and investment climate less attractive than it could be.[48] In addition, official policy and capital shortage may drive some of the external behavior that is most unpalatable from the American perspective. Especially for nonproductive units, policy and shortage encourage central and local authorities to encourage organizational self-financing. Consequently, it is thought that prison camps and, indeed, the entire public-security system should be self-supporting, and this provides an incentive for prison-labor (and military) exports.[49] Even universities are establishing workshops that make, for example, military drone aircraft for export.[50]

Second, the Chinese price and tax system encourages reduplicative investment in processing industries and underinvestment in raw materials and industrial crops. The result has been the formation of what are called "ducal" (or feudal or mercantilist economies) at the subnational level. Various regions ban the "export" of cotton, wool, tea, silk, and other important raw materials and build processing plants to turn these materials into finished products. Relatively efficient factories in Shanghai and other coastal areas are often starved of raw materials, forcing them to run at a loss. Meanwhile, interior provinces with limited comparative advantages in processing produce second-rate products and use raw materials less efficiently. This forces the coast to import agricultural products that might not be necessary in a more fully developed market economy.[51] (If market prices prevailed and interior enterprises produced at a profit, then importing raw materials for the coastal regions might be efficient if profits and exports exceeded the costs of imports and production—indeed, this would be comparative advantage at work.)

Finally, China's political economic attributes may have determined the whole course of reform and the open-door policy. It is well known that the economic reforms began in the countryside and were followed by reforms in foreign trade and investment and then in industry. This order roughly parallels the degree of success of the reforms. By 1984, Chinese agriculture had returned to a largely private basis, and the harvest of that year was the best in Chinese history. Indeed, it was so bountiful that the state had to renege on promises to buy surplus products brought to market. Having angered the peasants and risked dampening the dynamism of the countryside, it had to find an economic outlet for the rural economy. This it did by encouraging rural industry and, increasingly, exports from rural small-scale industry. These rural enterprises (coupled with foreign firms) have been the most energetic sector of the economy and of exports.[52] Indeed, the vitality of rural industry appears central to the China's strategy of economic reform—outgrowing the plan.[53] This strategy and China's increasing outward orientation are in important ways the outgrowth of the contradictions of its political economy and the results of the successes (and limitations) of rural reform.

China's political economy and the domestic reform program have profoundly shaped its involvement in the international system. This is not to say that international feedback from its opening to the outside world has not, in turn, profoundly affected China.[54] Nonetheless, there can be no denying that the structures, policies, and contradictions that characterize the Chinese political economy have generated important elements of Chinese external behavior, and will continue to do so for the next five to ten years. The international system will be yet another area where Chinese economic actors attempt to extract resources to serve their interests.

Profiting from the International System

The time has come to move beyond the debate over whether the international system or the domestic political system is more important in determining China's foreign policy behavior. Comparative study of the ability of states to extract resources from the international system and to minimize the constraints that the international system imposes on them is one way to proceed. Cost-benefit analysis of international involvement and domestic consequences should be possible and may reveal more interesting things about comparative foreign policy and international politics than do arguments about the sources of foreign policy behavior.

To carry out such a task, an index of external gains and costs might be constructed. Some of the relevant variables would include, on the external side, growth of merchandise exports, balance of trade, foreign indebtedness and hard-currency reserves, percentage of exports in industry, degree of trade dependency of the overall economy and specific economic sectors, and amount of foreign investment and aid. On the internal side of the ledger, key variables might include convertibility of the currency and, if convertible, fixed or floating exchange rates, degree to which domestic interest rates correspond to interest rates in major industrial economies, access to domestic markets and institutions, whether disputes can be arbitrated or adjudicated in other jurisdictions, extent of secrecy laws, and degree of legal codification. If such an index were to be constructed for China, it might in verbal form resemble the following:

China's ability to extract resources and obtain benefits from the international system while not being overwhelmingly constrained by the operations of the system is unique, and perhaps only Japan has been as successful. Since reform began in the late 1970s, China has moved from the world's thirty-second-ranked exporter to twelfth or thirteenth. On average, China's gross national product (GNP) has grown at about 9 percent per year since 1978, among the highest in the world during this period, and export and GNP growth continue. China has attracted a great deal of foreign investment over the same period, with amounts increasing dramatically over the past several years. It may receive more concessionary international financing than any other nation. It has enjoyed substantial trade surpluses for the past several years, and its international debts are within comfortable servicing standards. It has achieved many of these successes despite recessions among the advanced industrial economies, the brutality of the Tiananmen Massacre, and international disgust with the regime.

In exchange for these benefits, China has agreed to make certain institutional adjustments, for example, in the areas of intellectual property rights, prison inspections, and market access. It implicitly agreed to release some political prisoners at times that roughly corresponded to visits by leading U.S. officials or congressional debates about China's most-favored-nation trade status. It has said that it will abide by the Missile Technology Control Regime and the Nuclear Non-proliferation Treaty. It has also become much more open to foreign influences and outside ideas, especially in South China. Nevertheless, so far China has probably made fewer adjustments for the gains it has received from full involvement in the international system than has any other country (again with the possible exception of Japan). Political decision making is still highly autonomous from societal or international factors. The World Bank and the IMF have made numerous recommendations to the Chinese on many economic issues, but their advice has been only partially heeded. The United States is the only country for which most-favored-nation status for China is an issue.[55]

China's position as a UN Security Council veto power allows it to extract international strategic rents for acquiescing to actions that the United States would like to undertake multilaterally, for example, in the area of peace-keeping operations. The economic strength of overseas Chinese communities has allowed the Chinese government to absorb huge quantities of foreign investment without offering a very attractive investment climate.[56] China's economic successes have forced foreign corporations to rethink their China operations even if they had given up on the China market. The "myth" of the China market becomes less of a myth as the GNP increases by 10 percent annually.

China is being changed by its international interactions but in ways that are difficult to identify and quantify. If it is to extract greater benefits from the international system, it will have to continue to modify its internal structures, rules, and regulations. Some of these rationalizations of the political economy and the legal system might have happened in any case, as marketization and capitalism spread in China. International influences will only hasten this process.

But just as it is difficult to identify and quantify the effects of the international system on China, so too is it difficult to identify and quantify the effects of a dynamically growing China on the international system. The growing economic integration of Hong Kong, South China, and Taiwan can be expected to affect the international political economy, and the extremely rapid growth of China's already very large output and exports will have implications for international institutions. One may wonder whether world trade can survive the rise of another export-based economy in Asia, particularly an export-based economy with the world's largest population, and how the interactions of China, Japan, and the two Koreas will alter the international strategic environment.

The international system is changing China, but so far it appears that China has obtained the better of the deal. It is increasingly a force to be reckoned with in the international system, and this means that it is less and less susceptible to direct international pressure. As China grows, the international system will increasingly have to adapt to it. China may undertake more adaptations to the international system than the system may to China, but ten or fifteen more years of rapid Chinese economic growth will fundamentally alter the international system as well.

Notes

1. "U.S. Takes Lead Back in Exports," *New York Times* (hereafter *NYT*) (national edition), March 18, 1992, C1, C19, on export rank (citations to the *NYT* before September 1, 1991, refer to the

New York metropolitan edition; after that time, they refer to the national edition); United Nations Transnational Corporations and Management Division, *World Investment Report 1992* (New York: United Nations, 1992), pp. 311–315; Nicholas R. Lardy, "Chinese Foreign Trade," *China Quarterly* (forthcoming), on the Sino-American trade surplus; and "1991 Statistical Bureau Communiqué Released," Foreign Broadcast Information Service, *Daily Report—China* (hereafter FBIS-China), March 6, 1992, pp. 38–45, see p. 42.

2. For one of many examples, see Frank Gibney, Jr., "China's Renege Province," *Newsweek*, February 17, 1992, pp. 35–36.

3. This discussion is heavily influenced by Kenneth N. Waltz, *Theory of International Politics* (Reading, Mass.: Addison-Wesley, 1978).

4. Two of the major works explaining the importance of international institutions are Stephen D. Krasner, ed., *International Regimes* (Ithaca, N.Y.: Cornell University Press, 1983), and Robert O. Keohane, *After Hegemony* (Princeton, N.J.: Princeton University Press, 1984).

5. Some of the major statements on these issues are discussed in Peter Gourevitch, "The Second Image Reversed: The International Sources of Domestic Politics," *International Organization* 32:4 (Fall 1978):881–912.

6. Michael Doyle, "Liberalism and World Politics," *American Political Science Review* 80:4 (December 1986):1151–1169, and Henry A. Kissinger, *American Foreign Policy* (New York: Norton, 1969), chap. 1.

7. "Qian Qichen on the World Situation," *Beijing Review*, January 15–21, 1990, p. 16.

8. One example of a structuring impact of the international system on China's economy is David Zweig, "Internationalizing the Chinese Countryside: The Political Economy of Exports from Rural China," *China Quarterly* No. 128 (December 1991):716–741. Despite its title, this essay fails to discuss how external forces influence domestic politics. For a superb study of precisely this point, see Thomas G. Moore, "China in the World Market: International Sources of Reform and Modernization in Chinese Industry" (Ph.D. diss., Department of Politics, Princeton University, 1994).

9. For example, "Fighting Back," *The Economist*, March 7, 1992, p. 36, and Jim Mann, "China Seeks Russian Weapons," *Los Angeles Times*, July 12, 1992, pp. A1, A8.

10. See Nicholas D. Kristof, "As China Looks at World Order, It Detects New Struggles Emerging," *NYT*, April 24, 1992, pp. A1, A4.

11. Lawrence H. Summers, "The Rise of China," *International Economic Insights* (May–June 1992), p. 17, and "When China Wakes," *The Economist* (China Survey), November 28–December 4, 1992, inset, pp. 1–18.

12. Perhaps the best example of this is the "Memorandum of Understanding between the Government of the United States of America and the Government of the People's Republic of China Concerning Market Access," October 10, 1992. For analysis see Joseph Massey, "301: Successful Resolution," *China Business Review*, November–December 1992, pp. 9–11.

13. See Harold K. Jacobson and Michel Oksenberg, *China's Participation in the IMF, the World Bank, and GATT* (Ann Arbor: University of Michigan Press, 1990).

14. Two good studies of the difficulties in business dealings with China are Margaret M. Pearson, *Joint Ventures in the People's Republic of China* (Princeton, N.J.: Princeton University Press, 1991), and Jim Mann, *Beijing Jeep* (New York: Simon and Schuster, 1989). On China's external successes, see Nicholas R. Lardy, *Foreign Trade and Economic Reform in China 1978–1990* (Cambridge: Cambridge University Press, 1991); Ezra Vogel, *One Step Ahead in China* (Cambridge, Mass.: Harvard University Press, 1989); and Nicholas D. Kristof, "Foreign Investors Pouring into China," *NYT*, June 15, 1992, pp. C1, C6.

15. Scholars from the Chinese Institute of International Studies (attached to the Foreign Ministry) say that the imposition of conditional most-favored-nation status by the United States on China may mean that China will expand its arms sales, perhaps of missiles, prohibited by the Missile Technology Control Regime. Comments by Chinese scholars, the Asia Foundation, San Francisco, Calif., December 1, 1992.

16. In the second edition of *China and the World*, I discuss some of the other variables listed in this paragraph. See pp. 34–40.

17. I discuss these issues in more detail in "The Limits to Leadership in China," in *NBR Analysis*, Vol. 3, No. 3 (August 1992), *The Future of China*, pp. 23–35, esp. 24–32.

18. Again, these issues are discussed in more detail in Bachman, "The Limits to Leadership in China."

19. On Guangdong, see Gibney, "China's Renege Province"; Vogel, *One Step Ahead in China*; and the series of articles on the Shenzhen special economic zone in *Far Eastern Economic Review* (hereafter *FEER*), May 14, 1992, pp. 23–32.

20. This type of politics is discussed in David M. Lampton, "A Peach for a Plum: Bargaining, Interests, and Bureaucratic Politics in China," in Kenneth G. Lieberthal and David M. Lampton, eds., *Bureaucracy, Politics, and Decision Making in Post-Mao China* (Berkeley: University of California Press, 1992), pp. 33–58.

21. On border issues, for example, see Nicholas D. Kristof, "Mainland Threat Worrying Taiwan," *NYT*, February 10, 1991, p. A9; *Tibet Press Watch*, various issues; Michael Vatikiotis, "China Stirs the Pot," *FEER*, July 9, 1992, pp. 14–15; and "Qian Proposes Agreement on Sino-ASEAN Co-op," *China Daily* (hereafter *CD*), July 22, 1992, p. 1.

22. An excellent source on Chinese missile sales is Timothy V. McCarthy, "A Chronology of PRC Missile Trade and Developments" (processed, International Missile Proliferation Project, Monterey Institute of International Studies, released February 12, 1992). See also *Eye on Supply* (Emerging Nuclear Suppliers Project, Monterey Institute of International Studies), various issues; John Pomfret (Associated Press), "China Turns Guns into Butter—to Pay for Better Guns," *Seattle Times/Post-Intelligencer*, May 10, 1992, p. A4; and Sheryl WuDunn, "China Browses for Tanks, Aircraft, and Carrier in Ex-Soviet Lands," *NYT*, June 7, 1992, p. 8.

23. See Barbara Crossette, "China Signs Prison Labor Pact with U.S. Meant to Curb Prison Labor on Exports," *NYT*, August 8, 1992, p. 3.

24. On various aspects of Chinese trading practices drawing U.S. criticism, some of which appear to be the result of lack of central control, see James Bennet, "U.S. Accuses Chinese of Conspiring with Textile Firms in Trade Fraud," *International Herald Tribune*, May 8, 1992, p. 7, and Sheryl WuDunn, "In the Trade Wars, China Has Learned Guerrilla Tactics," *NYT*, Week in Review Section, June 9, 1991, p. 2. On Chinese–Hong Kong economic relations, see, for example, Sheryl WuDunn, "Hong Kong–China Fence: No Bar to Business," *NYT*, April 12, 1992, p. 7, and Carl Goldstein, "Ties that Bind," *FEER*, July 30, 1992, pp. 61–62. On provincial competition and foreign trade practices, see "Provincial Developments and Central Reactions," *China News Analysis* (hereafter *CNA*) No. 1463 (July 1, 1992); and "Learning the Rules of Foreign Trade," *CNA* No. 1464 (July 15, 1992).

25. On the links between China's release of political prisoners and U.S. debates about most-favored-nation trade status, see Harry Harding, *A Fragile Relationship* (Washington, D.C.: Brookings Institution, 1992), esp. chap. 8.

26. Fragmentation and bargaining are central themes in Lieberthal and Lampton, *Bureaucracy, Politics, and Decision Making*.

27. John Wilson Lewis, *Leadership Doctrines in Communist China* (Ithaca, N.Y.: Cornell University Press, 1963).

28. On the importance of redundancy, see Martin Landau, "Redundancy, Rationality, and the Problem of Overlap and Duplication," *Public Administration Review* 29 (July–August 1969):346–358, and Samuel P. Huntington, *Political Order in Changing Societies* (New Haven: Yale University Press, 1968), esp. chap. 1.

29. On central dimensions of the operation of the Chinese state system, see Kenneth Lieberthal and Michel Oksenberg, *Policy Making in China* (Princeton, N.J.: Princeton University Press, 1988); Lieberthal and Lampton, *Bureaucracy, Politics, and Decision Making*; Barrett McCormick, *Political Reform in Post-Mao China* (Berkeley: University of California Press, 1990); Avery Goldstein, *From Bandwagoning to Balance of Power Politics in China* (Stanford, Calif.: Stanford University Press,

1991); and Hong Yung Lee, *From Revolutionary Cadres to Party Technocrats in Socialist China* (Berkeley: University of California Press, 1990).

30. The Chinese call this the tendency to strive for "big and complete" and "small and complete" factories. On "big and complete," see Xue Muqiao, ed., *Almanac of China's Economy, 1981* (Hong Kong: Modern Cultural Company, 1982), pp. 175–193, esp. 181–182. Many of the defects of the bureaucracy are identified in "On the Reform of the System of Party and State Leadership," in *Selected Works of Deng Xiaoping (1975–1982)* (Beijing: Foreign Languages Press, 1984), pp. 302–325.

31. For a general analysis, see Shen Liren and Dai Yuanchen, "Formation of 'Dukedom Economies' and Their Causes and Defects," *Chinese Economic Studies* 25:4 (Summer 1992):6–24.

32. Kenneth Lieberthal, "Introduction: The 'Fragmented Authoritarianism' Model and Its Limitations," in Lieberthal and Lampton, *Bureaucracy, Politics, and Decision Making*, pp. 1–30, esp. 2–3 on the *xitong* in the late 1980s.

33. David Bachman, *Bureaucracy, Economy, and Leadership in China* (Cambridge: Cambridge University Press, 1991).

34. See Barry Naughton, "Hierarchy and the Bargaining Economy," in Lieberthal and Lampton, *Bureaucracy, Politics, and Decision Making*, pp. 245–279. See also *Zhongguo guding zichan Touzi tongji ziliao, 1950–1985* [Statistical Material on China's Fixed Capital Investment] (Beijing: Zhongguo tongji chubanshe, 1987), p. 155.

35. This incident and the general conditions of military arms sales are discussed in John W. Lewis, Hua Di, and Xue Litai's superb article, "Beijing's Defense Establishment: Solving the Arms-Export Dilemma," *International Security* (hereafter *IS*) 15:4 (Spring 1991):87–109, esp. 96 on the Saudi sale.

36. The scholars from the Chinese Institute of International Studies mentioned earlier suggested that there is now more coordination over arms sales, with Foreign Ministry input.

37. On the reports of these sales and other actions, see Nicholas D. Kristof, "U.S. Feels Uneasy as Beijing Moves to Sell New Arms," *NYT,* June 10, 1991, pp. A1, A8; Sheryl WuDunn, "China Backs Pact on Nuclear Arms," *NYT,* August 11, 1991, pp. 1, 10; Elaine Sciolino with Eric Schmitt, "Algerian Reactor Came from China," *NYT,* November 15, 1991, pp. A1, A7; idem., "China Said to Sell Parts for Missiles," *NYT,* January 31, 1992, pp. A1, A2.

38. The best study of China's missile programs, on which this paragraph is based, is John Wilson Lewis and Hua Di, "China's Ballistic Missile Programs," *IS* 17:2 (Fall 1992):5–40, esp. 33–39.

39. The strongest claim for the relative autonomy of the military system is found in Jonathan D. Pollack, "Structure and Process in the Chinese Military System," in Lieberthal and Lampton, *Bureaucracy, Politics, and Decision Making*, pp. 151–180.

40. This is implied in Hongda Harry Wu, *The Chinese Gulag* (Boulder, Colo.: Westview Press, 1992). See also Jan Wong, "In China's Siberia, Prison Means Business," *Seattle Times/Post-Intelligencer,* June 28, 1992, A3.

41. See Pomfret, "China Turns Guns into Butter," noting that the Palace Hotel (Beijing's best) is partly owned by the General Staff Department of the Chinese Army; other information comes from well-informed foreign businessmen, who report the involvement of the Ministry of State Security in at least one and possibly two joint-venture hotels.

42. See, for example, John Kamm's "Reforming Foreign Trade," chap. 11 in Vogel, *One Step Ahead in China.*

43. Examples of these points are found in Sheryl WuDunn, "To Cantonese a Little Graft Is Forgivable," *NYT,* May 7, 1991, p. A14; Carl Goldstein, "Strait Ahead," *FEER*, March 5, 1992, p. 54; and Nicholas D. Kristof, "Support for Move to Freer Markets Is Growing in China," *NYT,* June 28, 1992, pp. 1, 8.

44. Compelling evidence of the weakness of the Chinese planned economy is found in Barry Naughton, *Growing Out of the Plan: Chinese Economic Reform, 1978–1990* (Cambridge: Cambridge University Press, 1993), chap. 1.

45. This is the approximate figure that Barber Conable, former president of the World Bank and new president of the National Committee on U.S.-China Relations, was given during an inter-

view at the State Planning Commission in Beijing in May 1992. Information provided by one of the members of the delegation.

46. On these points, see Naughton, *Growing Out of the Plan*, and Christine P.W. Wong, "Central-Local Relations in an Era of Fiscal Decline," *China Quarterly* No. 128 (December 1991):691–715, among others.

47. See Naughton, "Hierarchy and the Bargaining Economy"; Wu Minyi, "Guanyu difang zhengfu xingweide ruogan sikao" [Certain Reflections on the Behavior of Local Governments], *Jingji Yanjiu* [Economic Research] (hereafter *JJYJ*) No. 7 (1991):56–60; and the Study Group on the Economic Abilities and Behavior of Local Governments … , "Difang zhengfu zai qiye yingyunzhongde jingji xingwei" [The Economic Behavior of Local Governments in Enterprise Operations], *JJYJ* No. 8 (1991):48–55.

48. See Jacobson and Oksenberg, *China's Participation*, pp. 173–175; Carl Goldstein, "Ties That Bind," *FEER*, July 30, 1992, pp. 61–62; and Pearson, *Joint Ventures*.

49. Wu, *The Chinese Gulag*, esp. pp. 135–141.

50. See the advertisement for the ASN Technical Group, the Northwest Industrial University, in *CD*, Business Weekly, July 20, 1992, p. 4.

51. Xia Yang and Wang Zhigang, "Zhongguo jingji 'geju' xianxiang chutan" [Preliminary Investigations of China's Economic "Warlordism"], *Liaowang* [Outlook] overseas edition No. 39 (September 26, 1988):2–5; Andrew Watson, Christopher Findlay, and Du Yintang, "Who Won the 'Wool War'?" *China Quarterly* No. 118 (June 1989):213–241; on aspects of regional development, Dali Yang, "Patterns of China's Regional Development Strategy," *China Quarterly* No. 122 (June 1990):230–257; idem, "China Adjusts to the World Economy," *Pacific Affairs* 64:1 (Spring 1991):42–64; idem, "Reforms, Resources, and Regional Cleavages," *Issues and Studies* 27:9 (September 1991):43–69.

52. On rural reform, the best study is Dali L. Yang, "Making Reform: Leadership, Societal Resistance, and Institutional Change in China" (Ph.D. diss. Department of Politics, Princeton University, 1992). On rural industry and exports, see Zweig, "Internationalizing the Chinese Countryside." On the dynamism of the "entrepreneurial sector," see Nicholas R. Lardy, "Redefining U.S.-China Economic Relations," *NBR Analysis*, Vol. 4, No. 5 (1991).

53. Naughton, *Growing Out of the Plan*.

54. This feedback is the focus of Zweig, "Internationalizing the Chinese Countryside."

55. On China's using the international system for maximum benefit but taking on minimal responsibilities, see Samuel S. Kim, "International Organizations in Chinese Foreign Policy," *Annals of the American Academy of Political and Social Science* 519 (January 1992):140–157. On specific examples of World Bank and IMF policy recommendations to China and China's responses, see Lardy, *Foreign Trade and Economic Reform*, pp. 119–120; and Wu Nianlu and Chen Quangeng, *Renminbi huilu yanjiu* [Studies on the Exchange Rate of the Renminbi] (Beijing: Zhongguo jinrong chubanshe, 1989), pp. 239–242 (my thanks to Nicholas Lardy for providing me with a copy of this book).

56. On the overseas Chinese, see "A Driving Force," *The Economist*, July 18, 1992, pp. 21–24.

3

Anti-Imperialism in Chinese Foreign Policy

EDWARD FRIEDMAN

Nationalism

The Communist Party led by Mao Zedong that conquered state power in China in 1949 seemed the embodiment of heroic anti-imperialist nationalism. A portrait of the Red Army as China's patriotic force contrasts its brave and bold response to imperialist invaders with the northeastern (Manchurian) warlords' surrender to Japan in 1931 and the failure of Chiang Kai-shek (Jiang Jieshi) and his Nationalist Party government to prevent the barbarous rape of Nanking (Nanjing) by the Japanese military. From this viewpoint, the only fighting patriots in China, the Communists, waged a courageous guerrilla war to protect China's people from the Japanese. This nationalist tale of modern Chinese resistance to foreign marauders is imagined as at one with the struggle of China's people throughout history to defend their land from foreign invaders. It links time, place, and people in a unifying grand narrative that begins with the building of a Great Wall of stone in ancient times to defend against wave after wave of barbarian plunderers, goes on to describe the successful fourteenth-century resistance of what became the Ming dynasty to its Mongol conquerors (the Yuan dynasty), and ends with the unifying liberation of China by a people's army—China's modern Great Wall of Iron.[1] This grand narrative of patriotic history is given its modern origin in 1839, with a failed popular defense against Britain's barbaric attempt to force civilized Chinese to buy British opium. This losing Chinese effort carried the historic lesson that Chinese should not try to imitate the seafaring pirate-merchants; Britain could not be defeated with ships on the sea, but on the nation's sacred soil invaders could be submerged and drowned in a sea of popular resistance.[2] A force that could mobilize Chinese villagers could defend China's independence. In this narrative of Chinese Communist national legitimation, the imperialist armies of Japan are finally defeated in 1945, when the Red Army of the Soviet Union comes to the aid of China's Communists, the people's guerrilla resisters, and helps to liberate Manchuria from the Japanese. The victory of Mao's anti-imperialist forces was the victory of an international socialist mission that alone was capable of unleashing the might of the Chinese people in pursuit of its independence. As Mao put it in 1949, at long last the Chinese people stood up.

Any historian can easily poke large holes in this pretended seamless fabric. In fact, ancient China rose through trade and cultural exchange with surrounding peoples. About half the students in the National Academy in the Tang dynasty capital (today Xian) were foreign. The Great Wall was built by the Ming dynasty and reflects a self-inflicted injury to Chinese development—a nativistic and isolationist turn that cost the Chinese people the potential benefits of openness to the early industrial revolution and thereby made them vulnerable to foreign attack. Modern astronomers were executed so that the emperor alone could comprehend and command the heavens. The communist Soviet Union helped detach Mongolia from the Chinese empire in the 1920s and thereafter fought to hold onto special (imperialist?) privileges in Manchuria. It was the United States that defeated Japan in World War II, in alliance with Chiang's Nationalists, who fought brilliantly in Burma. Many non-Communist forces in China courageously resisted the Japanese military occupiers. By the 1990s, as Chinese nationalism was being redefined, even Deng Xiaoping blamed Ming dynasty isolationism for China's modern weakness.[3] The controlled and censored film industry of China could, in the 1990s, present movies of non-Communist anti-Japanese resistance. Mao-style anti-imperialism has lost its credibility. An overview of Chinese foreign policy as an attempt to respond to imperialist challenges shows that Mao's policy perspective injured the Chinese people and is being discarded.

Understanding the degree to which the notion of communism as the national essence pursuing independence from imperialism is a temporally constructed and temporarily legitimating narrative makes it clear that the anti-imperialist national project depended on maintaining the popular credibility of this empowering mythos, celebrating and miming the nativistic and isolationist aspects of the Ming dynasty. Mao identified with the founder of the Ming.[4] The narrative of total mobilization for a war of defense is increasingly less capable of winning the allegiance of patriotic Chinese. In an era in which world market competitiveness seems to define national success, Maoist anti-imperialism engenders a crisis of post-Mao legitimation. A new national project is emerging from the renewed efforts of China's people, in the post-Mao era, to benefit from the common wealth of the entire human race, even to the point of pursuing potentially profitable business as far away as Peru and the United States. How can one legitimate anti-imperialism when China has become the top investor in the century-old British colony of Hong Kong?

Independence

"The Chinese people have stood up" is Mao's best-remembered phrase. With the establishment of the People's Republic of China on October 1, 1949, rulers and ruled looked forward to freedom from the incursions of imperialist powers. The new foreign policy makers saw themselves as engaged in a continuing struggle to free China from and defend it against imperialism in all its aspects—economic exploitation, military invasion, and cultural pollution. To counter imperialist challenges, a Communist Party dictatorship would strive to make China completely independent, that is, economically self-reliant, militarily strong, and, in matters of values and beliefs, pure. Freedom was sought not for individuals but for the new nation-state. In political practice, this meant all power to the dictatorial rulers of the Leninist state.[5]

State leaders had to transform their anti-imperialist project into workable policies. In the post-World War II bipolar, Cold War world, Mao concluded that China needed to ally itself with the Soviet Union to defend itself against the imperialist United States, allied with revanchist Japan and with counterrevolutionary armies loyal to the defeated side in China's civil war.

Compromising with the Soviet Union

Mao Zedong and the other rulers of Communist China believed that state power had been redefined by the U.S. use of atomic weapons in war. Even before establishing themselves in the restored national capital of Beijing, Mao's followers sent agents to an anti-American peace conference in Paris, the declared purpose of which was to ban the use of nuclear weapons. Ironically, the agents' mission was purchasing material so that China could one day build its own nuclear weapons. At the same time, Chinese agents approached Chinese scientists and engineers abroad, mainly in the United States, to persuade them to return home to work as patriots on a Chinese atomic bomb project. Mao's ruling group found that to be a great power in the age of nuclear weapons required possessing nuclear weaponry. Only the most advanced weapons would free the Chinese people from fear of invaders.[6] The Soviet Union was open to an alliance with China because World War II had ended with the United States occupying Japan and turning its military might in Japan toward Russia.

In addition to placing a high priority on restoring China's dignity and greatness through military might (a project that soon involved Chinese in learning from the Communist Party dictatorship in the Soviet Union, which exploded its first nuclear weapon in 1949), the new Chinese ruling group believed that it had to act immediately to stave off direct foreign threats of aggression on behalf of counterrevolution. Its concern was that the United States might try to overthrow the Leninist socialists and restore to power the defeated Nationalist Party led by Chiang Kai-shek (Jiang Jieshi).[7] Mao Zedong's belief in the need to resist imperialists supporting counterrevolutionary forces reflected his understanding of both global revolutionary history and Chinese anti-imperialist goals. For Mao, all of the modern revolutions—the 1789 French Revolution, the 1871 Paris Commune, the 1917 Bolshevik Revolution, the crushing of the Spanish republic by international fascism in the 1930s, and the Greek partisans of the 1940s—had been attacked by foreign-sponsored armies allied with domestic counterrevolutionaries, and China had since its origin been engaged in a continuous struggle to defend itself against invaders. Division at home made China vulnerable to foreign threats. Only the Leninist one-party dictatorship could resist imperialism by mobilizing Chinese resources against it. Consequently, anti-imperialist China's top priority was to smash all opposition to Mao's correct line and to prepare to defend China's revolution against expected imperialist invaders. This in 1949 meant the United States, which was seen as establishing itself next door to China in Japan.

Mao worried that an imperialist United States might join forces with a re-vanchist militarist Japan and Jiang Jieshi's counterrevolutionaries. Consequently, on Valentine's Day in 1950 China signed a pact with the Soviet Union that committed the latter to come to China's aid should it be attacked by Japan or any nation allied with Japan. This was a formula that appealed to popular anti-Japanese sentiment in China while actually targeting the United States, understood as not merely capitalist but a reembodiment of the barbarian invaders who had threatened China from time immemorial. The new regime's legitimation was based on its ability to defend against foreign enemies to China's national independence.[8]

The Korean War

War in Korea between June 1950 and July 1953 tested the alliance of Beijing and Moscow against Washington. The Communist forces in North Korea were beholden to the occupying army from the Soviet Union for their very existence. The Korean Communists[9] sought Moscow's support for a war to liberate the south from military occupation by U.S. imperialism and its client regime, headed by the patriotic tyrant Syngman Rhee. According to the 1980s memoirs of Russians and Koreans involved in the 1945–1950 events initiating the war, agents from Moscow planned the war, including a withdrawal of Russian advisers just prior to the initial attack to conceal their involvement, but Stalin checked with Mao before giving North Korea's dictator, Kim Il Sung, the go-ahead.[10] The Chinese allowed Korean troops then fighting with China's Communist armies to join the armies that invaded South Korea on June 25, 1950. A mock attack was staged to look like a thrust from the South so that the North could camouflage its offensive with a pretext, as the Nazis did in 1939 against Poland. The United States nonetheless won United Nations approval for military action to defend South Korea against aggression, and General Douglas MacArthur headed the UN force.

In August 1950, when U.S. forces finally held against the North Korean Communist armies at a beachhead in southeastern Korea, Mao began to worry that the North was overextended and a U.S. counterattack was possible. Concerned that the United States would move on to threaten China's revolutionary independence, he began sounding out colleagues about how China should respond.[11] Most Chinese leaders felt that the nation should build itself up before taking on the United States—that the Chinese people were exhausted from a century of war, plunder, and turmoil and needed tranquility. But Mao believed in getting the inevitable war with the United States over with as soon as possible. After MacArthur's maneuvers in September had isolated the North Korean forces from the rear, the general in October ordered a march north toward the Chinese border. Chinese signals aimed at deterring this advance went unheeded.[12] Because Stalin did not want to provoke the United States, Mao was largely on his own when he committed China to send troops into Korea to fight the largely U.S. troops. The United States responded by persuading the UN to declare China an aggressor, backing Chiang Kai-shek's regime on Taiwan, and intensifying its embargo against China. As Communists in China saw it, the imperialist United States had intervened in China's civil war on the side of reaction in an attempt to reverse the progressive verdict of history.

The logic of events seemed to lend credibility to Mao's political project of anti-imperialist war communism. Industry on the coast, being bombed and blockaded by Chiang's forces, was moved north and inland. A campaign to ferret out counter-revolutionaries who might aid imperialist invaders targeted southern elites. Cultural pollution in the form of foreign missionary education was brutally up-rooted. Schools were reorganized away from U.S. forms (treated as subversively capitalist) in the direction of a Soviet model, called socialist. All of China was to be mobilized to secure its independence from imperialist enemies.

A long, bloody stalemate and war of attrition ensued in which almost half a million Chinese gave their lives. The U.S. president, Harry Truman, tried to re-strict the fighting to Korea. In 1951 he fired MacArthur, who had insisted on ex-panding the war into China, using Chiang Kai-shek's troops from Taiwan, treat-ing the war as global, and rejecting limitations on weaponry and targets ("refusing to fight with one hand tied behind one's back"). Had MacArthur's pol-icies prevailed, Mao's worst fears would have been realized. Although specialists still debate how close MacArthur came to succeeding, it was close enough to strengthen the hold of Maoist presuppositions on Chinese patriots.

Even after the war was stalemated in mid-1951, an end to the fighting took an-other two years to negotiate. Mao insisted that China's dignity required that all Chinese prisoners be repatriated to the motherland—that they not be surren-dered to imperialism. Truman insisted that prisoners on both sides be free to choose not to return to totalitarian control. Finally, in late 1952, Mao decided that the draining war in Korea was increasing China's dependence on the Soviet Union and delaying its emergence as a great power, and therefore he conceded that the war in Korea could end with stalemate and free choice by prisoners on repatria-tion. But Truman could not meet China halfway. Only a Republican president might have had the anti-Communist credibility to compromise with Commu-nists in China.

In November 1952, Dwight Eisenhower was elected to replace Truman as presi-dent, and immediately after taking office he offered an exchange of wounded pris-oners. Mao readily agreed, and disengagement began. The final obstacle to peace was the opposition of the South Korean government, which wanted the United States to fight on at all costs. The United States allowed Mao's China to pound the South Korean antiarmistice forces into submission—an early sign that on a purely realpolitik basis, with neither Beijing nor Washington benefiting from war in Asia with each other, the interests of the two countries overlapped. This overlap was obscured by China's belief that only an all-out defense, including a willing-ness to risk nuclear attack, had saved China and the U.S. assumption that it was the threat of nuclear attack that had forced China to compromise in Korea.[13]

The Bandung Era

True to Communist anti-imperialist nationalism, Mao began to yield to pres-sure from the Chinese military for military action to liberate the southern off-shore islands held by the counterrevolutionary forces of Chiang Kai-shek.[14] The ultimate patriotic goal of the Leninists in Beijing was reunifying China, including Taiwan, and eliminating any remaining reactionary pretenders to Chinese state power that denied the People's Republic its rightful place as a great power. They also increasingly identified with a global anti-imperialist mission given meaning by Third World independence, seeking to participate in the first conference of independent states of Africa and Asia held in Bandung, Indonesia, in 1955. Moreover, to obtain the material goods required to construct an independent, strong, and prosperous China—one that would have the wherewithal to contribute to a global struggle against imperialism—the government in Beijing welcomed trade with any partner. This set of policies is often characterized as united front, peaceful coexistence, or détente. It included overtures to and talks with the United States in Geneva and Warsaw—participation in the 1954 Geneva conference to settle the wars against French imperialism in Indochina, in which China armed Ho Chi Minh's forces and urged similar compromises in a split Vietnam as in a split Korea. China's independence could be obtained by policies other than war mobilization.

These Bandung-era policies were still completely congruent with China's great-power, anti-imperialist ambitions. Mao's government cooperated with the Soviet Union to obtain nuclear weaponry and stepped up efforts to allow China to work on its own for nuclear bombs. It tried to keep imperialist forces away from China's borders in Korea, in formerly French Indochina, in the Fujian–Taiwan Strait region, in Burma, and on the Tibet/India border. In short, China was creating space and time in which to turn itself into a great power, a nation that could be truly independent of imperialist dangers and help other global forces that were similarly inclined.

Agrarian Socialism

By mid-1955, Mao had concluded that Chinese independence and great-power goals would not be served by following the Soviet path or intensifying economic or military dependence on the Moscow regime. After all, Soviet agriculture was a disaster. Rejecting the Soviet notion that collectivization required prior mechanization, China collectivized agriculture with no machinery inputs from modern industry—a project known by Communist critics in China as agrarian socialism. The tough, disciplined, heroic Chinese villagers who had fought the imperialist invaders could, in Mao's view, build agrarian socialism without tractors and diesel fuel from the Soviet Union. With such a devoted people, an agricultural surplus could be produced to fund the speedy military buildup that would allow an independent China to ward off any threat.

Pushing aside other leaders who criticized independent agrarian socialism as adventurism, in 1957 Mao launched a series of initiatives designed to make China independent, prosperous, strong, and great. Seeing the Soviet dictator Nikita Khrushchev as unworthy, Mao urged the crushing of the great October 1956 Hungarian revolution and insisted on reading Tito's Yugoslavia (which believed in détente, decollectivization, and other reforms) out of the communist movement. Disappointed that Moscow had done so little for Nasser's Egypt after the 1956 Suez Crisis, China tentatively challenged U.S. military commitments to Chiang Kai-shek over the islands of Jinmen (Quemoy) and Mazu (Matsu), across from Taiwan, islands occupied by almost one-third of Jiang's military. The posture seemed in Washington and Moscow to threaten a struggle of Mao's side against Chiang's that could drag America and the Soviet Union into a war that neither wanted. Mao meant to contribute with China's military to a global anti-imperialist effort; his shooting policy backfired.

Khrushchev saw Mao's initiatives as threatening to undermine the Soviet priority of détente with the United States to block a U.S.-backed militarization of West Germany. A Moscow-Washington agreement to avoid war required opposition to Taiwan-area globalizing policies premised on the power projects of Mao and Chiang. Suddenly Mao was faced with two possible outcomes that could weaken his nationalist cause: that Taiwan might be permanently split from China and that China might be left isolated against both the Soviet Union and the United States. Consequently, he changed his policy toward Chiang's troops on Fujian's offshore islands, pointing to their presence as evidence that the Chinese Revolutionary Civil War was unfinished and that only foreign interference had kept the People's Republic of China from incorporating Taiwan province. He also intensified efforts to resume talks with the United States on problems such as Taiwan.

To enhance their ability to defend China against potential invaders, all regions, down to the gargantuan militarized, multivillage collectives whose misnomer was "commune," were to become self-reliant. The intention here was to reduce the need for markets and money (the world's most deadly famine followed, leaving over twenty million Chinese dead) and to enhance the ability to survive as a socialist entity against any potential invasion. In the countryside, virtually everyone was ordered to become a soldier. Elements of culture that did not serve the purposes of the anti-imperialist regime came under attack. Textbooks were rewritten to read that dying in the defense of China against invaders was the ultimate glory. Rituals such as lineage burials and prolonged familial celebrations of the New Year were attacked for detracting from the primary purpose of mobilizing to win the anti-imperialist struggle.

Mao's insistence on his own, better way to build a great power alienated both other leaders of China's anti-imperialist cause and the rulers of the Soviet Union. In 1959 Moscow broke its commitment to help China build atomic bombs, and in 1960 it recalled all Soviet scientists and technicians working on that project and others in China. Mao responded by ordering full commitment to the most rapid development of the nuclear project, even if it meant—as it did—more starvation for ordinary Chinese.

In 1961, according to Hu Hua, a keeper of the Party archives, Mao prodded his new minister of national defense, Lin Biao, to suggest to the leadership that, with both Moscow and Washington as adversaries and tensions along China's Tibet border with India, it was necessary for China to mobilize in self-defense. China, he argued, should devote all its efforts to preparing to survive as the world's only true anti-imperialist socialist society, building locally self-reliant economies without market relations that could survive a blockade and support a war effort. Other leaders insisted, however, that recovery from the murderous 1959–1961 famine had to be priority number one, and Mao temporarily yielded to this consensus. The Soviet Union was blamed for the Mao famine and the other miseries caused by the disastrous policies of the Great Leap.[15] The deep presuppositional nature of a Chinese nationalism defended by martial anti-imperialism virtually guaranteed Mao the capacity to win massive support from Chinese patriots for subsequent initiatives in harmony with the grand anti-imperialist narrative.

The Third Front

By 1963 world events permitted Mao to persuade many fellow leaders that China was confronted by an imperialist United States in collusion with a revisionist Soviet Union and could become dangerously vulnerable if it did not act swiftly and fully in its own defense. Now China alone was the world's hope for anti-imperialist socialism. In 1962 Chinese rulers had found themselves responding to an advance of Indian troops, armed and supported by both Washington and Moscow, into Tibet. After China had forced the Indian troops back across the original border, both the United States and the Soviet Union had increased their military support for expansionist India, seen in China as a subimperialist power. In addition, the United States and the Soviet Union had signed treaties against atmospheric nuclear testing and for a halt to nuclear proliferation, and in the capital of the PRC, it seemed obvious that their goal was not peace but dominion. Their shared purpose was to keep China from succeeding in its costly pursuit of the nuclear military might that would supposedly permit it to act independently on behalf of anti-imperialism worldwide. U.S. President John Kennedy was even considering scenarios for destroying China's bomb-building installations before China could explode its first nuclear device. Chinese participants in a Pugwash Conference in the Soviet Union in 1963 found Americans and Russians wanting to discuss how to keep China from going nuclear. China increasingly seemed the target of military collusion by the superpowers.

Local events reinforced the overall threat. After a 1962 clash in China's far-western province of Xinjiang, an exodus of Turkic Muslims from China to the Soviet Union was welcomed by Moscow. The view there was that irrational Maoist economics would bring more famine in China and hungry people would be seeking land with food in Soviet territory. In 1963 the Soviet Army was therefore redeployed in greater numbers in China's border region, including Mongolia.[16] Already in 1962 Mongolia had been taken into the Soviet-run economic bloc, thus squeezing China out of Mongolia and making China's northern border a Soviet monopoly. At this time of danger, China's air force was weaker than Egypt's. If war came, it would be fought on China's soil.

Although the Soviet Union increasingly seemed the most active threat to China, it was not alone. Chiang Kai-shek's forces on Taiwan maneuvered militarily in May to spark a rebellion in China in 1962. Mao ordered a pullback of government institutions from the Taiwan Strait coast of Fujian and mobilization as far inland as Nanjing. U.S. President Kennedy halted Chiang's thrust. A consensus was developing among China's leaders that China had to defend itself against potential aggression from numerous directions.

Even south of China proper, in Indochina, the United States and the Soviet Union were increasingly involved against Chinese interests. A crisis in Laos permitted the Soviets to use their airlift capacity to supply the Communist Lao forces from the territory of North Vietnam in 1961–1962 and threaten to squeeze China out. The United States was backing a losing group in Laos and arming the Saigon regime in South Vietnam, far from China's borders, and therefore Chinese leaders did not envision a U.S. invasion from Indochina. As Soviet forces, arrayed in a half-moon to the north, west, and south, pressed hard against Chinese territory and broadcast into China on behalf of a military coup against Mao, the United States seemed to complete the encirclement from the U.S. bases in Japan, the Ryukyus, Taiwan, and the Philippines. Mao's policy initiative of 1961—Lin Biao's failed trial balloon—would seem wise to many Chinese leaders in 1964–1965.

With leaders in Washington and Moscow discussing how to destroy a purported Chinese threat to world peace, Mao won support in late 1964 for an all-out attempt to save China from a coming war that might be immediate, nuclear, and widespread. Facing the ultimate imperialist aggression, China reached out to any friend it could find. It armed liberation struggles at no charge against white racist Rhodesia and Portuguese colonial Mozambique. It reached out to anti-imperialists in Southeast Asia such as Sihanouk in Cambodia and Sukarno in Indonesia. It approached dissidents within the U.S. and Soviet camps, hoping to split each from within. Within the U.S. camp, France recognized China, amd Beijing hoped that Japan would follow. Within the former socialist camp dominated by the Soviet Union, China became the sole support of super-Stalinist Albania, pressing Tirana to persuade other East European regimes to break with Moscow.[17] China's October 1964 explosion of an atomic weapon earned it more stature in the Third World and more animus from Moscow and Washington. In both capitals more people in power were looking for ways to destroy China's growing military power.

Many Chinese anti-imperialist initiatives failed. Sukarno was overthrown in Indonesia. The Afro-Asian movement, after Ben Bella was overthrown in Algeria, adopted a more pro-Soviet orientation based on the prestige of Nehru in India and Tito in Yugoslavia. In response, China frantically offered arms free to all anti-imperialists. These Chinese efforts did, however, persuade Washington that U.S. intervention in Vietnam was needed to stop a Chinese policy of global subversion by proxy. More important, the post-Khrushchev rulers in Moscow from 1965 on saw nuclear-armed, economically irrational, antirevisionist (i.e., anti-Soviet) China as their major enemy, with Beijing wooing anti-imperialists in Africa, trying to subvert Moscow's hegemony in Eastern Europe, and working to cause Communists internationally to see Moscow as their major enemy and Beijing as their only friend. When Moscow responded to Mao's taunts about U.S.-Soviet détente by mocking China's accommodation with colonial Hong Kong, Mao snapped back, calling attention to czarist Russia's land grabs from China. The Brezhnev regime subsequently intensified military actions targeting Mao's government in China.

By 1965 China was moving military industry into its hinterland, away from both the Soviet border and the coast. First-line defenses were built on the west, north, and east, on China's long, exposed border with the Soviet Union and Soviet-occupied Mongolia and facing the U.S. military bases in the Pacific island chain. Second lines of defense were prepared in defensible mountain regions behind the first. A third front, the secure militarized hinterland, was prepared in China's southwest, not far from Indochina. Mao believed that if the United States invaded it would do so from the coast, not from the jungles of the south. More powerfully than ever, the premise of all-out anti-imperialist war mobilization of the entire people defined China's policy project.

With everyone mobilized for war communism, China's economy was grievously wounded. Moscow, rapidly building its forces on China's borders in aggressive array, was enemy number one. The Soviet Union's purportedly phony communism, called revisionism, was taken as the major enemy. Revisionists in China—opponents of Mao's mobilizational priority—were portrayed as traitors and potential allies of anti-imperialist China's major foe. Mao launched a series of movements, the Cultural Revolution being the best-known, to root out so-called revisionists and to institutionalize anti-imperialist economic policies so that each region of China could be self-reliant and survive war and invasion.

Mao's China became isolated from all but the most militant anti-imperialists. From countries all over the world these zealous Communists, dissatisfied with Moscow's détente with Washington and with the Soviet Union's grey stagnation, flocked to China for political lessons and military support on real revolution, total revolution, continuous revolution. The choice for them was between Maoism, whatever its unfortunate excesses, and global Armageddon. Revolutionary tourists came from annihilationist groups all around the world, from Pol Pot and his genocidal Khmer Rouge in Cambodia, from the Naxalites in India, from dissident Communists in Peru following Alberto Guzmán, who would form the monstrously murderous Sendero Luminoso. Tied to the international liaison office of the Party's Central Committee, led by the 110-percent Maoist Kang Sheng, a Maoist anti-imperialist international was in the making.

After the Soviet Union had crushed a Czechoslovak effort to build "socialism with a human face" in 1968 and announced its right to do the same to any nation undermining what Leonid Brezhnev called the socialist commonwealth, and after it had responded to a Chinese incursion in March 1969 with an overwhelming pummeling of the Chinese border area, Mao grew open to a tactical entente with the United States against it. Rulers in Moscow from 1968–1969 on debated whether to attack China.

Cooperation with Washington that would check the threat to Beijing from Moscow could also permit a Chinese opening to the U.S.-dominated world economy and, consequently, a reinvigoration of the Chinese economy, which had stagnated and declined because of third-front policies that imposed sacrifice on China's people. A political struggle in Beijing pitted Mao, who believed the Chinese people needed a respite from all-out struggle, against Defense Minister Lin Biao, who continued to promote mobilization against both the United States and the Soviet Union.

By 1970 what anti-imperialism meant to Mao was defeating the Soviet Union, perceived as the greatest danger because of the prestige it retained from its earlier era of true anti-imperialism. The key ally for this effort was the United States. President Richard Nixon's arrival in Beijing, after three years of secret negotiations, in February 1972 won Mao and China's people relief from third-front war mobilization pressures. Lin Biao, still committed to the third-front policies against both the United States and the Soviet Union, had fallen in the autumn of 1971. In the tremendous succession struggle that followed, Mao's continuing commitment to the war communism model precluded Maoist legitimation for the forces whose titular leader was the premier, Zhou Enlai, which were committed to policies of reform, openness, and international maneuvering aimed at making China a militarily strong, economically prosperous, socialist country. Under this leadership China normalized relations with Japan and imported means for promoting economic growth from capitalist imperialist countries, such as fertilizer plants from the United States. Anti-imperialism meant anti-Sovietism.

The Soviet Union grew ever angrier at this U.S.-Chinese détente but after 1974 increasingly blamed Washington rather than Beijing. Not until after Mao's death in September 1976, with the ascension of Zhou's protégé Deng Xiaoping in 1977–1978, were the policies of the third front legitimated by Mao's anti-imperialism finally reversed. But anti-imperialism remained the premise of the nationalism that still legitimated China's post-Mao Leninist rulers. China was to try to make itself the anti-imperialist center of the world not through mobilization of an armed, self-reliant people but through economic growth, providing the wealth to build a modernized, militarily powerful China that could not be bullied.

The grand narrative of Chinese history as popular mobilization against potential foreign invaders clashed, however, with increasing economic involvement with imperialist economies. If Great Walls and opposition to foreign commerce were no longer the building blocks of a modernizing and militarizing China, then how could the rulers of Leninist China legitimate their new policy direction?

Modernization and Legitimation

China's post-Mao leaders agreed that autarkic policies intended to make it strong and respected by maximizing distance from the world market had in fact left it poor and weak. Although the state had mobilized resources to manufacture nuclear weapons and rockets, the basic equipment of the military was copies of 1950s deliveries from the Soviet Union that even at the time had not been the most advanced weapons available. When in 1979 Deng Xiaoping dispatched China's army into northern Vietnam after Hanoi's Soviet-backed armies had toppled Pol Pot's Chinese-backed forces in Cambodia, Chinese soldiers paid a terrible toll for the country's military backwardness. It was clear to the leaders in Beijing that China's military required a modernization that could only be based on access to the world's most recent science and technology. This required opening commercial and cultural exchange relations with the advanced industrial democracies to gain access to their markets.

In general, the post-Mao leadership grew ever more aware that China under Mao had stagnated economically while the rest of East Asia had raced ahead. Mao's anti-imperialist policies of self-reliance had isolated China from the dynamic forces of economic progress. In a world in which the United States was still the leading economic, military, and political power, the Deng government could win access to the sources of growth only by normalizing relations with Washington, especially to win cheap loans from the international financial institutions in which China now participated. The Leninist anti-imperialist notion that dealing with capitalist international finance was surrender to a bloodsucking monster consequently lost credibility.

In mid-December 1978 Deng agreed to allow the United States to continue arms sales to Taiwan as the price of normalization of relations. The Beijing rulers were caught on the horns of a dilemma. Their basic legitimation had been nationalistic. To modernize, to create a dynamic economy, and to begin to satisfy the pent-up demands of Chinese people for the material benefits of modernity (washing machines, baby strollers, toilet paper, sanitary napkins, quality and style in everything) required changes that undermined prior anti-imperialist nationalist appeals. Since 1949, incorporating Taiwan into the People's Republic had been central to this legitimation. Yet if Taiwan kept obtaining weapons from the United States, why should it surrender to an amalgamation with the People's Republic? And if China's growth required foreign capital, foreign technology, and foreign trade, what did it mean to be a socialist anti-imperialist state? Success in modernization clashed with legitimation by anti-imperialism.

The political struggle in China seemed to foster a stable compromise. On the one hand, by not disbanding unprofitable state enterprises or allowing the private ownership and sale of farm land the state preserved the jobs of those loyal to the money-wasting Party-state machine. On the other hand, it welcomed, at local levels, the emergence of entrepreneurial efforts tied to foreign investment, especially by Chinese from Hong Kong and Taiwan, overseas Chinese from Southeast Asia and the United States, and others from the European Community and Japan. As money poured in, mainly via Hong Kong,[18] two very different Chinas seemed to develop—a flourishing, dynamic south tied to Chinese the world over and a conservative Confucian north ever more involved with Japanese loans, trade, and investment. To the extent that anti-Japanese sentiment had been the heartbeat of Maoist anti-imperialism, the north was at risk of losing legitimacy to the south.

In addition, with economic growth through openness to the world economy an overall policy priority, Beijing normalized relations with Moscow, eliminated the last remnants of the third-front policy, and instructed the military to earn funds through commercial transactions at home (e.g., selling motorcycles from Sichuan) and abroad (e.g., selling Silkworm missiles to Iran, nuclear technology to Pakistan and Algeria, rockets to Saudi Arabia and Iraq). There no longer seemed to be an imperialist threat to China against which to mobilize support except perhaps for the popular experience of exploitation by Japan.[19] The Deng government adopting the Japanese model of aggressive exporting to earn the foreign exchange to buy what it needed to modernize.[20] It abandoned its embrace of stagnant, miserable Stalinist North Korea to normalize relations with capital-rich South Korea, seen as selling Japanese-quality products at Third World prices. Likewise, to win friendly economic ties with the rapidly rising economies of Southeast Asia, Beijing stopped backing the Khmer Rouge and imposing military pressure on Vietnam.

And yet a tough nationalism still characterized the legitimating patriotism of China's ruling group. In negotiating with Britain for the return of Hong Kong to China in mid-1997, Beijing would tolerate no democratization or shared British rule. Although Beijing capital was heavily invested in a profitable Hong Kong, it would not guarantee Hong Kong the autonomy that its residents wanted and even threatened to send in its troops to keep Hong Kong in line. Increasingly, the hope of Hong Kong people was the rise of a Canton-based southern force that would not be a tool of Beijing's northern chauvinists. This growing regional identity was enhanced by the economic reforms, which strengthened regional forces against the old capital. Consequently, even the remnants of the old anti-imperialism as applied against Hong Kong were delegitimating for China's Leninist rulers because they seemed the antithesis of what was needed to permit Chinese to prosper.

The Leninist dictatorship's old guard still believed that its power rested on tough military chauvinism. It abandoned the conciliatory initiatives of the early post-Mao reformers toward the Tibetans and used harsh military means to crush them while an endless stream of trucks carried out of Tibet its precious timber and other resources. Similar force was used against a democracy movement in June 1989. The question remained whether economic modernization could combine with military chauvinism to buttress the old order. The consequences of this contradiction were manifest in Beijing's policy dilemmas over Taiwan. By 1990 investment from Taiwan had surged, but if Beijing could deal normally with Taiwan, then so could others. The United States, France, and Germany stepped up arms sales to Taiwan. Japan welcomed Taiwan's foreign minister as an "unofficial" guest. Taiwan politics became Taiwanized. Beijing condemned each and every one of these changes but also fostered the environment facilitating these actions by strengthening economic ties with Taiwan.

In the late 1980s, the political conservatives in Beijing committed themselves to the project of restoring China to great-power status. Hoping to free itself of unwanted human rights pressures from the United States or the European Community,[21] China would try to buttress shaky Leninist dictatorships elsewhere, for example, in Pyongyang, Hanoi, and Havana. It would seek to maximize beneficial economic relations with all nations (e.g., Russia was no longer a military superpower to be feared) and continue its open-door economic policy. It would make maximum use of economic ties with South Korea, Japan, Taiwan, Hong Kong, and Southeast Asia to modernize rapidly. The future seemed to lie in Asia.

By 1991 Japan was the world's number-one aid giver and the largest repository of capital in the world. The United States seemed in economic decline as Japan continued to rise. Beijing's rulers redefined China as the origin and center of East Asian Confucianism, the core dynamic that supposedly facilitated Asian economic growth and political stability. Their assumption was that no Asian nation wanted to deal with an economically mighty Japan that would also be a military superpower; China would act as a military-political counterweight to Japan. Economically, China would ally itself with Japan. Politically and militarily, however, it would ally itself with all others in Asia to check Japan. This combination of policies was expected to take China into the twenty-first century as the leading power of Asia, itself the leading region of the world. The humiliation and weakness caused by imperialism's oppression would become a matter only for history; China would finally have defeated imperialism.

Maneuvering between the two military superpowers was a thing of the past, with the United States in economic decline and the former Soviet Union having disintegrated. China in the 1990s was responding to very different international forces. Realization of its vision of a great China leading a great Asia in the Asian twenty-first century was, however, far from guaranteed. Regional forces[22] were pulling the economic center of China south and into a Chinese diaspora, and memories of a long, cruel war made many Chinese doubtful about Beijing's intimate adversary friendship with Japan. In a world where the logic of modernization had discredited the discourse of Leninist anti-imperialism, it was uncertain whether Beijing's failed Mao-era legitimations could inspire the loyalty of the Chinese people into the twenty-first century.

Notes

1. Arthur Waldron, *The Great Wall of China: From History to Myth* (Cambridge: Cambridge University Press, 1990).

2. This view was popularized by Wei Yuan, the most influential writer of the times on foreign policy.

3. Chinese historians in the 1990s do credit the contributions of noncommunist resisters in the anti-Japanese struggle.

4. A grandson of Mao is said to be writing a biography of the Ming founder to highlight Mao's understanding of the identities of the two state leaders.

5. A Leninist state is an overlapping of four institutional networks legitimated by anti-imperialism: (1) a militarized, secret Party based on a hierarchy of cells, (2) a pervasive police covering residence, work, travel, and all other aspects of life, (3) a command economy in which the central government imposes prices, runs industrial production, and distributes inputs and outputs, and (4) a *nomenklatura*—a list of names of the politically loyal who can be appointed or promoted to official positions by various levels of the state-party hierarchy rather than being chosen on the basis of merit, exam, election, or seniority.

6. John Wilson Lewis and Xue Litai, *China Builds the Bomb* (Stanford, Calif.: Stanford University Press, 1988), contend instead that China's atomic bomb project was a response to the 1954–1955 Taiwan Straits crisis threat of American nuclear blackmail. Mark Ryan, *Chinese Attitudes Toward Nuclear Weapons* (Armonk, N.Y.: M. E. Sharpe, 1989), details how China's presumed nuclear war was inevitable from the outset. See also Chong-pin Lin, *China's Nuclear Weapons Strategy* (Lexington: D. C. Heath, 1988).

7. For an overview of the foreign policy of the Nationalist Party on Taiwan, see Hong-mau Tien, *The Great Transition* (Stanford, Calif.: Hoover Institution Press, 1989).

8. Book-length studies of Chinese foreign policy capturing this essence include Peter Van Ness, *Revolution and Chinese Foreign Policy* (Berkeley: University of California Press, 1970), and Gerald Clark, *In Fear of China* (Melbourne: Lansdowne Press, 1966).

9. The writings of Bruce Cumings are the best sympathetic guide to the calculations of North Korea's rulers.

10. These memoirs of the pro-Moscow faction of North Korea's Communist Party have been regularly reported on in *Moscow News*. These individuals were given asylum in the Soviet Union at the end of the 1950s to escape a murderous purge of faction members by the North Korean tyrant Kim Il Sung. South Korea has been systematically mining the now open Russian archives, the best new, rich source on Chinese foreign policy.

11. In the post-Mao era, military memoirs by now retired Chinese army commanders have been full of details on Mao's strategic thinking.

12. Compare Allen Whiting, *China Crosses the Yalu* (New York: Macmillan, 1960), and Edward Friedman, "Problems in Dealing with an Irrational Power," in Edward Friedman and Mark Selden, eds., *America's Asia* (New York: Pantheon, 1969), pp. 207–252. The best overall study of Chinese security calculations is Harvey Nelsen, *Power and Insecurity: Beijing, Moscow, and Washington, 1949–1988* (Boulder, Colo.: Lynne Rienner, 1989).

13. On peacemaking in Korea, see John Lewis Gaddis, *The Long Peace (New York: Oxford University Press,* 1987), and Edward Friedman, "Nuclear Blackmail and the End of the Korean War," *Modern China* 1:1 (January 1975).

14. Scholars in China with access to the military agree on this.

15. There is a large and diverse literature on the causes of the Moscow-Beijing split, with analysts varying on when the rift became unhealable, ranging in date from 1955, when Mao began to criticize the Soviet Union in internal Chinese statements, to 1963, when Moscow began dispatching troops to the Chinese border. The first solid book on the topic was Donald Zagoria, *The Sino-Soviet Conflict, 1956–1961* (Princeton, N.J.: Princeton University Press, 1962). A more recent study is Gordon Chang, *Friends and Enemies: The United States, China, and the Soviet Union, 1948-1972* (Stanford, Calif.: Stanford University Press, 1990).

16. Good introductions to Soviet views are Roy Medvedev, *China and the Superpowers* (New York: Basil Blackwell, 1986), and Arkady Shevchenko, *Breaking with Moscow* (New York: Knopf, 1985). For a more propagandistic presentation of Moscow's views, see G. Apalin and U. Mityayev, *Militarism in Peking's Policies* (Moscow: Progress Publishers, 1980).

17. The supposed memoirs of Enver Hoxha, *Reflections on China,* 2 vols. (Tirana: 8 Nentori, 1979), are a good introduction to China's attempt to split the Soviet-led bloc.

18. Ezra Vogel, *One Step Ahead in China* (Cambridge, Mass.: Harvard University Press, 1990); Yung-wing Sung, *The China–Hong Kong Connection: The Key to China's Open Door Policy* (Cambridge: Cambridge University Press, 1991); Wang Gungwu, *China and the Overseas Chinese* (Singapore: Times Academic Press, 1991).

19. See Allen Whiting, *China Eyes Japan* (Berkeley: University of California Press, 1989) and "China and Japan," *Annals of the American Academy of Political and Social Science* 519 (January 1992):39–51.

20. Paul Kennedy, *The Rise and Fall of the Great Powers* (New York: Random House, 1987), pp. 447–458, concluded that China was succeeding and would become a superpower. Kennedy's book was quickly translated and published in China.

21. See Peter Van Ness, *Analyzing the Impact of International Sanctions on China* (Australian National University, Department of International Relations, Working Paper 1989/4), and "Human Rights and International Relations in East Asia," *Ethics and International Politics,* July 1992, pp. 43–52.

22. See *Dædalus* 120:2 (Spring 1991).

PART TWO

Interactions

4

Sino-American Relations: Testing the Limits of Discord

STEVEN I. LEVINE

The 1990s are a time of trial for China and the United States. The tempered optimism concerning Sino-American relations that the leaders of both countries expressed throughout most of the 1980s had given way by the end of the decade to mutual recrimination and wrangling. Washington condemned China for abusing human rights, engaging in unfair trading practices, and violating arms limitation agreements. Beijing responded by charging the United States with interfering in Chinese internal affairs and attempting to subvert China's socialist system. Buffeted by the winds of international change as well as by domestic political strife, in recent years the once sturdy structure of Sino-American relations has fallen into what appears to be a state of serious disrepair. Until the winds abate, however, it will be difficult to determine whether the damage incurred is structural or merely superficial. In either case, as joint tenants China and America must ultimately decide, singly or in tandem, whether to repair and remodel or demolish and replace the existing structure of Sino-American relations.

Two singular events reshaped the bilateral and international environment of Sino-American relations at the end of the 1980s. First, the Beijing Massacre of June 4, 1989, shattered the positive U.S. image of China as a reform-minded Communist state, forcing a significant change in the terms of the U.S. debate over China policy. Second, the collapse of European communism and the end of the Cold War, which had structured Sino-American relations since 1949, spurred policy makers in both Beijing and Washington to reexamine their existing international relationships. Old enmities evaporated and time-tested friendships dissolved as national leaders struggled to come to terms with the fluid global environment of the post–Cold War world.

Even before these traumatic events, the natural evolution of Sino-American relations in the 1980s had already pointed to the desirability of a thorough reevaluation of the relationship. Particularly in the United States, where China policy is subject to periodic public scrutiny, the need to articulate a new rationale to undergird U.S.-China relations became evident. America's China policy debate placed Beijing increasingly on the defensive after 1989. Consequently, China's policy toward the United States became predominantly reactive. In bilateral relations Chinese leaders coped with what they perceived as a continuous barrage of arbitrary and capricious actions by their American counterparts. Meanwhile, on the broader stage of world politics, China sought to accommodate without submitting to the paradoxical reality of a multipolar world in which the United States still exerted disproportionate influence, particularly in the realm of security affairs.

A Glance Backward

In the early 1970s, parallel concerns about the rise of Soviet global power led Chinese Communist Party Chairman Mao Zedong and Premier Zhou Enlai to join with President Richard M. Nixon and National Security Advisor Henry Kissinger in ending the twenty-two-year Sino-American Cold War confrontation.[1] A common interest in combating the "Soviet threat"—the focus of China's and America's shared obsession—served as the creation myth of Sino-American relations, sanctioning the development of what eventually became an elaborate network of Sino-American economic, political, military, cultural, academic, and scientific and technological exchanges. As the relationship expanded beyond its original strategic focus, the mutual suspicion that had initially permeated the marriage of convenience between the self-proclaimed "revolutionary" society of Mao's China and what Chinese leaders saw as their "reactionary" American ideological adversary gradually dissipated. Post-Mao China's acceleration onto the fast track of economic reform coincided with the establishment of diplomatic relations between China and the United States in early 1979. "Normalization," as this step was called, facilitated a decade of explosive growth in every area of interaction.[2] By 1988 trade had grown to $13.5 billion; thirty thousand Chinese students were studying at U.S. colleges and universities; an endless flow of official and unofficial delegations crossed the Pacific; and an archipelago of luxury tourist hotels—many built with joint-venture capital—annually sheltered more than a quarter of a million American tourists from the insalubrious realities of Chinese life.

The development of Sino-American relations was facilitated by three important agreements concerning Taiwan (the Republic of China). Since 1950 the United States had protected this island territory governed by the Chinese Nationalists from Beijing's threats to incorporate it, by force of arms if necessary, into the Chinese Communist state. In the 1972 Shanghai Communiqué, President Nixon agreed not to challenge Beijing's claim that Taiwan is a part of China. It was not until seven years later, however, that President Jimmy Carter accepted China's demands that the United States break *official* relations with the Republic of China and abrogate the 1954 U.S.-ROC Mutual Security Treaty as the price for normalization. Congress, uneasy about jettisoning an old ally, passed the Taiwan Relations Act of April 1979 establishing the *quasi-official* American Institute on Taiwan to replace the American embassy and asserting a continuing American interest in Taiwan's security.

When Taiwan failed to yield to the mixture of blandishments and implied threats that constituted China's appeal for reunification, Beijing blamed the

United States for Taipei's stubbornness and pressured Washington to terminate all American arms sales to Taiwan. Protracted negotiations yielded a bilateral agreement in August 1982 in the form of a joint communiqué according to which the United States agreed to "reduce gradually its sale of arms to Taiwan, leading over time to a final resolution," in exchange for Beijing's assurance that its strategy of peaceful reunification was a "fundamental policy."[3] PRC leaders saw this agreement as merely one step along the road toward their long-term reunification goal.

By the late 1980s changes in the relations among China, the Soviet Union, and the United States had progressed to the point where it was no longer feasible to sustain the old Mao-Nixon anti-Soviet strategic rationale as the basis for Sino-American alignment. For a generation of American global strategists the Sino-Soviet conflict had been like an old security blanket, but once Beijing and Moscow normalized relations it became a hand-me-down for historians and social scientists.[4] Meanwhile, a new era of cooperative Russian-American relations commenced. Beijing and Washington now faced a vital question: Were shared strategic concerns the indispensable foundation of U.S.-China ties, as many observers had long asserted, or were they merely a scaffolding that could now be dismantled without jeopardizing the completed structure of the relationship?

In practical terms, Sino-American political, military, economic, cultural, and other links had expanded so rapidly during the 1980s that there should have been no question about either the durability or the resilience of the overall relationship. Sino-American relations seemed like a bridge suspended by thick cables consisting of interwoven common interests in many different fields of activity. A further protection, it seemed at the time, was that plural interests operated like independently suspended shock absorbers cushioning the vehicle of Sino-American relations from the bumps and potholes in the road.[5] By the mid-1980s, as Harry Harding has observed, American interest in promoting Chinese modernization appeared to have replaced strategic cooperation as a mutually acceptable basis for Sino-American relations.[6]

In order to understand the impact of the Beijing Massacre on Sino-American relations, it is necessary to consider briefly some perceptual dimensions of the relationship. Fundamentally, China's Communist leaders viewed the United States as an imperialist power addicted to military intervention but one that nevertheless was a useful, if sometimes problematic, partner that could help China to achieve such goals as deterrence in the 1970s and economic modernization in the 1980s. The attraction that China's educated, urban youth felt toward America's "degenerate, bourgeois" culture was an unwanted side-effect of the U.S. connection but one that most Chinese leaders believed posed no immediate threat to Communist Party rule. It should be noted that the formulation of Chinese policy toward the United States, far from being a matter of open political conflict or public contention, was the exclusive prerogative of the inner circle of power holders.[7]

Not so in the United States. America's sentimental attachment to China, leavened by memories of the bitterly partisan "Who Lost China?" debate following the Communist victory in 1949, made China policy a potentially explosive political issue even though it was rarely at the center of public attention. Therefore, to be acceptable to Congress and the public, the president's China policy had to be grounded in an explicit and easily understood rationale rooted in America's informal ideology or political value system.[8] Initially, the U.S. global contest with the USSR, interpreted as a struggle against malevolent communism, provided just such a rationale. Nixon's strategic alignment with the PRC in the 1970s was generally accepted in the United States as a necessary exercise in realpolitik, but it was not until 1979 that a majority of the American public came to view China favorably.

Deng Xiaoping's market-oriented reform policies in the 1980s, which persuaded many Americans that the PRC was abandoning socialism in all but name, provided an alternative rationale for U.S. China policy. China's postrevolutionary mood of avaricious individualism, mirroring that of American society during the Reagan years, convinced many American observers that China was launched on a trajectory toward capitalism and democracy. These were objectives that Americans could enthusiastically support. When huge student-led demonstrations filled Tiananmen Square in the spring of 1989, invoking Jeffersonian slogans and deploying familiar-looking symbols such as the Goddess of Democracy, American public opinion eagerly anticipated the Second Coming of Chinese Democracy. But the brutal suppression of the popular movement on the terrible night of June 3–4, 1989, rendered American illusions about China secondary victims of the massacre.[9]

In retrospect, it is clear that neither the creation myth (the anti-Soviet strategic rationale of the 1970s) nor its replacement (the proreform rationale of the 1980s) provided a stable foundation for long-term Sino-American ties. Rather, by accepting and disseminating such simplifying notions, American political and public opinion leaders, especially the mass media, obscured the complex realities of China, fostering exaggerated and unrealistic expectations that the Sino-American relationship could not possibly fulfill.

The Contours of Sino-American Relations

After June 4, Chinese Communist Party (CCP) hard-liners condemned the United States for supposedly having called the signals from the sidelines of what they quickly labeled a "counterrevolutionary rebellion." (Actually, Americans had been more like cheerleaders for the political protest movement.) Reflecting the American public's instinctive revulsion from the repression ordered by China's top leaders, Congress pressured President George Bush to sharpen his characteristically cautious response to the widely publicized killing. Washington's imposition of a series of economic, political, and military sanctions against the PRC further fueled Beijing's ire. Among other measures, Washington canceled all high-level exchanges with China, cut off arms transfers and military-related sales, suspended financial credits and economic assistance, and conditioned their restoration on substantial evidence of Chinese progress toward political reform.[10]

Beijing's inevitable indignation at these actions was partially alleviated when it learned that in President Bush it had a powerful partner who was determined to check the free fall of Sino-American relations. Confident of his own China expertise, Bush took personal charge of U.S. policy, brushing aside widespread criticism from within his own Republican party as well as from opposition Democrats. The president asserted that it was only through active engagement that Beijing's repressive behavior could be meliorated.[11] For the remainder of Bush's term, Chinese leaders, never comfortable with Congress's wild-card foreign policy role in any case, looked to the White House as a bulwark against efforts on Capitol Hill to influence China's conduct via punitive legislation. Even when the president gradually toughened his stance toward the PRC during his final year in office, Chinese leaders were reluctant to criticize Bush personally because they considered the alternatives much worse.

For this reason, Democrat Bill Clinton's victory in the 1992 presidential election raised questions about the future of Sino-American relations similar to those that Ronald Reagan's victory had posed in 1980. As had Reagan, the new president had sharply criticized his predecessor's China policy during the campaign. After taking office in 1981, however, Reagan had rapidly adjusted his personal views to accord with the prevailing bipartisan China policy consensus. Essential continuity was maintained. The problem in the early 1990s was that there was no American consensus on China policy.

Chinese leaders hoped that President Clinton would pursue what they considered a realistic China policy, by which they meant that the United States would refrain from meddling in Chinese domestic affairs and respect China as a major power with significant geopolitical and economic interests. They also meant that Washington would tacitly acknowledge that the Chinese Communist Party reformers, who emerged from the Fourteenth CCP Congress in October 1992 in a strengthened position, were the best judges of the direction and speed of China's further economic and political evolution. Alternatively, Beijing feared that Clinton might choose to conduct a crusade against Chinese communism. Such a crusade, which was favored by an unusual coalition of congressional liberals and ultraconservatives, human-rights lobbyists, and anticommunist ideologues, spelled intensified American interference in Chinese internal affairs, confronting Beijing on such contentious, value-laden issues as human rights, population control, political reforms, and Tibet.

Underlying the uncertainty of Sino-American relations in the 1990s is that neither the Chinese nor the Americans can agree among themselves or with each other as to just what a normal Sino-American relationship should look like. The use of unrealistic objectives such as harmony (a Chinese ideal) or a stable equilibrium (an American one) as criteria for assessing the current state of the relationship results in unduly pessimistic conclusions. If both sides could only recognize that Sino-American relations are *necessarily* in a state of protracted transition, then the Chinese tendency to posit harmony and the American tendency to posit a stable equilibrium as a goal might both be seen for the chimeras they are. This is because the ordinary uncertainties of any relationship between two large and powerful states are compounded by the extraordinary challenges of domestic and international political change and economic readjustment that China and the United States both currently confront. Each item on the long list of issues that constitutes the contemporary agenda of Sino-American relations is an element in this larger process of change and readjustment. None of these issues can be readily resolved, or even successfully managed, over the longer term apart from this larger process; therefore, it is vain to expect harmony or a stable equilibrium anytime soon.

If both sides accept the entirely commonplace proposition that normal Sino-American relations include conflict as well as cooperation, and if they can avoid pushing the panic button when disagreements inevitably appear, it will be easier to manage the specific differences. At the same time, it must be emphasized that because the issues on which China and the United States regularly clash are expressions of deeply rooted political, social, economic, and value differences, it would be foolish to suppose that they can be made to disappear by a combination of goodwill and political sleight of hand.

China and the United States in the New World Order

Throughout the Cold War, Chinese leaders viewed the United States in the context of an international system defined by the competition of the superpowers for global hegemony. Although significantly weaker than either of the superpowers, China was adept at extending its own influence in international politics beyond the limits of its tangible power by playing upon American and Soviet hopes and fears.[12] The end of the Cold War and the collapse of the Soviet Union terminated this game.

In the first phase of the post–Cold War world, Chinese leaders encountered a curious paradox. In what was intrinsically a multipolar international system, the United States was inclined, nevertheless, to act as the sole hegemonic power. Brandishing American "victory" in the Cold War, the Bush administration proclaimed a New World Order. Under this new dispensation, on such occasions as it chose to exert its will Washington could orchestrate international responses to the separatist, ethno-religious, territorial, civil, and other conflicts that were, at least in part, the turbulent legacy of the end of Cold War bipolarism.[13] The U.S.-led coalition that defeated Iraq in the 1991 Gulf War provided one model of post–Cold War American military intervention in the Third World. The international effort to provide civil-war-ravaged Somalia with humanitarian relief under military protection suggested a new and potentially even broader role for American military power in the world's "failed states."[14]

China's leaders viewed the Bush administration's post–Cold War foreign policy activism as a significant political, if not a direct military, threat to the security of the world's last major Leninist state. In April 1990, with the United States in mind, Deng Xiaoping warned his comrades that "the international hostile forces have focused their attention on China. They will try by every means to stir up trouble and bring more difficulties and pressures on China."[15] One concrete expression of this profound paranoia was the ensuing CCP campaign to inoculate China's intellectuals and urban youth against the subversive cultural influence of the United States supposedly targeted at undermining Chinese socialism through a strategy of promoting "peaceful evolution."[16]

Washington's success in mobilizing a broad international coalition during the Gulf War suggested that Beijing simply could not afford to oppose the United

States directly in the global arena without risking renewed international isolation or marginalization. Chinese leaders were hardly ready, however, to give unqualified endorsement to American-led military interventions. Fortunately for them, in order to avoid the appearance of unilateralism Washington resorted to the United Nations to provide international authorization for its war against Iraq. As one of the five permanent members of the UN Security Council, China was in a position to deny Washington a UN umbrella by vetoing the resolution authorizing the use of force, but had it done so it would have incurred a prohibitive cost in terms of its international standing. Instead, simply by abstaining on this critical vote, Beijing gained Washington's gratitude. Its subsequent criticism of American military operations helped to sustain its reputation in the Third World as an independent great power.[17]

Chinese observers argued that over the longer term the United States would be unable to implement its post–Cold War hegemonic global strategy because of the inherent multipolarity of world politics as well as the limits imposed by American domestic problems.[18] Meanwhile, the major short-term challenge facing China's foreign policy and security elite in the 1990s was how to accommodate American power without submitting to it. China employed a multipronged strategy toward this end.

In bilateral terms, Chinese leaders frequently emphasized their desire for improved Sino-American relations and denied that any fundamental conflicts of interest existed between the two countries. For example, meeting with a U.S. congressional delegation on November 30, 1992, CCP General Secretary Jiang Zemin called for "more mutual trust and less problems, more cooperation and no confrontation," between China and the United States, which shared "major responsibilities ... to maintain peace and stability in the Asia-Pacific region and the whole world."[19] Beijing also tried to assuage American concerns by belatedly signing the 1968 Nuclear Non-Proliferation Treaty (NPT) as well as announcing its adherence to the Missile Technology Control Regime (MTCR). China likewise cooperated in international efforts to end the civil war in Cambodia and reduce tensions on the Korean peninsula.

Such reassuring gestures, however, went hand in hand with redoubled efforts to equip the People's Liberation Army (PLA) with expensive high-tech weaponry—including major purchases of advanced fighter aircraft and other weapons systems from Russia—to enable China to fight limited conventional wars on its periphery and become a truly modern world-class military power early in the next century.[20] China's active diplomacy vis-à-vis its major Asian neighbors— Japan, Vietnam, Korea, and India—also strengthened its claim to Asian great-power status and implicitly challenged Washington's globalism.

China and the United States are both major components of the emerging multipolar structure of international power and have a common interest in maintaining a peaceful environment in the Asia-Pacific region. But the economic dynamism of this region is matched by the fluidity of its security arrangements. It seems unlikely that a multilateral regional security structure will be created anytime soon. Therefore, bilateral security arrangements will continue to predominate as they have since World War II. Chinese power is likely to grow incrementally over the coming decades, since China will be unconstrained by multilateral regional security obligations and unlikely to enter into restrictive bilateral arrangements.

Although the United States will remain a significant factor in the regional security equation, it is by now only one of many players, having lost its once-dominant position. Moreover, it is very likely that regional security questions will increasingly be decided among the states of the region themselves without reference to any overarching global struggle. Numerous factors will combine to accelerate the Asianization of Asian-Pacific security politics. Among these are China's emergence as an authentic regional military power, Japan's slowly growing foreign policy assertiveness, the appearance, sooner or later, of a unified Korea, the end of Vietnam's international isolation, and the likelihood of a revitalized Russian role in Asia in line with Moscow's historic interests once that country's internal problems have been sorted out. This may stimulate the reappearance of historic rivalries that were muted during the past half-century.

How China and America relate to each other under such circumstances will very much depend on how each of them relates to other states in the region. For example, should China decide to use its air and naval power to enforce its expansive territorial claims to the islands and waters of the South China Sea, other claimants, including even Vietnam, might appeal to the United States to counterbalance Chinese power. Should Japan someday veer away from its security relationship with the United States in the direction of armed unilateralism, conceivably Beijing and Washington might draw together to contain Tokyo.[21]

A chronic problem in Sino-American relations with major implications for regional security is the question of Taiwan. For many years China and the United States managed to avoid a collision over Taiwan through the adroit diplomacy of "creative ambiguity"—employing diplomatic formulas that each side interpreted as it chose. This has become much more difficult now. Chinese leaders were outraged when, in September 1992, President Bush approved the sale of up to 150 F-16s to Taiwan. His action gutted the 1982 Sino-American agreement limiting arms sales to Taiwan and shattered the international taboo on major arms sales to the island. In order to avoid exacerbating already badly strained relations with Washington, however, Beijing kept its anger in check. Furthermore, recent trends in Taiwan's democratized politics, including legalization of the advocacy of Taiwan independence and electoral gains by the Democratic Progressive Party, which favors an independent Taiwan, run counter to Beijing's goal of peaceful reunification. Washington hopes that growing functional links between China and Taiwan will culminate in reunification and spell the end of the "Taiwan problem," but this may not happen. If at some point Beijing exerts coercive pressure vis-à-vis Taipei, Washington may be forced to choose between its legal commitment to Taiwan's security under the Taiwan Relations Act of 1979 and its desire to avoid a major crisis in relations with China, which by that time may well have become a full-fledged Asian superpower. The destabilizing effects on Asian-Pacific security of such a scenario are obvious.

It is not only in Asia that Chinese and American security interests differ. Beijing and Washington have frequently been at odds over Chinese arms sales to the Middle East and its supplying of nuclear technology to several countries in Asia and North Africa. A constant, if often scarcely noticed, player in Middle

Eastern politics since the mid-1950s, China began selling short- and intermediate-range ballistic missiles to Iran, Iraq, and Saudi Arabia in the 1980s. Under intense pressure from the United States—which is itself by far the largest supplier of weapons to the region—China reluctantly agreed to terminate its missile sales but repeatedly dragged its feet on implementing its promises. Similarly, notwithstanding Beijing's assurances to the contrary, Washington feared that China's sale of nuclear reactors to Pakistan, Iran, North Korea, and Algeria increased the danger of nuclear weapons proliferation.[22]

In broader terms, such contemporary bilateral issues in Sino-American security relations are significant in pointing toward an even more fundamental question. How will China and the United States relate to each other in the Asia-Pacific region and the world if China's continuing development substantially reduces the historical inequality of power between them? (In this connection, we should recall that during the Cold War the United States felt mortally threatened by the Soviet Union, which was a significantly weaker state.) The answer to this question lies as much in the realms of economic, political, and cultural relations as it does in the sphere of security affairs.

Economic Relations

Since the late nineteenth century American merchants, hoping to gain hundreds of millions of Chinese customers, have been drawn to the fabled if perennially disappointing China market. It is ironic, then, that the primary focus of contemporary Sino-American economic relations is on America as a market for Chinese goods. This is because, beginning in 1979, Deng Xiaoping's economic reform program transformed China from a typical state socialist economy with minimal foreign trade into a rapidly developing mixed economy in which foreign trade accounts for more than a third of the gross national product (GNP).

Two-way Sino-American trade shot up from $2.3 billion in 1979 to over $25 billion in 1991. Since the late 1980s the United States has been the largest market for China's exports. These consist largely of inexpensive consumer goods such as apparel, toys and sporting goods, consumer electronics, and footwear, manufactured for most part in China's nonstate sector, which is most highly developed in the booming southern provinces of Guangdong and Fujian. Large-scale private capital investment from Hong Kong and Taiwan in these two provinces fuels double-digit annual growth rates. Chinese imports from the United States consist largely of aviation and aeronautical equipment, heavy machinery, chemicals (fertilizers), raw materials, and agricultural commodities.[23]

China's export surge turned a positive American trade balance with China up to the early 1980s into what, according to American statistics, is a chronic and rapidly growing trade deficit that reached nearly $13 billion in 1991 and over $18 billion in 1992.[24] By the late 1980s the growth of China's exports to the United States, which followed the earlier trajectory of Japanese, Korean, and Taiwanese goods on the American market, began to elicit accusations of unfair trading practices similar to those that Americans have regularly voiced since the 1970s against their other major Asian trading partners. The critical element that transformed a rather ordinary trade dispute into an explosive political issue between the two countries was the change in the American public's perception of China that the 1989 Beijing Massacre evoked. Since then Sino-American economic relations have been closely linked with political considerations.

In the early 1990s the annual question of whether or not to renew China's most-favored-nation status and if so under what conditions became the fulcrum of conflict between the Bush White House and congressional opponents and public interest groups.[25] President Bush supported the unconditional extension of the status, arguing that Sino-American trade not only was mutually beneficial but also indirectly helped the cause of China's political reform by accelerating the growth of its nonstate sector. He warned that revoking most-favored-nation status or burdening it with conditions might trigger a trade war and precipitate a general crisis in U.S.-China relations. Another powerful argument was that the prosperity of Hong Kong and, to a lesser extent, Taiwan, which are major participants in U.S-China trade, would be badly hurt.[26] Congressional majorities, spearheaded by Democrats but including many Republicans as well and supported by an increasingly effective China human-rights lobby, insisted that the extension of most-favored-nation status should be made conditional on the easing of political repression in China and improvements in China's abysmal human-rights record.[27] Beijing, of course, praised the wisdom of President Bush's position while exiled leaders of the Chinese democracy movement split on whether political conditions should be attached to the extension. Although for three consecutive years (1990–1992) large majorities in both the House and the Senate voted for various forms of conditionality, Congress was unable to muster the two-thirds majority needed to override Bush's vetoes.

In China the most-favored-nation issue pressed upon a sensitive nerve of national pride; public interest in it, as in U.S.-China relations generally, dwarfed that in the United States. The possibility that the United States might "reject" and "punish" China by withdrawing the status activated the negative pole of that deep-seated ambivalence toward American power and culture that many, particularly well-educated, Chinese have long felt. As a new administration took office in Washington, Beijing reiterated its opposition to conditionality, but there remained some hope that an acceptable compromise might be worked out.

Bush and Beijing, bedfellows on this issue, clashed over concrete trade policy. Charging that China's huge trade surplus with the United States was the result of unfair Chinese trade practices including bureaucratic barriers, closed markets, dumping, evasion of quotas, and currency manipulation, in the early 1990s the United States threatened to impose exorbitant tariffs on a broad range of Chinese products under Section 301 of the U.S. Trade Act. Beijing threatened retaliation in kind. Washington's high-profile strategy of economic brinksmanship, in which negotiations took place under the gun of U.S.-imposed deadlines, was probably designed in part to counter the impression that Bush was "soft" on China and reinforced feelings in China and throughout Asia that U.S. trade policy was highhanded.

Protracted and contentious negotiations on intellectual property rights and market access yielded two agreements in 1992. Responding to American complaints of widespread Chinese piracy, in January Beijing consented to provide copyright protection to computer software and chemical patents as well as to print publications. In October, China agreed to cut tariffs, eliminate most of the quotas and other import-licensing restrictions on American goods over a period of several years, and publish the hitherto secret trade laws, statutes, and regulations that had long frustrated American companies.[28] These measures were expected to facilitate American access to the China market and eventually rectify the trade imbalance. China's long-term plans to upgrade its industrial technology and develop its economic infrastructure also brightened the prospects for American exports.

In fact, despite the political chill between the two countries and the war of words over trade, Sino-American economic relations have flourished in recent years. Chinese leaders apparently see that by increasing imports from the United States they may effectively signal their interest in improving relations. For example, shortly after Clinton's election Beijing closed a $2 billion deal to purchase American wheat. In 1992 alone China signed a $1.2 billion deal with McDonnell Douglas to assemble civilian aircraft in Shanghai from imported American parts, agreed to purchase American communications satellites worth more than $650 million, approved a $1.2 billion project with ARCO to market offshore natural gas, contracted with the Crestone Energy Corporation to explore for oil in the South China Sea, and allowed AIG, America's largest commercial insurance company, to reopen its old office in Shanghai, where the company had originated in 1919. By 1992 U.S. direct foreign investment in China amounted to $6.6 billion, third behind Hong Kong and Japan.[29]

Despite its interest in boosting American exports, Washington hesitated to approve the sale of supercomputers and other high-tech equipment to China because of evidence that Beijing had violated the pledges it gave in November 1991 to curtail the sale of Chinese missiles and weapons technology. U.S. officials were also concerned lest China misuse American technology for unauthorized military and intelligence purposes.[30] Meanwhile, Beijing's application to rejoin the General Agreement on Tariffs and Trade (GATT), pending since 1986, has been held up by China's unwillingness to pledge to complete the transition to a full market economy and until then to refrain from below-market price exports (dumping). The United States insists that Beijing must meet these and other conditions before being let back into the GATT.[31]

The most visible evidence of American commercial success in China is the fast-food industry. That the world's largest McDonald's and Kentucky Fried Chicken franchises are located in the heart of downtown Beijing is, of course, more of a cultural than a culinary statement. The Chinese, who possess the world's finest cuisine, are eating American culture. Another sign of American chic is the success of a Beijing restaurant specializing in that perfect marriage of the familiar and the exotic—steaming bowls of so-called California noodles. The ne plus ultra of Sino-American economic relations is the contract signed by the Wonton Foods Company of New York, a titan in the fortune cookie industry, to build a fortune cookie plant in Guangzhou from which it intends to introduce "Chinese fortune cookies"—actually an American product—to the Chinese market. Donald H. Lau, the vice-president of Wonton Foods, a high-tech company that stores its fortunes on computer disks, expressed confidence that the fortunes supplied to Chinese consumers would not be subjected to censorship by Chinese political authorities.[32] It is perhaps worth noting that the ancient Chinese profession of fortune-telling, although often winked at by local officials, is a proscribed occupation in the People's Republic.

Human Rights and the Value of Values in U.S.-China Relations

What role do political and cultural values play in Sino-American relations? Does raising value-oriented issues such as human rights jeopardize the relationship by needlessly introducing irreconcilable perspectives? Proponents of Sino-American reconciliation in the 1970s considered values irrelevant to the pursuit of their strategic objectives. Until 1989 most Americans virtually ignored China's persistent and systematic human-rights abuses, but the Beijing Massacre reawakened Americans to the repressive realities of Chinese-style socialism. Enjoying greater access to Congress and the media, human-rights groups such as Asia Watch and Amnesty International succeeded in placing political repression, imprisonment for political activities, torture, and prison-labor exports on the agenda of U.S.-China relations. Americans also took sympathetic notice of the long struggle of Tibetans, inside and outside their homeland, against oppressive Chinese colonial rule. In April 1991 President Bush met briefly with the Dalai Lama, as did President Clinton two years later, and in July 1992 the Senate held hearings on the situation in Tibet.

Although Chinese officials are clearly discomfited by the widespread attention accorded Chinese human-rights abuses in the American media and on Capitol Hill, they have felt compelled to respond. As James Seymour's chapter on human rights (Chapter 10) clearly demonstrates, Chinese authorities view human rights not as a legitimate issue for Sino-American dialogue but as a cudgel brandished by foreigners who are hostile to Chinese socialism. Yet the variety of Chinese responses he delineates reflects alternative assessments by different Chinese political groupings of how best to handle these issues. China has repeatedly rejected foreign criticism of its human-rights record as constituting unacceptable interference in its internal affairs. Recently Beijing has also aggressively defended its own human-rights record, arguing that Chinese socialism has done a superior job in guaranteeing the vital social and economic rights that capitalism neglects. After the April 1992 Los Angeles riots, for example, Chinese newspapers had a field day denouncing the American judicial system, condemning racial discrimination, and pointing out that the rampant violence and drug abuse of America's inner cities are the fruits of economic despair.[33] (It is worth noting, incidentally, that as the largest foreign supplier of guns and ammunition, including semiautomatic assault rifles such as the AK-47, to the American market, China contributes to the violence in America that it piously condemns.)[34] Chinese government officials have also periodically discussed human rights with their American counterparts as well as with representatives of U.S. nongovernmental organizations. In these ways, an intermittent and often discordant dialogue of sorts has taken place.

Does a dialogue that is often marked by mutual recrimination serve any useful purpose in Sino-American relations? Many thoughtful Chinese and American observers worry that the fragile structure of Sino-American relations may collapse under the weight of value dissonance. Ideological conflicts between Chinese state socialism and Americal liberal capitalism, they argue, should be set aside in line with former Chinese Premier Zhou Enlai's injunction to "seek common ground while reserving differences" (*qiu tong cun yi*). Unfortunately, past experience suggests that ignoring the essential differences between China's Leninist and America's liberal political system is a defective formula for Sino-American stability.

In order to win long-term acceptance by Congress and the American people, U.S. policy toward China must be rooted in America's democratic political culture, which accords a high value to human rights, particularly political and civil rights. This is realism not idealism. Furthermore, rather than being an incitement to ideological warfare or an excuse for restricting relations, the affirmation by each side of its own values can be the point of departure for a new and much needed realism. Stripping away the sentimentalism and phony friendship of "special relationships" of any sort facilitates the search for real common interests as well as the sober discussion and prudent management of real points of conflict. It thereby reduces mutual expectations to realistic proportions.

Democratic political and civil rights are not the parochial expressions of American culture but universal values that are increasingly being recognized and implemented by culturally diverse members of the international community. In this connection it is worth noting that the most powerful challenges to Chinese Leninism have come not from the outside world but from within China itself. China is inherently, if not officially, pluralistic. The values of state socialism proclaimed by the regime have by now been abandoned by large numbers of Chinese, including many members of the Communist Party itself, who are attracted to pluralist and democratic values. Moreover, China's political system is intrinsically unstable and in the process of transition, although it is impossible, of course, to predict its future.[35] Precisely because of this uncertainty, it is important to the future of Sino-American relations that Chinese and Americans establish a wide variety of contacts with each other. For the United States this means having contacts with Communist power holders, domestic dissidents, and China's exiled democratic opposition alike. China itself, incidentally, long ago set the precedent for such broad-spectrum relations when it cultivated officials such as Nixon and Kissinger while simultaneously embracing American radicals and anti–Vietnam War critics.

In sum, the inclusion of values such as human rights on the agenda of Sino-American relations serves to legitimate U.S. China policy to Americans, encourages realism by clarifying the limits and possibilities for interaction, promotes universal values and challenges both sides to improve their performance, and acknowledges the pluralism of Chinese as well as of American society in order to prepare for a range of future political contingencies.

Since the early 1970s, cultural, educational, and scientific and technical exchanges have been an important component of Sino-American relations. To the dismay of Chinese conservatives, American popular culture and consumerist ideology as well as democratic ideas have been a potent force for change in Chinese society. Introduced onto Chinese television in 1986, Mickey Mouse and Donald Duck quickly became widely disseminated Chinese cultural icons whose individ-

ualism, irreverence, and pleasure ethic implicitly challenged such paragons of col-
lectivist virtue as the nerd soldier Lei Feng.[36] American rock music inspired cultural iconoclasts such as the rock singer Cui Jian, whose daring lyrics probed the
personal and political despair of contemporary Chinese society.[37]

America remains the destination of choice for outward-bound Chinese students. More than forty thousand Chinese students attend colleges and universities in the United States, and Chinese constitute the largest contingent of foreign
scholars and researchers in American research institutions and laboratories. The
study of English is a national pastime in urban China and taking the Test of English as a Foreign Language an important rite of passage for ambitious Chinese
college students.[38] Even though most Chinese intellectuals remain committed to
the idea of serving China, they are increasingly cosmopolitan, and many are
drawn to Western notions of intellectual autonomy, unfettered criticism, and
democratic norms.[39] Appealing to their patriotism and desire for security, reform-minded Chinese officials are trying to attract larger numbers of Chinese
students to return to China when they have completed their studies in the United
States.

The educational, cultural, and intellectual exchanges between the United
States and China, most of which take place through nongovernmental channels
on the American side, tend to promote decentralizing tendencies in China itself.
These exchanges often implicitly challenge the official Chinese penchant for orthodoxy and control, but the experience of other authoritarian societies suggests
the futility of trying to control the dissemination of universal values in today's information age.

Increasing numbers of legal Chinese immigrants, most of whom settle in San
Francisco and New York, have helped to nearly treble the Chinese population of
the United States from 435,000 in 1970 to over 1.2 million in 1990, strengthening
the human link between China and the United States but aggravating urban social
problems and stirring anti-Chinese prejudice. In the early 1990s, additional tens
of thousands of illegal Chinese immigrants paid Chinese and Hong Kong crime
syndicates up to $50,000 per person to smuggle them into the United States
aboard wretched vessels that often resembled slave ships. This traffic poses yet another challenge to American and Chinese authorities.[40]

Conclusion

Sino-American relations have been particularly tempestuous since 1989, but
what all the sound and fury signifies is by no means immediately obvious. Are
Sino-American relations inherently fragile and/or in crisis?[41] Or is it a case, as a
Chinese proverb puts it, of "leisheng da, yudian xiao," loud thunder but little
rain?[42]

Supporting the latter assessment is the fact that the volume of economic, cultural, and academic interactions among Chinese and Americans has actually increased since 1989. There is dialogue on contentious issues, and agreements continue to be reached, often after a lot of posturing and numerous threats. All of this
suggests that the angry accusations, recriminations, and other alarming noises
that reverberate through the structure of the Sino-American relationship are not

the rumblings of impending collapse but the sounds of animated engagement between two countries whose relations remain as substantial as they are often conflictive.

This is not to argue that there is no cause for concern about contemporary Sino-American relations. The main danger is that, for domestic political reasons, leaders on both sides may push disagreements over issues of basic values, economic advantage, international politics, and arms sales and arms control beyond the limits of their capacity to work out compromises. As China and the United States proceed with their national agendas of economic renewal and pursue their separate and inherently different post–Cold War foreign policies, it will take concerted efforts by Chinese and American political leaders to recognize the dangers and avoid senseless and provocative actions that could indeed jeopardize the Sino-American relationship.

Notes

I thank Andrew J. Nathan and James D. Seymour for their critical reading of an earlier draft of this chapter.

1. Henry Kissinger, *The White House Years* (Boston: Little, Brown, 1979), pp. 684–787; Walter Isaacson, *Kissinger: A Biography* (New York: Simon and Schuster, 1992), pp. 333–354.

2. Harry Harding, *A Fragile Relationship: The United States and China Since 1972* (Washington, D.C.: Brookings Institution, 1992), pp. 138–172.

3. *Department of State Bulletin* 82:2067 (October 1982):20.

4. Steven M. Goldstein, "Diplomacy amid Protest: The Sino-Soviet Summit," *Problems of Communism* 35:5 (September-October 1989):49–71.

5. Both of these images are from Steven I. Levine, "Sino-American Relations: Renormalization and Beyond," in Samuel S. Kim, ed., *China and the World: New Directions in Chinese Foreign Relations* (Boulder, Colo.: Westview Press, 1989), pp. 93–94.

6. Harding, *A Fragile Relationship*, p. 215.

7. David Shambaugh, chapter on U.S.-China relations, in Thomas W. Robinson and David Shambaugh, eds., *Chinese Foreign Policy: Theory and Practice* (New York: Oxford University Press, 1993); also David Shambaugh, *Beautiful Imperialist: China Perceives America, 1972–1990* (Princeton, N.J.: Princeton University Press, 1991).

8. For this concept see Michael H. Hunt, *Ideology and U.S. Foreign Policy* (New Haven: Yale University Press, 1987).

9. Demonstrations in support of reform occurred in several score Chinese cities, but the American media focused almost exclusively on the movement in Beijing. See Stephen R. MacKinnon, "The Role of the Chinese and U.S. Media," in Jeffrey N. Wasserstrom and Elizabeth J. Perry, eds., *Popular Protest and Political Culture in Modern China* (Boulder, Colo.: Westview, 1992), pp. 206–214.

10. Harding, *A Fragile Relationship*, pp. 224–234.

11. Ibid., p. 279; "President's Report on MFN Status for China," *U.S. Department of State Dispatch* 2:24 (June 7, 1991):430–432; see also Richard H. Solomon, "U.S. Relations with East Asia and the Pacific: A New Era," *U.S. Department of State Dispatch* 2:21 (May 27, 1991):388–389. In 1974–1975, at a time when Kissinger directly controlled China policy, Bush headed the U.S. Liaison Office in Beijing.

12. There is an immense literature on the three-cornered Sino-Soviet-American relationship. See, for example, Ilpyong Kim, ed., *The Strategic Triangle* (New York: Paragon House, 1987), and

Beyond the Strategic Triangle (New York: Paragon House, 1992); Lowell Dittmer, *Sino-Soviet Normalization and Its International Implications* (Seattle: University of Washington Press, 1992).

13. James Rosenau, *Turbulence in World Politics* (Princeton, N.J.: Princeton University Press, 1990).

14. Gerald B. Hellman and Steven R. Ratner, "Saving Failed States," *Foreign Policy* No. 89 (Winter 1992–1993):3–20.

15. *Zheng Ming* (Hong Kong) No. 151 (May 1, 1990):6–8; Foreign Broadcast Information Service, *Daily Report—China*, May 1, 1990, p. 12.

16. On this campaign, see, for example, Liang Yuntong et al., *Meiguo heping yanbianzhanlue* [America's Peaceful Evolution Strategy] (n.p.: Jilin renmin chubanshe, 1992).

17. China voted for the UN resolution authorizing the deployment of foreign military forces in Somalia to protect relief operations.

18. Wang Haihan, "Meiguo de quanqiu zhanlue mianlin yanzhong tiaozhan" [America's Global Strategy Faces Fundamental Challenges], *Guojiwenti yanjiu* [International Studies] No. 4 (October 1992):19–24.

19. *Beijing Review* 35:49 (December 7–13, 1992):9. The Chinese for this was "zengjia xinren, jianshao mafan, fazhan hezuo, bu gao duikang." *Renmin ribao* [People's Daily] overseas ed., December 1, 1992.

20. See the discussion in David Shambaugh, "China's Security Policy in the Post–Cold War Era," *Survival* 34:2 (Summer 1992):103–104.

21. For further discussion, see Ronald N. Montaperto, "Whither China? Beijing's Policies for the 1990s," *Strategic Review* 20:3 (Summer 1992):23–33.

22. Shambaugh, "China's Security Policy," p. 95; John W. Lewis, Hua Di, and Xue Litai, "Beijing's Defense Establishment: Solving the Arms Export Enigma," *International Security* 15:4 (Spring 1991):87–109; Richard A. Bitzinger, "Arms to Go: Chinese Arms Sales to the Third World," *International Security* 17:2 (Fall 1992):84–111.

23. "U.S.-China Trade," *China Business Review*, May-June 1992.

24. Ibid.; see also Harding, *A Fragile Relationship*, Table A-2, p. 364. China's statistics, which are calculated very differently, continue to show an American surplus. For a discussion, see Jan Prybyla, "How Should Future American-Chinese Economic Relations Be Managed?", unpublished conference paper, "New Ideas and Concepts in Sino-American Relations," American Enterprise Institute, November 18–20, 1992, pp. 5–8.

25. Most-favored-nation status is accorded virtually all U.S. trading partners and actually conveys no special treatment. It is the denial of the status that is unusual.

26. The concept of a "Greater China"—an economic macroregion comprising China, Hong Kong, and Taiwan—is invoked in this argument. See Harry Harding, "The U.S. and Greater China," *China Business Review*, May–June 1992, pp. 18–22; and David M. Lampton et al., *The Emergence of "Greater China": Implications for the United States* (New York: National Committee on United States–China Relations, 1992).

27. David Zweig, "Sino-American Relations and Human Rights: June 4th and the Changing Nature of a Bilateral Relationship," in William T. Tow, ed., *Building Sino-American Relations: An Analysis for the 1990s* (New York: Paragon House, 1991), pp. 57–92.

28. *Far Eastern Economic Review*, January 30, 1992, pp. 37–38; *New York Times* (hereafter cited as *NYT*), national edition, October 10, 1992, pp. 1, 5.

29. *Beijing Review* 36:17 (April 26–May 2, 1993):12.

30. *NYT*, December 5, 1992, p. 5.

31. *Far Eastern Economic Review*, March 11, 1993, pp. 56–57.

32. *NYT*, November 7, 1992, pp. 1, 10.

33. *Far Eastern Economic Review*, May 21, 1992, pp. 26–27.

34. *Washington Post National Weekly Edition*, April 12–18, 1993, p. 6.

35. See Roderick MacFarquahar, "Deng's Last Campaign," *New York Review of Books* 39:21 (December 17, 1992):22–29; and Steven M. Goldstein, *China at the Crossroads: Reform After Tiananmen* (New York: Foreign Policy Association, 1992).

36. See James Lull, *China Turned On: Television, Reform, and Resistance* (London and New York: Routledge, 1991).

37. Andrew F. Jones, *Like a Knife: Ideology and Genre in Contemporary Chinese Popular Music* (Ithaca, N.Y.: Cornell University, East Asia Program, 1992).

38. Passing this test is often a prerequisite for studying in the United States.

39. See Perry Link, *Evening Chats in Beijing* (New York: W. W. Norton, 1992).

40. On immigration, see David Reimers, *Still the Golden Door: The Third World Comes to America* (New York: Columbia University Press, 2nd ed., 1992), pp. 93–117. On the problems of Asian-Americans, see United States Commission on Civil Rights, *Civil Rights Issues Facing Asian-Americans in the 1990s* (Washington, D.C., 1992). On illegal immigration, see Grace Kinkead, *Chinatown* (New York: Harper Collins, 1992), pp. 159–166; Lena Sun, "The Contraband Companies of China," *Washington Post National Weekly Edition,* March 23–29, 1992, p. 11.

41. Harding, *A Fragile Relationship,* passim; Michel Oksenberg, "The China Problem," *Foreign Affairs* 70:3 (Fall 1991):1–16.

42. Steven I. Levine, "China and America: The Resilient Relationship," *Current History* 91:566 (September 1992):241–245.

5

China and Russia: New Beginnings

LOWELL DITTMER

The People's Republic of China's relationship with the (former) Soviet Union has been significant from its beginnings, in part because of the seminal role Moscow played in the Chinese Revolution. The Chinese Communists always regarded Moscow as *fons et origo* of Marxism-Leninism qua doctrine of state, at first seeking to model themselves after their more mature patron, later rebelling against the Soviet precedent, but always implicitly acknowledging the Bolshevik Revolution as an ancestor of their own and of the anticipated world revolution. The USSR was also strategically important to the PRC, initially by providing it extended nuclear deterrence in the face of the Western blockade, later as the major threat to its security. The national identity issue complicated the relationship for both powers, as each sought to demonstrate the unique relevance of its own revolution and subsequent nation-building experience to other developing countries, in the process launching complex encirclement and counterencirclement drives that complicated Soviet strategy with the prospect of a two-front war, diverted Chinese efforts from modernization to a massive (and, in retrospect, wasteful) defense buildup in its interior, and forced Third World countries and parties to make irrelevant choices on fine points of doctrine. Not until Mao's death in 1976 and the advent of Deng Xiaoping's reform regime in December 1978 did it become possible to contain and mend this breach. Gradually the national security issue was brought under control without unduly alarming such third parties as the United States, and even the national identity quandary seems to have become manageable. By late 1992 the relationship had become more amicable than at any time since the heyday of Sino-Soviet friendship in the early 1950s.

It would be misleading to give the impression that Sino-Soviet relations abruptly and dramatically improved upon the death of Mao. Chinese foreign policy, and particularly Sino-Soviet policy, actually underwent the first stages of "reform" during the terminal stages of Mao's tenure, making this the first policy arena to undergo this form of rationalization. This was partly due to the good offices of the moderate Zhou Enlai, perhaps, but even more to the fact that the nation's sovereignty, even its survival, was put at risk, obliging policy makers to

94

subordinate ideology to *raison d'état*. When the ideological polemics of the 1960s resulted in the mutual escalation of border forces, culminating in a Chinese-initiated border clash at Zhenbao (Damansky) Island on the Chinese side of the main channel of the Wusuli (Ussuri) River on March 2, 1969, the Russians not only retaliated massively (producing, according to recent revelations, thousands of Chinese casualties)[1] but subjected the Chinese to a sustained siege of diplomacy by force. For the next-half year they provoked a series of clashes along the entire length of the border, augmented by both veiled and public warnings to the effect that the USSR was considering a preemptive nuclear strike against the nascent Chinese first-strike force.[2] Meanwhile, the American conflict with Vietnam was still at a delicate stage, when U.S. strategic bombing of Hanoi and Haiphong and the "incursion" into Cambodia made the possibility of Chinese intervention quite real. The PRC, finding itself on the brink of confrontation with both superpowers at once (in the context of which Moscow was suggesting Soviet-American collusion), was obliged to calculate its national interest very carefully. The Soviets did under these circumstances succeed in driving the Chinese to the negotiating table—border talks began in Moscow in October 1969, alternating between capitals on a semiannual schedule for the next decade—though they did not win many concessions from them there. The Americans achieved a much more meaningful breakthrough, signaled by the February 1972 Nixon visit and the opening of trade, defense consultations, and implied U.S. protection from Soviet nuclear blackmail—in return for which China sharply scaled down its support for the Vietnam War. In point is the fact that the Chinese leadership responded to this security dilemma by allowing considerations of national interest to override ideological considerations almost entirely. Following this "deradicalization," China would chart its course according to a more conventional national interest calculus, compromising with capitalist countries, for example, in order to gain entrée into the international market system.

This chapter is concerned with China's relations with its northern neighbor(s) during the reform period, beginning with the Third Plenum of the Eleventh Central Committee in December 1978 but focusing on the most recent developments. It is chronologically divided into three sections. The first adumbrates the process of normalization culminating in the historic Beijing summit meeting of May 1989. The second examines the postnormalization phase—although it has been anything but "normal," approaching miscarriage at least twice before regaining a certain stability. The third section, with much less water under the bridge, is concerned with the course of developments since the dissolution of the Soviet Union in December 1991.

The Reform Regime

Sino-Soviet relations were conducted during the reform decade within the framework of what has come to be known as the "strategic triangle," playing within limits set during the late Maoist era. Triangularity meant that each bilateral relationship was contingent upon each participant's relations with the third. The essence of this relationship[3] was not simply "two against one" but one *playing* the other two (or two playing the third) in a variety of ways.[4]

This was the insight behind the American "romantic triangle" with China and the USSR inaugurated by the Nixon administration in the early 1970s. Whereas the Sino-Soviet antagonism could be successfully manipulated by Washington in the 1970s, during the early 1980s the revival of the Cold War made it possible for China to manipulate Soviet-American antagonism to its own advantage. Reassured by the Reagan arms buildup, Beijing was able to reduce arms spending by about 7 percent per annum as a proportion of gross national product (GNP) from 1979 (the year of the Vietnam invasion) to 1989. Both superpowers in the course of their confrontation, however, began experiencing economic difficulties (most acute in the Soviet case) due to overburdened arms budgets and neglected civilian economies. This eventually led to revival of Soviet-American détente, beginning with the Intermediate-Range Nuclear Forces (INF) treaty of December 1987 and continuing through the Strategic Arms Reduction Treaty (START) talks (successfully concluded in July 1991), unilateral Soviet withdrawal from Eastern Europe, and conventional arms reduction talks. Meanwhile Sino-Soviet normalization talks began in 1982, followed by a relatively steady growth of trade (particularly cross-border trade, which resumed in 1982). The process, held to a funereal tempo by a Chinese leadership intent upon wringing maximal concessions from both sides, culminated in "normalization" with Mikhail Gorbachev's May 1989 visit to Beijing. But while the disappearance of antagonistic relationships facilitated cooperation among all three players, it deprived the triangle of leverage and ultimately of structure, and it soon vanished as well.

After Tiananmen

Sino-Soviet relations from the May 1989 summit until the dissolution of the Union in December 1991 may be divided into roughly four stages. In the first, from June to October 1989, the Soviets seemed likely to reap windfall profits from Beijing's adverse reaction to Western sanctions. During the second stage, from October 1989 through the spring of 1990, relations frayed in the harsh light of Chinese criticisms of Gorbachev for "deviating from the path of socialism" by promoting reforms that exposed the bloc to capitalist subversion. During the third stage, inaugurated by Li Peng's successful April 1990 visit to Moscow, Chinese leaders took a somewhat more tolerant second look at Soviet developments, concluding that Gorbachev had to be dealt with as the "least worst" in a regrettably limited range of options. In the fourth stage, launched by the Gulf War (January–February 1991), Sino-Soviet relations warmed considerably in response to a threatening New World Order, moving toward an ideologically based affinity without formal alliance. This came to grief with the August coup, with dissolution of the empire coming as an anticlimactic fillip.

The First Stage

The 1989 summit, Foreign Minister Eduard Shevardnadze's suggestion at the eighth round of the semiannual normalization talks (held in Moscow in April 1986), put a ceremonial capstone on a seven-year bilateral normalization process. Whereas in the early (1982–1986) phase of normalization the Chinese seemed most forthcoming (by agreeing to talks and other exchanges in the absence of any Soviet response to Chinese demands), in 1986–1989 the Soviets made a series of tangible concessions: in Gorbachev's July 28, 1986, speech in Vladivostok he agreed to settle the riverine Ussuri-Amur boundary along the thalweg (the deepest point of the channel), and at the ninth round (October 6–14, 1986) the Soviet Union agreed to discuss Cambodia, thereafter entering into intensive discussions with the Chinese to resolve the issue (from September 1988 until issuing a joint statement in February 1989, Chinese and Soviet foreign ministers held no fewer than five rounds of talks on a Cambodian settlement). As the Chinese were unsatisfied by a 1988 Soviet pledge that Vietnam would withdraw all troops from Cambodia by 1990, in April 1989 Vietnam announced withdrawal of all remaining troops by the end of September regardless of whether a satisfactory political settlement had been achieved. By May 1989 the so-called Three Obstacles had been "essentially" eliminated.

The Soviets meanwhile launched a domestic reform program that seemed at first to have been stimulated by the successful Chinese experience but soon veered off in a quite different direction, focusing on politics as a precondition for economic reform. This development—which had a dramatic impact on politics but few visible positive economic effects—split Chinese observers: whereas unofficial commentary waxed enthusiastic, official commentary drew attention to the gap between formulation and implementation of policy. The Soviet emphasis on political reform at its January 1987 Plenum seems to have coincided with the Chinese Communist Party's (CCP's) decision, after a few rather tepid experiments, to forgo that route—as symbolized by the suppression of the December 1986 student movement and the January demotion of General Secretary Hu Yaobang. Yet Gorbachev's political reform continued to inspire the Chinese journalistic and intellectual community: The Shanghai vanguard reform publication *World Economic Herald* closely followed the progress of Soviet political reforms, which achieved a dramatic breakthrough in the multicandidate elections to the restructured Supreme Soviet just before the summit (March 1989). Indeed, the demonstrations were to some extent stimulated by the visit: although the demonstrators refused to clear the Square, they asked Gorbachev, a reform hero to whom Zhao Ziyang was then hopefully compared, to address them, and Gorbachev even asked permission to do so (the CCP leadership refused).

The summit—which Deng heralded as "ending the past, opening up the future"—thus had both domestic and foreign policy ramifications. Gorbachev told Deng that neither Karl Marx nor Vladimir Lenin had the answer to today's problems for the USSR and the PRC, signaling his interest in the cooperative pursuit of socialist reform. He also revealed some of the details of Soviet military cutbacks for Asia. Most of the promised cuts were in border garrisons facing China, with far less change in the lineup against American/Japanese forces: of the twelve divisions and eleven air force regiments to be withdrawn from the Soviet Far East by 1991 (totaling about 200,000 troops), 120,000 would come from the border with China. In addition, sixteen battleships would be removed from the Red Pacific Banner Fleet. Already in progress was the removal of all SS-20 missiles from the Soviet Far East, as promised in the INF treaty, and the withdrawal of 75 percent of the ground forces in Mongolia. Going beyond these agreed-upon reductions,

Gorbachev proposed the complete demilitarization of the border, the details of which would be arranged in the bilateral troop reduction talks under way at the vice foreign ministerial level since February 1987. Though both sides agreed that Sino-Soviet friendship was directed against no third country, the inclusion in the final joint communiqué of an "antihegemony" provision (previously directed against Soviet "social imperialism") at least proved that the USSR was no longer the triangle's pariah.

What was most striking was how much the meeting's meaning was transformed by the mass movement and culminating massacre that framed it. This was apparent in a subtle reversal of the symbolism that the two sides attached to the meeting: before, the USSR had attempted to highlight the occasion while the PRC played it down; afterward, the USSR sought to play it down while the PRC emphasized its wide-ranging implications. Soviet disappointment was understandable; after all, Gorbachev had come to visit what was identified as a reform regime—indeed, perhaps the most successful exemplar of socialist reform in the world. Two weeks after he left that reputation had been besmirched. President Bush announced four sanctions on June 5, and most other Western countries followed suit. Western tourism, trade, and investment plunged (the value of all foreign investment in China dropped 22 percent during the first half of 1990).

The Soviet summiteers (Gorbachev himself, Foreign Minister Shevardnadze, and Gorbachev's personal foreign affairs adviser Aleksandr Yakovlev, as well as the China experts in the Communist Party of the Soviet Union (CPSU) Central Committee's international department) were no less disconcerted by the denouement of the demonstrations they had witnessed[5] but remained discreet in public, and momentarily it seemed that the Soviet Union might draw strategic dividends from China's ostracism. It is reported that in internal discussions, Politburo Standing Committee members Li Peng and Yao Yilin, both members of the growing pool of Soviet-returned students in the emergent leadership, advocated the need to counterbalance China's economic relations with the capitalist world with closer economic cooperation with socialist countries. Both planned and free (i.e., border) trade expanded: total bilateral trade turnover was U.S.$3.95 billion for the year (an 18 percent hike over 1988's $3.26 billion), having increased one and a half times in the past decade (1980–1990), amounting to 8 percent of China's total trade; the Soviet Union had become China's fifth-largest trade partner.[6]

The Second Stage

During the fall and winter of 1989–1990, old Chinese suspicions of a threat from the north combined with new fears of the upsetting repercussions of Soviet reform efforts to bring to an abrupt end the summer's honeymoon. China had since the mid-1950s recurrently criticized Soviet occupation of Eastern Europe, on the one hand hoping to build a united front against Moscow within the bloc, on the other fearing that the Brezhnev doctrine might provide a precedent for a Soviet expedition to discipline China. Thus when Warsaw Pact forces invaded Czechoslovakia in 1968, the CCP joined the Kremlin's critics; China even publicly supported German reunification (on Bonn's terms) in the 1960s and 1970s. Yet in the wake of Tiananmen the CCP leadership had second thoughts. At a small discussion group with Yang Shangkun, Wan Li, and the six formal members of the Politburo Standing Committee during the four-day Fifth Plenum of the Thirteenth Central Committee in early November, Deng Xiaoping attacked Gorbachev's "new thinking," accusing him of pursuing a path "not in conformity with true Marxism-Leninism." In November 1989 Politburo member Qiao Shi attended the Fourteenth Congress of the Romanian Communist Party; in his talks with Ceaucescu and with newly appointed General Secretary of the Bulgarian Communist Party Petar T. Mladenov, Qiao stressed the maintainance of strict ideological orthodoxy. When Gorbachev condemned both the Czech invasion and its legitimating doctrine in Italy in early December 1989, the CCP took an evasive stand. These expressions of unease in response to the collapse of ruling communist parties along the northern tier reached a much higher decibel level in early December, when the Bucharest regime collapsed after waging desperate resistance (notwithstanding the recent visit of the Chinese security chief, Qiao Shi, who no doubt advised the leadership on how to implement the "Chinese solution"). The ensuing execution of the Ceaucescus threw elderly CCP veterans into great indignation. Deferring earlier plans to lift martial law by Christmas Eve, troops were placed on first-degree alert in late December 1989 and precautions taken to monitor student activity.

The CCP convened a series of high-level meetings at which Deng, Li Peng, and Jiang Zemin vied in denouncing Gorbachev and forecasting his imminent political demise. After the February 1990 Soviet Central Committee Plenum that renounced the CPSU's monopoly of power and opened the way to a multiparty parliament, an expanded CCP Politburo meeting was held in which a directive on Sino-Soviet relations was approved for dissemination through the ranks; this document called for "thoroughly educating" CCP members on the true nature of Soviet "revisionism." The possibility of internal collapse via socialist reform qua "new thinking" was perceived to be even more virulent than the threat of "peaceful evolution" posed by the West. In January–February a government-made videotape entitled "Eastern Europe in Turmoil," which recorded in graphic terms the fall of communist parties in Poland, the German Democratic Republic, and Romania, was shown at state organs and at Beijing municipal Party committee organs for "study." Retreating from a statement by Vice Premier Yao Yilin in mid-1989 that China should develop relations with the USSR as a "counterbalance" to Western sanctions, foreign trade units were instructed by the central government to be "more cautious" in developing trade and economic relations with Soviet companies.[7] In diplomatic response to the prospect of the defection of Eastern Europe, Deng gave his blessing to a rapprochement with Vietnam in December 1989 and sent Jiang Zemin to Pyongyang in the spring to cement that alliance: "The three socialist countries of Asia must protect and uphold the flag of socialism."

Beijing's paranoia nearly provoked a revival of public polemics. The Propaganda Department compiled seven hundred thousand characters of "black" materials, and Propaganda Department "adviser" Deng Liqun submitted a six-thousand-character draft resolution (which had been personally reviewed by Wang Zhen) to the Politburo before the Sixth Plenum in early March 1990 proposing a systematic public demolition of Soviet revisionism. But Deng Xiaoping held the line at "internal" criticism: "First of all we should mobilize the entire Party to do our own work well," he said. "I do not favor issuing documents like the 'first to ninth commentaries on the CPSU'" (written in the early 1960s). He also advised Jiang Zemin against trying to play a major role in the international communist movement, as China could not afford to be cast in that light. Three factors conceivably influenced his decision. First, the Soviets dispatched several emissaries to Beijing asking them not to do this because it would hurt bilateral relations. In late December, Gorbachev sent his envoy, Valentin Falin, with a personal missive for Jiang Zemin, but this fence-mending visit apparently did not suffice (Jiang Zemin indefinitely postponed his reciprocal visit to Moscow). Thus Vice Foreign Minister Igor Rogachev was dispatched to Beijing January 9–11, 1990, and he succeeded in fixing a date for a visit by Li Peng in April 1990. Second, Gorbachev himself made two statements during the February 1990 CPSU Central Committee Plenum that had a redeeming impact: he reaffirmed his commitment to socialism; moreover, despite having approved legislation renouncing the Party's "leading role," he declined calls by reformist supporters to resign as CPSU general secretary. Third, Taiwan was at this time energetically pursuing dollar diplomacy aimed at diplomatic recognition, establishing relations with eight small developing countries in 1989–1991, and as the former satellites lost no time in recognizing South Korea upon their self-emancipation it was clear that they might also recognize Taiwan unless the PRC quickly buried the ideological hatchet. Thus China promptly recognized all the postcommunist East European regimes (now addressed as "Messrs.," rather than "comrades").

The Third Stage

From the spring of 1990 till the spring of 1991 Chinese Soviet policy had a differentiated two-tiered, external/internal structure. The "internal" aspect consisted of a continuing but somewhat toned-down critique of the Soviet reform program designed to "educate" the CCP and deter possible Chinese emulators. It had become clear that the overthrow of communism in Eastern Europe would not necessarily discredit the CCP regime, because neither democracy nor capitalism would prove a panacea for these countries—their economic difficulties were not to be speedily solved. The CCP leadership deemed the Soviet situation to have greater relevance, and their internal critique continued. As late as October 1990 the CCP issued a document conveying Jiang Zemin's criticisms of the Soviet Union, in which he held that Gorbachev was practicing not socialism but social democracy, that his thinking was a refurbished version of the revisionism of the Second Communist International.

As Chinese denunciations of the Soviet leader intensified, Moscow's assessment of the PRC split. To such ardent reformers as Sakharov, China was now the bête noire; on the first anniversary of the May 1989 hunger strike in Beijing, students in thirty-six Soviet cities staged commemorative hunger strikes. In contrast, conservatives around Gorbachev pointed with admiration to China, urging their chief to discontinue perestroika and "put the Soviet house in order." As Gorbachev's difficulties with Lithuania and other would-be breakaway states mounted in the spring amid growing popular discontent with the economy, he began to surround himself with military/security types and to curb his liberal wing (e.g., on April 10 the CPSU Central Committee published an open letter criticizing reformers within the Party)—moves that the CCP leadership, concerned about separatist tendencies in China's own autonomous regions, heartily welcomed. Gorbachev's odyssey to the economically dynamic Pacific Rim, after a promising beginning heralded by the recognition of South Korea on January 1, suffered a clear setback in his April 1991 visit to Tokyo. China seemed his best chance in Asia.

Thus both ideological and geopolitical factors helped the relationship to thaw in the course of the year. Based on an understanding that the two would not form a military alliance, engage in public ideological disputes, or interfere in each other's internal affairs,[8] the process of bridge-building resumed. Li Peng's visit to Moscow (April 23–26, 1990) was a major icebreaker, resulting in six important agreements, including the Agreement on Strengthening Trust in the Military Realm as a Guilding Principle, which made provision for "confidence-building measures" and renewed military cooperation. Hitherto China's military modernization efforts had relied on Western technology, but as U.S. sanctions continued in force the Chinese saw a chance to teach Washington a lesson. General Xu Xin, deputy chief of the Chinese general staff, accompanied Li Peng in April, and on May 30 a military delegation led by Liu Huaqing, vice chair of the CCP Central Military Commission (CMC) and a 1958 graduate of the Voroshilov Naval Academy in Leningrad, visited Moscow for two weeks to discuss the possible transfer of Soviet military technology. During Liu's meeting with Soviet Defense Minister Dimitri Yazov (the highest-level bilateral military contact since the early 1960s), the Soviets indicated that they might be willing to provide help in the modernization of Chinese defense plants constructed on the basis of Soviet technology in the 1950s (the visit coincided with Beijing's decision to cancel a U.S.$550 million deal with the United States for avionics to upgrade fifty Chinese F-8 fighters). Reciprocating this visit, the first Soviet army delegation to visit China in thirty years arrived in Beijing on June 1, led by Rear Admiral Vladimir Khuzhokov, head of the external relations department of the Soviet defense ministry, and including alternate Politburo member (and, with Yazov, future coup conspirator) Boris K. Pugo, whose visit implied the improvement of Party-to-Party relations. Military cooperation would progress rapidly: by fall 1990 China had agreed to buy from the USSR twenty-four troop-carrying helicopters capable of operating in high-altitude climates (the United States had refused to permit sale of such weapons systems because they might be used in Tibet).

Meanwhile economic, cultural, and educational exchanges continued. Although total Soviet foreign trade dropped 6.4 percent for the year, Sino-Soviet trade volume increased to U.S.$5.3 billion, a quarter of which was border trade, in 1990, topping the 1989 record level by 26 percent, as the USSR overtook Germany as China's fourth-largest trade partner. The State Council approved the designation of Heihe City, which overlooks Blagoveshchensk (the third-largest city in the Soviet Far East) across the Amur/Heilong River, as a special economic region.[9] Some two hundred cooperative projects were initiated between localities of the two countries, and China dispatched some fifteen thousand citizens to the Soviet Far East for labor service; some twenty Sino-Soviet joint ventures were established in the USSR and a few in China—personnel from the Soviet Union became involved in cocoa production on Hainan Island. There were three hundred exchanges of scientific and technological delegations in 1990. The Soviet Union sent 809 exchange students to China between 1988 and 1990, while 1,307 Chinese postgraduate students went to study in the USSR.[10]

The Fourth Stage

By the time of the 1991 Spring Festival, Sino-Soviet relations had warmed noticeably, for two reasons. The first was the Gulf War: China played its vote in the Security Council debates shrewdly, exchanging its abstention for a relaxation of U.S. diplomatic sanctions. But China's prognosis had been pessimistic, advising more time for economic sanctions to work and forecasting a Vietnam-type stalemate in the event of war; it was therefore taken aback by the unexpectedly swift allied triumph and dismayed by the subsequent emergence of an essentially unipolar New World Order. According to a paper drafted by a key adviser to Li Peng and circulated among senior cadres after the war, the U.S. goal was world domination, in the context of which "the United States has decided it must thoroughly destroy the existing order of China" by encouraging internal disorder and sapping the country's strength by forcing democratization.[11] The implication was that only with the help of a renascent Soviet superpower could that distasteful prospect be averted. Second, though it could easily contain its enthusiasm for Gorbachev, the CCP leadership found no viable alternative. According to Chinese Kremlinologists, the three main factions contending for power were Ligachev on the "left," Yeltsin on the right, and Gorbachev in the middle. The CCP would have preferred Ligachev, but after sending a "Party-worker delegation" to make investigations in the Soviet Union, it concluded that he had no following at all and that Yeltsin's influence was increasing. Gorbachev had to be embraced as the only alternative to Yeltsin, who would enlarge the ideological gap between them and increase China's isolation.[12]

Thus Sino-Soviet relations enjoyed improvement in both public and private aspects during this period. Internal documents on Soviet domestic problems circulating within the CCP around New Year's 1991 were all critical in tone, particularly concerning Gorbachev, but they were less negative than those of the previous year. The CCP Central Committee issued a document to cadres at section-chief level and above throughout the country in the spring of 1991 that represented a major shift in tone and content since the fall of 1990. It made three points: (1) the Soviet Union is still adhering to the socialist road; Gorbachev is opposed to Yeltsin's idea of restoring capitalism across the board and also opposed to separatism; (2) Sino-Soviet cooperation is important to counter the impact of U.S. "Bushism" since the Gulf War; and (3) the border issue should be approached realistically; China cannot require the Soviet Union to return territories occupied by czarist Russia.[13] The CCP began to give publicity to Sino-Soviet friendship, praising Soviet fraternal assistance in the 1950s. More than twenty Soviet novels of that vintage, censored until 1990, suddenly became required reading material for political education, including *How Steel Is Tempered* and *An Iron Torrent;* large numbers of Soviet feature films were released. Jiang Zemin finally reciprocated

Gorbachev's 1989 visit in April–May 1991, bearing 80 tons of gifts for the children and old people of Moscow and Leningrad. Greeted with Brezhnev-type bear hugs and tirades against U.S. foreign policy, Jiang nostalgically tendered the CCP's desire to recover the spirit of the 1950s.[14] Though there were no new accords, Jiang and Gorbachev signed an agreement on the eastern borders in which China gained sovereignty over the symbolically significant one-square-mile Zhenbao (Damansky) Island (where the 1969 clash had started) and a few other river islands on the Chinese side of the channel (though the fate of Heixiazi [Black Bear] Island remained moot). In accordance with agreements made during Li Peng's earlier visit, trade was transformed on January 1, 1991, from escrow trade to trade based on cash settlement; although this liberated trade from government regulation, the lack of foreign exchange in the Soviet Union, China, and Eastern Europe meant that trade declined to U.S.$3.9 billion in 1991 (although border trade, still on a barter basis, continued to boom, and China agreed to extend U.S.$715 million in concessionary credits to the Soviet Union for the purchase of badly needed Chinese agricultural commodities).[15] The two countries also stepped up military contacts. Negotiations for the purchase of Sukhov Su-27 fighters, under way since early 1990, culminated in the purchase of twenty-four at a "friendship" price (U.S.$700 million), with an option to buy an additional forty-eight, reversing a mutual thirty-year freeze on arms sales. There was also tentative agreement on Chinese coproduction of MiG-31s, as well as "widespread reports" of Chinese interest in buying Soviet T-72 tanks, Il-76 transport planes, an aircraft carrier, and refueling technology to give its bombers a range of more than a thousand miles. Beijing also expressed interest in acquiring Soviet space technology and the Soviets in China's success in converting military factories to civilian production.[16] Beginning in the second half of the year, China planned to send military personnel to study in the Soviet Union; a number of pilots were gathered for concentrated preparations for studies in the USSR in June, where they would undergo a training course of one to one and a half years.

The August Coup and Thereafter

Despite the undertaking on both sides throughout this period not to interfere in each other's internal affairs, the Chinese leadership did not shrink from doing what it could to promote the actors and policies most compatible with its interests. Jiang Zemin's April visit was a gesture of support for Gorbachev; he also held a private meeting with Vice President Yanayev, later a key figure in the coup, while spurning Yeltsin's request for a meeting. Upset by the margin of Yeltsin's victory in his June 1991 election as president of the Russian Republic, the PRC invited his hard-line opponent, Ivan Polozkov, a member of the CPSU Politburo and chair of the Russian Republic's Party Committee, to Beijing for a ten-day visit that coincided with Yeltsin's talks with Bush in the United States.[17] From May through August, three top CCP leaders, including not only Jiang but Li Peng and People's Liberation Army (PLA) Chief of Staff Chi Haotian, visited the Soviet Union on separate occasions.

This stepped-up diplomatic activity naturally gave rise to suspicions that Chinese leaders had had advance notice of or even aided and abetted the August coup by CPSU hard-liners, suspicions that have since been denied by both countries. It is true that Chi's visit came the week before the coup (August 7–12), and that it included secret talks with Yanayev and Yazov. There are reports that Yazov inquired (during his May visit) whether the PRC would supply grain and foodstuffs to the USSR in the event that some incident should lead to a suspension of Western aid (to which he received an affirmative answer), but there is no sign of collusion on the coup itself. Upon hearing news of Shevardnadze's formation of a new party in July, the CCP Central Committee disseminated a document to central and regional officials warning that the Soviet Union might well "go capitalist" by the fall of 1991 and calling upon cadres to "raise our vigilance … make sure cadres and members will not be shocked as they were by events in Romania."[18] Chinese news coverage of the coup was prompt and sympathetic; at a time when Western leaders were refusing to recognize the new Soviet regime, the PRC was promising that Sino-Soviet relations would enjoy "continued development."

The inside story is, unsurprisingly, that CCP leaders were delighted by the coup and disappointed by its swift collapse. The CCP quickly geared up for emergency decision making and issued a rapid series of mutually contradictory top-priority circulars in the course of the State of Emergency Committee's (SEC's) seventy-hour life span. The first was on August 19, the day of the coup, when Deng Xiaoping and other leaders rushed back to Beijing (from Beidaihe, where they were enjoying their summer vacation) to hear Chi Haotian report on his talks with Yazov. Chi urged the CCP openly to express its support for the SEC at once, but Deng advised it to "remain composed and watch what happens." The coup was certainly a "good thing," he added; we must "not be visibly pleased but only be delighted at the bottom of our hearts." On August 20, Jiang Zemin convened the CCP Secretariat to draft a Central Committee document to the effect that the Soviet Union would strengthen its internal and external policies again and that the coup would therefore contribute to the consolidation of socialism (and that the PRC should recognize the SEC regime).[19] Before that document could be issued, however, the leadership got word (on the evening of August 21) that the coup had been canceled; another emergency enlarged Politburo meeting was convened. The Politburo now confined itself to noting that Gorbachev had resumed his duties (congratulations were clearly not in order) and offered to readjust relations with the Soviet Union on the basis of noninterference in each other's internal affairs. The SEC were "the real Marxists," but they had committed various tactical blunders, such as naively relying on legal procedures (e.g., waiting for a parliamentary session to endorse their putsch) and failing to take "resolute measures" to quell protests, arrest Yeltsin, and control the army. The CCP should draw a lesson from the Soviet experience and guard against similar events in China. These guidelines were conveyed orally to all State Council ministries and to all Party, government, and PLA organs on August 22. The PLA was placed on first-degree combat alert, all troops on leave (particularly border troops) ordered to return and stand by.

But the final blow was soon to fall: on August 24, Yeltsin ordered the disbandment of the Russian CPSU and Gorbachev "voluntarily" resigned from his post as general secretary. The CCP Politburo Standing Committee convened its third emergency session the following day. Attention was drawn to three disquieting domestic trends: (1) the CCP had been influenced by "social democratic" tendencies, and many Party members had advanced proposals calling for "pluralism," implying a renunciation of CCP leadership; (2) the individual economy had expanded greatly, with the number of individual households and their economic power surpassing what existed before socialist transformation in 1953; and (3) "bourgeois liberal" ideas were having an insidious effect on the people's values. The leadership adopted a strategy of "five upholds and five oppositions": uphold the Party's leadership, the Party's absolute control of the army, the people's democratic dicatorship, the socialist road, and the economic legal system based on public ownership; oppose any multiparty system, the PLA's involvement in politics, the parliamentary system, social democracy, and privatization. Yang Shangkun argued during the meeting that Soviet developments proved that the measures taken by the CCP during June 3–4, 1989, were correct. The leadership agreed that the collapse of the coup could be attributed to the lack of a "core force" of veteran proletarian revolutionaries and a poor choice of successors. "It is necessary to choose well successors to leadership at various levels," Deng Xiaoping concluded. "Politically unreliable elements must be resolutely ousted. Do not be afraid of opinions against groups and strata of young aristocrats. ... The root cause of the problem in the CPSU was that their choice of succeeding leadership was bad and imprecise and hence allowed bourgeois individualistic careerists to grasp political power." On Deng's instructions, the Central Committee Organization Department officially notified localities that they should not deliberately exclude children of cadres in choosing cadre candidates and that they should choose cadres with a strong Party spirit and sense of political responsibility at the second and third echelons, allowing a long period to observe and test them. Chen Yun agreed: "This is not only a life-and-death situation concerning our Party and State but also a life-and-death question concerning our wives, children, and ourselves."[20]

In the next several months, a clear distinction reappeared between China's public and its "internal" Soviet policy. The former remained cautious. The CCP's official policy would remain one of noninterference in Soviet internal affairs: no public debates on ideological differences would be conducted. The media should gradually pass on to the people the information that the Soviet Union had "deteriorated" (*bian zhi*), but they should not publish this in a conspicuous position on the page so as to give offense, nor should the current Soviet authorities be criticized directly. A Central Committee document was issued orally to department- and bureau-level cadres on August 29, conveying the twenty-four-character instruction formulated by Deng Xiaoping at the August 25 Politburo meeting: "Observe the development soberly, maintain our position, meet the challenge calmly, hide our capacities and bide our time, remain free of ambitions, never claim leadership." Meanwhile, the Party conducted an internal campaign to drive home the lesson that the ultimate consequences of Gorbachev-style reform were disastrous, reciting ample objective evidence to bolster its case. Whereas the public media focused on how hard life had become for the common people, the internal media stressed the disaster befalling leaders and cadres. The Central Committee Propaganda Department issued a classified document criticizing the spineless Communist leaderships of the various Eastern European countries and moralizing about their humiliating ends: Honecker and Wolf facing trial in German courts, an erstwhile prime minister serving as a train conductor, some leaders becoming peddlers, some homeless, all of course losing jobs and the perquisites of office.[21] The Central Committee's General Office issued an internal document on November 1 excerpting perhaps the most trenchant critique of the consequences of Soviet reform from a speech by Bo Yibo, vice chairman of the Central Advisory Committee of the CCP:

> The Soviet Union was a military and economic superpower in the 1970s and 1980s, but it has now disintegrated as a state. All Soviet officials, from the president of the Soviet Union to the president of the Russian Republic and government ministers, have been sent to the United States, Western Europe and Japan to beg for economic aid and grains so that they can get through their difficulties this cold winter.[22]

Although it is arguable that the USSR's collapse was in the PRC's national interest, the CCP leadership identified with the Soviet regime to such an extent that its fate filled them with a "sense of crisis" (*weiji gan*), and they denounced Gorbachev as a "superbeggar," a "traitor to Marxism-Leninism, a source of disaster to the Soviet people, and the biggest traitor in the history of the international communist movement."

China and the Post-Soviet Republics

Despite this inauspicious beginning, the new leadership of the Republic of Russia quickly made clear its intention to continue to foster good relations with China (under the mantle of inheritor of the international commitments of the USSR), and the Chinese regime reciprocated. The PRC promptly recognized both the eleven republics now constituting the Commonwealth of Independent States (CIS) and the four that opted not to join (partly for fear that they would otherwise recognize Taiwan; in fact, Latvia did establish consular relations with Taipei—an attempt at compromise that Beijing spurned, breaking relations).

Although one might have expected the Soviet collapse to lead China to quarantine its borders to forestall the spread of separatist tendencies among its own minority populations, trade has continued to wax. Lack of hard currency has hindered program trade somewhat (the trade balance has been in China's favor, but China cannot offer much credit because of its own budget deficit), but border trade has grown in explosive fashion (by 1991 it made up 60 percent of total trade and is projected to make up 80 percent in 1992). In May 1992 three economic development zones (similar to the special economic zones) were established to lure foreign capital in Urumqi, Shiheizi, and Kuitun in Xinjiang, all sited on the Eurasia railway near inner Asian Islamic countries; similar arrangements were planned for Suifenhe in Heilongjiang, Huichun in Jilin, and Manzhouli in Inner Mongolia. Moscow finally dubbed Vladivostok an "open city" in early 1992, welcoming not only Chinese but Korean and Japanese capital and technology. Chinese "special households" (*getihu*) have been permitted to travel to the adjoining republics quite freely, and thousands of Chinese traders have been shuttling back and forth selling Chinese leather jackets, down coats, and wool sweaters in Siberia (trains from Beijing now arrive in Irkutsk three times weekly) and small tractors

in Kyrgyzstan and Kazakhstan; these traders come home with tales of dismal economic conditions across the border, which get great media play.[23] But Russians,
Ukrainians, and others also began flocking into China to sell their wares out of
duffel bags and accumulate enough currency to purchase consumer goods to take
home and resell at a profit: they came in such numbers that "Foreign Guest Special Business Counters" had to be set up at two Beijing markets (Hongqiao and
Dongdaqiao) to "avoid disorder."[24] Thus the entire sixth floor of the Guotai Hotel
was turned into a sort of mini-mall, with all doors open and all rooms filled with
clothing for sale to Russian customers in mass quantities. Local labor organizations in northern China hire out lumberjacks, vegetable farmers, and construction workers—by the summer of 1992, some twenty thousand Chinese workers
were working in Siberia.

The various forums established under the aegis of normalization have continued to function smoothly. The first economic and trade agreement since the
breakup of the Union was signed in early March 1992, and on March 16–17 Russian Foreign Minister Andrei Kozyrev—the highest-level visitor since Gorbachev—visited China to discuss developing new channels between the two countries. In August the Russian defense minister, Pavel Grachev, met with Chinese
Defense Minister Qin Jiwei to discuss military cooperation and further arms
sales. Yeltsin himself came to China in December 1992. Border talks continue, albeit now complicated by the fact that China has borders not only with Russia but
with Kazakhstan, Kyrgyzstan, and Tajikistan. China and the Soviet Union had
fortunately agreed on 93 percent of their 5,500-kilometer border (including nearly
all of the eastern quadrant) prior to the latter's dissolution. The major area still in
dispute between Russia and China is Heixiazi Island, a large (with a second island,
a total of 700 square kilometers) but strategically insignificant island at the confluence of the Amur/Heilong and Ussuri/Wusuli rivers, where many of the leading
citizens of nearby Khabarovsk have their dachas. About 3,500 kilometers of the
Sino-Soviet border was with Russia, ca. 1,000 kilometers with Kazakhstan, 800 kilometers with Kyrgyzstan, and 400 kilometers with Tajikistan; yet whereas 99 percent (by Russian calculation) of the Sino-Russian border has been demarcated,
less than 30 percent of the border with the other three republics has been agreed
upon. Sino-Kazakh borders, although long, pose no major problem; the most serious difficulty seems likely to be the Sino-Tajik border, where the Pamir region is
mountainous and difficult to demarcate. The Chinese are somewhat unnerved by
the prospect of a spillover of ethno-religious politics in Tajikistan (63 percent of
the population is Tajik, 24 percent Uzbek) into Xinjiang—which has experienced
anti-Chinese unrest sporadically, most recently in 1989. In any case, the resumption of border negotiations was formally agreed upon in September 1992, and by
the following month two joint delegations representing the four former Soviet republics (under Russian leadership) were in Beijing negotiating the border and
economic/scientific cooperation, respectively.

The reason neither side seems to take these border issues too seriously is that
the national security dilemma seems to have virtually vanished. Russia has been
steadily cutting troop levels in the strategic area abutting North China: in recent
years troop levels in the region have been cut from more than half a million to two
hundred thousand. Huge armaments factories in the Khabarovsk industrial re-

gion have been closed, precipitating unemployment rates nearing 30 percent in some towns. In June 1992 the last remaining combat troops were withdrawn from Outer Mongolia (which hosted some sixty-five thousand troops in the 1960s).[25] This force reduction is based on a redefinition of national security that carries the logic of Gorbachev's "new thinking" to radical conclusions: to rely as Brezhnev did on an impregnable military for national security only increased regional suspicions and diverted the economy from more productive investments: "Power politics swallowed up tremendous resources and weighed heavily on the country without paying any dividends. Not only did the threat to our security not diminish, it actually increased. ... Meanwhile, the Soviet Far East lagged increasingly behind in economic development."[26]

China's military burden has, needless to say, been greatly relieved by the disappearance of what had for decades been the major threat to its national existence. Not only has the border issue been neutralized but the antagonism that had been indirectly generated by Soviet alliances with China's southern neighbors has been defused, leading to substantial improvements in Sino-Indian, Sino-Mongolian, and Sino-Vietnamese relations. Indeed, according to some Chinese analysts China's national security outlook has not been brighter since the Opium War. But the policy implications have been less clear. Though some have argued for further troop demobilization and retrenchments of military expenditures, the trend since 1989 has been in the other direction (from 1989–1992 Chinese military spending increased some 50 percent). The reasons for the buildup are no doubt largely domestic, as the regime needs a firm hand to compensate for its loss of ideological legitimacy and navigate between the aftermath of Tiananmen and an impending succession. Yet China has also sought to project power beyond its shores—by acquiring air-refueling capability for its fighter aircraft, by building a blue-water navy, possibly by acquiring an aircraft carrier.[27] The 1979 Vietnam War taught the PLA that it was unprepared to execute local wars; to cope with future threats on its periphery, China thus emphasizes the creation and modernization of "special purpose" elite units.[28] Whereas previously this could be rationalized in terms of the Soviet threat, Chinese territorial designs on a large region of islands and ocean in the South China Sea are now being seen in somewhat more sinister perspective.

The "internal" Chinese interpretation of the Soviet collapse is of course more difficult to fathom. The initial reaction seems to have been that the Soviet disintegration confirmed the correctness of the Tiananmen hard-liners' "line" and the folly of any liberal alternative. Given the demonstrated bankruptcy (or at least mortal peril) of political reform (and Yeltsin's reforms are far worse than Gorbachev's, dismissed as "utopian capitalism"), China can only bank on redoubled economic efforts. "Only through our development can we convince disbelievers of the superiority of the socialist system," as Deng put it in late 1991. "They will be a bit more clear-headed when we have reached the level of small-scale prosperity by the end of the century. If, by the next century, we become a socialist country with a medium-level prosperity, the majority of the disbelievers will have realized their mistakes."[29] Yet whereas in the immediate aftermath of the coup the hard-liners threatened to reverse economic as well as political reform in a sweeping campaign against "peaceful evolution" (*heping yanbian*), by fall 1990

Deng was able to create a pragmatic sanctuary for economic reform as a "core." By the summer of 1992, in the context of Deng's trip to the south in preparation for yet another comeback qua leader of the reform forces, a slightly revised interpretation had appeared according to which the disaster befalling the Soviet Union could be attributed not to reform itself but to the fact that the Brezhnev leadership had delayed for too long, walling the Soviet Union off from economic and technological developments in the outside world. The policy implications of this line of analysis were that more reform, not less, would be necessary for China to avoid the fate of the USSR.

Conclusions

What is most striking about China's relations with the Soviet Union and its successor republics is not that there have been abrupt vicissitudes, for indeed there has been a nonstop rollercoaster of changes over the last several years in the context of which each regime could make a good case for having been doublecrossed by the other. The Chinese crackdown on vocal reform advocates at Tiananmen was at least politically inconvenient to Gorbachev and the Soviet reform contingent, the sustained Chinese critique of his own efforts at liberalization still more so. True, the Chinese kept their criticisms "internal," but we need only suppose the Soviet intelligence network to be as competent as Western reporters to assume the Kremlin to have been fully apprised of the Chinese crititique. Gorbachev must have felt again betrayed by Chinese support for the SEC in the August coup. And if Gorbachev had reason to feel betrayed, Yeltsin never had any particular reason to feel grateful to a regime that had snubbed him before the coup and excoriated him afterward. For their part, the Chinese felt betrayed by a regime whose policies they had often criticized but now expected to provide ideological bedrock in a turgid international environment. This was particularly true for a regime undergoing succession in which many hailed from Soviet schools, from Yang Shangkun and Chen Yun in the revolutionary generation to Li Peng and Jiang Zemin among the heirs apparent.

What is mysterious, then, is how the relationship has been able to survive and improve while being buffeted by so many reversals. The new friendship's mysterious tenacity places previous explanations of the fractious history of the relationship in a new light. One of the leading theories of the origins of the schism traced it to ideology. Yet if ideological disputes were adequate to explain the original dispute, such differences would certainly doom the current relationship. Never has the ideological gap been wider—Kozyrev even raised human-rights concerns during his March 1992 visit, to his hosts' dismayed surprise. There are supporters of the Chinese "road" in Moscow, but they are hard-liners totally out of tune with political developments since 1989 and rather unlikely to regain power.

We may also conclude that geostrategic explanations of the antagonism were greatly exaggerated. The Sino-Soviet border has been divided among four sovereign republics, but the Russian portion of that border—some 3,500 kilometers— is still the longest in the world. Yet contrary to prevailing expectations for twenty years, neither country now regards the other as a national security threat, and the border is at peace. True, demilitarization is far from complete, but that seems to be only a matter of time, and mutual economic needs are gradually turning a once impenetrable barrier into a commercial artery. China is now pushing for the revival of a hydroelectric power plan dating back to the days of Sino-Soviet friendship, for instance, which would include construction of twelve dams, seven very large ones on the Amur River moving upriver from the Khingan Gorge and five more on its tributaries.[30] Most of the power would be sold to China.

Whatever the origins of the dispute, there are two explanations for its reconciliation that seem, prima facie, to stand up fairly well. The first has to do with the passing of the strategic triangle. The eclipse of the triangle is the result of a long-term evolution that brought the Cold War to an earlier (but less complete) conclusion in Asia than in the West. The triangle dissolved because of the declining credibility of the nuclear weapons monopoly that had symbolized the primacy of the triangular powers. The waning credibility of nuclear weapons may in turn be attributed to the continuing efficacy of low-threshhold conventional weapons (for example, in national liberation wars), the futility of nuclear confrontations when both sides have second-strike capability, and the ideological deradicalization of Marxism-Leninism, divesting postrevolutionary leaderships of an ideal *casus belli*. Thus it is not coincidental that the wave of popular insurrections that began in the heart of Beijing and riffled domino-like through Eastern Europe in 1989 followed Soviet-American détente and coincided with the normalization of Sino-Soviet relations, which neutralized the last antagonistic relationships within the triangle.

An explanation in terms of the passing of the strategic triangle is necessary but insufficient to account for the current cordiality of the relationship. The sufficient cause is the strategy of diplomatic bridge building by small steps, an approach inaugurated by the resumption of normalization talks in 1982. When such talks had first been undertaken in the 1970s, China had accepted under duress, placing both sides in a situation in which the flexibility necessary for compromise did not exist. By the time talks resumed in 1982, China had acquired a secure second-strike capability and independent access to Washington. Bilateral links grew through accretion, creating a multistranded network of meeting forums and economic and cultural exchanges. There are now two "land bridges" consisting of railroad lines linking China to Western Europe, the first of which is between Dalian and Moscow via the trans-Siberian express, the second (which opened in June 1992) from Lianyungang port in southern Jiangsu via Urumqi and Alma Ata all the way to Rotterdam (a thirty-three-hour trip). Thousands of traders, workers, and entrepreneurs now cross the border every day. Any disruption would impose a tangible penalty on sizable constituencies on both sides.

Whether the future relationship fits into a larger regional or global configuration as clearly defined as the triangle seems dubious, but a few trends are worth noting. China is likely to have a significant role to play in a world in which economics rather than nuclear power is the ultima ratio. China is not the most advanced industrial economy in the Asia-Pacific region—that is a distinction that Japan will claim for some time to come. Technologically, it lags behind the Four Tigers and perhaps even some of the Association of Southeast Asian Nations (ASEAN) countries. Yet China's dominant position in the region seems ensured by its population, geostrategic centrality, and role as looming East Asian "growth pole." A nation of more than a billion people projected by World Bank economists to have the region's most rapid growth over the next decade, China cannot be ignored. The future role of Russia in the region is still being debated (for the immediate future, intra-CIS relationships seem likely to preoccupy Moscow), but it seems likely in any event to be greater than during the Cold War. Russia is now a much more Asian country than during the heyday of the empire. Its new borders are more than 1,000 kilometers east of Europe, where many of its neighbors are in ethnic turmoil and economic depression, with less than friendly feelings for their former occupier; to many Russians even the fate of Western Europe seems uncertain. East Asia has been the world's most dynamic region for the past two decades; capital and technology seem to be flowing from west to east. Some 80 percent of Russia's natural resources and less than 20 percent of its population are east of the Urals. This could be Russia's new frontier, a land bridge between Orient and Occident, where the Russian Far East's vast natural resources could form a profitable symbiosis with the industrial dynamism of the newly industrialized countries. In that case, China might function as Russia's passport to a key role in the Pacific century.

Notes

1. Major-General Vitaly Bubenin, who was a Border Guard lieutenant on the scene, recalled the clashes in an interview with the newspaper *Vostok Rossii*, attributing the March 2 clash to a Chinese ambush but admitting that on March 15 Soviet forces launched a calculated counterattack using huge salvoes of rockets. James Flannery, reporting from Khabarovsk in a Reuters dispatch, June 3, 1992.

2. See Thomas Robinson, "China Confronts the Soviet Union: Warfare and Diplomacy on China's Inner Asian Frontiers," in Roderick MacFarquhar and John K. Fairbank, eds., *The Cambridge History of China, Vol. 15, The People's Republic, Part 2: Revolutions Within the Chinese Revolution 1966–1982* (New York: Cambridge University Press, 1991), pp. 218–301.

3. For a more detailed exposition, see my *Sino-Soviet Normalization and Its International Implications, 1945–1990* (Seattle: University of Washington Press, 1992).

4. The first attempt to deal with the logic of the triangle systematically, Theodore Caplow's *Two Against One: Coalitions in Triads* (Englewood Cliffs, N.J.: Prentice-Hall, 1968), is strategically limited to this sort of balance-of-power weighting.

5. According to an anonymous memoir by a senior Russian China specialist, as cited in *Far Eastern Economic Review* (hereafter *FEER*), June 11, 1992.

6. Gu Guanfu and Chun-tu Hsueh, "Sino-Soviet Ties Grow Steadily," *Beijing Review* 36 (September 3–9, 1990):8–12. Total trade for the five years 1986–1990 amounted to 22 billion Swiss francs, double that for the entire decade of the 1970s.

7. *South China Morning Post* (Hong Kong) (hereafter *SCMP*), February 17, 1990, p. 12; Lo Ping, "Notes on a Northern Journey," *Zheng ming* No. 150 (April 1, 1990):6–8.

8. *Pravda*, March 1, 1990, p. 5.

9. *SCMP*, September 3, 1990, p. 12. In 1990, Heihe negotiated trade contracts worth about U.S.$140 million in 1990.

10. *Zhongguo qingnian bao* [China Youth Daily], May 13, 1991, p. 2.

11. He Xin, "The Gulf War and China," in Foreign Broadcast Information Service, *Daily Report—China* (hereafter FBIS-China), February 27, 1991, pp. 5–6.

12. Liu Zhixun, *Guang jiao jing*, June 16, 1991, pp. 20–23.

13. See Ho Boshi, in *Dangdai* (Hong Kong) No. 3 (June 15, 1991):18.

14. "We intend to return to the state of relations we had in the 1950s," Jiang said. "These are the relations among allies." *Christian Science Monitor*, May 27, 1991.

15. Liu Guangjun and Chen Baojiu, "A New Change in China's Economic Relations and Trade with the Soviet Union," *Jingji cankao* [Economic Reference] (Beijing), July 5, 1990, p. 1.

16. Since summer 1991, China has recruited a few hundred senior Soviet scientists to work on new weapons technology, offering them a monthly salary of 1,200 yuan plus free housing and a paid annual home leave. Guocang Huan, "The New Relationship with the Former Soviet Union," *Current History*, September 1992, p. 254.

17. *SCMP*, June 20, 1991, p. 9.

18. *SCMP*, July 16, 1991, p. 10.

19. Cai Yongmei, in *Kai fang* (Hong Kong) No. 15 (September 15, 1991):22–24; He Boshi, *Dangdai* No. 6 (September 15, 1991):8–12; *Bai xing* (Hong Kong) No. 247 (September 1, 1991):15.

20. Lo Ping, in *Zheng ming* No. 167 (September 1, 1991):6, 8; He Boshi, in *Dangdai* No. 6 (September 15, 1991):8–12.

21. *Bai xing* No. 248 (September 16, 1991):6–7; Jan Wong, in *Toronto Globe and Mail*, September 7, October 28, 1991; Yvonne Preston, in *The Age* (Melbourne), October 29, 1991.

22. *Zheng ming* No. 170 (December 1, 1991):22–23.

23. David R. Schweisberg, United Press International (UPI), July 27, 1992; *Moscow Times*, September 17, 1992; Reuters, June 24, 1992.

24. UPI, June 10, 1992; Reuters, June 24, 1992.

25. James Flannery, in Reuters, June 3, 1992; also Reuters, June 17, 1992.

26. Ye. Bazhanov, "Reflections on Soviet Policy in the Asia-Pacific Region," *Pravda*, January 16, 1990, p. 5, as trans. in *Current Digest of the Soviet Press* 42:3 (1990):10.

27. Nicholas Kristof, "As China Looks at World Order, It Detects New Struggles Emerging," *New York Times*, April 21, 1992, pp. A1, A4; on the naval buildup, see David G. Muller, *China as a Maritime Power* (Boulder, Colo.: Westview Press, 1983), and Rosita Dellios, *Modern Chinese Defense Strategy: Present Developments, Future Directions* (New York: St. Martin's Press, 1990).

28. See He Chong, "Let Some Units Modernize First," *Jiefangjun bao*, February 5, 1988, in *Joint Publications Research Service-CAR*, February 19, 1988, p. 85, as cited in Yitzhak Schichor, "Defense Policy Reform," in Gerald Segal, ed., *Chinese Politics and Foreign Policy Reform* (London: Kegan Paul International, 1990), pp. 77–99.

29. New China News Agency, October 9, 1991; *Jingji ribao* (Beijing), November 22, 1991; see also *SCMP*, August 26 and December 14, 1991.

30. Daniel Sneider, in *Christian Science Monitor*, August 27, 1992.

6

Japan and Europe in Chinese Foreign Relations

DONALD W. KLEIN

China's focus on economic modernization virtually ensures a continuing emphasis through this century on its already extensive ties to the three centers of industrial and economic strength—North America, Europe, and Japan. Until the Soviet collapse in late 1991, China's relations with the industrial West had a strategic element that surely matched their economic component. The emerging New World Order of the 1990s seems certain, however, to see an ever-increasing economic focus in the conduct of its international relations.

This chapter deals with Japan and Europe and focuses on the post-Mao era and the events since the Tiananmen tragedy of 1989, but some space must be given to the earlier years. A preliminary observation is in order: Throughout the postwar era, Japan and Western Europe have been closely allied with the United States, and thus any analytical framework that ignored the U.S. role would lead to muddled thinking and faulty conclusions. This point was particularly salient before the breakup of the Soviet Union, and it will surely be a major consideration in the years ahead.

The Early Years: Legitimacy in the 1950s

During the bipolar 1950s, when Moscow and Beijing were tightly linked in a strategic, economic, and ideological alliance, China unabashedly viewed Japan and Europe as contemptible lackeys of the United States. From China's perspective, this was understandable. Japan and Europe were closely tied to the United States through anticommunist pacts—in the Atlantic region by the North Atlantic Treaty Organization (NATO) and in the Pacific by defense pacts that linked the United States with Japan, South Korea, Australia, and New Zealand. For China these links were no mere abstraction. No fewer than seven NATO nations fought against China during the Korean War (Belgium, Canada, France, Greece, Luxembourg, the Netherlands, and Britain), although most of these countries' contributions were small or largely symbolic. Moreover, four of these nations (Britain, France, Australia, and New Zealand) allied in 1954 with the United States and three Asian countries (Pakistan, the Philippines, and Thailand) to form the Southeast Asian Treaty Organization (SEATO), clearly an "anti-China" pact. Finally, although Japan contributed no troops during the Korean War, it served as an exceptionally important logistic base for the U.S. forces that waged war against Chinese troops in Korea.

Beyond the strategic threat, China's very legitimacy was challenged by most European nations and Japan: they recognized Taiwan but not the People's Republic. Diplomatic recognition came at first only from Britain, Sweden, Denmark, and Switzerland. Norway and the Netherlands were added to the list in 1954, but a full decade passed before another European nation, France, recognized Beijing. This lack of recognition had a crucial by-product: the denial of the China seat in the United Nations. With few exceptions, European nations and Japan supported the U.S. position that kept Beijing out of the UN until 1971.

What was true about legitimacy also applied roughly to trade. By dollar value or percentages, China's trade with Europe and Japan during the 1950s was marginal. From the viewpoint of European countries and Japan, most of them great trading nations, the China trade was virtually nil. For a brief period coinciding with the Bandung era (roughly 1955–1957), it appeared that the PRC's trade with Europe and Japan might improve markedly, but this was quickly dampened (especially with Japan) when China's Great Leap Forward (1958–1961) propelled it into a period of marked hostility toward the industrialized world.

The 1960s

When China emerged from the Great Leap disaster it encountered and helped shape a very different world. Relations with Moscow and Washington were almost entirely hostile. Not only had China lost the Soviet defense connection; trade with the USSR was also careening downhill, and Soviet technology transfer to China was falling with equal speed.

The 1960s saw the high point of China's sponsorship of Third World radicalism. This period, after all, witnessed Beijing's endorsement of Indonesia's effort to form a "revolutionary United Nations." The Chinese strongly supported the emerging Palestine Liberation Organization (PLO) and tried to engineer a second Bandung Conference (which ultimately aborted). But most of all, Defense Minister Lin Biao's "Long Live the Victory of People's War" (September 1965) was a clarion call for an increasingly radical foreign policy. Yet virtually all these steps were verbal; relatively little action matched the revolutionary rhetoric. For example, Chinese foreign aid went to the Pakistan government (not to a leftist guerrilla force trying to overthrow that government) and to Vietnam. Beijing's verbal radicalism abroad was matched at home by the Cultural Revolution's extreme turbulence. The Chinese, now portraying themselves as the sole defenders of Marxist purity, renewed their ardor for the doctrine of "self-reliance."

If the 1960s seemed an unpropitious time for improving relations with Europe and Japan, other imperatives challenged Chinese decision makers during this stormy decade. Revolutionary rhetoric aside, this was in fact the time when China moved to improve relations with Europe and Japan. Important needs dictated this change, which in many ways was probably repugnant to Mao. First, a need for large-scale food imports sent China into the international grain market, then dominated by the United States, Australia, and Canada. U. S. grain was out of the question in the 1960s, and therefore a simple supply-and-demand situation led to huge purchases from both Canada and Australia—a trade that has flourished from 1961 to the present.

Apart from grain, China needed to establish trade with nations that could sell medium- and high-level technology and provide profitable markets for China's products. Europe and Japan nicely fit this profile, and thus by the mid-1960s they emerged as the PRC's chief trading partners. The disparity between revolutionary rhetoric and economic imperatives is neatly illustrated by China's foreign trade in 1966, a year of tremendous turbulence caused by the Cultural Revolution. In that year seven of China's ten leading trading partners were European countries, Canada, Australia, and Japan, and its trade with them represented no less than 44 percent of the total even though the dollar figure was a modest $1.9 billion. A quarter of a century later (1990), the percentage had dropped to 30 percent (owing in large part to China's booming trade with Hong Kong) but the dollar figure soared to nearly $39 billion.

In short, beneath the highly visible layer of revolutionary rhetoric was the more important layer known as realpolitik. One assumes that Mao approved of these concrete actions vis-à-vis Europe and Japan. They came a full decade before his death and well before the 1969 border clash with the Soviet Union that apparently convinced him that some gesture toward the United States was necessary to balance the "more dangerous" superpower.

The Impact of the Nixon Visit

The Kissinger and Nixon trips to China in 1971–1972 were epochal events that substantially reshaped China's relations with Europe and, even more, with Japan. It's easy to forget that Sino-Japanese relations in the late 1960s and early 1970s were still quite strained, notwithstanding Japan's rank then as China's leading trading partner. For example, Premier Zhou Enlai castigated Japan in his much-publicized interview with *New York Times* journalist James Reston in mid-1971.[1] Then, in the Shanghai Communiqué signed during Nixon's February 1972 visit to China, the Chinese bluntly asserted their opposition to the "revival and outward expansion of Japanese militarism." Yet Beijing soon set aside its tough talk toward Japan, and by the early fall of 1972 the two nations had established formal diplomatic relations (Japan simultaneously breaking its formal—but not its informal—ties with Taiwan). Of special interest is the fact that China formally renounced "its demands for war indemnities from Japan," although in the late 1980s and early 1990s ostensibly unofficial demands for reparations were made.[2]

In the meantime, China moved swiftly on the diplomatic front to establish diplomatic relations with a flock of industrial nations, and in almost all cases this meant breaking ties with Taiwan. For example, in the 1970–1973 period China formalized relations with Canada, Italy, Austria, Belgium, Japan, West Germany, Australia, and Spain. Then, in 1974, formal relations were established with the European Economic Community (EEC). In brief, by 1979, China had formal relations with *all* of Western Europe, Canada, and Australia. Because much attention has been paid to China's orientation toward the West since Mao's death in 1976, it is worth noting that all these events happened before he died—and surely had his approval.

Another Chinese turnabout predating Mao's death concerns military relations. China moved gingerly on this issue, apparently trying to remind the then-hostile Soviet Union that military ties with Europe were possible without antagonizing it further. Beijing began to talk in quite favorable terms about NATO and sent arms-purchasing missions to Europe. In the event, few arms were bought (they were too expensive), and after Mikhail Gorbachev took power in 1985 China's need to play the European card sharply diminished.

Enough has been said to show that China had developed increasingly substantial ties with Europe and Japan by the time of Mao's death. In particular, there is a clear line of continuity during the late Mao and post-Mao periods in China's geopolitical posture toward the industrialized West, and this is equally true for economic relations.

Post-Mao Relations with Europe and Japan

Crucial changes in China's relations with Europe and Japan took place before Mao's death, but even more important ones were to come after his passing. Perhaps most important was China's willingness to accept economic aid and direct foreign investments. Sharply altering its previous "self-reliance" policy, it became an eager recipient of Western economic aid. As recently as 1979, World Bank figures for official development assistance reveal that Beijing received a mere $17 million. This figure rapidly ballooned to $940 million in 1985 and then more than doubled to $2.15 billion in 1989, by which year China was the world's leading recipient. As a result of world anger over the June 1989 Tiananmen Massacre official development assistance was cut back (but only marginally) to $2.08 billion in 1990, thereby dropping China to third place behind Egypt and Bangladesh.[3] All signs, including repeated pronouncements by China's most senior leaders, indicate that Beijing will continue its avid quest for such funds, most of which come directly (or indirectly through multilateral organizations) from Europe and Japan.

In addition to foreign aid, post-Mao China has witnessed a huge flow of foreign money in the form of direct foreign investment. For example, at the end of 1991 it claimed that some thirty-seven thousand foreign-funded enterprises had poured in over $26 billion since it had begun accepting such funds in 1979.[4] By a wide margin, most of these investments come from Overseas Chinese in Hong Kong and Macao, but China constantly presses Europe and Japan to increase their investments.

Still another post-Mao development has been the spectacular leap forward in what Western political scientists call transnational relations. Most notable have been the dispatch of tens of thousands of Chinese students and scholars abroad for advanced study and the dramatic rise of tourism in China. By the end of the 1980s and the early 1990s, Chinese students (overwhelmingly in the natural sciences and engineering) were a common sight in the West. The international scientific community is dominated by the United States, Europe, and Japan, and thus it would seem that these (mainly graduate) students will provide China with a link to the West for decades to come. Unfortunately for China, however, many of these same students have refused to return home in the wake of the Tiananmen Massacre.

In the late Mao years and for a brief period afterward, China actively engaged in what it dubbed "people-to-people" diplomacy. These were very inexpensive visits, and China probably lost money on them. Those days are long gone, having been replaced by an unblushing tourism designed to earn foreign currency. In 1991 tourist earnings netted China over $2.8 billion from more than 33 million visitors. Overseas Chinese from Hong Kong and Macao were by far the largest contingent, followed unsurprisingly by the peripatetic Japanese, 458,000 of whom visited China in that year. This flood of foreigners, especially those from the West and Japan, is plainly a mixed blessing for Chinese officialdom. Beijing welcomes the huge sums of money, yet it clearly feels the need to remind its citizens about the alleged risk of corruption in hosting foreigners.

The Tiananmen Impact

China's ties to Europe and Japan would seem, at first glance, to have been thrown under a dark cloud in June 1989, when the world witnessed—live and in color—the Tiananmen Massacre. In mid-1989, few would have doubted that this tragic event would be the "story of the year" or perhaps even the "story of the decade." Foreign policy analysts are usually reluctant to include luck as a factor, but China was indeed lucky in that the Tiananmen story was dwarfed that autumn by the tumbling of the Berlin Wall—again, live and in color—and the long-playing story of Gorbachev's ouster and the Soviet Union's collapse. Nor should we forget that Iraq's invasion of Kuwait came only fourteen months after Tiananmen and that the world for the next half-year was transfixed by the Persian Gulf War.

In response to Western outrage concerning Tiananmen, China immediately declared that it would brook no outside interference in a "domestic" affair. Yet just as quickly it assured the outside world that it still heartily welcomed Western trade, aid, and investment; in other words, it tried to strengthen the economic links to the West so carefully cultivated during the previous decade. Equally if not more important, it took several important steps to demonstrate that it was a "good international citizen." For example, it went along with the various anti-Iraqi sanctions imposed by the United Nations, and although it abstained on the resolution to use force against Iraq it at least did not hinder the operation by using its Security Council veto. It also began cooperating in global efforts to move toward a peaceful settlement in Cambodia. In this instance, China played a crucial role as chief backer of the notorious Pol Pot faction, and thus its cooperation was not merely useful but vital. Another post-Tiananmen diplomatic move concerned North Korea, long supported by China. The evidence is inconclusive, but it appears that Beijing has applied some pressure to curb the often erratic behavior of the Kim Il Sung regime in Pyongyang. This seems to include inducing North Korea to continue its high-level talks with South Korea and persuading Pyongyang to agree to enter the United Nations together with South Korea in

1991.[5] Still another gesture to the West and Japan was China's 1992 ratification of the Nuclear Non-Proliferation Treaty.

There is little doubt that Tiananmen damaged China's normative standing. The damage has probably been more severe in the public mind than in the more hard-hearted world of international diplomacy and global business. Western diplomats are more mindful than the public at large of such things as China's help in solving the Cambodia problem, and the business community seldom ignores the huge China market.

There were certainly short-term setbacks for China regarding its economic links with the West, but it is now clear that these were not in fact too damaging. Most important is that China in the early 1990s is more militarily secure than it has been since the Communists took power in 1949. The drama of Tiananmen in June 1989 tends to obscure the crucial fact that Gorbachev's visit to China in the previous month had largely settled the long-term Sino-Soviet dispute. At a minimum, the likelihood of a Soviet attack on China is vastly diminished in contrast to a decade earlier when the Soviets invaded Afghanistan, a country that borders on China. Moreover, the Soviet collapse has meant that Vietnam has lost its Kremlin support, and thus Hanoi has been forced to come to terms with China. In brief, as Beijing today surveys it borders, it can feel a general sense of security unknown to China for well over a century and a half.

Relations with Europe and Japan:
Costs and Benefits

At the purely political level, China now enjoys formal diplomatic relations with all European governments. This includes those East European governments that have broken away from the Soviet Union and are now attempting to integrate themselves into the Western European system (including EEC membership). For much of the late 1970s and the early 1980s, China applauded NATO as a bulwark against Soviet power. This, however, is a thing of the past. China has also pushed to institutionalize its political links to Europe since the 1970s by sending its most senior officials (especially the premier and the foreign minister) to Europe. For example, the three premiers since Zhou Enlai's death in 1976 (Hua Guofeng, Zhao Ziyang, and Li Peng) have all traveled there. On the European side, virtually all European countries sent a president, prime minister, or foreign minister to China in the 1970s or 1980s. Such visits abruptly halted after Tiananmen, but by 1990 they had been renewed without fanfare. Similarly, Chinese officialdom was no longer welcome in Europe after Tiananmen, but less than two years later senior Chinese officials were again visiting Europe. For example, Chinese Foreign Minister Qian Qichen traveled to Spain, Portugal, and Greece in early 1991, and a year later Premier Li Peng was in Italy, Switzerland, and Spain.

In terms of economic links, Europe has been a fruitful partner for China. For the past three decades, about 13 to 20 percent of China's trade has been with Europe. Apart from percentages, the sheer volume is impressive. Chinese-European trade in 1986 was $13.5 billion, about double the amount for 1983, and in 1989 (the Tiananmen year) moved up to $15.9 billion. One might have expected that the outrage occasioned by Tiananmen would have seen a drop in 1990, but the figure rose to $16.8 billion and then to $17.5 billion in 1991. Further trade increases seem likely, because from Beijing's perspective Europe is an ideal alternative to Japan or the United States—a source of the good trading terms and long-term loans that are virtually a form of foreign aid. For the most part, China's economy and the European economies are complementary, and therefore there is little likelihood of the sort of trade dispute that often darkens the commercial horizon between Japan and Europe.

Closely related to trade is the matter of technology transfer. Here too the Sino-European connection has been useful to China. Europeans have regularly taken out patents in China, and large numbers of Europeans (especially from Germany, Britain, and France) have gone to China as economic and technical experts.

In addition to trade and technology, China is especially eager to attract European investment. Although the results have been disappointing, a Chinese source indicated that the "Big Four" European states (Britain, Germany, France, and Italy) had negotiated by 1991 to invest about $3.5 billion in China.[6] This sum is far below that of investment from Hong Kong and Macao (the biggest investors by a wide margin) and also below U.S. and Japanese investment, but the Europeans are still among China's major investors.

The disadvantages in China's dealings with Europe seem very few indeed. Europe clearly poses no strategic danger. A sharp deterioration in Sino-American ties might cause Washington to pressure its European allies to lessen their ties to China, but in the post–Cold War era this seems very unlikely. There are obviously no border disputes between China and Europe. In the two situations involving territory—the colonies of Hong Kong and Macao—an agreement was reached with the British in 1984 that Hong Kong would revert to China in 1997, and a similar Sino-Portuguese accord in 1987 provided that Macao would become part of China in late 1999. In the interim, China continues to profit enormously from the current situation, and precipitous action seems unlikely.

European relations with Taiwan might be a problem. In recent years, Taiwan's trade with Europe has roughly matched PRC-European trade, thus giving the Europeans a large stake in continuing their trade with Taiwan. Virtually all European nations have so-called unofficial trade offices in Taiwan, and Taiwan has counterpart offices all over Europe. Beijing's response to this situation has been grudging acceptance provided that trade and investment do not lead to "official" diplomatic recognition. From time to time European officials have made "unofficial" trips to Taiwan. Beijing quickly registers an "official" objection, but there the matter rests.

Not surprisingly, China is more sensitive to European sale (or proposed sale) of weaponry to Taiwan. China and the Netherlands had a problem in the 1980s when the Dutch sold two submarines to Taiwan. Similarly, China quite vigorously protested a possible sale of six French warships to Taiwan in early 1990. In this instance, France canceled the sale, and that ended the matter. Almost three years later, however, the issue of French weaponry sales to Taiwan arose again. Perhaps emboldened by the U.S.-Taiwan agreement of November 11, 1992, to sell 115 American F-16 jets (worth nearly $6 billion) to Taiwan, France agreed a week later to sell Taiwan 60 Mirage 2000-5 jet fighters and 1,000 missiles (worth $2.6 billion). Beijing immediately protested the proposed French sale, declaring that it would "react strongly." In reporting on these developments, the *New York Times* noted that Germany might sell submarines to Taiwan.[7] At about the same time, however, Beijing reported on the visit of the German foreign minister, pointedly noting that he had "refuted allegations that Germany would supply military equipment, including submarines, to Taiwan."[8] It seems that more will be heard from the Chinese on these large-scale weapon sales.

Notwithstanding the Tiananmen troubles and the possibility of further European weapon sales, most other signs point to a continuing good relationship with Europe. The relationship has been in the main an economic one, and it is worth emphasizing that China has relatively little economic leverage to use against the Europeans. By way of a rough comparison, Japan's 1991 trade with Europe was over six times greater than China's, and U.S.-Europe trade was almost thirteen times greater.

Japan is vastly more important to China than any European nation. Except for the United States and perhaps the former Soviet Union, China's most important bilateral relationship is with Japan. For well over a century, East Asian interstate relations have hinged largely on Sino-Japanese affairs, and from China's viewpoint this relationship was generally very bad indeed.

Whatever Sino-Japanese problems exist today, it should be emphasized that the relationship is now better than at any time in well over a century. Moreover, it is likely that Japan will play *the* most significant role of any nation in China's long and arduous pursuit of economic modernization. Indeed, this seems more probable in the early 1990s than it did only a few years ago. The reasons are fairly straightforward: The United States has severe economic problems of its own and is therefore not inclined to offer much economic assistance to China. Europe, facing staggering financial burdens in assisting both the East European nations and the Commonwealth of Independent States, is similarly disinclined to assist China. It seems very unlikely that this situation will change significantly for the rest of this century. In any case, whatever the Sino-Japanese problems, one would be hard-pressed to find two major nations with more complementary economies. China has many natural resources that Japan needs and, potentially, a vast market for Japanese products. Japan has the technology and the money to assist China and a rich market for Chinese goods. Proximity adds another positive element that, among other things, holds down transportation costs.

Japan replaced the Soviets as China's top trading partner in 1965 and held that position until 1987, when Hong Kong displaced it. Japan's trade with China during the 1965–1986 period was usually much greater than its trade with the number-two contender (which for many years was Hong Kong). For most of this period, Sino-Japanese trade was usually about 50 percent greater than China's trade with Europe. By the late 1980s, however, China's trade with Japan and Europe was roughly the same, partly, it seems, because of Beijing's desire to avoid overdependence on Japan. A similar pattern characterizes a comparison of China's trade with Japan and with the United States. As recently as the mid-1980s, Beijing's trade with Japan was about double its trade with the United States, but by the late 1980s the trade was roughly equal. Through the 1970s and early 1980s, oil-exporting Saudi Arabia was Japan's number-two trade partner (behind the

United States). The Saudis were displaced by the Chinese in 1985, but by 1989–1990 China had fallen back to fifth place among Tokyo's trade partners.

Problems naturally arise when the volume of trade reaches Sino-Japanese levels. Massive trade imbalances in Japan's favor were among the thorniest issues from Beijing's point of view. These reached record levels in the mid-1980s and led to bitter Chinese complaints. As have many nations, China had difficulty penetrating the Japanese market. Yet, as a state-controlled economy, it had the capability and will to lower trade volumes, and it did exactly that. By the late 1980s. Sino-Japanese trade was in rough balance. Interestingly, the 1990–1991 trade figures indicate that China has begun to run substantial trade surpluses with Japan.

None of these ups and downs in Sino-Japanese trade should obscure the central fact that it has been highly profitable to both sides. Accordingly, while we can expect China to avoid an overdependence on Japan, we can also expect a continued very high volume of commodity trade in the years ahead.

Beyond trade matters, other economic links add testimony to Japan's importance to China. Beginning in 1982, China for the first time became the top recipient of Japan's official development assistance. It held this position until 1988–1989, when Indonesia replaced it and it moved back to second place. Moreover, Japan is the largest supplier of bilateral aid. In 1988, for example, Japan provided 54 percent of the total official development assistance received by China. France was the next-largest contributor (11 percent).[9] Beyond this direct assistance, Japan's Overseas Economic Cooperation Fund, in two loan packages (1979 and 1984), committed over $3.5 billion for various construction projects focused on improving China's rail network and ports.[10]

Predictably, Japanese aid was "suspended" in the wake of the Tiananmen crisis, in large part because of Western (and especially U.S.) pressure. Tiananmen was obviously a human-rights violation, but given Japan's guilt over its own wartime human-rights violations in China, the Japanese are always very reluctant to push this point vis-à-vis China. Moreover, the Japanese argued, it was in no one's interest to see China isolated. Accordingly, Tokyo urged its Western allies to lift the ban on aid to China. In any event, aid was back in the pipeline by 1990, and late that year the two sides signed documents for Japan's third loan package, worth about $7 billion for the 1990–1995 period. The renewal of "normalized" relations was indicated in the summer of 1991 when Japanese Prime Minister Kaifu Toshiki became the first head of state among the industrialized nations to visit China since Tiananmen.

China has been particularly eager to attract direct foreign investment from Japan's business community. To date, however, the results have been extremely disappointing. As of 1991, Japan was the third-largest investor—far behind Hong Kong and Macao and also behind the United States. By early 1992, Japanese business had cumulative investments in China of $3.4 billion, only about 1 percent of Japan's global investment. That year saw a strong surge in Japanese investment, and from preliminary figures it appears that another $1 billion or more will be added.[11]

The Japanese government's well-known ability to put pressure on its business community has its limits. It's one thing for Japanese business to conduct commodity trade with China and quite another to induce firms to pour vast, long-

term sums into China. In addition to such difficulties as corruption and ineffi-
ciency, there are increasingly attractive investment opportunities elsewhere in
Asia. Accordingly, and notwithstanding persistent Chinese complaints, no huge
flow of Japanese long-term investments should be expected.

Another area of Chinese disappointment with Japanese performance is technology transfer. By 1986, however, some 10,000 foreign experts were working in
China, of whom about 40 percent were from Japan.[12] Japan has moved rapidly to
increase the number of Chinese students in Japan. In the brief period from 1987 to
1991, the number jumped from 5,700 to 19,600,[13] and scores of technical groups
conduct inspection missions in both nations.

Another source of Japanese money is tourism. This is an instance in which the
costs of Tiananmen can be measured in some detail. In 1988 (the year before
Tiananmen), 477,000 Japanese traveled to China. This fell abruptly to 395,000 in
1989 and then down to 367,000 in 1990. Interestingly, however, the numbers rose
in 1991 to 458,000—a figure not far below the record year of 1988.[14]

Sino-Japanese ties are regularly reinforced by visits between the two countries'
cabinet-level ministers. Virtually all senior Japanese political leaders, including
the staunchly conservative Liberal Democratic Party chiefs, have visited China.
Beginning with Prime Minister Tanaka Kakuei in 1972, six prime ministers have
visited China while in office (Tanaka, Ohira Masayoshi, Suzuki Zenko, Nakasone
Yasuhiro, Takeshita Noboru, and Kaifu Toshiki). On the Chinese side, paramount
leader Deng Xiaoping visited Japan in 1978 and 1979, followed by visits in 1980,
1982, and 1989, respectively, by Premiers Hua Guofeng, Zhao Ziyang, and Li Peng.
Also, former Communist Party General Secretary Hu Yaobang visited Japan in
1983, and the current holder of that post, Jiang Zemin, was there in 1992 (the first
top-ranking Chinese leader to visit Japan after Tiananmen). The United States
has roughly matched these high-level exchanges, but no European nation comes
even close to official Japanese contacts with China. In a word, senior-level Sino-
Japanese communication has been fairly well routinized over the past two decades.

Despite the extensive economic linkages and the fairly intensive and regularized contacts between political leaders, problems do exist. Some are essentially bilateral in nature, while others are part of the larger Northeast Asian geopolitical
scene. The former category derives in some measure from a peculiar Japanese ob-
tuseness toward Chinese sensitivities. A few well-publicized cases are illustrative.
In 1982, changes in school textbooks in effect whitewashed Japan's invasion and
predatory occupation of China during the 1930s and 1940s. Japan promised to
rectify the situation only after strenuous Chinese objections. Three years later,
Prime Minister Nakasone angered Beijing by visiting Tokyo's Yasukuni Shrine—
the burial place of Japan's military men. China saw this as a visit to the graveyard
of war criminals and vigorously protested. (No Japanese prime minister has repeated this performance.) In 1986, Japan's Education Minister Fujio Masayuki
made some remarks that minimized Japan's wartime actions in China. Beijing
protested; Fujio was fired.

It may be that Beijing almost welcomes these blunders as a way of keeping a
kind of psychological upper hand in dealing with Japan. In any case, China shows
no reluctance to remind Japan of its past war crimes from time to time. In 1987,

for example, when China commemorated the fiftieth anniversary of Japan's full-scale attack, the Chinese press scathingly denounced Japan's past misdeeds. A former Japanese cultural attaché in Beijing has commented that the new Japanese generation has a weaker sense of historical guilt and therefore "China may not be able to continue with this stratagem for long."[15]

Other problems derive from the very different political systems. For example, Japan has an independent judiciary, whereas China does not. The ownership of a student dormitory in Kyoto claimed by both China and Taiwan has languished in Japan's court system for years. To Beijing this is purely a political case—the work of "certain circles" in Japan that foster a "two-Chinas" policy; to the Japanese, it is a matter for the courts.

Some of the geopolitical problems that troubled the Beijing-Tokyo relationship have, in the post–Cold War era, sharply diminished. In Korea, for example, Japan recognizes only South Korea, but it has moved actively to improve relations with North Korea. China, of course, has long had formal relations with North Korea. From the late 1980s strong Sino–South Korean commercial ties were developed, and this led in August 1992 to the establishment of diplomatic relations. The so-called two-Chinas problem is apparently less troublesome than it was only a few years ago. As with South Korea, China in recent years has developed elaborate economic ties with Taiwan and is thus less inclined to badger Japan about its extensive economic links to Taiwan. In any event, many senior members of Japan's ruling Liberal Democratic Party hold very pro-Taiwan views, and public opinion polls reveal a Japanese public that hopes Taiwan can remain independent. Beijing has presumably concluded that Japan's powerful business establishment is unlikely to budge on this issue. Similarly, the "Soviet issue" is far less troublesome than a few years ago. China resented Japan's fairly active trade relations with Moscow, but because Beijing has essentially made its peace with the Russians this issue has also been defused.

China continues to be concerned (or pretends to be concerned) about Japanese "militarism." For example, it issued some sharp cautionary remarks in 1987 when Japan's defense budget slightly passed the self-imposed (since 1976) 1-percent-of-gross-national-product "barrier." Similar remarks were made in 1991 during the Persian Gulf crisis while Japan's parliament was considering a bill to allow Japanese military forces to be dispatched abroad. However, Beijing has difficulty in claiming the higher moral ground on this issue because China's military establishment is vastly larger than Japan's. Not only that, but the Chinese defense budget has surged in the 1989–1991 years, growing by 52 percent.[16] Moreover, China has been buying huge amounts of advanced weaponry from the former Soviet Union, including Su-27 jet fighters, MiG-31 interceptors, and missile-guidance technology. According to one report, these arms sales could reach $2 billion by 1994.[17]

Problems have already arisen concerning jurisdictional disputes over the continental shelf that involve fishery questions and oil-drilling rights. The most important of these disputes is about sovereignty over the uninhabited Diaoyu (Senkaku) Islands not far north of Taiwan. Back in 1978, Deng Xiaoping told the Japanese that this could be settled peacefully at some future time. The issue flared up again in late 1990, when Japan built a lighthouse on one of the islands. In February 1992 China passed a law explicitly placing the islands in Chinese territorial waters and providing China the right to use military force to repel any foreign incursion. The Japanese embassy in Beijing immediately lodged a protest, claiming that the islands were "without doubt" Japanese territory.[18] China rejected the protest. Interestingly, however, when Communist Party General Secretary Jiang Zemin visited Japan two months later, he suggested (in the fashion of Deng Xiaoping) that the issue be shelved. He did so in the context of repeating Beijing's invitation to the Japanese emperor to visit China to mark the twentieth anniversary (1992) of the establishment of Sino-Japanese relations. The new Chinese law, seen in the context of Beijing's growing military (and especially naval) strength, suggests that the issue may well aggravate Sino-Japanese relations in the years ahead.

Notwithstanding these very real irritants, the overall positive aspects of Sino-Japanese relations and the general improvement in the Northeast Asian geopolitical situation would seem to augur well for the balance of this century.

Concluding Remarks

Setting aside what appears to be the relatively short-term damage resulting from the Tiananmen tragedy, China has profited enormously from its elaborate linkage with Europe and especially Japan. Both Europe and Japan, on the one side, and China, on the other, would suffer great losses should their relationships founder. Moreover, the crucial geopolitical changes of recent years have also greatly benefited China; it is more strategically secure today than at any time in the past century and a half.

An important lesson that can be drawn from this analysis is that despite much Chinese rhetoric about hegemonism and imperialism, Beijing quite relentlessly pursues its ties with Europe and Japan. Regardless of zigzags, the basic links—trade, investments, aid, technology transfer—remain in place. Once again ignoring Chinese rhetoric in praise of "self-reliance," willingness, indeed eagerness, to accept Western aid seems to be an enduring policy. Many foreign analysts focus on real or fancied Chinese "sensitivity" to Western criticism. The Chinese were certainly hectored in the strongest terms after the Tiananmen Massacre—and most of this hectoring came from the Western world. Call it opportunism or whatever, but we have learned that China was willing to absorb considerable verbal punishment to maintain its economic links with the West.

This analysis of China's relations with Europe and Japan is plainly optimistic in tone. From Beijing's viewpoint, this optimism is well founded. The 1970s and 1980s were spectacularly successful: China emerged from partial isolation to become an acknowledged member of the world community, and its links to Japan and Europe certainly contributed much to this emergence. China surely suffered a setback in the wake of Tiananmen, but by the early 1990s most Sino-Japanese and Sino-European links had been restored.

It is important to remember, however, that the most striking element of Chinese foreign policy is its volatility. In its four-decade history, the People's Republic of China has had extreme swings of policies with *every* important nation with which it has dealt. For instance, in some period between 1949 and the early 1990s

China has had cordial relations with the (former) Soviet Union, the United States, India, and Vietnam, but in this same span of years it has fought all four on the battlefield. This cannot simply be attributed to Mao—witness the 1979 Sino-Vietnamese War. Nor is a distinction between communist and noncommunist countries an adequate explanation: Two of the nations just mentioned are communist and two are not.

We should also remember the fundamental point of China's claim to sovereignty over Taiwan. European nations and Japan ritualistically pay lip service to the "claim" of China's sovereignty, yet all of them—and especially Japan—have very extensive dealings with Taiwan. China's own ties to Taiwan are now so extensive that it would seem foolhardy for it to take any precipitous action. Still, the PRC has never categorically renounced the use of force to "liberate" Taiwan at some future point.

These issues aside, what other domestic or foreign considerations should command our attention? In domestic affairs, the 1980s and early 1990s have been centered on achieving the Four Modernizations—of industry, agriculture, science and technology, and national defense. Virtually all signs point to a continuation of this policy through this century. It is very unlikely that these goals can be achieved without Japanese and European cooperation. Beijing's leaders know quite well that the lion's share of direct and indirect aid to China comes from Europe and even more so from Japan.

Could China's relations with Japan and Europe weather the turbulence of another Cultural Revolution? (Given the age of "paramount leader" Deng Xiaoping—89 years old in 1993—this is not a completely hypothetical question.) China's economic ties to Europe and Japan remained largely intact not only through the Cultural Revolution but also through the Vietnam War, the heyday of the Gang of Four in the mid-1970s, and even the Tiananmen crisis. (Of course, the intensity of economic links today is vastly greater than during the period from the 1960s to the early 1980s.) Occasional flurries of strident nationalism or "puritan communism" might well inflict limited damage on China's relations with Europe and Japan. But both Europe and Japan have some of the world's most experienced business executives, accustomed to such excesses from governments of the left or right around the world.

What is the likelihood of ideological clashes between the communism of China and the capitalism of Europe and Japan? Nationalism has proven to be one of the twentieth century's most potent forces. Nationalism destroyed the great Western colonial empires, and we have seen its power in the dismemberment of the "worldwide communist movement," not to mention the former Soviet Union. The capitalist nations, however painfully, have adjusted to this development, so it seems unlikely that ideology will significantly damage Chinese ties to Europe and Japan in future years.

At the most basic strategic level, do Europe and Japan threaten China? Distance alone answers the European question. Japan is the only conceivable threat. Yet, in this case, China is by no means alone. It is no exaggeration to say that *all* Asian nations are apprehensive about Japanese remilitarization, and none have any qualms about articulating their unease. Equally important is the fact that Japan's ruling elite is fully aware of these anxieties. Accordingly, Japanese military action against a militarily powerful China seems no more likely than a renewal of Franco-German hostilities in Europe. Yet, as Voltaire once said, "Doubt is not a very agreeable state, but certainty is a ridiculous one."

Notes

1. *New York Times, Report from Red China* (New York: Avon Books, 1971), 81–106.

2. For a brief review of China's technically unofficial requests for reparations, see *Far Eastern Economic Review* [hereafter *FEER*], November 5, 1992, p. 13. The issue arose in connection with Japanese Emperor Akihito's visit to China in October 1992. There was much speculation at the time concerning the wording of the emperor's "apology" to China for wartime atrocities, and this in turn led to press speculation about reparations. However, the issue did not arise in any formal sense during the emperor's visit.

3. World Bank, *World Development Report 1992* (New York and London: Oxford University Press, 1992), p. 256.

4. Those familiar with foreign investments in China recognize the difficulty of finding consistent figures. Although figures cited in the text come from *Beijing Review* No. 12 (March 23–29, 1992):41, later in the year this same source (No. 32 [August 10–16, 1992]:21) claimed that by the end of 1991 more than forty thousand foreign-funded enterprises had been approved and total "foreign investment" involved was "about US$50 billion, with more than US$20 billion put into use." This $20 billion utilization figure appears to be roughly consistent with Margaret M. Pearson's study, which lists a utilization figure of $15.61 billion through 1989. Margaret M. Pearson, *Joint Ventures in the People's Republic of China* (Princeton, N. J.: Princeton University Press, 1991), p. 70. The $20 billion also appears to be in rough accord with a United Nations report on world investments (*World Investment Report 1992: Transnational Corporations as Engines of Growth* [New York: United Nations, 1992], p. 315.)

5. Because of the secrecy involved in Chinese–North Korean relations, it is extremely difficult to gauge the leverage (if any) that Beijing is able to apply in its relations with Pyongyang. Most analysts use guarded language concerning this important relationship, but there does seem to be a sense that Beijing has in fact tried to temper North Korean foreign policy. A South Korean scholar, for example, wrote in 1992 that "there is reason to believe that Beijing has made it clear to Pyongyang that it would object to any terrorist or military provocation." Ahn Byung-joon, "Prospects for Sino-Korean Relations: A Korean Perspective," *Journal of East Asian Affairs* (Seoul) 1 (Winter/ Spring 1992):56. Referring back to 1984, another Korean professor paraphrased a statement made by Deng Xiaoping as follows: "the North would never invade the South and had no strength or force to do so." The professor also wrote (in 1991) that "China will induce Pyongyang to take a more conciliatory policy toward South Korea." Hwang Byong-moo, "The Evolution of ROK-PRC Relations: Retrospects and Prospects," *Journal of East Asian Affairs* 1 (Winter/Spring 1991):33, 47. An American-based Korean scholar asserted, in reference to PRC Premier Li Peng's May 1991 trip to North Korea, that he "reportedly told North Korea [that China] would not exercise its veto to block [South Korea's] admission into the United Nations, thereby enticing North Korea to reverse its stance on the separate UN membership." Young Whan Kihl, "North Korea's Foreign Relations: Diplomacy of Promotive Adaptation," *Journal of Northeast Asian Studies* 3 (Fall 1991):37. Japanese writers at Tokyo's Research Institute for Peace and Security commented on a 1990 meeting of Soviet and Chinese foreign ministers in Harbin that the "two agreed on the necessity for maintaining 'peace and stability' on the Korean peninsula. Such a pointed reference was the outward sign of the hidden pressures both were applying to North Korea, and this pressure apparently moved Pyongyang to accept the necessity for talking with the South." Research Institute for Peace and Security, *Asian Security 1991–92* (New York: Brassey's, 1991), p. 27. The same writers also noted "China's refusal to assure North Korea that it would veto an expected South Korean application for a seat in the UN" (p. 90). Harry Harding wrote in less qualified terms: "[China] successfully encouraged

North Korea to accept membership in the United Nations, together with South Korea." Harry Harding, "China's American Dilemma," *Annals of the American Academy of Political and Social Science* 519 (January 1992):22.

6. *Beijing Review* (hereafter *BR*) No. 12 (March 23–29, 1992):41.

7. *New York Times,* November 20 and 29, 1992.

8. *BR* No. 46 (November 16–22, 1992):4.

9. Ministry of Foreign Affairs, *Japan's Official Development Assistance: 1990 Annual Report* (Tokyo, 1991), p. 163.

10. Nicholas R. Lardy, *China's Entry into the World Economy* (Lanham, Md.: University Press of America), p. 10.

11. *FEER*, October 22, 1992, p. 53.

12. *BR* No. 2 (January 12, 1987):26–27.

13. *Daily Yomiuri* (Tokyo), February 8, 1991, plus information supplied by the Japanese Consulate-General, Boston.

14. *Look Japan* No. 437 (August 1992):4.

15. Kazuaki Kotake, "A Sense of Place," *Look Japan* No. 437 (August 1992):7.

16. Samuel S. Kim, "China as a Regional Power," *Current History,* September 1992, p. 248.

17. *FEER*, November 26, 1992, pp. 24–25.

18. Kim, "China as a Regional Power," p. 249; *FEER*, March 12, 1992, pp. 8–9; *Japan Quarterly,* April–June 1992, p. 282.

7

China and the Third World in the Changing World Order

SAMUEL S. KIM

The Place of the Third World

To capture the place of the Third World in Chinese foreign policy thinking and behavior has perhaps never been more difficult than today. China, the Third World, and the international system have become moving targets on turbulent trajectories, subject to contradictory pressures and undergoing profound metamorphoses. With the ending of the Cold War, the East-West conflict has suddenly withered away, and other embedded ethnonational, social, economic, and ecological conflicts have become more salient. The overwhelming majority of these are "internal conflicts" and "state-formation conflicts."[1] This new global setting presents challenges to China and the Third World as they individually and collectively redefine their roles in the changing world order.

From the very beginning, the Manichaean element in Mao's image of world order made it difficult, at least in theory, to accommodate "nonaligned" or "third" global actors between the imperialist and the socialist camp. All Chinese without exception, Mao confidently declared in 1949, "must lean either to the side of imperialism or to the side of socialism. Sitting on the fence will not do, *nor is there a third road.*"[2] Of course, much has changed since then as Beijing began to experiment with playing a variety of roles on the world stage. It was not until the early 1970s that China seemed to have made peace with itself as a member of the Third World. Ever since, the centrality of the Third World has been ensured by three recurring themes in China's foreign policy pronouncements: that China is a socialist country *belonging* to the Third World; that support for and solidarity with the Third World is a basic principle of Chinese foreign policy; and that such identification will continue undiminished even if China becomes a rich and powerful (non–Third World) state. Yet China has emerged in the course of its international relations as the most independent actor in global group politics, a veritable Group of One, by refusing to join the two leading Third World caucuses—the 129-member Group of Seventy-Seven (G-77) in global developmental politics and the 108-member Non-Aligned Movement (NAM) in global geopolitics. In both the International Monetary Fund (IMF) and the World Bank, China has refused to join the Group of Twenty-Four—more formally, the Inter-governmental Group of Twenty-Four on Monetary Affairs, formed in 1971 of finance ministers from Third World member states of the IMF.

At first blush it may seem anachronistic to be concerned about China's relationship with the Third World in the post–Cold War setting. Indeed, it has recently become commonplace and even faddish to dismiss the Third World as dead or irrelevant. Even before the "endism" debate of 1988–1989 and the collapse of the second (socialist) world, some argued that with the rise of the East Asian newly industrializing/industrialized countries (NICs) the Third World was already extinct.[3] Others who espouse the New World Order from a narrow ecological perspective view North/South relations as of no particular concern in the next phase of international life.[4] With the collapse of the Soviet Union and the end of bipolarity, we are told nowadays, the concept of a "third" global force has lost whatever symbolic and geopolitical leverage it may have had during the long Cold War years of East-West rivalry.

What all of this suggests is that Third Worldism as a critique of unevenness and hierarchy in international life is not to be confused with the power and plenty that shape and control the global political economy. It has become evident that, even during its heyday, the united front of the Third World, associated with the call for a New International Economic Order (NIEO), was more symbolic than substantive. The cleavages in the South between fast-growing and stagnant, small and large, coastal and landlocked, left and right, and democratic and authoritarian made any claim of a unified Third World movement seem a curious mixture of rhetoric and wishful thinking. The number of "Fourth World" countries—the least-developed of developing countries—has actually increased from thirty-six in the mid-1970s to forty-six today, even as Third World debt has skyrocketed to $1,340 billion. The uneven and differentiated performance in economic growth and social equity has introduced a measure of distortion to the holistic image of the Third World.[5]

At the same time, deconstructing the symbolism of the Third World as an independent force in world politics, if carried too far, can be just as misleading as the earlier claims on behalf of its negotiating solidarity. A more valid critique is normative and conceptual. The term "Third World" is increasingly challenged by those claiming to represent that world, who prefer such terms as "nonaligned" and "South" to a designation they see as unwittingly legitimating a hierarchy in the global political system.[6] Without completely rejecting this critique, I retain the label "Third World" partly because it persists in Chinese policy pronouncements and partly because it is emblematic of the common identity and shared aspiration that still link the countries and peoples of the poor South in an essential but elusive struggle to escape from poverty and underdevelopment. Despite the distortions generated by the NIC phenomenon, the term "Third World" has gained universal currency as a shorthand expression for the developing countries in Asia (minus Japan), Africa, and Latin America. At least on this concept there is no difference between Chinese and Western usage. Besides, any substitute term runs the twin risks of being a mere semantic quick-fix and of being misunderstood.

Paradoxically, the declining geopolitical leverage of the Third World seems to be strengthening its solidarity in the domain of global low politics. The ending of the Cold War has made it more relevant in the emerging world order, involved in such major world-order issues as UN peacekeeping, peacemaking, the global political economy, global human-rights politics, global green politics, and the management of the global commons. To a significant extent, the post–Cold War challenge of preventing, controlling, restraining, weakening, or encapsulating regional armed conflicts has devolved on the United Nations, where the Third World can still exert its power of numbers through the G-77 and the NAM.

Without prejudging the degree of effectiveness and importance the Third World actually commands in the post–Cold War global politics and Chinese foreign policy, this chapter proceeds from the premise that the Third World is an integral part of an increasingly interdependent and interactive world[7] and that there is perhaps more to China's Third World policy than meets the eye. China's Third World policy and its global policy are overlapping if not identical. Moreover, China's Third World policy may be seen as reflective of its shifting strategy of world order. What, then, is the "basic line" (*jiben luxian*) guiding China's Third World/global policy? What types of changes have occurred in its theory and practice, and why?

The scope of this chapter is largely limited to the most recent developments since Tiananmen (mid-1989 to early 1993). For historical perspective, however, a sense of shifting role playing may be conveyed by scanning the stages of post-Mao foreign relations: (1) the "continuity" period (September 1976 to May 1978), when Mao's three-worlds theory staged a comeback with a vengeance; (2) the "entente" period (May 1978 to mid-1981), when the three-worlds theory lost significance as China and the United States moved on parallel anti-Soviet tracks; (3) the "independent line" period (mid-1981 to mid-1984), during which the three-worlds theory made a partial but only temporary recovery as China adopted an independent policy and again reasserted its symbolic identity with the Third World; (4) the "world peace/development line" period (mid-1984 to mid-1989), when the Third World was once again marginalized in the intensified status/modernization drive; and (5) the post-Tiananmen period (mid-1989 to early 1993) when the Westphalian (and pre-Nuremberg) notion of sovereignty-bound international order coupled with the rhetoric of global economic interdependence became the lingua franca of Chinese international relations in a frantic quest for international legitimation. As ways of capturing the complex and multifaceted nature of China's Third World/global policy at various systemic levels, three broad issue areas—political/diplomatic, military/strategic, and economic/functional—have been selected for close examination. By way of conclusion, several antinomies and paradoxes of Chinese sovereignty-bound foreign policy thinking are suggested.

The Political/Diplomatic Domain

Since its inception in the mid-1950s, China's Third World policy has been a function of its siege mentality—the instrument of an insecure state in search of a united global front. Here more than in any other aspect of Chinese international relations one could see a close connection between superpower and Third World policy—the higher the frustration level in superpower relations, the greater the importance of the Third World. The life cycle of Mao's three-worlds theory is illustrative of the shifting basic line guiding China's diplomatic and political relations with the Third World. The three-worlds theory had no easy or immaculate conception. Its genesis was in Mao's recognition in the mid-1950s of the increasing insufficiency of his 1949 declaration of the lean-to-one-side policy. Even before the Sino-Soviet split, Mao's initial two-camp (and two-world) theory had already been modulated by the fuzzy notion of intermediate zones. His continuing attempts during the 1960s to define and redefine the notion of intermediate zones against the backdrop of the dual-adversary strategy vis-à-vis both superpowers led to his advocacy of proletarian revolutionary internationalism and domestic self-reliance. In the end, his heroic defiance of the logic of the international system only exacerbated China's national identity and security dilemma. He had to bend China's principled stand to the logic of uncongenial geopolitical realities through Sino-American rapprochement (1971–1972). In early 1974, however, he also sought to resolve the identity crisis by casting China's lot, at least in theory, with that of the Third World.

The three-worlds theory experienced several gyrations in the post-Mao era before its purported final demise. During the continuity period, when the "whateverism" faction of Hua Guofeng was still in power, the theory was revived in a more virulent form. In the brief entente period, however, it disappeared from major Chinese foreign policy pronouncements. One result of the official reassessment of Mao Zedong in mid-1981 was the rediscovery of this theoretical legacy. This partial, almost forced, rediscovery was part of a renewed search for a more ideologically balanced and politically viable line between the practical requirements of de-Maoification and the normative requirements of re-Maoification. Yet Mao's three-worlds theory vanished again almost as quickly as it had reappeared. From 1982 on, references to it practically disappeared for a third time from foreign policy pronouncements. The demise of the three-worlds theory can be understood as a shift from a system-transforming to a system-maintaining approach. The three-worlds theory, as a theory of struggle, is obviously incompatible with China's growing enmeshment in the capitalist world system.

If the three-worlds theory no longer serves as the basic line, what has replaced it is the Five Principles of Peaceful Coexistence: (1) mutual respect for sovereignty and territorial integrity, (2) mutual nonaggression, (3) mutual noninterference in internal affairs, (4) equality and mutual benefit, and (5) peaceful coexistence. At the very least, the Five Principles are claimed to be identical with the primary principles and purposes of the UN as well as with the fundamental principles of contemporary international law.[8] They are also characterized as a sort of successful joint Sino–Third World normative venture. "The initiation, implementation, and development of the five principles," writes a leading Chinese scholar-diplomat, "were great contributions by the independent states of the Third World to contemporary international relations and international law. Our country played a positive role and did its share in the common effort."[9] China's contribution is said to be threefold: (1) having initiated the Five Principles in 1954 (with India and Burma) and later publicized them at the 1955 Bandung Conference, (2) having adhered to them over the years through its diplomatic practices, and (3) having advanced new principles (e.g., the principle of opposition to hegemonism) in their progressive development as the fundamental norms of contemporary international relations.[10] Despite this claim of principled continuity, it was not until the inauguration of an independent foreign policy that the Five Principles were restored to the status they had enjoyed in 1954–1958, but their revival brought a globalization, embracing East and West and North and South, in the 1980s.

In the wake of the Tiananmen carnage, state sovereignty acquired shrill resonance in Beijing's multilateral diplomacy, with its repeated calls for a "new international political and economic order" based on the Five Principles. There is no alternative to the Five Principles, we are told, given the structural reality of two social systems and three categories of countries—modern capitalist, socialist, and nationalist—coexisting and competing over a fairly long period without being able to replace or eliminate each other. Deng Xiaoping set in motion another round of the "imperial word game" with a fundamentalist pronouncement at the June 30, 1989, meeting of the National People's Congress (NPC) Standing Committee: "The storm was bound to come sooner or later. This was determined by the macro climate of the world and the micro climate of our country. Its inevitable arrival was independent of man's will."[11] This "imperial edict" was a green light for an all-out revival of fundamentalism reminiscent of the Stalinist two-camp theory in its attack on so-called peaceful evolution (*heping yanbian*). In his speech at the Fifth Plenum of the Thirteenth Central Committee on November 9, 1989, General Secretary Jiang Zemin declared: "The struggle between international hostile forces and socialist countries will exist for a long time on the levels of infiltration and counter-infiltration, subversion and counter-subversion, and 'peaceful evolution' and the effort to counter it."[12] Spates of policy pronouncements and polemical essays on peaceful evolution were published from mid-1989 to 1991, to disappear only in the wake of another imperial signal emanating from Deng's much publicized trip to southern China in early 1992.

China's sovereignty-bound thinking is most persistent and resonant in the domain of human rights. With unprecedented clarity, Tiananmen dramatized to the global audience—and in global prime time—the widening chasm between popular sovereignty and state sovereignty. The most basic, recurring theme in Chinese human-rights thinking is the primacy of state sovereignty—*no state sovereignty, no human rights*. Conveniently, the argument rests, in part at least, on the historically and culturally grounded notion that communities come before individuals, duties and obligations before rights and privileges; hence, human rights inhere not so much in individuals as in collectivities. Even the much-touted "right to development," one of the central themes in post-Mao China, inheres solely in the state, not in the individual. This theme, along with the theory of cultural and economic relativism—had receded in the 1980s, as China began to participate in UN human-rights politics, only to return with renewed vigor in post-Tiananmen foreign relations.

The proposition that individuals have finally become subjects of international law in the post-Holocaust and post-Nuremberg era is ruled out of court on all counts in the Chinese international law literature and policy pronouncements. It is considered both theoretically untenable and practically infeasible because it pits the principle of state sovereignty against the principle of human rights. The principle of state sovereignty is always prior and superior to the principle of human rights because only the former can guarantee the implementation of the latter:[13] "Although theories advocating the supremacy of human rights abound in the world, *modern* international law is *still* centered on national sovereignty and the nature of international relations *still* rests on the balance and coordination of interests between national states."[14] Inconsistent with the claim that the international community can intervene only in situations of "large-scale human rights violations" (i.e., apartheid, colonialism, foreign aggression), the right to *national* self-determination has been nullified by the first principle of *state* sovereignty. If a nation within a state demands independence or self-government, according to leading Chinese international law scholars, this is also a matter of the domestic jurisdiction of that state, and the principle of national self-determination is not applicable.[15]

All the same, by 1981 China seemed to have recognized that human rights had become an integral part of global normative politics and decided to participate in the work of the UN Human Rights Commission in Geneva. Since 1980 it has acceded to nine UN-sponsored multilateral human rights conventions, mostly on collective or group human-rights treaties with regard to women, racial discrimination, refugees, apartheid, genocide, torture, and children. The classical Westphalian notion that the way in which each state mistreated its own citizens was not a matter for international concern gradually became less compelling. Post-Mao China's apparent acceptance of the proposition that a country's human-rights performance was inextricably linked with its international image and reputation was manifest in its incremental modification and expansion of the concept of human rights, its greater participation in the activities of UN human-rights forums, and its increasing acceptance of certain select global human-rights principles and norms. Post-Tiananmen China seemed initially to have taken a great leap backward on human rights, but it is important to note the shift from the defensive to the offensive in 1991 with the publication of a first-ever "White Paper on Human Rights in China." The implications of the white paper seem obvious— that there is no longer any escape from human rights as a legitimate global issue and as a challenge to Chinese foreign policy.

Immediately after the June 4 crackdown, the Politburo held a secret meeting and issued a new directive that in tone and substance is quite revealing about the place of the Third World in Chinese foreign policy thinking:

> In the past, China's relations with Western countries have been overheated, giving a cold-shoulder to the Third World countries and old friends (meaning Africa). Judging from the events in this turmoil, it seems that at a critical moment it was still those Third World countries and old friends which gave China the necessary sympathy and support. Therefore from now on China will put more efforts in resuming and developing relations with these old friends and Third World countries.[16]

At this critical moment of self-inflicted national-identity/legitimation crisis, China once again turned to the Third World for help. High-level and high-profile visits to Third World countries, which had become less frequent in the preceding years, were renewed as ways of demonstrating to the home audience that China was not isolated. Foreign Minister Qian Qichen, Premier Li Peng, and President Yang Shangkun visited African, Southwest Asian, and Latin American countries, respectively, in the latter half of 1989 and much of 1990. The most notable aspect of this shuttle diplomacy was an attempt to form a new socialist/Third World united front against the unipolar world order. Pax Sinica via acceleration of Sino-Soviet, Sino–North Korean, Sino-Vietnamese, Sino-Cuban, Sino-Romanian, and Sino–East German cooperation briefly became ways of countering the Western "peaceful evolution" strategy. In early 1991, faced with the collapse of socialism in Europe and the clear and continuing danger of the collapse of socialism in the Soviet Union, Beijing quietly adopted a new strategy of establishing a Beijing-Pyongyang-Hanoi socialist united front.[17] In the wake of the aborted Soviet coup in August 1991, China's interest in South-South cooperation and the NAM suddenly became livelier than ever. And yet, with the virtual demise of Western sanctions and the collapse of the Soviet Union by the end of 1991, the Third World factor seems once again considerably attenuated. The official state visits, all in the latter half of 1992, of the South Korean president (hardly a typical Third World country), the Japanese emperor, and the Russian president were widely publicized as among the crowning achievements of post-Tiananmen diplomacy.

The pattern of post-Tiananmen renewal of ties with Third World countries is a bizarre mixture of symbolic and political hype and substantive marginality. Having virtually phased out its foreign aid since 1978, Beijing is now stressing the importance of political and diplomatic rather than economic and strategic ties. Because of the two Chinas' international diplomatic-recognition race, however, Beijing can hardly afford to turn its back on the Third World. Its unusually swift recognition in December 1991 of twelve newly independent states in the wake of the collapse of the Soviet Union was prompted by fear that Taiwan would outperform it in the international diplomatic-recognition race (Table 7.1). The greatest leverage Beijing had in this connection was its veto power in the Security Council and the threat to use it in blocking the entry of any of these newly formed states into the world organization: no acceptance of the Beijing Formula (Hallstein Doctrine), no UN entry.[18]

The two Chinas' flexible diplomacy battle sets limits to what is possible and permissible in Beijing's official international relations. In every case of a nation's setting up diplomatic relations with Taipei, Beijing has severed ties. In the intermediate case of "official but not diplomatic" consular ties, as in the case of Latvia, Beijing "suspended" ties. In countries such as Bolivia, where Taiwan-representative offices now use the official name of the Republic of China (ROC), Beijing has not retaliated, and in the unusual case of Vanuatu, it actually rewarded the government after it "officially recognized" Taiwan.[19] High-level official visits to Taiwan have generated protests from Beijing, but only in the case of repeated trips by Philippine cabinet secretaries has it taken action, rotating its ambassador home a year early. While no industrialized nation has yet to match the daring of Fiji and other small Third World states that have dispatched prime ministers and foreign ministers to Taiwan, increase in the level of Western visitors to the ministerial one will likely continue. What all of this reveals is the marginality of the small, weak Third World states, which ironically enables them to get

TABLE 7.1   Number of Countries Recognizing the PRC and the ROC (1969–1992)

	PRC	ROC	UN Membership
1969	49	67	126
1970	54(+5)	67	127
1971	69(+15)	54(−13)	132
1972	87(+18)	41(−13)	132
1973	89(+2)	37(−4)	135
1974	96(+7)	31(−6)	138
1975	105(+9)	27(−4)	144
1976	109(+4)	26(−1)	147
1977	111(+2)	23(−3)	149
1978	113(+2)	22(−1)	151
1979	117(+4)	22	152
1980	121(+4)	22	154
1981	121	23(+1)	157
1982	122(+1)	23	157
1983	125(+3)	24(+1)	158
1984	126(+1)	25(+1)	159
1985	127(+1)	23(−2)	159
1986	127	23	159
1987	127	23	159
1988	130(+3)	22(−1)	159
1989	132(+2)	23(+1)	159
1990	136(+4)	28(+5)	160
1991	140(+4)	29(+1)	167
1992	154(+14)	29	179

Sources: For the PRC, PRC Ministry of Foreign Affairs, *Zhongguo waijiao gailan 1992* [Survey of Chinese Diplomacy 1992] (Beijing: Shijie zhishi chubanshe, 1992), pp. 481–487, and, for 1992, Liu Huaqiu, "China's Diplomatic Achievements in 1992," *Beijing Review* 35:52 (December 28, 1992–January 3, 1993):8. For the ROC, Department of Treaty and Legal Affairs, Ministry of Foreign Affairs, Republic of China. For the UN, UN Press Release, ORG/1156 (19 January 1993).

away with a greater volume and intensity of interaction with Taiwan than industrialized states such as France and Britain.

At the global level, the UN General Assembly affords an indispensable forum for the projection of China's symbolic identification with the Third World. The UN's recognition of the People's Republic in late 1971 as the "sole legitimate government of China" allowed Beijing access to the chief global arena for the politics of collective legitimation and delegitimation. Because of the enduring two-Chinas problem and China's essential quest for national identity via absolute international legitimation, the General Assembly as a quasi-parliament serves as the global stage upon which China dramatizes its role for domestic and international audiences. There is ample evidence that the Chinese government sees this organ as the most suitable platform from which to project its national identity (e.g., Mao's three-worlds theory was unveiled, ironically enough, by Deng Xiaoping in a major plenary speech at the Sixth Special Session of the General Assembly in April 1974).

That China's international influence is growing by the day and that China is playing its "proper and unique role" in the Security Council is a recurring theme in post-Tiananmen Chinese foreign policy pronouncements. The decision to hold the first-ever Security Council summit meeting in New York in January 1992 came as a godsend for the Li Peng government in the search for international legitimation, as an army of reporters from the *People's Daily*, the Xinhua News Agency, Central Chinese Television, the Central People's Broadcasting Station, and Radio Beijing was sent to cover what the local press called "China's triumphant diplomatic breakthroughs" in the prime global arena of high politics. With the recent and unexpected revival of Taiwan's diplomatic campaign to reenter the United Nations, Beijing's permanent membership and veto power have been publicly touted as the impregnable fortress that defends the integrity of People's China as the only legitimate Chinese government in the world organization.

China's international egalitarianism has suffered substantial slippage in the post-Mao era. During the Maoist period of 1971–1976, China stood out as the only member of the Permanent Five supporting charter review and revision. In the post-Mao era, Chinese references to charter review have vanished. Instead, China seems to be enjoying its self-styled role as the only developing country among the Permanent Five fighting for the causes of the Third World, ensuring through its veto power that only a Third World candidate will be elected secretary-general. Ling Qing, a former UN ambassador, even claims that China's veto "ultimately belongs to the Third World. This gives China special influence in the Third World."[20] The fight for a Third World candidate for the post of secretary-general is well suited to China's maximize-benefits/minimize-constraints code of conduct. On the one hand, such posturing enhances, to a degree, the credibility of its claim of assuming rhetorical championship without behavioral leadership; on the other hand, it papers over or at least compensates for its amibiguous stand on the long-standing Third World demand for more equitable representation among the Council's permanent members (e.g., India, Brazil, and Nigeria). "No more additional members and no more changes to the UN Security Council," Foreign Minister Qian Qichen is reported to have declared in Jakarta on September 3, 1992.[21] As might have been expected, the official position of the Chinese government is framed in safer and more ambiguous language—that it favors a proper adjustment of the composition of the Security Council at a proper time to bring it more in line with changes in the internationl system, with due regard to the principle of fair geographical distribution.

Despite Beijing's pursuit of absolute international legitimation in the world of international intergovernmental organizations (IGOs), the flexible diplomacy battle in the economic IGOs is no longer a zero-sum game. In the past the question was who would represent China. Each IGO was asked to choose between the two competing governments, and the predictable outcome was that Taiwan either withdrew or was expelled. However, since 1986, when the Asian Development Bank (ADB) decided to admit Beijing without expelling Taipei, the game has become a matter of names in which only the status of the ROC is at stake.[22] Will it be "Taipei" or "Taiwan," before or after "China," with or without a comma, hyphen, or parenthesis? Given the hierarchy and the unevenness of authority structures of the keystone international economic institutions, what the Third World can do for Beijing here is rather limited.

There is little doubt that Beijing has expended considerable diplomatic capital in the post-Tiananmen years in shoring up its position in the Third World. It has also advanced the unabashed claim of Third World leadership, especially in global human-rights and environmental politics, that it had previously declined as evidence of its antihegemonic pledge. As if to bridge the widening gap between policy pronouncements and policy performance, Beijing in the 1980s pointed to its decline as a Third World leader as proof that it had kept its pledge never to be or act like a hegemon in international relations: "Our state policy of never seeking hegemony dictates that *we cannot and shall never become the leader of the third world or of any bloc of countries.*"[23] In a renewed search for Third World leadership, in 1992 Beijing departed somewhat from its long-standing posture as a Group of One by asking the NAM for and being granted *observer* status.

In the global domain of human-rights politics, China has positioned itself as the Third World's most vociferous (anti-)human-rights "champion." Paradoxically, North-South tensions have sharply increased as East-West conflicts over human rights have waned. At the same time, UN human-rights activity in the post–Cold War setting has shifted from a promotional (standard-setting) to a protectionist (implementation and enforcement) phase. Tiananmen made it possible, even if temporarily, for the UN to censure China for its human-rights abuses at home. In August 1989 the Subcommission on Prevention of Discrimination and Protection of Minorities, a subordinate expert body of the UN Human Rights Commission, passed by a secret vote of fifteen to nine the first resolution in UN history criticizing one of the Permanent Five for human-rights abuses at home. In February 1990, the International Labour Organization added international delegitimation by endorsing the findings of an expert committee extremely critical of China's mistreatment of workers who had supported the prodemocracy movement. Since the forty-sixth session of the fifty-three-member commission in early 1990, China has managed to piggyback on the Third World's power of numbers to escape international censure. Vote on a draft resolution to "take no action" on the human-rights situation in China has not changed much between 1990 (seventeen to fifteen, with eleven abstaining) and 1993 (twenty-one to seventeen, with twelve abstaining). The worst has thus been avoided, only just, because of a combination of factors—the Iraqi invasion of Kuwait that suddenly preempted center stage, China's putative support for or at least refusal to veto Security Council Resolution 678 in the Gulf-crisis pro forma motion of the Western powers, and abstention by a dozen or so democratic Third World states.

Against this backdrop China has adopted a "divide and demolish" strategy in its global human-rights diplomacy. An official white paper on human rights "accepts" international human-rights principles by redefining them in terms of state sovereignty and cultural, economic, and social relativism.[24] Although the relativism thesis is greatly overstated, as China is still far behind in terms of some of the rights claimed (e.g., childbearing women are too often dehumanized as livestock to be rendered infertile as a way of enforcing the one-child policy, and China stands in 101st place with 0.566 in global "human development ranking"),[25] it signals an acknowledgment that the best defense is a good offense. Indeed, the white paper's final section contains an exaggerated account of how active China has been in the drafting of most of the human-rights agreements of recent decades and of how constructive a role it has played in promoting human rights not only for Palestinians and South Africans but (less convincingly) in Cambodia—where the PRC actually bankrolled the genocidal Khmer Rouge to the tune of $100 million per year. The bottom line of China's "right to development as an inalienable human right" seems simple enough: "If one really intends to promote and protect human rights ... then the first thing for him to do is to help remove obstacles to the development of developing countries, lessen their external debt burden, provide them with unconditional assistance."[26] It is precisely this proposition of unconditional aid that is sweet music to the Third World, even though China has always received special treatment in getting the lion's share of bilateral and multilateral aid with virtually no strings attached.

The logic of China's "divide and demolish" strategy is to slice up the concept of universality little by little, region by region, to the point where there is little left of the UN human-rights monitoring and implementation regime. China has led the way on behalf of some of the most oppressive Third World countries to keep the UN human-rights regime small, fragmented (regionalized), ineffective, and abstract. Efforts to alter the structure and terms of reference of a World Conference on Human Rights to be held in Vienna in June 1993 to conform with its own minimalist view received little support.[27] The Chinese delegation was also extremely active in the Third World Committee and Fifth (Financial) Committee debate about financing the UN Human Rights Centre, attempting to alter its plans and reduce the resources available but again with little success. However, China pressed successfully for the General Assembly to include the relationship between development and human rights as one of the priority topics at the 1993 conference as well as to hold regional preparatory conferences. As a result, Asia's first regional human-rights conference was held in Bangkok in late March 1993, attended by governmental delegates from forty-nine countries stretching from the Middle East to the South Pacific. The thirty-point Bangkok Declaration that emerged from the conference is full of contradictions and ambiguities papering over serious intraregional cleavages. That the chief delegates from China, Burma, and Iran, three notorious human-rights offenders, made up the drafting committee speaks volumes about China's "leadership" role in this first Asian human-rights conference. Much to its credit, Japan voiced serious reservations about the content of the Bangkok Declaration, restating its stand that expressions of concern about human-rights violations do not constitute interference in a nation's internal affairs. Sino-Japanese confrontation was avoided and the declaration adopted by "consensus" largely through the solidarity of delegates from the Association of Southeast Asian Nations (ASEAN), who formed a bridge between Japan, at one extreme, and China, Burma, and Iran, at the other.[28]

On the eve of the world conference, China was poised to lead a pack of the worst Third World offenders in an attack on the core principle of *universal* human rights. As a self-styled Third World champion, it declared that the final conference document should be based on the declarations of the three regional preparatory meetings (Bangkok, Tunisia, and San Jose), with emphasis on state sovereignty, territorial integrity, and noninterference in the internal affairs of states, rather than on the working paper proposed by the UN Secretariat, with emphasis on the strengthening of the global human-rights regime.

The Military/Strategic Domain

The most significant theoretical change in the post-Mao era has been the gradual demise of the Leninist/Stalinist inevitability theory of war. China persisted, with varying degrees of intensity and consistency, in the inevitability theory during much of the Maoist era. It was during the world peace/development-line period that the theory began to be drastically downgraded. The catalyst for the official deconstruction of the theory was the enlarged meeting of the Central Military Commission (CMC) in June 1985. Clearly, the inevitability theory was an obstacle to the CMC's decision to reduce the army by a million troops. Once again it required an "imperial edict" from Deng for this theoretical revisionism to be rationalized in Chinese scholarship. "As long as the forces for peace continue to expand," Deng said at the CMC meeting, "it is possible that world war will not break out for a fairly long time to come, and there is hope of maintaining world peace."[29] In April 1986, in a talk with a visiting former Japanese prime minister, Deng publicly singled out the inevitability of theory of war as a grave error in judgment and declared its demise.[30]

What followed in the wake of Deng's pronouncements was a mixture of realist and functionalist arguments. The Leninist inevitability theory was undoubtedly correct until World War II, we are told, but it has become increasingly outmoded in today's nuclear era. Clearly, Lenin's vision of the final stage of imperialist rivalry in which the slicing of the Chinese melon would take place is now a doctrinal and practical liability. At the same time, the long peace in the Western capitalist world is explained in terms of intercapitalist mutual interdependence through the globalization of their production and capital. In an era of global interdependence, war can no longer be considered a practical means for resolving conflict; economic bargaining has become its functional equivalent. In short, capitalism is no longer the cause of war or socialism the cause of peace. The new factors negating the inevitability of a world war in the postwar international system are said to include (1) the scientific and technological revolution and the nuclear balance of terror, (2) the decline of the superpowers and the rise of multipolarity (although there is no Chinese scholarly consensus on this point), (3) the rise of the Third World as a peace force in global politics, and (4) global economic interdependence. What has emerged is "neorealist theory with Chinese characteristics." Following Western realist theory, national interests—conflicts of state interests rather than class struggle—have become the locus of the question of war and peace in our time. The political contents of war are said to have shifted from class struggle to contradictions of state interests. Hegemonism, not imperialism, explains the many different kinds of war in the Third World since World War II. Unlike imperialism, hegemonism is said to have no special implications of a social system or class character because it is defined in behavioral (non-Gramscian) terms. This explains Chinese assaults on hegemonic behavior rather than on the hegemonic state per se.

If a world war is no longer inevitable, the same cannot be said about local wars. In terms of military doctrine and strategy, the 1985 CMC meeting put an end to the principle of preparing against "an early war, a big war, and even a nuclear war" adopted in 1965. What has emerged is a new military doctrine and strategy more capable of responding to the most likely type of armed conflict: intense local/partial wars in and around China's expansive regional security perimeter. The most significant effect of this change in strategic doctrine is the gradual decoupling of local and regional conflicts from superpower rivalry. It will be recalled that China had justified its war against Vietnam in 1979 in terms of *global* security imperatives, not as a matter of *bilateral* or even *regional* conflict.

The ending of the Cold War and the disintegration of the Soviet Union have accelerated this delinkage process. This does not mean that the center of gravity has shifted from "hard" globalism to "soft" regionalism. Instead, China's regional security thinking seems to have become a function of its nationalism-unilateralism in bilateral clothing. The world peace/development line has been not so much replaced as overlain by technocratic realism pivoting around the notion of comprehensive national strength. Without sufficient military power, according to China's strategic analysts, it will be impossible to enhance the country's status as a world power or play a decisive role in global politics. The Gulf War demonstrated with particular clarity the type of warfare with which the Chinese armed forces were tasked in the CMC's 1985 directive. Thus, the military has been called on to take up a new mission at variance with the Maoist doctrine of protracted struggle: limited war to achieve a quick, decisive high-tech military victory in a matter of days.

Apparently, the emergence of power vacuums is not a danger to be avoided or managed through regional or global conflict-management mechanisms but an opportunity to be unilaterally exploited. As if to legitimate China's gunboat diplomacy in the South China Sea, it is claimed that all countries have taken the capability of coping with regional conflicts as the major objective of military modernization. The 1985 strategic decision requiring the People's Liberation Army (PLA) to redirect its military thinking and policy from preparation for general war to preparation for the more probable local and regional wars on China's periphery has become a more credible and potentially practicable scenario. China today regards the disputed but oil-rich Paracel and Spratly Islands in the South China Sea in terms all too reminiscent of the Third Reich's *Lebensraum* imperial policy. A recent internal Chinese document states that these island groups, some of them situated nearly 1,000 kilometers south of China's Hainan Island province and most of them subject to conflicting jurisdictional claims, could provide *Lebensraum* (*shengcun kongjian*—literally, "survival space") for the Chinese people.[31]

The most significant conceptual effect of the momentous changes in the world situation in recent years is to accelerate the process of decoupling local and regional conflicts from global superpower rivalry. The new foreign policy line—as confirmed by Jiang Zemin's political report to the Fourteenth Party Congress in 1992—may be characterized as a comprehensive national strength line. Bipolarity is pronounced to have ended. Multipolarity is cast in a new light as giving China more leverage opportunities and more space than before. At the same time, the military "should attach importance to quality construction; should enhance combat strength in an all-around way; should more successfully shoulder the lofty mission of defending the country's territorial sovereignty over the land and in the air, as well as its rights and interests on the sea; and should safeguard the unification and security of the motherland."[32]

China's security behavior seems fraught with ambiguity and contradiction as it attempts to balance geostrategic and normative concerns. As we have seen, the unstated code of conduct guiding China's consecutive and simultaneous participation in multiple security games on the global, regional, and bilateral chessboards is the maximization of security benefits and the minimization of normative costs. Three major issues in the post–Cold War setting—collective security, arms control and disarmament, and the global arms trade—may suffice to show the rather tenuous nature of China's contribution to the shaping of a more peaceful world order. If China in theory is part of the global solution, it has become in practice part of the global problem.

The charter-based world-order system premised in the revitalization of UN peacekeeping and peacemaking offers a concrete real-world case for assessing Chinese world-order strategy. China's position on UN peacekeeping has shifted over the years, although remaining within the context of state sovereignty, evolving through four distinct periods: (1) opposition/exclusion (1949–1970), (2) opposition/nonparticipation (1971–1981), (3) support/participation (1982–1989), and (4) retreat/participation (1990–present). Throughout the exclusion period, both ideology and experience dictated a negative attitude toward UN peacekeeping operations. After its entry into the United Nations in 1971, however, China's opposition became more verbal than real, as Beijing opted "not to participate" rather than cast negative votes on authorizing resolutions. As the Security Council moved away from the charter system of collective security to consensual peacekeeping, China adhered—conveniently and safely—to the charter system's grandiose notion of a clear distinction between aggressor and victim. Nonetheless, this conceptual conflict between the two was resolved by allowing China to have it both ways—by meshing its "principled stand" (expressed as nonparticipation and dissociation) with tacit "cooperation" (expressed as noninterference [nonveto] in the authorization and implementation process).

A policy change in late 1981 was part of Beijing's opening to the outside world, ushering in the support/participation period. Progressively, Beijing "safely" projected itself as a champion of UN peacekeeping. This change can be better explained as tactical and situational adaptation than as normative conversion. It was part of China's renewed identification with the Third World and strategic detachment from the United States. Given an altered international situation and the evolution of the role of UN peacekeeping operations, Ambassador Ling Qing stated in the General Assembly in late November 1981 that the Chinese government had decided to adopt a *flexible* attitude toward UN peacekeeping. Ling admitted that the demands of China's Third World friends and a desire to avoid any confrontation on its payment arrears had played a role in its decision to pay, starting on January 1, 1982, its share of the assessed expenses for UN peacekeeping operations. Pakistan as China's closest Third World ally played a crucial role in the behind-the-scenes consultations to work out a face-saving formula for preventing another constitutional/financial crisis over Beijing's arrears.[33] China's resumption of its financial obligations related to peacekeeping would be extremely modest, especially in the mid-1980s, when UN peacekeeping was in its deepest recession. A biennial UN peacekeeping budget for 1986–1987 amounted to only $364 million, as compared with $3,827 million for 1992–1993. Its support of UN peacekeeping operations in 1981–1989 was convenient, cheap, and safe. It was simply a continuation by another name of its quest for international legitimation as a *responsible* Third World champion in the Security Council—a well-calculated move to demonstrate its role as a global power on the world stage.

The 1990–1991 Gulf crisis marks the beginning of the retreat/participation period. Despite the publicly expressed support for UN peacekeeping between 1982 and 1989, the first litmus test showed that the maxi/mini strategy disguised in the principle of state sovereignty remained the bottom line. Despite its initial ambiguous posturing, Beijing soon awakened to the possibility of seizing on the crisis to show its indispensability in the management of regional conflicts in the Security Council and to divert the world's attention from the repressive reality of post-Tiananmen China itself. The crisis came as a geopolitical blessing in disguise. China succeeding in altering the draft Security Council Resolution 678 to eliminate any explicit reference to "the use of military force." Then it abstained from voting on the resolution (which authorized the use of "all necessary means to uphold and implement" all relevant Council resolutions) on November 29, 1990. Thus it allowed itself ample space for multiple interpretations of its "principled stand"—another demonstration of its multiprincipled diplomacy of projecting itself as all things to all nations.

Despite the repeated pronouncements in the course of the Security Council proceedings that "China does not have nor wishes to seek any self-serving interests in the Middle East region," China managed to extract maximum payoffs from the United States with minimum support. In the end, through its fence-straddling strategy it managed to force Washington into the position of an overanxious supplicant. A Washington quid for a Beijing quo exemplified the maxi/mini code of conduct. The Bush administration, ignoring a crackdown on political dissidents, agreed to resume of high-level diplomatic intercourse (a long-sought White House visit by Foreign Minister Qian was granted) and to support the World Bank's first non–basic-human-needs loan since Tiananmen. All the same, China seized the Gulf crisis as a way of neutralizing the pressures of the unipolar world order.

In the face of the growing number of UN peacemaking and state-making activities in 1991–1992, China began to retreat by redefining its stand in contingent and sovereignty-bound terms. Suddenly it is argued that peacekeeping operations can be established and conducted only in compliance with the principle of noninterference in internal affairs, as the UN Charter does not authorize involvement in the internal disputes of its member states.[34] To appreciate the logic of this shift calls for a brief look at the Security Council. In the post–Cold War setting, the Security Council has haltingly and at times selectively responded to the growing recognition in the world community that the principle of state sovereignty and the principle of noninterference no longer provide a legitimate shield for the violation of human rights or the rejection of UN peacekeeping, peacemaking, or humanitarian interventions. Having extricated itself from the destructive pattern of East-West confrontation, the Security Council has decided not to let state sovereignty get in the way of its intervening in situations perceived to be threatening international peace or the collective moral consciousness of the world community. With the end of the Cold War came an irresistible pressure not to paralyze the Council with a veto—there have been no such vetoes since May 31, 1990. In this spirit of ad hoc judgment and consensus, eight of the thirteen current operations have been established in just the past two years (1991–1992)—and the number of peacekeepers has increased from 15,000 to 55,000 and the biennial peacekeeping budget from $364 million in 1986–1987 to $3,827 million in 1992–1993—as the Security Council has redefined its roles and functions in relation to series of sanguinary conflicts in trouble spots around the world from Central America to the Balkans through Africa and the Middle East to Indochina.

Against this backdrop and at the request of the first-ever Security Council Summit (January 1992), Secretary-General Boutros Boutros-Ghali issued six months later a landmark report, entitled "An Agenda for Peace," calling upon the member states, in particular the Permanent Five, to redefine state sovereignty to strengthen the world organization's capacity for "preventive diplomacy, peace-making, peace-keeping, and post-conflict peace-building."[35] While paying mandatory lip service to the principle of state sovereignty, the secretary-general made clear what is required for the organization to meet the rising demands of people's security: "The time of absolute and exclusive sovereignty, however, has passed; its theory was never matched by reality."[36] Once again, the question of state sovereignty is back in the news and on the agenda of a New World Order and UN reform, as the Security Council shifts by fits and starts from peacekeeping to "peacemaking" and "peace-enforcing."

In China's foreign policy thinking and behavior, the Security Council is an important *arena* for demonstrating its status as a global power and pursuing its maxi/mini realpolitik but not a world-order *actor* in the promotion of collective security. There is, deep down in Chinese world-order thinking, little concern for or commitment to revitalizing the UN Security Council as the principal instrument for preventing, abating, or even managing regional conflict. Of the Permanent Five, China has already assumed the most skeptical posture toward the secretary-general's new peace agenda, proposing the revitalization of the global collective security system envisioned in the UN Charter.[37] The secretary-general's report contained too many sovereignty-diluting features for Beijing; instead, according to the foreign minister, "UN reform should contribute to maintaining the sovereignty of its member states. Sovereign states are the subjects of international law and the foundation for the formation of the United Nations. The maintenance of state sovereignty serves as the basis for the establishment of a new international order."[38]

In effect, it is not so much the defense of state sovereignty anywhere or anytime as fear of a precedent's being established for possible use against the multinational Chinese state that seems to serve as the unstated code of conduct. Having extracted maximum geopolitical mileage out of the Cambodian crisis, China had no sovereignty-bound qualms about participating in the UN's state-making activity in Cambodia. As suggested by the nomenclature itself, the United Nations

Transitional Authority in Cambodia (UNTAC) is anything but a typical UN peacekeeping operation. By far the most comprehensive and expensive operation the world organization has ever undertaken at a cost of $1.5 billion, UNTAC has been authorized to supervise the administration of the entire war-torn country, organize and supervise free and democratic elections, disarm three separate factional militias, remove innumerable mines, and resettle a large number of displaced refugees. China also voted for the Security Council resolution authorizing the deployment of foreign military forces in Somalia to protect relief operations—a textbook case of humanitarian intervention. Yet in 1992 Beijing decided that it had to resist UN efforts to protect Iraq's ethnic minority regions for fear that this would constitute a precedent of another kind whereby one day the international community might be forced to work against China's own ethnic minority regions, such as Tibet, Inner Mongolia, and Xinjiang. China expressed its stronger reservations—and shock—on the unfolding of the Bosnian crisis not about the genocide but about the dangerous precedent that the Security Council was establishing for "humanitarian intervention" via the UN Protection Force (UNPROFOR). The Chinese press at home and representatives in the Security Council repeatedly issued warnings about the clear and continuing danger of a shift from Chapter 6 (nonmandatory pacific settlement provisions) to Chapter 7 (mandatory enforcement measures) of the UN Charter. China's "do-nothing" minimalist stand in the Security Council on the Bosnian crisis is particularly damaging in an enraged Muslim world of fifty countries and more than one billion inhabitants readying itself to become involved in the Balkan war with clenched fists and whispers of *jihad* (holy war).[39] China's credibility as a self-styled champion of the Third World in the Security Council has been badly shaken, as five NAM member states have already adopted a united Third World stand pressing Western states to take more decisive collective enforcement measures on behalf of the Muslim victims of Serbian aggression.

In the highly sensitive domain of arms control and disarmament, China's official public position has progressively shifted in tone and style from initial nonparticipation to reluctant participation to active participation in global forums, especially in the Conference on Disarmament in Geneva. As if to demonstrate that there is more than meets the suspicious eye in such posturing, however, China in 1982–1992 has acceded to ten of the twelve multilateral arms control and disarmanent conventions.[40] Still, its stand is expressed in the espousal of differentiated responsibilities in the global processes involved. Since the two superpowers account for 95–97 percent of all nuclear warheads in the world, we are told, it is they who must bear the primary responsibility by drastically reducing their nuclear arsenals before other nuclear weapons states can join the disarmament process. In this way, China projects its role as a constructive and positive player in the UN disarmament game without constraining its own nuclear development. At the Second Special Session on Disarmament in mid-1982, China somewhat modified its ambiguous stand: the superpowers should reduce their nuclear weapons by 50 percent before China and the other nuclear powers would join in further nuclear disarmament negotiations. This concession was probably made on the safe assumption that such an agreement was still far beyond reach in an atmosphere of Soviet-American strategic rivalry. Yet the 1987 Soviet-American Intermediate-Range Nuclear Forces (INF) treaty seems to have come as a rude awakening to the idea that Beijing may have committed the cardinal sin of premature specificity. While welcoming the INF as the first genuine disarmament treaty of the postwar era, China rather quickly relapsed into a "Who, me?" refrain. A 50-percent reduction would no longer meet its new measure of a "drastic reduction."

At the same time, an old Chinese arms control and disarmament line has been resurrected: Although the superpowers have the special *responsibility* for drastic nuclear disarmament, all countries, big and small, strong and weak, have the *right* to take part in any future disarmament negotiations. Not surprisingly, the Third World's long-standing demand for a halt to nuclear tests has fallen on China's deaf ears; China remained in recent years the only nuclear-weapons state not to pledge or adopt a moratorium on nuclear testing. Since a comprehensive nuclear test ban and nuclear disarmament are linked, the United States and Russia "have the obligation to take the lead in halting all nuclear tests *and* carrying out drastic nuclear disarmament so as to create conditions for a comprehensive ban on nuclear tests."[41] Even as Chinese diplomats routinely deny that China has ever engaged in the nuclear arms race, Chinese military strategists at home are warning that "once an agreement is reached banning the use and testing of nuclear weapons, we will lose our position as a nuclear power."[42]

The Strategic Arms Reduction Treaty (START) and START-II, which will reduce each nuclear superpower's strategic arsenal by about three-fourths (to fewer than 3,500 warheads), seems to have had no discernible impact on China's behavior. While acknowledging these treaties as "some initial progress," China insists that the two nuclear superpowers still have a long way to go in the process of nuclear disarmament. Pending the realization of "complete prohibition and thorough destruction of nuclear weapons," however, all nuclear-weapons states should undertake the following commitments: (1) not to be the first to use nuclear weapons and to conclude an international agreement on the no-first-use principle; (2) not to use or threaten to use nuclear weapons against nonnuclear-weapons states and nuclear-weapon-free zones and to conclude an international agreement in this regard; and (3) to support the proposals for the establishment of nuclear-weapon-free zones and undertake the corresponding obligations.[43] Once again, China has defined and projected its position on nuclear disarmament issues in a self-serving way, asking others to do as it says, not as it does. Even more tellingly, science and technology are defined as the common wealth of mankind, to be shared and used for mankind's benefit. And such scientific and technological sharing is expected to be carried out in such a way as to contribute to confidence in the global nuclear disarmament process![44]

After years of providing arms free of charge, mostly to its three Asian allies (North Korea, North Vietnam, and Pakistan), post-Mao China decided in 1979 to join the global arms trade. However, it was not until September 1988 that it was finally compelled to enunciate its "three principles of arms sales." These principles are expressed in so amorphous and elastic a way as to remove any normative constraints on China's burgeoning arms trade practice: that arms export should be for legitimate national defense only, for enhancing regional stability without in any way infringing upon any country's sovereignty.[45] When the General Assembly adopted a resolution on Transparency in Armaments (A/Res/46/36L) establishing a UN Registry of Conventional Arms on December 9, 1991, with a recorded vote of 150 to 0, with 2 abstentions (Cuba and Iraq), China expressed its displeasure by absence. The Permanent Five met several times to formulate guidelines for arms transfers to the Middle East but failed because of China's recalcitrance. In the third Permanent Five meeting in May 1992, for instance, China broke with the rest on the questions of prior notification of arms shipments (that information should be exchanged *only after* arms transfers are made) and whether ballistic missiles (Beijing's main military exports) should be included in the restrictions.[46]

Here more than in any other world-order problem area, a decisive shift from Mao's normative foreign policy to Deng's interest-driven foreign policy is apparent. In effect, China has no principles, only interests, driving its arms sales to the Third World. Here is the strongest Sino–Third World linkage at the bilateral level; about 80 percent of Chinese arms sales in the 1980s, valued at more than $15 billion, have been channeled to the Middle East, not only to warring Iran and Iraq but also to Egypt, Syria, Libya, and Saudi Arabia. In the process, China emerged as the world's fourth-largest military exporter—and the Third World's largest exporter—in the period 1987–1991. The ending of the Iran-Iraq War caused shrinkage in absolute terms without affecting global ranking. China surpassed France in 1991 as the world's third-largest arms exporter (see Table 7.2) even as it began to participate in international arms trade control forums.

China has a definite comparative advantage in those weapons systems—in particular, intermediate-range ballistic missiles and nuclear weapon technology—whose proliferation has been highly circumscribed or banned by various multilateral conventions and regimes. The evidence shows that between 1966 and 1976, at a time when China was publicly supporting proliferation as a means of breaking the superpower nuclear duopoly, it provided no nuclear assistance to Third World countries—except for training North Korean scientists in nuclear technology. In the 1980s, however, China's proliferation policy pronouncements and policy performance have sharply diverged (Table 7.3). While making repeated pledges of nonproliferation, Beijing has been held responsible for helping, either directly or indirectly, the nuclear weapons programs of over half a dozen nuclear-threshold states.[47]

The pattern of perfidious Chinese behavior in the sale of military equipment and technology, especially in the nuclear weapons and missile field, seems clear enough to justify a few generalizations. Of the eight post-Mao arms trade corporations, the Comprehensive Science and Technology Corporation, a unit directly under the PLA and the CMC, is the sole agent in the marketing of weapons systems ranging from strategic nuclear-warhead missiles to satellites for military purposes and precision radar systems; hence it is safe to assume Deng's knowledge and approval of such transactions. The leadership probably knew it was fighting fire with fire in selling proscribed weapons of mass destruction to rogue regimes and therefore took extraordinary precautions to elude international detection by relying on Third World intermediaries (e.g., North Korea, Pakistan, Jordan, possibly Syria and Libya). Only in the face of irrefutable evidence directly linking Beijing to Third World customers has it confirmed missile or nuclear technology sales. Once such evidence is uncovered, Beijing either cites its non-

TABLE 7.2 Leading Exporters of Major Conventional Weapons to the Third World, 1987–1991 (U.S.$millions at constant 1990 prices)

Rank	Exporter	1987	1988	1989	1990	1991	1987–1991
1	USSR	13,420	10,761	10,869	6,845	3,516	45,412
2	United States	6,966	4,609	3,454	4,364	4,224	23,618
3	France	3,403	1,652	2,065	1,617	650	9,028
4	China	2,917	1,866	865	954	1,127	7,729
5	U.K.	2,006	1,516	1,968	1,261	847	7,599
Total		32,162	24,054	21,735	16,720	12,336	107,007

Source: Adapted from Stockholm International Peace Research Institute (SIPRI), *SIPRI Yearbook 1992: World Armaments and Disarmament* (New York: Oxford University Press, 1992), p. 272.

TABLE 7.3   China's Nuclear Sales and Transfers, 1950s–February 1992

Recipient and Time Period	Nature of Transaction
1 Algeria 1983–1991	Under a secret agreement, supplied a nuclear reactor large enough to make weapons-grade plutonium.
2 Argentina 1981–1985	Sold at least 60 metric tons of heavy water to run reactors capable of making plutonium, uranium concentrate (possibly 45 tons), low-enriched uranium hexafluoride, and about 12 kg of 20-percent-enriched uranium as fuel for research reactors.
3 Brazil 1984	Sold uranium enriched to 3 percent, 7 percent, and 20 percent in three shipments totaling 200 kg.
4 India 1982–1987	Sold at least 130 tons of heavy water through Alfred Hempel, a West German broker.
5 Iran 1985–1990	Under a secret cooperation agreement, trained several Iranian nuclear technicians in China and may have supplied technology for reactor construction. May have contracted to sell a research reactor.
6 Iraq 1989–1990	Helped Iraq manufacture special magnets for stabilizing ultrahigh-speed centrifuges for enriching uranium. Agreed, in violation of UN trade embargo, to sell 7 tons of lithium hydride, which can be used in the manufacture of nuclear weapons.
7 North Korea 1950s–1960s	Trained North Korean scientists in nuclear technology.
8 Pakistan 1983–1989	Supplied a reliable bomb design, enabling Pakistan to make a warhead weighing less than 400 lb. Reportedly supplied enough highly enriched uranium for two atomic bombs. Aided Pakistan's efforts to enrich uranium at its Kahuta plant. Sold tritium gas capable of boosting the yield of fission bombs. Provided special magnets for centrifuges at the Kahuta plant, which produces nuclear weapon fuel. May have scheduled a nuclear test for Pakistan in 1989 at its Lop Nor testing ground. Agreed to supply a 300-megawatt nuclear power station despite an international nuclear supply embargo.
9 South Africa 1981	Sold 30 tons of 2.7-percent- and 30 tons of 3-percent-enriched uranium through Alfred Hempel.
10 Syria 1992	Syria indicated intent to import small research reactor from China.

Source: Christian Science Monitor, March 10, 1992, p. 3, compiled from Carnegie Endowment and Wisconsin Nuclear Project.

proliferation pledges since 1984 or more recently its accession to the Nuclear Non-Proliferation Treaty (NPT) regime as prima facie evidence of its full compliance with the regime norms or insists that the arms sold have been for peaceful uses only. It then seeks to shift responsibility for ensuring the peaceful uses of its nuclear technology to its customers and the International Atomic Energy Agency (IAEA). All the same, China often argues that its NPT commitment cannot take effect retroactively (e.g., that the Algerian nuclear reactor need not be placed under IAEA rules, since it agreed to those rules only just after its export) and/or that the specifications of the missiles it has sold fall outside the scope of the regime (e.g., the M-11 missiles to Pakistan need not be placed under Missile Technology Control Regime [MTCR] rules because the missile's range is 290 kilometers while the MTCR considers only missiles of 300-kilometer range and above). It even insists on redefining the Middle East for purposes of arms sales limitations so as to exclude its own major customers (Algeria and Libya) but to include Turkey (a major U.S. customer).[48]

Given this pattern of denial, double-talk, and responsibility shifting, Beijing's recent decision to finally accede to the NPT commands little international credibility. In fact, the NPT issue was skillfully exploited as a bargaining chip in removing the Western sanctions imposed in the wake of the Tiananmen bloodletting. In 1991, France, Japan, the United States, and the IAEA put heavy pressure on China on the nuclear proliferation issue. On June 3, 1991, President François Mitterrand announced his far-reaching disarmament plan, including a commitment to become a party to the NPT. France left no doubt that it was making this commitment as a way of drawing in China. Its decision exposed China as the last officially acknowledged nuclear weapons state outside the NPT regime, depriving Beijing of any fig leaf on the nuclear proliferation issue. The issue became embarrassing with the revelation, first denied and then admitted, that China had secretly collaborated with Algeria for eight years in the construction of a nuclear reactor large enough to make weapons-grade plutonium. In the summer of 1991, the IAEA inspection team's disclosure that China had assisted the Iraqi nuclear weapons program came as another embarrassment. Against this backdrop Beijing announced in August 1991 that it would become a party to the NPT regime, but this decision was first made known to visiting Japanese Prime Minister Kaifu as a kind of reward for his leadership in Group of Seven politics in phasing out the Western sanctions as well as resuming Japan's large-scale aid program for China. The formal acceptance of the NPT and a commitment to abide by the MTCR guidelines are now routinely cited as prima facie evidence of China's full compliance with the nonproliferation norms in ongoing Sino-American negotiations.

With the collapse of the strategic triangle the temptation to use, by way of substitution, whatever other instrumentalities Beijing possessed became well-nigh irresistible. It was in this context of post–Cold War and postcommunist world politics that the Chinese leadership found that arms sales, especially in the nuclear and missile field, were another way of demonstrating its status as a global power and that regional conflicts in the Third World, especially in the Middle East, could not be resolved without China's participation and tacit cooperation. The conventional view that Chinese arms sales patterns and directions follow the logic of market demand—and that economic power in post-Mao China grows out of cash sales on the arms barrelhead—is not so much wrong as incomplete. China's missile sales to Saudi Arabia—Dong Feng 3 (CSS-2) intermediate-range ballistic missiles—earned not only hard currency but also a long-sought diplomatic shift from Taipei to Beijing (on July 21, 1990). Despite its refusal to recognize Israel until the Palestinian question is solved, Beijing has maintained covert military ties with that country since 1980 and finally established official diplomatic relations with it in early 1992. It is widely believed that Israel helped China to improve the accuracy of the intermediate-range Silkworm missiles that have been sold to Saudi Arabia, putting Tel Aviv within firing range of Riyadh. Since Tiananmen, Israel has emerged as China's leading foreign supplier of advanced technology, becoming in effect China's "back door" to U.S. technology.[49]

If Beijing's active involvement in the global arms trade has well served its political, economic, and military/strategic interests in the Middle East, the same cannot be said about East Asia. Since Tiananmen official defense spending has been increasing at double-digit rates. Outside estimates of China's actual military spending, including the income earned by the PLA from investments in businesses, arms sales abroad, and research and development expenditures, range from $12 billion to $24 billion, as against the $6–7 billion of official figures. Remarkably, Beijing seems to have recovered rather quickly from the reality shock of the collapse of the Soviet Union, turning Russia into a wholesale arms bazaar for advanced weapons systems (e.g., China bought $1.8 billion of weaponry from Russia in 1992, including twenty-four advanced Su-27 fighters). All of these changes, coupled with China's unilateral legislative move, made the disputed Paracel and Spratly Island groups the most dangerous flashpoint in the Asia-Pacific region. No fewer than six states—Brunei, China, Malaysia, the Philippines, Taiwan, and Vietnam—have competing jurisdictional claims to the potentially oil-rich Spratly Islands. These and the Paracels also straddle sea-lanes vital to East Asian states including Japan, adding a geostrategic dimension to the simmering conflict. China, Taiwan, South Korea, and Japan are also locked in dispute over the Diaoyu (Senkaku) Islands, farther north in the East China Sea. To possess the five Diaoyu (Senkaku) Islands, some 166 kilometers northeast of Taiwan, is to have legal jurisdiction over about 21,645 square kilometers of the continental shelf believed to be one of the last unexplored hydrocarbon resource areas in the world (up to 100 billion barrels of oil).

What gave rise to the China threat theory in recent years is assertive nationalism and unilateralism in bilateral clothing. Beijing quashed various Soviet, Australian, Canadian, and Japanese proposals for a multilateral Asia-Pacific security conference. Likewise, Beijing categorically rejected any international conference, let alone the establishment of a multilateral regime for handling territorial disputes, maintaining instead that disputes should be resolved by the countries directly involved on a bilateral basis. On February 25, 1992, the National People's Congress adopted the Law of the People's Republic of China on its Territorial Waters and Contiguous Areas "in order to enable the People's Republic of China to exercise its sovereignty over its territorial waters and its rights to exercise control over their adjacent areas, and to safeguard state security as well as its maritime rights and interests" (Article 1). The new law stipulates China's territorial sovereignty as including "the mainland and its offshore islands, Taiwan and the various affiliated islands including Diaoyu Islands, Penghu Islands, Dongsha Islands, Xisha [Paracel] Islands, Nansha [Spratly] Islands, and other islands that belong to the PRC" (Article 2). Furthermore, it claims the right to "adopt all necessary measures to prevent and stop the harmful passage of vessels through its territorial waters" (Article 8). It empowers "PRC military ships or military aircraft carriers … to chase" violators out to the open sea (Article 14).[50] It was the first time China had claimed direct sovereignty through such unilateral legislative sleight of hand.

Whatever its motivations and intentions, Beijing rather quickly backed off when it looked as if the new law might jeopardize its chances for a visit from the Japanese emperor in the latter half of 1992. The visit was viewed by the Chinese as a litmus test of Sino-Japanese relations and was threatened by the right-wing opposition that the new law had generated in Japan. Rather than risk giving such groups ammunition, an official of the Ministry of Foreign Affairs softened the law's impact, stating that its passage was a "normal domestic legislative process" and that "it doesn't mean any change in China's policy of 'leaving aside the controversy and jointly developing the islands with the countries involved in the dispute.'"[51] The official also claimed that a law addressing China's territorial claims had been in the works for ten years and that the timing was not meant to be offensive: "[China's] position on the islands issue and its policy of settling it by peaceful means will not change ... since the law simply reiterates its long-standing position." To further reassure the Japanese, CCP Chief Jiang Zemin reconfirmed the shelving of the issue on April 1, 1992, as a precursor to his own scheduled trip to Japan. Beijing's reactions to Tokyo's passage of the so-called peacekeeping operation bill in mid-1992 were remarkably restrained, as *Reference Materials*, a daily internal news digest for senior party leaders, recommended that "public comment should be restrained in view of China's need for Japanese aid."[52]

Although the desire to receive the emperor was part of China's motivation in softening its maritime policy, a further factor was the desire not to create too many enemies at one time. The new law had already offended many of China's Southeast Asian neighbors, who also claimed many of the other islands that Beijing had included in its proclamation, and reports of Chinese aggressive militarization were sparking anti-Chinese rhetoric in the region. Thus a relaxation of its line with Japan would prevent China from being encircled by doubters, as well as undermine any efforts by the Japanese right wing to use the dispute to justify Japanese remilitarization.

The Economic/Functional Domain

During the post-Mao era, especially since the Third Plenum of the Eleventh Party Congress, China's dominant developmental line has remained steadier than its geopolitical one. Gradually, it seems to have shifted from dependency theory to a neorealist theory of global interdependence. Its linkage with the NIEO can be accepted as the bellwether of this shift. The NIEO represented the Maoist line in China's engagement in global developmental politics just as the three-worlds theory represented the Maoist line in its engagement in global geopolitics. As a collective consensus package, the NIEO embodied a wide range of Third World claims and demands, a kind of birthday wish-list. It represented a mixture of dependency theory in its diagnosis and postwar international liberalism in its prescription. The logic of dependency theory stresses the maximization of internal autocentric development (self-reliance), the minimization of external dependency, and the transformation of the capitalist world economy. Conversely, the logic of international liberalism calls for world economic integration based on an international division of labor and the principle of comparative advantage. For

Maoist China, the NIEO was a globalization of its own self-reliance developmental model.

The self-reliance model remained intact during the continuity period. In the entente period, China's support for the NIEO continued, though in a drastically revised and muted form under the pressure of the born-again modernization drive. Maoist China's unique style of expounding its principled stand on world development issues in support of the system-transforming NIEO model had begun to be replaced by a more self-serving reformulation of the global political economy. The NIEO was redefined as an integral part of its global antihegemonic (anti-Soviet) geopolitics. The two bêtes noires of the Maoist era—global interdependence and the division of labor and specialization—were embraced as integral parts of the new open-door policy. In line with its growing enmeshment in the capitalist world economy, post-Mao China abandoned its model projection in Third World policy and drastically downgraded its system-transforming role in the global political economy.

The most significant conceptual change in China's bilateral relations with Third World countries in the 1980s was a shift from aid to exchange. Premier Zhao Ziyang's eleven-nation African tour in December 1982–January 1983 provided an occasion to bridge the gap between the authorized and the actual. Zhou Enlai's Eight Principles of foreign aid (mostly expressing China's altruistic and egalitarian norms) were drastically revised in content and reduced in number to become the Four Principles of Sino-African Economic and Technological Cooperation: equality and mutual benefit, emphasis on practical results, diversity in form, and common development. In the context of global North-South relations, China has redefined its support of the NIEO in terms of South-South cooperation (collective self-reliance). South-South cooperation and North-South dialogue are said to be interrelated aspects of the same process of transforming the old economic order and establishing a new one. South-South cooperation is not an alternative to the NIEO but a more realistic path toward building independent national economies, strengthening Third World solidarity, increasing the South's bargaining power, and generating new momentum for the stalled global negotiations.

The world peace/development-line period witnessed the emergence of the concept of global interdependence, in which all countries, North and South, East and West, are becoming increasingly interdependent and interpenetrable in the context of one world market. By 1984 the Chinese had come to the conclusion that the NIEO was a spent movement. By extension, China's message for the North was a sweet variation on the theme of global interdependence: "Now it is high time [for] the prosperous North [to] realize that it could not do without global prosperity, which in turn required global co-operation between North and South."[53] China's message for the South, for the first time, had a critical and sour note: "But the South has only itself to blame for some of its poverty. Factors such as failed policies and improper management can be held responsible to varying degrees in particular countries. It is not practical to blame the North for all the South's troubles, though exploitation is truly a root cause of the situation."[54]

One might be tempted to believe that Tiananmen dealt the concept of global interdependence a lethal blow, but it has become apparent that the return of Stalinist fundamentalism, as far as Chinese foreign economic policy is concerned, was more domestic smoke than external fire. The policy of reform and opening to the capitalist world continued undiminished. The world economy is still said to be an "inalienable whole," and the "global division of labor in industrial production is becoming a more and more important part of international cooperation."[55] Faced with the suspension of normal lending by the World Bank in the wake of the Tiananmen Massacre, China has taken a desultory approach to controlling the damage. In May 1990 Beijing even advanced the functionalist argument: Liu Zhongli, the Chinese vice minister of finance, attacked the error of certain countries in obstructing "the independent decision-making of the World Bank" and called upon all member states to act to prevent the bank from being "politicized" in this way.[56] At both the ADB's twenty-third annual meeting in New Delhi and its twenty-fourth in Vancouver, Li Guixian, state councillor and governor of the People's Bank of China, called on it to resume loans to China, arguing that as an economic institution it should not be influenced by politics. The irony is that it was politics, not economics, that had made Beijing's grand entry into the World Bank Group possible in 1980 and allowed it to impose the one-China principle on the ADB in 1986. In actuality, the post-Mao leadership has followed neither a classical Marxist nor a neo-Marxist dependency, nor a Western liberal global interdependence model. Rather, its development strategy reflects a neomercantilist, state-centered, and state-empowering model. The concept of global interdependence has been narrowly construed, confined to the global political economy, and treated as an opportunity to receive benefits without incurring any political, economic, military, and cultural costs.[57]

In the post-Mao era, the science and technology component of China's Four Modernizations (the others being industry, agriculture, and national defense) has begun to transform both the style and the substance of its Third World/global policy. The turning point came in late 1978, when China suddenly shifted from aid giving to aid seeking; it broke with tradition by seeking United Nations Development Program (UNDP) technical aid. That this request from a poor Third World country was received in the UN community as a complete surprise and with mixed reactions suggests China's ambiguous status in the global political system. Having thus crossed the Rubicon, the post-Mao leadership quickly plunged into the race for aid from trilateral countries, corporations, commercial banks, and UN economic and technical assistance agencies.

Such aid-seeking "neorealist" diplomacy soon caught up with the budgetary process. In 1979 China shocked the General Assembly's Committee on Contributions by presenting "complete national income statistics" with the request that its scale of assessment be revised downward. Despite the considerable controversy surrounding the accuracy of the Chinese statistics, its assessment was reduced from 5.5 percent to 1.65 percent (for a few transitional years) and finally to 0.77 percent. This has decisively changed the cost-benefit equation in Chinese international organization participation because it applies to all the organs and specialized agencies of the UN system.[58] At 5.5 percent, China was among the top five or six largest contributors to the UN budget in 1974–1978 (even ahead of the United Kingdom at 4.4 percent). At 0.77 percent, it is not even the largest Third World contributor, as Brazil (1.59 percent), Saudi Arabia (0.96 percent), and Mexico

(0.88 percent) have all surpassed it. China and Iran (0.77 percent) are now tied as the fourth-largest Third World contributors. That China's switch on UN peace-keeping *followed* a drastically reduced assessment also speaks directly to the logic of post-Mao neorealism-cum-neofunctionalism. Although the five permanent members of the UN Security Council are categorized as top-ranking Group A for UN peacekeeping assessment purposes, contributions to peacekeeping expenditures are still closely keyed to the regular UN scale of assessments. As a result, China, as the third-largest economy in the world, after those of the United States and Japan, contributed a pittance of $4,762,700 in 1991 for UN peacekeeping, as compared with $151,031,600 for the United States, $60,343,900 for Russia, $37,757,900 for France, and $29,361,800 for Britain.[59]

In the course of a few years, post-Mao China managed to transform itself from the only developing member state declining any multilateral aid to one of the largest aid recipients. Between 1979 and February 1983, China received $230 million in grants from the UNDP, the UN Fund for Population Activities, and UNICEF. In contrast, China's contributions to the UNDP amounted to only $5.8 million for the period 1973–1983. By 1989 China had become the world's largest recipient of official development assistance from all sources ($2,153 million). Tiananmen had only a slight impact; China's ranking dropped from first to third ($2,076 million), behind Egypt and Bangladesh.[60]

China has been exceptionally successful in securing World Bank financial assistance to fuel its modernization/status drive without too many strings. From 1981 to the end of June 1987, World Bank lending to China amounted to $5.5 billion for 52 projects. The World Bank, as the largest single source of concessionary multilateral aid, speaks louder than any other international organization. During the period 1981–1993 it has approved 124 projects for a total of committed loans and credits valued at $16.5 billion. For two consecutive years, China recaptured the number one ranking, receiving $2.56 billion in 1992 and $3.17 billion in 1993. Tiananmen had short-term consequences (for a modest interval of less than eighteen months) but no significant long-term repercussions. The World Bank has allowed China to reassert its claim to even more than its previous share of the total multilateral pie for the Third World.[61]

Although China initially claimed that it wanted to join the ADB in order to do its part to promote the economic expansion of developing countries in the Asia-Pacific region, this euphemistic rhetoric has really been a mask for its insatiable appetite for foreign capital. A year after its admission, it began seeking loans from the ADB's Ordinary Capital Resources fund. From 1986 until the June 1989 massacre, the ADB provided China with seven loans valued at $416 million, twenty-two technical assistance projects in the amount of $8.42 million, and a $3-million private-sector investment equity line to the Shanghai SITCO Enterprise Co., Ltd. ADB lending increased from $133.3 million in 1987 to $282.9 in 1988, then dropped to $39.7 million in 1989 and $50 million in 1990. On November 30, 1990, the ADB approved its first loan to China since Tiananmen, its operations in China returning to normal. Post-Tiananmen lending has, in fact, shot up dramatically, to $496.3 million in 1991 and $903 million in 1992, and the bank plans to lend China $1.1 billion in 1993, $1.5 billion in 1994, and $1.6 billion in 1996.[62]

At the same time, China's aid practice with regard to the Third World has generally been outpacing any policy or theoretical debate. The drastic revision of the principles guiding China's foreign economic relations with the Third World is a case in point. Although China shifted in 1978 from aid giving to aid seeking and stopped aid to two of its largest recipients (Albania and Vietnam), it was not until January 1983 that the guiding principles were revised in line with the new practice.[63]

The sound and fury of post-Tiananmen Third World policy, to borrow a popular saying in China, amount to "a lot of thunder but little rain" as far as aid practice is concerned. The *People's Daily* widely publicized thirteen "aid" projects for small Third World countries between mid-1989 and mid-1990, all designed to maximize symbolism and minimize costs.[64] Even when challenged by Taiwan's "dollar diplomacy" in the international diplomatic-recognition race, Beijing stayed close to the bottom line. In a forty-one-day diplomatic tug-of-war between Beijing and Taipei in mid-1992 when Niger maintained recognition of both Chinese governments as a way of seeking the highest bidder, Taipei won by outbidding Beijing (e.g., a loan for $50 billion and other developmental assistance). Liberia had received $140 million in aid from Taiwan in 1988 and only $20 million in aid over twelve years from China.[65]

Foreign trade made a great leap forward and outward in the post-Mao era, playing a crucial role in the modernization/status drive. It has been growing at an average annual rate of 12.9 percent—exports at an average rate of 15.1 percent—in 1979–1992. The share of foreign trade as percentage of gross national product (GNP) rose from less than 10 percent in 1978 to 27.3 percent in 1988. Tiananmen seems to have had only a slight and temporary effect, with the foreign trade share of GNP dropping to 26.3 percent, then rapidly rising to 31.4 percent in 1990, 36.7 percent in 1991, and 38.5 percent in 1992. The post-Tiananmen years 1990–1992, paradoxically enough, witnessed an unprecedented rise in foreign trade (and surplus), foreign direct investment, foreign exchange reserves, and economic growth rate. The persistent trade deficit of the 1980s turned into a comfortable surplus in these years. In the process, China's ranking as a global trade power rose from thirty-second in the world in 1978 to fifteenth by the end of 1991 and to eleventh by the end of 1992, for the first time ahead of Taiwan (twelfth) and South Korea (thirteenth) but still just behind Hong Kong (tenth).[66]

China has enjoyed a strong comparative advantage in its trade with the Third World. Although its Third World imports are largely primary commodities, most of its Third World exports are finished industrial products. Thus, the composition of its rapidly growing trade with the Third World is analogous to that of other developed countries. As a result, it has maintained a favorable trade balance with the Third World on the order of $5.9 billion a year, a total of $41.6 billion in the period 1980–1986. In 1990–1992, China's Third World annual trade surplus shot up to about $14.3 billion per year, doubling its annual trade surplus of $5.9 billion in the 1980s. Its Third World exports increased substantially, from $8.9 billion (49.5 percent) in 1980 to $44.2 billion (61.5 percent) in 1991 and $52.2 billion (59.4 percent) in 1992, while its Third World imports increased from $4.0 billion (20.7 percent) in 1980 to $29.6 billion (46.4 percent) in 1991 and $37.8 billion (46.2 percent) in 1992 (Table 7.4).

TABLE 7.4 China's Trade with Industrialized and Developing Countries and Selected Regions, 1980–1992 (U.S. $millions and, in parentheses, percentage of total trade)

	1980	1982	1984	1986	1988	1989	1990	1991	1992
World total	18,139ᵃ	21,865	24,824	31,366	47,663	52,914	64,500	71,986	86,206
	19,505	18,920	25,953	43,503	55,352	59,140	54,449	63,957	81,735
Industrialized Countries	8,110	9,371	10,407	12,235	17,470	19,023	21,901	25,028	30,675
	(44.7)	(42.9)	(41.9)	(39.0)	(36.7)	(36.0)	(34.0)	(34.8)	(35.6)
	14,356	13,029	17,912	28,852	30,571	31,767	26,860	31,544	37,976
	(73.6)	(68.9)	(69.0)	(66.3)	(55.2)	(53.7)	(49.3)	(49.3)	(46.5)
Developing Countries	8,980	11,783	13,281	17,015	27,701	30,443	39,294	44,273	51,193
	(49.5)	(53.9)	(53.5)	(54.2)	(58.1)	(57.5)	(60.9)	(61.5)	(59.4)
	4,029	4,331	6,416	11,775	20,398	21,820	24,291	29,653	37,793
	(20.7)	(22.9)	(24.7)	(27.1)	(36.9)	(36.9)	(44.6)	(46.4)	(46.2)
Africa	482	760	543	574	1,642	608	1,188	784	1,014
	(2.7)	(3.5)	(2.2)	(1.8)	(1.3)	(1.5)	(1.8)	(1.1)	(1.2)
	285	261	310	254	245	394	357	376	412
	(1.5)	(1.4)	(1.2)	(0.6)	(0.4)	(0.7)	(0.7)	(0.6)	(0.5)
Asia	6,530	7,222	9,347	12,935	22,359	26,825	34,523	41,008	46,921
	(36.0)	(33.0)	(37.7)	(41.2)	(46.9)	(50.7)	(53.5)	(57.0)	(54.4)
	1,700	2,540	4,140	8,196	15,700	16,842	21,204	26,508	33,934
	(8.7)	(13.9)	(16.0)	(18.8)	(28.4)	(28.5)	(38.9)	(41.4)	(41.5)
Europe	770	548	507	1,034	1,381	1,256	1,513	345	417
	(4.2)	(2.5)	(2.0)	(3.3)	(2.9)	(2.4)	(2.4)	(0.5)	(0.5)
	985	661	799	1,624	1,951	1,817	966	602	677
	(5.1)	(3.5)	(3.1)	(3.7)	(3.5)	(3.1)	(1.8)	(0.9)	(0.8)

	1980	1982	1984	1986	1988	1989	1990	1991	1992
Middle East	*803*	*2,725*	*2,435*	*2,109*	*2,089*	*1,410*	*1,430*	*1,568*	*1,966*
	(4.4)	(12.5)	(9.8)	(6.7)	(4.4)	(2.7)	(2.2)	(2.2)	(2.3)
	985	*272*	*280*	*150*	*577*	*579*	*477*	*809*	*1,044*
	(5.1)	(1.4)	(1.1)	(0.3)	(1.4)	(1.0)	(0.9)	(1.3)	(1.3)
South America	*395*	*528*	*449*	*363*	*231*	*344*	*640*	*567*	*873*
	(2.2)	(2.4)	(1.8)	(1.2)	(0.5)	(0.7)	(1.0)	(0.8)	(1.0)
	716	*597*	*888*	*1,550*	*1,925*	*2,188*	*1,287*	*1,358*	*1,724*
	(3.7)	(3.2)	(3.4)	(3.6)	(3.5)	(3.7)	(2.4)	(2.1)	(2.1)
USSR and	*1,050*	*707*	*1,129*	*2,101*	*2,381*	*2,866*	*2,827*	*2,678*	*3,610*
	(5.8)	(3.2)	(4.5)	(6.7)	(4.1)	(5.4)	(4.4)	(3.7)	(4.2)
Others	*1,121*	*1,186*	*1,393*	*2,530*	*2,830*	*3,043*	*2,859*	*2,516*	*4,321*
	(5.7)	(6.3)	(5.4)	(5.8)	(5.1)	(5.2)	(5.3)	(3.9)	(5.3)

[a]Export figures are italicized; import figures are in roman type.

Source: Adapted from International Monetary Fund, *Direction of Trade Statistics Yearbook 1987* (Washington, D.C.: IMF, 1987), pp. 136–138 for the 1980-1986 figures; *Direction of Trade Statistics Yearbook 1992* (Washington, D.C.: IMF, 1992), pp. 134–135 for the 1988-1991 figures, and *Direction of Trade Statistics* (June 1993), p. 33 for the 1992 figures.

The defining characteristic of China's Third World trade is its highly skewed regional concentration and distortion. In 1992, for example, Sino-Asian trade amounted to about 91 percent of total Third World trade, followed by trade with the Middle East (3.4 percent), Latin America (2.9 percent), and Africa (1.6 percent). Even in the Asian context, Japan and Hong Kong together accounted for annual averages of 45 percent of China's global trade and 86 percent of China's Asian trade in the period 1982–1988.[67] In 1992, China's top five trading partners (Hong Kong, the United States, Japan, Taiwan, and South Korea) dominated the foreign trade aspect of the reform and opening to the outside world, taking up over 71 percent of the total volume. The overall marginality of China's Third World trade, except in the global arms trade field, is underscored by the volume and composition of trade with ASEAN, on the one hand, and with just one East Asian NIC, the Republic of Korea (ROK), on the other. Although Sino-ASEAN trade increased from $1.85 billion in 1980 to $6.6 billion in 1989, it is still modest (about 4–6 percent of the global total and about 10 percent of the Asian trade), marked more by competition than by complementarity, as both parties are more concerned with the major developed economies than they are with each other. In contrast, indirect trade between China and the Republic of Korea started slowly from a zero base (about $40,000 in 1978) and increased to $461.6 million in 1985 and, after the 1986 Asian Olympic Games in Seoul, $1.49 billion in 1986 (about 80 percent of Seoul's total trade volume with all socialist countries at the time), $3 billion in 1989 (nearly ten times the value of China's trade with North Korea), $3.8 billion in 1990, $5.8 billion in 1991, and $8.22 billion in 1992; it is currently projected to top $20 billion by 1995. The volume of Sino–South Korean trade in 1992 at $8.22 billion was over five times that of Sino-African trade ($1.6 billion) and nearly three times that of Sino–Latin American trade ($2.9 billion). Its composition also defies the typical Sino–Third World pattern, with China exporting coal, minerals, raw materials, and agricultural products and importing steel, industrial products, petrochemical items, advanced machinery, and electronic parts and technology. Dramatic increases in this trade in the past two years were made possible by a most-favored-nation trade agreement signed in February 1992 and the establishment of diplomatic relations on August 24, 1992.

If we remove the Four East Asian Tigers from the category of "developing countries," the marginality of the Third World in Chinese foreign trade becomes even more obvious. In a sense, Hong Kong, Taiwan, and South Korea have been drawn in as indispensable players in the implementation of Zhao Ziyang's coastal developmental strategy. The crucial role of Hong Kong in the development of Guangdong, especially Shenzhen special economic zone, needs no elaboration here.[68] In the late 1980s Taiwan started transferring its production lines to nearby Fujian province, creating another major export-launching base. Surely it is no mere coincidence that from 1987 to 1992 both Hong Kong and Taiwan reduced their trade surpluses with the United States as China's trade surplus suddenly ballooned. The combined trade deficit of the United States with "Greater China" has remained at about $28 billion, with only the relative proportions shifting from Taiwan and Hong Kong to China. Now, South Korea is poised to enter the game to transform Shandong province, which lies across the Yellow Sea from the Korean peninsula, into another export-launching platform. Foreign direct investment is flowing into Shandong from South Korea, China's plentiful supply of cheap labor being attractive to South Korean entrepreneurs who face rising production costs in their own country.[69]

Since 1979, China has joined Third World competition to export cheap labor under the guise of promoting "international labor cooperation" (*guoji laowu hezuo*). The total number of Chinese workers abroad under such contracts increased from about 18,000 between 1979 and 1981 to 31,000 in 1983 and 59,000 by the end of 1985. From 1979 to 1985, the total value of labor service contracts was $5.1 billion. Between 1979 and 1988, China signed 7,164 labor service contracts with 117 countries, earning $10.3 billion. Since 1988 labor export has proceeded at a faster pace, with an annual volume of 70,000 workers on average. Between January and October of 1992, China dispatched 128,000 workers overseas, an increase of 40 percent over the corresponding period in 1991. Not only the Middle East but also Japan, Singapore, South Korea, and the Commonwealth of Independent States (CIS) are among the new magnets for China's labor exports. In 1992, construction and labor projects contracted by China with foreign countries totaled $6.3 billion, up 75 percent, and operational revenue reached $2.8 billion, up 18.5 percent. By the end of 1992, there were 130,000 people implementing contracts abroad.[70]

In foreign direct investment, too, China stands out as an exceptional Third World country. In global flows of such investment, the developing countries have been getting a steadily smaller share, from 31 percent in 1968 down to 17 percent in 1988–1989. Moreover, most foreign direct investment is concentrated in relatively few developing countries, well over one-third of it flowing into China, South Korea, Indonesia, Singapore, Malaysia, and Thailand.[71] Asia's share of total foreign direct investment inflows for the Third World rose from 25 percent in the early 1980s to over 50 percent in the early 1990s, surpassing Latin America, the traditional stronghold. In this area, too, 1992 was a vintage year, with $11.16 billion representing 27 percent of all such investment committed to China since 1979—and almost the same as was lured by the United States, the world's biggest economy—and including substantial increases from Taiwan, Thailand, Singapore, the ROK, and Canada. For the first time, the amount of foreign direct investment exceeded the total foreign capital introduced in the form of foreign loans, compensation trade, and international leasing.[72] No Third World country came anywhere near this figure in 1992, and no Third World country can ever expect to, since a substantial portion, probably over 80 percent, is coming from Hong Kong, Taiwan, and Macao. With a huge domestic market, natural resources, lower taxes, more lenient pollution laws, and abundant and cheap labor, China has managed to lure an estimated twelve thousand enterprises with $8 billion in Taiwanese investments to operate on the mainland. Taiwan is now the largest foreign investor in China, surpassing both the United States and Japan. Taiwanese investors have found Xiamen special economic zone in Fujian province especially attractive because of its proximity and the uniformity of local dialects.

The greening of world politics in recent years and the universal awareness of China's status as an environmental giant afforded Chinese leaders another opportunity to apply their maxi/mini code of conduct in foreign policy. A close fit between Chinese and Third World interests on ecodevelopment and the shared fear of environmental conditionalities in aid and trade allowed Beijing to reassert its Third World leadership role in this quintessentially functional domain. China's environmental diplomacy was aimed at maximizing foreign aid and technology transfers and minimizing the international normative and material costs of the Tiananmen crackdown. The maxi/mini strategy has led Beijing to adopt a "cash first, cooperation later" posture in its global environmental diplomacy. China has contributed to global warming faster than any other major country,[73] but its "principled stand" on the global campaign to protect the ozone layer was thinly disguised blackmail: it refused to sign the 1987 Montreal Protocol without a promise of substantial funds and greater "flexibility" on the use and production of chlorofluorocarbons (CFCs). In June 1991 Beijing finally signed an amended Montreal Protocol. Apparently, a series of amendments adopted by the June 1990 London Conference satisfied the maxi/mini principle of differentiated responsibilities and rights, including provisions regarding technological transfers "under equitable and most favorable conditions, and abolishing some clauses that discriminated against developing countries," and the establishment of a multilateral environmental fund ($200 million) to help developing countries gradually reduce the production and consumption of CFCs. At the Chantilly Conference in February 1991, Chinese representatives openly opposed any international action to set emission ceilings with the claim that such ceilings would violate the principle of state sovereignty.[74] Yet it was announced in late April 1993 that the UNDP would assist China in developing a $2.1 billion program to phase out use of ozone-depleting substances by the year 2010, drawing upon the multilateral fund set up under the Montreal Protocol.[75]

In preparation for a more serious challenge at what was billed the first Earth Summit (the United Nations Conference on Environment and Development in Rio de Janeiro, Brazil, in June 1992), the Chinese government sponsored a two-day Ministerial Conference of Developing Countries on Environment and Development in Beijing in June 1991. Although only forty-one developing countries participated, China seems to have realized, with the adoption of the Beijing Declaration, its main objective of projecting its own party line as the united principled stand of the Third World. China's commitment to the global effort for environmental protection and sustainable development is keyed to various preconditions stated as "principles": (1) differentiated responsibilities, (2) differentiated obligations, (3) state sovereignty and equality, (4) untied aid, (5) differentiated capabilities, and (6) preferential treatment.[76] Once again Premier Li Peng headed a huge delegation in a bid for Third World leadership at the Earth Summit, presenting over a million characters' worth of position papers and documentation for negotiation in the name of "the Group of Seventy-Seven plus China."

Sovereignty Revived or Perforated?

The interplay of China and the Third World in the changing world order is complex and often surprising. The dialectical style of Chinese international conduct and the tendency to try to be all things to all nations on all global issues make generalization and prognostication hazardous. Nonetheless, several distinctive antinomies and paradoxes of China's sovereignty-bound global policy are readily apparent.

Despite routine lip service to the twin identifications with the Third World and as a socialist country and the shared common interests and solidarity, China's Third World policy has been marked by the strategy of enhancing its own status with little if any global responsibilities. Despite all the changes and shifts, China's global role as a Group of One persists. In the post-Mao era, its Third World identity and its revolutionary and socialist identities have suffered steady burnout. Third World identity made a comeback of sorts in post-Tiananmen China, to be sure, as Beijing in 1989–1990 intensified its rhetorical identification with the Third World and increased its shuttle diplomacy and aid programs in the context of growing alienation from both superpowers. By the end of 1992, however, its Third World policy seems to have relapsed into the more comfortable Jekyll and Hyde pattern combining rhetorical support with free-riding on its self-proclaimed Third World status as a way of maximizing preferential treatment in aid, trade, foreign direct investment, and technology transfer.

Post-Tiananmen China has more or less disqualified itself as a Third World country by what it *is* and what it *does* in global politics. To be "Third World" is to acknowledge the reality of "global apartheid" symbolized and structured by extreme unevenness, hierarchy, and deprivation in the global political economy (i.e., the richest 20 percent of the world's population preempts 82.7 percent of the total world income while the poorest 20 percent receives only 1.4 percent) and to promote global system transformation for a just and equitable world order. Measuring the world's economies in terms of the so-called purchasing-power parities (PPP) of each nation's own currency rather than by its dollar exchange value has catapulted China from the ranks of Third World nations to those of economic powerhouses. Under PPP calculations introduced by the IMF in May 1993, China's economy is four times larger than most previous estimates, making it the world's third-largest, after those of the United States and Japan. Yet the confirmation of China's new "first world" economic status obscures the rise of a two-tier economy that is rapidly widening the gap between rich coastal China and poor interior China even as many Chinese refer to the latter (four-fifths of the nation) as "China's third world."[77]

The idea of an egalitarian international order is a powerful ideological weapon in the antihegemonic struggle of the Third World for world-order transformation. Yet in the post-Mao era socialist egalitarianism has suffered slippage beyond redemption. In global politics China advances its own national interests disguised as abstract international principles. The credibility of antihegemonic struggle is also belied by the recent return of Sinocentric cultural arrogance and "big-nation chauvinism." Traditionally, the Chinese regarded Africans as even more barbaric than Westerners.[78] The outbreak of Chinese racism against African blacks studying in China—the only unsuppressed student demonstration (riot) of the post-Mao era—speaks directly to the progressive decay of normative foreign policy. The rise of China's standing in an American-led hegemonic world order and its unique status as a "poor global power" entitled to special treatment can also be explained by the putative change in China's national identity from a revolutionary antihegemonic actor to a neorealist system-maintaining status quo actor. The irony is that the world's principal aspirant to great-power status has been none other than the world's principal critic of superpower hegemony and that the world's principal antihegemonic champion has become the principal security and economic beneficiary of America's hegemonic structural power.

Although it inflicted little if any damage on China's bilateral relations with Third World countries, the June 1989 massacre dealt a severe blow to the credibility of the make-believe moral regime in global normative politics. Tiananmen made it possible, even if temporarily, for the United Nations to accomplish a human-rights "mission impossible"—condemning the self-styled champion of the Third World and self-styled permanent representative of the Third World in the Security Council for massive human-rights abuses at home. It is true that there were not many teeth in the international sanctions. Yet the greatest damage is not so much from the content or duration of the sanctions as from the collapse of credibility that they reflected. That China has managed to take advantage of the Third World's power of numbers to wriggle off the hit list of the UN Human Rights Commission since 1990 has a lot to do with the new Sino–Third World partnership of human-rights misery against Western linkage politics in international institutions—linking multilateral aid to democratization and environmental protection. In a sense, there is global interdependence between China and the Third World, but it is what Maoist China once likened to an asymmetrical interdependence "between a horseman and his mount."

There is much irony in this so-called new China's constantly invoking the "old" Westphalian principle of state sovereignty in the name of a "new" international order. It seems equally revealing that China has had to rely on the Western principles of state sovereignty and state equality to define and project its own conception of world order—world order with Chinese characteristics. The concepts of state sovereignty and state equality—essentially Western in origin—entered China's long and well-chronicled history relatively late. It took nothing less than a traumatic encounter with Western imperialism in the nineteenth century to force the disintegrating empire to sieze upon state sovereignty with a vengeance. Once again, in the wake of the Tiananmen tragedy, the comprehensive-national-strength thesis legitimated by the principle of state sovereignty has been revived as the only way of compensating for sagging domestic legitimacy. What makes state sovereignty all the more compelling in the Chinese case is the unresolved unification problem. Lacking co-optive power, ideological appeal, or a unifying value system, Beijing instinctively raises the sword of state sovereignty in its unrelenting efforts to maintain its control over Hong Kong, Tibet, Inner Mongolia, Xinjiang, and Taiwan. Yet all these sovereignty-bound pronouncements merely underscore the abiding antinomies between the traditional obsession with autonomy and self-reliance and the normative pressures generated by China's growing dependence on foreign aid, foreign direct investment, foreign trade, and the foreign science and technology needed to fuel its modernization/status drive. Chinese world-order thinking seems conditioned by the tyrannies of the past while tempted by the promise of modernity—the latest version of the persistent tension between the temptations and fears of external dependency and the long-standing pursuit of national identity via civilizational autonomy and political and intellectual self-sufficiency. The antinomies between the shadows of the past and the shadows of the future, apparently incapable of being resolved, hinder more positive Chinese engagement in global politics.

Despite the twin blows of the Tiananmen tragedy at home and the collapse of communism in Eastern Europe, the Soviet Union, and Mongolia, with all of their ominous implications, the record of Chinese economic achievements since those events has proved far more impressive than many had expected. For almost a decade, from 1980 to mid-1989, Beijing successfully applied a strategy of extracting maximum rights and payoffs while minimizing responsibilities and penalties, but this leaves its stellar post-Tiananmen economic performance unexplained. The answer, or at least one of the answers, to this paradox lies in the widening gap in Chinese development between the claims of state sovereignty and the realities of perforated sovereignty.

With the growing globalization of the Chinese political economy, the devolution of power at home, and the fragmentation of authority and decision-making structures at the apex during the post-Mao era, the center has been forced to make a series of decentralizing compromises enabling the Party-state's central planners to maintain the appearance that they were still controlling the economic reforms and opening to the outside world. In effect, the center has allowed the camel's nose of market-based competition to enter the tent of central planning, releasing the enormous entrepreneurial energies of sovereignty-free actors (mostly ethnic Chinese entrepreneurs from Hong Kong, Taiwan, Macao, and Southeast Asia) who have transformed the process of economic development with their own pace, logic, and direction. Ironically, the center has relaxed its control to cause such an unprecedented economic growth only to lose, by installments, its sovereign power over the economy. Today well over half of China's economy, especially the most robust part, has already escaped the control of central planners in Beijing. The center no longer controls the economically dynamic and prosperous southern peripheries. It lacks the interest rates and other monetary tools by which other countries control investment and currency growth. As economic power slips out of its hands, so too does political control. Moreover, nearly one-third of China's national income today depends on the world capitalist system, whereas during the era of Western imperialism only 2 percent of its national income came from foreign trade and investment.[79] Yet the impressive economic performance coupled with the reality of compromised economic sovereignty makes it virtually impossible for the center to turn the clock back to the heyday of orthodox Marxist self-reliance without causing a major economic crash landing and serious political risks.

Today sovereignty is constantly penetrated by the forces of supranational globalization from above and substate local and regional fragmentation from below. Modern communications, transportation, highly specialized technologies of space and oceans, interdependencies in currencies, human migration, commodity pricing, international trade, the traffic in drugs and terrorism, transnational AIDS epidemics, and environmental pollution are only a few of the new phenomena that defy the logic of national borders or state sovereignty and are steadily undermining the foundations of the sovereignty-centered international order. At the same time, a silent global information/transparency revolution is under way in China, even in the remote hinterlands. This revolution both reflects the globalization of increasingly intertwined political, economic, social, and normative structures and values and fosters the rapid mobilization of people's needs, demands, frustration and intolerance—indeed, the second "revolution of people power." In a sense, China has lost its sovereignty over global human-rights politics. With its increasing participation in human-rights politics, the shrinkage of social and geographical distances, the emergence of global human-rights standards and norms, and the proliferation of human-rights nongovernmental organizations providing a steady flow of information on human-rights violations, it is very difficult for China to maintain a policy of "do as I say, not as I do." Governmental oppression can no longer be concealed and the Chinese government's treatment of its people is no longer just a domestic matter.

The Tiananmen tragedy at home and the collapse of international communism at its epicenter have conflated domestic and international legitimation crises as never before. The sound and fury of state sovereignty cannot belie the unpleasant reality that China today is a weak, fragmented state. This changed domestic and international environment presents a clear and continuing danger to the leadership, because it threatens to take away the Party-state's last remaining source of—and indeed its ultimate claim to—legitimacy grounded in the national-identity-enacting mission of restoring China's great-power status in the world. The defining feature of a weak state is the high level of internal threats to the government's security. External events are seen primarily in terms of their effects on the state's internal stability. The idea of national security, which refers to the defense of core national values against external threats, becomes subverted to the extent that the Chinese Party-state is itself insecure. In short, China no longer has a legitimating and unifying ideology of sufficient strength to dispense with the large-scale repressive use of force in domestic life. The tension between nationalism and internationalism can be seen as entering full force into the national identity crisis, with serious implications for the peaceful resolution of many territorial disputes with neighboring Third World states in East Asia.

Although at this juncture nothing is more uncertain than the future of one coherent, unified, and fully sovereign China, the notion that an engaged and strong China is an irreducible prerequisite to any approach to world order is likely to remain central to Chinese global thinking. It seems safe to project, moreover, that the immediate future will be more or less like the immediate past. China's determination to increase its comprehensive national strength and to reassert itself as a great power is a grand strategy designed to shore up its sagging domestic legitimacy, restore a sense of national pride and purpose, and command a greater level of international attention and respect.

Notes

1. See Karin Lindgren et al., "Major Armed Conflicts in 1990," in Stockholm International Peace Research Institute (SIPRI), *SIPRI Yearbook 1991: World Armaments and Disarmament* (New York: Oxford University Press, 1991), pp. 345–379.

2. *Selected Works of Mao Tse-Tung*, Vol. 4 (Peking: Foreign Languages Press, 1961), p. 415, emphasis added.

3. Nigel Harris, *The End of the Third World: Newly Industrializing Countries and the Decline of an Ideology* (London: I. B. Tauris, 1986).

4. See Lester Brown, "The New World Order," in Lester R. Brown et al., *State of the World 1991* (New York: W. W. Norton, 1991), pp. 3–20; and Paul Kennedy, *Preparing for the Twenty-First Century* (New York: Random House, 1993).

5. This situation has led some scholars to classify Third World countries into various subcategories. J. Ravenhill, for instance, identifies five separate types of "developing" countries in assessing the varied potential of societies in Asia, Africa, and Latin America. In its most recent annual report, the World Bank, relying on 1990 gross national product (GNP) per capita income figures, uses a fourfold typology of national economies: (1) low-income ($600 or less), 2) lower-middle-income ($601–$2,465), (3) upper-middle-income ($2,466–$7,619), and (4) high-income ($7,620 or more). J. Ravenhill, "The North-South Balance of Power," *International Affairs* 66:4 (1990):745–746; World Bank, *World Development Report 1992: Development and the Environment* (New York: Oxford University Press, 1992), pp. 306–307.

6. See, e.g., the Report of the South Commission, *The Challenge to the South* (Oxford: Oxford University Press, 1990), esp. 1–24, and the earlier Brandt Commission Report, *North-South: A Program for Survival* (Cambridge, Mass.: MIT Press, 1980).

7. "The South's vision has to embrace the whole world," as the South Commission put it, "for it is part of that world. It cannot isolate itself; nor should it wish to isolate itself from the rest of the world." *The Challenge to the South*, p. 9.

8. Wang Tieya, ed., *Guojifa* [International Law] (Beijing: Falu chubanshe, 1981), pp. 81–82.

9. Sun Lin, "Heping gongchu wu xiang yuanze—xiandai guoji guanxi de jiben zhunze" [The Five Principles of Peaceful Coexistence—The Fundamental Norms for Modern International Relations], *Hongqi* [Red Flag] (hereafter cited as *HQ*) No. 11 (June 1, 1984):23.

10. Ibid., pp. 23–24.

11. Quoted in Lowell Dittmer, "The Tiananmen Massacre," *Problems of Communism* 38 (September–October 1989):3.

12. *Beijing Review* (hereafter cited as *BR*) 32:49 (December 4–10, 1989):17–22; quote on p. 22.

13. Wang, *Guojifa*, pp. 267–268.

14. Yi Ding, "Upholding the Five Principles of Peaceful Coexistence," *BR* 33:9 (February 26–March 4, 1990):16, emphasis added.

15. Wei Min et al., eds., *Guojifa gailun* [Introduction to International Law] (Beijing: Guangmin ribao chubanshe, 1986), p. 247.

16. Quoted in Lo Ping, "A Disaster for CPC's Foreign Affairs," *Cheng Ming* No. 144 (October 10, 1989), in Foreign Broadcast Information Service, *Daily Report—China* (hereafter cited as FBIS-China), October 3, 1989, p. 3.

17. Lo Ping and Lai Chi-king, "Secret Talks Between Chinese, Vietnamese Communist Parties and Between Chinese, Korean Communist Parties," *Cheng Ming* No. 166, (August 1, 1991), in FBIS-China, August 1, 1991, pp. 1–2.

18. Latvian Foreign Minister Janis Jurkans specifically mentioned this point during his visit to Taipei in December 1991. See James L. Tyson, "Taiwan, Besting China, Sets Up Ties to Baltics," *Christian Science Monitor* (hereafter cited as *CSM*), December 27, 1991, p. 8; *Free China Journal*, January 31, 1992, p. 1.

19. On September 24, 1992, Vanuatu Foreign Minister Serge Vohor signed a joint communiqué with Republic of China (ROC) Foreign Minister Frederick Chien whereby each side "officially recognized" the other. The next day, back in Vanuatu, PRC Vice Foreign Minister Wang Wendong reportedly stated the PRC did not object to "trade ties" between Vanuatu and Taiwan and a few days later signed a $3.6 million interest-free loan agreement with Vanuatu Prime Minister Maxime Carlot. See *China News Analysis* (hereafter *CNA*), September 24, 1992, in FBIS-China, September 1992, p. 67; and Radio Australia (Melbourne), September 30, 1992, in Foreign Broadcast Information Service, *Daily Report, East Asia*, October 2, 1992, p. 42.

20. See Ling Qing's interview, in *Ban Yue Tan* 6 (March 25, 1986), in FBIS-China, April 18, 1986, pp. A4–A6; quote on p. A5.

21. Jakarta ANTARA, September 3, 1992, in FBIS-China, September 4, 1992, p. 1.

22. See Yun-han Chu, ed., *The Role of Taiwan in International Economic Organizations* (Taipei: Institute for National Policy Research, 1990).

23. "China Will Never Seek Hegemony," *BR* 26:6 (February 7, 1983):18, emphasis added.

24. The white paper was issued by the State Council and translated as "Human Rights in China" in *BR* 34:44 (November 4, 1991):8–45, and FBIS-China, supplement, November 21, 1991, pp. 1–29. For more discussion, see chap. 10 in this volume.

25. Paul Lewis, "New U.N. Index Measures Nations' Quality of Life," *New York Times* (hereafter cited as *NYT*), May 23, 1993, p. 14.

26. "The Right to Development: An Inalienable Human Right," *BR* 35:51 (December 21–27, 1992):13.

27. This is the first global conference on human rights in twenty-five years. The General Assembly decided to convene such a conference via its Resolution 45/155 of December 18, 1990.

28. Gordon Fairclough, "Standing Firm," *Far Eastern Economic Review* (hereafter cited as *FEER*), April 15, 1993, p. 22.

29. Deng Xiaoping, *Jianshe you Zhongguo tese de shehui zhuyi* [Building Socialism with Chinese Characteristics] (Beijing: Renmin chubanshe, 1987), p. 112.

30. *Renmin ribao* [People's Daily] (hereafter cited as *RMRB*), April 24, 1986, p. 1.

31. See the cover story, "South China Sea: Treacherous Shoals," *FEER*, August 13, 1992, pp. 14–20, and John W. Garver, "China's Push Through the South China Sea: The Interaction of Bureaucratic and National Interests," *China Quarterly* No. 132 (December 1992):999–1028.

32. See the final version of Jiang's Political Report, in FBIS-China, October 21, 1992, supplement, pp. 1–21, esp. 15–16.

33. See the statement of Pakistan's representative on the behind-the-scenes "consultations" in Beijing and New York and Ambassador Ling's statement in the Fifth Committee of the General Assembly on November 27, 1981, in UN Doc. A/C.5/36/SR.56 (27 November 1981), pp. 5–8.

34. Hu Yumin, "UN's Role in a New World Order," *BR* 34:23 (June 10–16, 1991):12–14.

35. "An Agenda for Peace: Preventive Diplomacy, Peacemaking, and Peace-Keeping," UN Doc. A/47/277 and S/24111 (17 June 1992).

36. Ibid., p. 5.

37. Paul Lewis, "U.N. Set to Debate Peacemaking Role," *NYT*, September 6, 1992, p. 7.

38. This point is made in Foreign Minister Qian Qichen's major speech at the Forty-sixth Session of the UN General Assembly, which comes close to being China's annual state of the world report. FBIS-China, October 1, 1992, pp. 4–8; quote on p. 7.

39. Sassam Tabatabai, "Muslim World and Bosnia," *CSM*, May 11, 1993, p. 18.

40. See *SIPRI Yearbook 1992: World Armaments and Disarmament* (New York: Oxford University Press, 1992), pp. 600–615.

41. See "Working Paper: China's Basic Position on the Process of Nuclear Disarmament in the Framework of International Peace and Security, with the Objective of the Elimination of Nuclear Weapons" (hereafter cited as "Working Paper"), UN Doc. A/CN.10/166 (24 April 1992), p. 3, emphasis added.

42. Zhang Qinsheng and Zeng Guangjun, "Long Live the Interests of the State," *Jiefangjun Bao*, July 15, 1988, in FBIS-China, July 29, 1988, p. 30.

43. "Working Paper," p. 4.

44. For China's stand on arms control and disarmament issues in recent years, see UN Docs. A/CN.10/95 (8 May 1987); A/CN.10/116 (9 May 1989); A/CN. 10/118 (12 May 1989); A/CN.10/146 (25 April 1991); A/CN. 10/150 (26 April 1991); A/CN.10/152 (29 April 1991); "Working Paper"; and Li Weiguo, "Tiaozheng zhong de hei zhanlue yu hei caijun zhong de xin wenti" [New Issues in the Readjustment of Nuclear Strategies and Nuclear Disarmament], *Guoji wenti yanjiu* [International Studies] No. 3 (July 1992):42–47.

45. See Xinhua in FBIS-China, September 8, 1988, p. 1; "China Responsible for Its Arms Sales," in *BR* 35:9 (March 2–8, 1992):33.

46. See John Tessitore and Susan Woolfson, eds., *A Global Agenda: Issues Before the 47th General Assembly of the United Nations* (New York: University Press of America, 1992), pp. 133–134, and Lincoln Kaye, "Back in the Game," *FEER*, June 11, 1992, p. 9.

47. For a thoroughgoing analysis and documentation of this point, see Jag Mohan Malik, "Chinese National Security and Nuclear Arms Control" (Ph.D. diss., Australian National University, 1990), chap. 4.

48. John Calabrese, "Peaceful or Dangerous Collaborators? China's Relations with the Gulf Countries," *Pacific Affairs* 65:4 (Winter 1992–1993):471–485; John W. Lewis, Hua Di, and Xue Litai, "Beijing's Defense Establishment: Solving the Arms-Export Enigma," *International Security* 15:4 (Spring 1991):87–109; Shirley Kan, "China's Arms Sales: Overview and Outlook for the 1990s," in Joint Economic Committee, *China's Economic Dilemmas in the 1990s*, Vol. 2 (Washington, D.C.: U.S. Government Printing Office, 1991), pp. 696–711; Kaye, "Back in the Game," p. 9; and Eden Y. Woon, "Chinese Arms Sales and U.S.-China Military Relations," *Asian Survey* 29:6 (June 1989):601–618.

49. Richard A. Bitzinger, "Arms to Go: Chinese Arms Sales to the Third World," *International Security* 17:2 (Fall 1992):84–111.

50. Xinhua, February 25, 1992, in FBIS-China, February 28, 1992, p. 2.

51. "Legislation Doesn't Mean Policy Change," *BR* 35:13 (March 30–April 5, 1992):10.

52. Nayan Chanda, "Japan: Why They Worry," *FEER*, June 25, 1992, p. 18.

53. She Duanzhi, "United Nations: Rallying Around Common Interests," *BR* 29:38 (September 22, 1986):12.

54. Tong Dalin and Liu Ji, "North-South Co-operation for Mutual Prosperity," *BR* 28:26 (July 1, 1985):19.

55. *RMRB*, overseas ed., September 29, 1990, p. 4.

56. Xinhua, May 9, 1990, in FBIS-China, May 9, 1990, pp. 1–2.

57. See George T. Crane, *The Political Economy of China's Special Economic Zones* (Armonk, N.Y.: M. E. Sharpe, 1990); Robert Kleinberg, *China's "Opening" to the Outside World: The Experiment with Foreign Capitalism* (Boulder, Colo.: Westview Press, 1990); and chap. 9 in this volume.

58. For a graphic presentation of this change in China's assessments, see *Shijie zhishi* [World Knowledge] No. 21 (1985):9.

59. See Shijuro Ogata and Paul Volker, et al., *Financing an Effective United Nations: A Report of the Independent Advisory Group on U.N. Financing* (New York: Ford Foundation, 1993), p. 32, and Tim Weiner, "C.I.A. Says Chinese Economy Rivals Japan's," *NYT*, August 1, 1993, p. 6.

60. World Bank, *World Developmemt Report 1992*, p. 256.

61. Xinhua, July 8, 1993, in FBIS-China, July 12, 1993, p. 16. For a more detailed analysis, see chap. 11 in this volume.

62. The United States, however, has questioned the need for such high levels of lending to China in light of Beijing's $41 billion in foreign exchange reserves and large trade surplus. See Gene Linn, "U.S. Treasury Official Challenges Bank on Loans to China," *Journal of Commerce*, May 6, 1992, p. 2A.

63. China's aid commitments have fluctuated over the years. Though there have been several turning points, one fact is indisputable: China has been by far the largest non-OPEC (Organization of Petroleum Exporting Countries) Third World country donor, with a cumulative total of $9.3 billion in bilateral aid in the period 1953–1985. For a most comprehensive study, see Organization for Economic Cooperation and Development, *The Aid Programme of China* (Paris: OECD, March 1987).

64. See "China and the Third World: Eternal Friends?" *China News Analysis* (Hong Kong) No. 1412 (June 15, 1990), Table 2, p. 6.

65. Hong Kong Agence France Presse in English, in FBIS-China, October 16, 1989, p. 64.

66. See *The Economist* (London), April 10, 1993, p. 112; Xinhua in FBIS-China, March 17, 1993, p. 57.

67. For details, see John Frankenstein, "China's Asian Trade," in Joint Economic Committee, *China's Economic Dilemmas in the 1990s*, pp. 873–894.

68. See Crane, *The Political Economy of China's Special Economic Zones*.

69. Nicholas D. Kristof, "China's Newest Partner: South Korea," *NYT*, April 5, 1993, pp. D1, D6.

70. See Xinhua in FBIS-China, December 4, 1992, p. 25, and "Statistical Communiqué of the State Statistical Bureau of the PRC on the 1992 National Economic and Social Development," *BR* 36:10 (March 8–14, 1993):37.

71. United Nations Development Program, *Human Development Report 1992* (New York: Oxford University Press, 1992), pp. 52–54; Transnational Corporations and Management Division, Department of Economic and Social Development, United Nations, *World Investment Report 1992* (New York: United Nations, 1992).

72. Xinhua, February 18, 1993, in FBIS-China, February 18, 1993, p. 32.

73. China now releases 9.5 percent of global greenhouse-gas emissions, following the United States and the former Soviet Union but ahead of Japan, India, and Brazil. It is estimated that China generates 50 percent of the sulphur ion emissions that cause acid rain in Japan. See Robert Delfs, "Poison in the Sky: China Tops List of Acid Rain Suspects," *FEER*, February 4, 1993, p. 16.

74. For further analysis and documentation of Chinese global environmental diplomacy, see Samuel S. Kim, *China In and Out of the Changing World Order* (Princeton, N.J.: Center of International Studies, Princeton University, 1991), pp. 40–42.

75. Xinhua, April 24, 1993, in FBIS-China, April 26, 1993, p. 34.

76. For the full text of the Beijing Declaration embodying these principles and preconditions, see *BR* 34:27 (July 8–14, 1991):10–14.

77. See *The Economist* (London), May 15, 1993, pp. 15, 83, and Sheryl WuDunn, "As China Leaps Ahead, the Poor Slip Behind," *NYT*, May 23, 1993, p. 3, and International Monetary Fund, *World Economic Outlook* (Washington, D.C.: IMF, May 1993), pp. 8, 116–119.

78. Philip Snow, *The Star Raft: China's Encounter with Africa* (Ithaca, N.Y.: Cornell University Press, 1988), pp. 206–212.

79. Lucian Pye, "China: Erratic State, Frustrated Society," *Foreign Affairs* 69 (Fall 1990):60.

PART THREE

Policies and Issues

8

Force and Diplomacy: Chinese Security Policy in the Post–Cold War Era

PAUL H.B. GODWIN

In the late 1960s, China's military weakness demanded a critical review of Beijing's defense and foreign policies.[1] The need to deter a threatening Soviet Union ultimately caused Beijing to reject a policy of largely self-imposed isolation that over a decade had left China weak and vulnerable. Rapprochement with the United States in 1972 led finally to Beijing's call for a loose coalition of states opposed to "hegemonistic" goals of the USSR. The process of shifting from rapprochement with the United States to an anti-Soviet global coalition was not without its own divisive disputes.[2] Nonetheless, by the late 1970s, China was not only leaning toward the United States but encouraging the formation of an "antihegemonistic" front based on the United States as the "best-qualified country" to block what Beijing saw as the expansionist objectives of Soviet foreign policy.[3]

In 1981, even as the advantages of this strategy were being proclaimed in the Chinese press, Beijing began to show sensitivity to charges that China was dependent upon the United States for its security against the USSR[4] and that its links with the United States and Western powers had undermined its commitment to the Third World.[5] The dissension between Washington and Beijing that emerged in the early years of the Reagan administration over arms sales to Taiwan and the problems associated with technology transfers and trade restrictions served merely to exacerbate growing tensions in Sino-American relations.

As these problems were developing. policy makers in Beijing were beginning to perceive a shift in the balance of military power between Moscow and Washington. Beijing concluded not only that the balance of military power was shifting but that the edge passing to the United States would continue into the 1990s and perhaps into the twenty-first century.[6] A firmer U.S. policy toward the USSR made it easier for China to soften its relations with the Soviet Union in 1982 and to reopen negotiations on the issues that divided them.

As China was restructuring its relations with the USSR and the United States, analysts in Beijing were reevaluating their view of the long-term dynamics of global politics. Their reassessment concluded that the global influence of both the United States and the Soviet Union was declining and would continue to do so into the 1990s. The importance of their economies would decrease as those of Japan, Western Europe, and the Third World became stronger. Consequently, the dominant pattern of future global political dynamics was seen as multipolar.[7] This multipolarity, however, was interpreted by China's security analysts as containing quite specific dangers. Whereas the balance of power between the United States and the USSR, although favoring the United States, would not permit either to conduct war with the other, therefore minimizing the probability of a world war, the growing military strength of local and regional powers would increase the incidence of local wars.[8]

Beijing's interpretation of the global military balance led to the conclusion that the military capabilities of the superpowers in Europe and Asia had created a stalemate between them. As a consequence, China was not faced with a major military threat, and the trends of global politics indicated that this low-threat environment would continue into the twenty-first century. A low-threat security environment permitted Beijing to deemphasize the military component of its security policy and focus on political strategies consonant with its interpretation of the enduring trends in world politics.

In the spring of 1985, the Central Military Commission (CMC) of the Central Committee of the Chinese Communist Party ordered a critical change in the strategic guidance directing the People's Liberation Army's (PLA's) military strategy and training. The new guidance directed the armed forces to refocus their strategy formulation and operational training away from preparation for an "early, major, and nuclear war" and toward what the CMC declared the most likely form of conflict in the foreseeable future—local limited war (*jubu zhanzheng*) around China's borders.[9]

The "strategic shift" directed by the 1985 CMC meeting was announced more than a year prior to Gorbachev's July 1986 speech in Vladivostok, and therefore there is no connection between the Soviet Union's implementation of a more conciliatory policy toward China and the change in Beijing's threat perceptions. The central factor was Beijing's assessment that there had been a shift in the global power balance over the years 1978–1985. By the mid-1980s, Beijing saw the military threat to China as very low and judged that its national military strategy should be focused on military contingencies on its periphery. The CMC's directive to China's armed forces remains in force today within a drastically changed security environment.

Defining the Post–Cold War
Security Environment

The May 1989 Deng-Gorbachev summit in Beijing formalizing the normalization of Sino-Soviet relations was swiftly followed by the collapse of the Soviet empire in Eastern Europe that fall and the disintegration of the USSR over the years 1990–1991. These events came as a distinct shock to Beijing. The balanced and

steady deterioration of superpower influence in the international system anticipated by China's security analysts had not occurred. What is more, the devastat-
ingly swift military victory by an American-led multinational coalition in the
Gulf War suggested that the United States had become the world's preeminent
diplomatic and military power. This event recast China's anticipated multipolar
international system as one containing the potential for unipolarity dominated by
the United States, while the bloody suppression of demonstrators around
Tiananmen Square during the early morning hours of June 4, 1989, condemned
China as a pariah state in the eyes of the West. There were no major military
threats to China's security, but Beijing faced a far more complex international environment than it had anticipated in the years since 1985.

The potential role of the United States is central to Chinese analysts' views of
the emerging international system. Although the Cold War rationale for the Sino-
American alignment had weakened considerably with the revisions in Soviet security policy undertaken by Gorbachev, the disintegration of the USSR removed
any remaining leverage the Chinese might have retained within the so-called strategic triangle. This situation, combined with what many Chinese analysts interpreted as the American objective of building a post–Cold War collective security
system dominated by the United States, created a "new hegemonism" in the international system.[10]

Since the Gulf War, Chinese analysts examining the U.S. role in the post–Cold
War world have focused very specifically on the challenges to American hegemony in a world in which the United States is the only superpower.[11] In essence,
these analysts seek to demonstrate that the pattern of multipolarity that they have
anticipated since the early 1980s continues to emerge and that, no matter how
powerful the United States may be, it cannot prevent the redistribution of global
power into a multipolar pattern.

The role of military power in this emerging multipolar system is viewed by
Chinese analysts as less important than it was in the years of direct Cold War
competition but still significant. In the twenty-first century, comprehensive national strength, the nation's economic, technological, and scientific capabilities,
will become the most important measure of its power. The anticipated technological revolution of the next decade will have a fundamental effect on all phases of
economic and military development.[12]

The importance of the technological facet of warfare was underscored by the
speed of the Iraqi military collapse in the face of overwhelming American air
power and American operational and technological superiority in the ground
war. This brought into sharp focus the position taken by the Chinese armed
forces some seven or more years before: that on the modern battlefield technology
plays an absolutely critical role. The Gulf War was precisely the type of warfare—
limited in objectives and scope, intense, and brief—that the Chinese armed forces
were charged with preparing for in Beijing's 1985 redirection of its national military strategy.[13]

Clearly present as an undertone throughout the many Chinese appraisals of
the post–Cold War international system is the anxiety stemming from the reality
that China no longer wields the influence it did when the Cold War dominated
global politics.[14] Although the Soviet menace has evaporated, the leverage the

Cold War once provided China in Moscow and Washington has also disappeared. China therefore entered the post–Cold War era with its influence seriously curtailed even as Beijing's concern over its future role in this era was increased by the rise of American "hegemonism." That Chinese analysts predict that the U.S. goal of dominating the post–Cold War world will ultimately founder on the rocks and shoals of multipolarity does not appear to ease Beijing's concerns.

China and Asia:
The Immediate Security Environment

In his June 1992 address to the New Zealand Institute of International Affairs, Foreign Minister Qian Qichen contrasted the relative stability of the Asia-Pacific region with the turbulence of the Middle East and the territorial, ethnic, and religious disputes found in Europe and the republics of the former USSR. He talked positively about the potential for peaceful settlement of the Cambodian conflict, the process of reconciliation on the Korean peninsula, and a solution to the Afghanistan question. The prospects for peaceful settlement in these disputes were bolstered, in Qian's view, by the political stability and dramatic economic development of the region as a whole.[15] A May 1992 analysis in *Liberation Army Daily*, the official newspaper of the PLA, came to similar conclusions, classifying the political stability and military situation in the region as the best it has been since World War II.[16] Noting that the interests of the United States, Russia, Japan, and China converged in the Asia-Pacific region, the author concluded that the "military pattern" would be one of mutual cooperation. A similar pattern of cooperation was predicted for Southeast Asia, where the Association of Southeast Asian Nations (ASEAN) states (Thailand, Malaysia, Singapore, the Philippines, Indonesia, and Brunei) were perceived as working toward greater security cooperation.

Views such as these do not, however, go unchallenged. Other Chinese analysts assert that there is little room for optimism despite the potential demonstrated by easing political and military tensions in Southeast and Northeast Asia. Dangers in Asia had little to do with the global conflict between the USSR and the United States. The end of the Cold War and a reduced military presence by the former Soviet Union and the United States may result in regional arms races as more traditional mutual distrust surfaces within the region. The issues inhibiting solutions to the Cambodian situation and Korean reunification cannot be easily overcome, they contend. What is more, Japan's economic strength and its intention to play the role of a major political power may well become the source of aspirations to play a major military role, especially if the United States reduces its forces in the region too quickly.[17]

The contrasting views presented in Chinese official statements and journals raise the distinct possibility that the radical change in China's security environment created by the collapse of the USSR has generated dissonance among China's security analysts and in Beijing. Although there is clear recognition that China's security environment is now far less threatening than it has been for the past hundred years, the future stability of the Asia-Pacific region is disputed. The sources of this disagreement are the potential roles to be played by the United States and Japan.

The United States and Japan

U.S. security policy in Asia is of fundamental concern to Beijing because of its links to and influence over the future role of Japan in the region. Equally significant, however, are U.S. influence over the future of Taiwan, developments on the Korean peninsula, settlement of the Cambodian impasse, the future security policies of ASEAN and the Indochina states, and developments in South Asia.

Whereas China is confident that its northern borders are secure and that Russia will not present a viable military threat for at least a decade, Japan's potential role in Asia is of special concern to China's security analysts. China's fears of Japan have been evident for many years, but with the United States committed to force reductions in the region, the potential for Japan to become a major military power in Asia has received increased attention. The U.S.-Japanese linkage is seen as especially important in restraining what many Chinese analysts see as Japan's "natural" evolution into a military power.

There does seem to be a consensus among Chinese analysts, although not necessarily supported by those who focus specifically on military security issues, that the security treaty between Washington and Tokyo will remain in force for at least the next decade and will continue to restrain any rapid expansion of Japanese military power. For the United States, the security treaty is seen as a way of constraining Japan and retaining a military presence in the region that preserves American standing as a major military and political power.[18] Nonetheless, Chinese analysts remain wary of Japan's future role in Asia and are concerned that the Washington-Tokyo bond could fray. Chinese concern over Japan's potential to play a major military role in Asia was seen in Beijing's response to the Japanese government's efforts to pass legislation permitting Japanese forces to participate in UN peacekeeping operations. Although recognizing that Tokyo was under intense pressure from the United States, some Chinese commentaries insisted that the legislation was designed to shatter Japan's constitutional limitation on dispatching Japanese forces overseas, thereby preparing the way for Japan to fill the vacuum to be created by the reduction of Russian and American forces in the region.[19]

Other Chinese Security Concerns in Asia

Chinese concerns are not limited to Japan. India is viewed as increasing its military capabilities through the acquisition of more advanced weapons from Russia, France, and Switzerland. Some analysts believe that the Indian navy will increase its capabilities by augmenting its force of missile frigates and submarines and producing a 47,000-ton aircraft carrier in cooperation with France. In addition, India is seen as potentially developing strategic nuclear weapons with a range of 5,000 kilometers.[20]

The ASEAN states are viewed as changing their primary military focus from internal security to protection of their maritime interests. These changes are accompanied by increased defense cooperation within and without ASEAN itself. Chinese analyses note that this pattern of increased cooperation—including joint naval patrols, information exchanges, joint training and exercises—was accompanied by increased defense spending of about 5 percent throughout the 1990s.[21]

South Korea is also viewed as engaged in a rapid force modernization program. A Chinese analysis pointed out that South Korea has allocated some U.S.$24.03 billion to purchase arms and equipment from the United States and other sources in the years 1990–1995. These purchases include light, medium, and heavy transport helicopters, 120 F-16 fighters, most assembled in South Korea, 5 submarines, and 10 destroyers.[22]

Chinese security analysts are therefore reflecting the views expressed by Beijing's leaders that the transition to a post–Cold War world creates turbulence and instability. Although trends in Asia are primarily positive and moving toward political stability and continued economic growth, there remain sources of tension. China's diplomatic skills have been employed in defusing tension through efforts to resolve border issues with India, Russia, and the new Central Asian states. Similarly, China now has diplomatic relations with all the states of Southeast Asia for the first time since 1949. Nonetheless, Beijing's conservative military leaders continue to focus on the potential for conflict in China's complex border areas.

Chinese Defense Policy and Military Modernization

No state in the region can threaten China with the military capabilities demonstrated by the United States in the Persian Gulf War. Whereas China's military analysts can analyze that particular conflict and stress the importance of high technology in future wars, there is no indication that China faces such a war in the foreseeable future. Even though many Asian states are acquiring advanced weapon systems, they are not purchasing them in quantities that present a threat to China. Furthermore, although Russian military capability in East Asia remains a cause for caution, Moscow's domestic difficulties are viewed as removing that potential threat from emerging at any time within the decade.

China is the only Asian power with a triad of sea-, air-, and land-based nuclear weapons. It also maintains Asia's largest air, ground, and naval forces. Since the 1985 decision changing its military strategy, these forces have been systematically trained to conduct limited war on the periphery. The most significant constraints faced by these forces lie in their inability to conduct sustained military operations far from China and the relatively low technological level of their weapon platforms, systems, and equipment. For the most part, China's forces deploy weapons based on technologies from the 1950s or early 1960s. Although these limitations affect the vast majority of China's military systems, in the past decade there has been an upgrading of Chinese military technology from a variety of sources, including the United States, France, Britain, Italy, and Israel. Most troublesome to Asia and the United States are China's emerging military technology linkages with Russia.

Despite the generally low technology of their weapons and equipment, their sheer numbers and the deployment of nuclear weapons make Beijing's armed forces the most powerful in the region. Japan's Self-Defense Forces certainly have major technological advantages over China's forces but lack the numbers required to present a major threat to the PRC. Moreover, Japan does not deploy nuclear forces. India's armed forces, although large (but not as numerous as Beijing's) and equipped with more sophisticated weapons than China's, tend to be deployed primarily against Pakistan. India does have a nascent nuclear weapons program and is developing the capability to produce ballistic missiles that could carry nuclear warheads. For the moment, however, it is not known to deploy nuclear weapons in any form.

The role of the armed forces in China's security policy cannot, however, be analyzed solely from the perspective provided by speculative current and near-term military threats. To do so would miss a critical component of China's defense policy and military logic. China's ancient and modern history has created a strategic culture that is critical to Beijing's view of the world.

China's Strategic Culture

When the People's Republic emerged in the earliest days of the Cold War, its leaders brought with them traumatic memories of China's inability to determine its own fate in the preceding hundred years. China viewed itself then, as it does now, as the victim of Western and Japanese imperialism. In the nineteenth century, China fell prey to an imperialist external world because political decay, technological backwardness, and economic weakness had eliminated any capability it had had to defend itself. This frailty was in stark contrast to Chinese elites' vision of the Middle Kingdom as a major world power built on a superior culture extending back for millennia. Nationalism as much as Marxism-Leninism drove China's vision of its role in the world in the years following 1949. Chinese leaders then as now did not seek merely to build a China that would be secure within its Asian regional context. In the realm of global politics, they sought and continue to seek great-power status.

The "hundred years of humiliation," as Chinese refer to the century between the first Opium War and the victory of the Chinese Communist Party (CCP) in the civil war of 1946–1949, made the preservation of national sovereignty and integrity a crucial component of China's strategic culture. The Chinese People's Liberation Army (PLA), as all four armed services are collectively designated, is viewed both as a symbol of China's rebirth as a great power and as a defender of China's integrity and sovereignty. The PLA therefore has within it not only its tradition as a "people's army" born in the crucible of the Chinese Revolution but also the mission to restore China to its former greatness and ensure its independence and security. The defense modernization program under way since 1979 reflects this perspective more than it does a response to an immediate military threat. Asia, however, has a different perspective.

China's military modernization is now viewed with greater suspicion and concern than ever. Throughout Asia and in the United States, serious misgivings focus on three principal areas. There is apprehension that defense budget increases since 1989 reflect the intent to undertake a major military buildup, that China is developing a close relationship with Russia in order to advance the technological modernization of its armed forces, and that the purpose of its defense modernization is to establish a dominant military position within Asia, especially in the South China Sea and over Taiwan.

Defense Budgets, Arms Sales, and Arms Purchases

Immediately following the 1989 Tiananmen Massacre, China's defense budget was increased 14.9 percent over the previous year, following an 8.2 percent increase in 1988. The 1989 increment was the largest since 1979, when the budget was raised by 20.2 percent to defray the cost of the war with Vietnam. The 1989 increment was followed by increases of 14.6 percent in 1990, 13.8 percent in 1991, and 12.2 percent in 1992.[23] Chinese analysts argue that these increases were necessary because the defense budget had not kept pace with the rate of inflation, causing a degradation in soldiers' living conditions, lack of maintenance for buildings and equipment, and a retardation of defense modernization. The consequences were a significantly diminished level of morale and combat effectiveness within the armed forces.[24] When adjusted for the devaluation of its currency over the past decade, China's defense budget has hovered around U.S.$6 billion for the past decade even though in Chinese currency (renminbi [RMB]) the budget climbed from RMB17.87 billion in 1982 to RMB37.0 billion in 1992.

A major complicating factor in estimating the Chinese defense budget is the U.S. intelligence community's belief that the published defense budget may well represent less than 50 percent of actual expenditures. Funds from extrabudgetary sources will include revenue from arms sales and PLA-run businesses and from defense-related allocations in other government expenditures.[25] Nonetheless, these sources agree that, when adjusted for inflation, budgeted defense spending fell 21 percent from 1984 to 1988 but has risen 22 percent since 1988.[26]

A significant but unknown portion of the increase is being used to improve the living standards and morale of the soldiers, which had declined quite dramatically with inflation and as a consequence of the Tiananmen suppression of demonstrators. The cost of retirement benefits has also risen with the reduction in force from 7 million men in the late 1970s to fewer than 4 million today. Equally significant, additional funds are now required for equipment maintenance as the ratios of tanks, armored fighting vehicles, trucks, and other matériel increase as modernization proceeds and to maintain and operate the more advanced equipment being introduced to the air and naval forces. Some amount will also be allocated to increasing the quality of the People's Armed Police, including the equipment for their internal security role.[27]

The defense budget also became a more important source of revenue for weapons, equipment, and technology purchases as Chinese arms sales shrank with the end of the Iran-Iraq War. Chinese arms deliveries to the Third World, primarily Iraq and Iran, were estimated to be U.S.$6.2 billion over the period 1984 to 1987 and U.S.$7.4 billion from 1988 to 1991. Deliveries in 1991 are believed to have been only U.S.$900 million. (Soviet deliveries to the Third World are estimated to have been U.S.$55.8 billion for the period 1984–1991, U.S. deliveries U.S.$42.588 billion, French deliveries U.S.$25.0 billion, and U.K. deliveries U.S.$22.7 billion.)[28] The decline of 80 percent in Chinese arms sales since the end of the Iran-Iraq War is likely to continue because the Gulf War demonstrated the effectiveness of high-technology weaponry against the type of low-technology weapons sold by China. With the end of the Cold War, there is now a virtual glut of advanced weaponry available from the West and the republics of the former Soviet Union.[29]

Chinese purchase of the American F-15-equivalent Su-27 fighter bomber from Russia is one product of this glut. It is believed that this purchase of twenty-four aircraft was made possible by the very favorable terms offered by Russia; evidently Moscow was willing to accept a substantial part of the cost in barter trade.[30] Possibly only 35–40 percent of the cost will be paid in hard currency, the remaining costs to be reimbursed in goods that Russia would otherwise have to purchase with convertible currency on the world market. Russia's need for food and consumer products can be easily filled from China's overstocked shelves.

Of greater concern to Asia and the United States are the indications that Russia and China may well be establishing a more permanent military technology relationship. During his December 17–19, 1992, visit to China, President Yeltsin indicated Russia's willingness to sell "the most sophisticated armaments and weapons" to Beijing.[31] With Russian military needs shrinking, its defense industries are in dire need of sales of existing equipment to keep their production lines open. Furthermore, international agreements to reduce the number of weapons in the European theater will require Moscow to destroy significant quantities of military equipment if it cannot be sold. There are also signs that Ukraine and other Commonwealth of Independent States (CIS) republics are entering the international arms market and offering weapons at reduced prices.[32]

The possibility that a Sino-Russian military technology link of major proportions may be emerging is suggested by frequent exchanges of senior military officials[33] and continuing reports of additional military sales. Among those most frequently mentioned are the purchase of the American F-16-equivalent MiG-29, the MiG-31 advanced long-range interceptor, the Il-76 AWACS (Airborne Warning and Control System aircraft), and air defense missile systems. There were also numerous reports, denied by both Chinese and Russian officials, of China's desire to purchase the 67,000-ton aircraft carrier *Varyag*.[34] Shortage of funds allegedly made it difficult for Russia to complete the contract, and the ship is now a major liability for Ukraine's Chernomorsky shipyard. In addition, there are reports that Russia is considering licensing the production of advanced weapon systems in China.[35]

It would clearly be unwise to overlook the possibility that hard-currency revenue from past arms sales, China's U.S.$43 billion foreign exchange reserve, and favorable terms offered by Moscow make major purchases plausible.[36] The Chinese military has pressed for arms and equipment modernization for many years, and the opportunity to acquire advanced weapons, equipment, technology, and licensed production at bargain-basement prices on excellent terms may well have been an opportunity the Chinese government could not afford to pass up. This would be especially so since the Gulf War so clearly demonstrated the advantages of high-technology arms over the weaponry deployed by the Chinese armed forces. These factors, combined with the current regime's greater dependence on the military following the Tiananmen debacle, could well have caused the leadership in the Zhongnanhai compound to grasp an opportunity that might someday disappear.

Frequent Russian and Western reports of Chinese arms and technology transfers from Moscow are of considerable concern in Southeast Asia and Taiwan. No matter how often Chinese diplomats may stress that a tranquil international environment is essential for Beijing to proceed with its domestic economic goals, Chinese defense policy is carefully and skeptically analyzed throughout Asia. China's defense modernization goals combined with a national military strategy and military exercises devoted to developing the capabilities necessary to conduct limited war on China's periphery arouse severe apprehension in the region, especially in Southeast Asia.

The South China Sea

China's claims to the Spratly and Paracel island groups in the South China Sea involve the PRC in territorial and maritime disputes with Vietnam, Malaysia, the Philippines, and Brunei. Taiwan, on the principle that there is only one China, supports "China's" claims. Beijing's 1974 seizure of (South) Vietnamese-held islands in the Paracel group began the current friction. At the time, the U.S. Seventh Fleet stayed away, despite appeals from Saigon. The U.S. position was that it did not wish to get involved in a territorial dispute. In addition, Washington's rapprochement with Beijing was barely two years old, and there was concern that the new relationship not fall afoul of a minor territorial dispute. With the defeat of Saigon in April 1975, the new Socialist Republic of Vietnam quickly took control of islands in the Spratlys occupied by South Vietnamese troops.

On March 14, 1988, Chinese and Vietnamese naval vessels were involved in a minor engagement in the Spratlys.[37] What probably led to the action was an attempt by Hanoi to observe the construction under way on two small reefs about 250 miles from Vietnam. In December 1987, Beijing had dispatched about a thousand troops with a fifteen-ship flotilla patrolling the islands. A month or so later, construction began on the reefs. Because these reefs are submerged part of the year, China would need the construction to permit continuous occupation. Vietnam does have troops permanently stationed on ten small islands in the area, but China had never established a permanent garrison. Other states actually stationing troops on various disputed islands in the area are Malaysia, the Philippines (on the atolls close to Palawan Island in the eastern Spratlys), and Taiwan (on the biggest island in the group, Itu Aba [Tai Ping]).[38] In recent years, soldiers from Vietnam, Malaysia, and the Philippines have all increased their presence in the islands.[39]

Since August 1990, China has offered to hold the sovereignty question in abeyance while supporting joint economic development of the oil and gas resources believed to be present. However, in February 1992 it passed a territorial law that included the Paracel, Spratly, and Diaoyu (Senkaku) Islands (the latter, off Okinawa, claimed by Japan and the source of minor clashes in the past). The new law specified Beijing's right to use military force in the protection of China's territorial waters and airspace and to punish those who violate them.[40] In May 1992, China leased an oil exploration area adjacent to a Vietnamese offshore oil field to the Crestone Energy Corporation of Denver, Colorado. In June and July, China landed troops on islands claimed by Vietnam. These recent Chinese actions have been interpreted as indications of Beijing's intentions to enforce China's sovereignty claims militarily despite its diplomatic posture. One plausible explanation for the increased military activity throughout the Spratlys is that states laying claim to the reefs and islands undoubtedly seek ensured access to the potential oil and gas reserves. Establishing a military presence in the islands is probably undertaken to ensure that in any future negotiations over oil and gas rights, fishing rights, and the right of naval and commercial passage the claims of each state will have to be recognized.

Whatever China's intentions, the increasing capabilities of the Chinese navy and its marine corps, combined with Beijing's recent assertiveness, have raised concerns throughout the region. The ASEAN foreign ministers' meeting of July 1992 issued a declaration calling for peaceful settlement of the dispute. Chinese Foreign Minister Qian Qichen, present at the ministerial talks, supported the declaration and urged settlement of the disputes through negotiations "when conditions are ripe."[41]

That said, regional anxieties about China's future course in the South China Sea were increased by the purchase of Russian Su-27s, which can reach the area from the Paracels without refueling, and by China's acquisition from Iran a few years ago of midair-refueling capabilities that would give the shorter-legged MiG-29 regional range. These factors, combined with China's construction of better-equipped destroyers and the deployment on Hainan Island of a six-thousand-man marine brigade trained for amphibious operations, have all tended to arouse regional fears.[42]

Taiwan

China's purchases of military equipment from Russia and signs that Sino-Russian military technology cooperation is increasing resulted in a new and major U.S. arms sale to Taipei. Although President Bush's September 1992 agreement to the sale of up to 150 General Dynamics F-16s over the next decade was a response to the coming presidential election and French efforts to sell Taiwan the Mirage 2000, the consequences of growing Sino-Russian military cooperation were also involved in his decision. In fact, Taiwan's armed forces, especially its navy, had already begun to upgrade their capabilities with considerable assistance from the United States. Thus the decision to sell advanced fighter aircraft should be viewed within the context of an already expanding U.S.-Taiwan military relationship.

The Taiwanese surface navy is based upon twenty-two destroyers and nine frigates originally constructed by the United States in the 1940s. Their antisubmarine warfare systems are twenty years old. To upgrade Taipei's capability to defend itself against a PRC naval blockade, the United States has transferred to Taiwan the technology necessary to construct Perry-class frigates with upgraded antisubmarine warfare capabilities. For surface warfare, these ships will use a Taiwan-produced Israeli Gabriel antiship missile system. A twelve-ship construction program is now under way, with the first vessel to be delivered for sea trials in 1993 and subsequent ships scheduled for delivery on an eleven-month schedule. The United States also approved the lease of three Knox-class frigates, which will be turned over to Taiwan as soon as their crews can be trained.[43] This lease was declared "totally unacceptable" by China. Beijing charged the United States with violating the Sino-U.S. Joint Communiqué of August 1982, in which the United

States agreed to limit the quantity and quality of arms sold to Taiwan and ultimately end its arms sales to the island.[44]

Taiwan's efforts to increase its military strength have not been restricted to the United States. In 1991, Taiwan arranged to purchase sixteen unarmed Lafayette-class frigates from France. The first two will be French-built, the remainder constructed in Kaohsiung's yards. Taiwan's European naval shopping list also includes Dutch submarines and German frigates, but thus far these efforts have proved unsuccessful,[45] in large part because of China's resistance and threats to retaliate against governments that permit the sales. When, the in face of Chinese objections, France agreed to sell sixty Mirage 2000-5s to augment Taiwan's air defense capabilities.[46] Beijing ordered the French consulate in Guangzhou closed and banned French companies from participation in the city's projected subway system.[47]

The U.S. agreement to sell Taiwan F-16s was recognized by the Bush administration as a major change in U.S. policy, although its having permitted licensed production of Perry-class frigates and the lease of Knox-class vessels would indicate that the change had been under way for more than a year. What must be noted is that the F-16 sale comes after a decade of frustrated Taiwanese efforts to purchase advanced air defense fighters. In 1982, the Reagan administration refused to sell either the F-16 or the F-20 Tigershark under development by Northrop. Thus the F-16 will replace the island's forty-year-old F-104s and thirty-year-old F-5Es. Administration spokesmen took the position the F-16 sale was required by China's acquisition of Russian Su-27s to ease regional fears about China's growing military power. "We hope it doesn't mean a new arms race," an official observed.[48]

More significant than the air defense capability provided by the F-16 sale is the change in U.S. policy, which demonstrates a heightened U.S. commitment to sustaining Taiwan's military strength at a time when, over the next decade, China's own military power could increase dramatically. Nonetheless, there have been no indications that China intends to use military force to bring Taiwan under its control. Over the past five years, Taiwan has become a major investor in the economic development of South China and is now engaged in far more political and cultural exchanges with the mainland than at any time since 1949.[49] Indeed, the close commercial ties between Taiwan and the mainland, increasing trade ties, and indirect political contacts through a variety of ad hoc political fora on both sides of the Taiwan Strait all make the use of military force less probable than at any time since 1979, when the United States severed its formal diplomatic ties with Taiwan. The critical change in Taiwan's fortunes is, in fact, tied to Washington's changing perceptions of China's role in its own Asian national security strategy.

Sino-American Relations
in the Post–Cold War Era

Whereas in the days of the Cold War the United States was willing to overlook China's transgressions in many sensitive areas, in the post–Cold War era it believes that it can no longer do so. China's human-rights record and suspicion that Beijing intends to circumvent its responsibilities as signatory to the 1968 Nuclear Non-Proliferation Treaty and its acceptance of the guidelines provided in the

Missile Technology Control Regime have tended to create a series of significant frictions in Sino-American relations.[50] These frictions have served to compound American concerns over what appears to be a significantly enhanced Chinese defense modernization program and Asian reactions to increasing Chinese military capabilities.

The American position on China's recent reassertion of claims to territories in the South and East China Seas has been clearly stated. Assistant Secretary of State for East Asian and Pacific Affairs Richard H. Solomon observed in May 1992 that among the most significant areas of uncertainty in Asia's security "is the future of China's international role and, with it, the future of Sino-American relations."[51] Solomon specifically raised China's territorial claims in the East and South China Seas as among the most unsettling of Asia's security problems. In the same speech he described the American military posture in Asia as providing a balance "to prevent a strategic 'empty space' from developing, to reassure allies, and to provide a working presence in the case of regional contingencies."[52] Perhaps in response to this reference to a military vacuum, Foreign Minister Qian Qichen's speech at ASEAN's July 1992 postministerial conference contained a specific denial that China planned to "fill up the vacuum" created by the post–Cold War diminution of Russian and American forces in the region.[53]

The latest iteration of the Pentagon's East Asia Strategy Initiative (EASI) stresses that a key American post–Cold War objective in the region is to "discourage the emergence of a regional hegemon."[54] Without identifying China as a major military threat to Asia, the EASI's authors do provide measures against which Beijing's future intentions in the region will be assessed, including China's policies toward the Spratly Islands, Vietnam, Taiwan, Hong Kong, and Korea. Particular mention is made of China's readiness to use force in the Spratly dispute.[55]

It is also evident that Beijing now sees the United States as a potential adversary,[56] and there would also seem to be a clear sense in Washington that China now has the potential to be a destabilizing force within Asia. This perception further compounds American apprehensions over Beijing as a likely proliferator of nuclear and missile technology.

Retrospect and Prospect

The driving force for Beijing's military modernization programs is not any sense of an immediate military threat. These programs are a reflection of a strategic culture derived from China's "century of humiliation" and the directly related intent to become a major power in global politics. Military power combined with a vibrant economy is viewed as indispensable for China to regain its status as a major world power and to defend against any military threats to its sovereignty and integrity.

Chinese pronouncements clearly recognize that regional desires for a continuing American military presence in Asia reflect apprehensions over the future policies of Beijing as much as those of Tokyo. In the eyes of many, the balance in China's use of force and diplomacy is swinging toward force. Beijing clearly recognizes this, and this endows its strategists with a profound dilemma.

Current Chinese security analyses state that a U.S. security objective is "to establish a U.S.-dominated new order in the Asia-Pacific region."[57] Despite China's desire for a continued American security relationship with Japan that serves to restrain any future military ambitions Tokyo may harbor, Beijing does not want the United States to continue its dominant military role in the region. Rather, it seeks a future regional security environment in which Beijing plays the preeminent role. It does not yet have the economic and military capability to fulfill such a role and repeatedly denies any intent to pursue a hegemonic policy in Asia. Throughout Asia, these pronouncements are viewed with skepticism, and this skepticism lies behind the demand by many Asian countries that the United States retain a significant military capability in Asia.

Thus Beijing's search for wealth and power as it endeavors to restore China to its proper place in the world generates precisely what it would diminish. Where this dilemma will lead Sino-American relations over the next decade is a troublesome question.

Notes

The opinions expressed in this chapter are those of the author and are not to be construed as those of the National War College, the National Defense University, or any other agency of the U.S. government.

1. See Thomas Gottlieb, *Chinese Foreign Policy Factionalism and the Origins of the Strategic Triangle*, R-1902-NA (Santa Monica, Calif.: RAND Corporation, November 1977).

2. Jonathan Pollack has analyzed the complexities of this dispute in *The Sino-Soviet Rivalry and Chinese Security Debate*, R-2907-AF (Santa Monica, Calif.: RAND Corporation, October 1982).

3. Qi Ya and Zhou Jirong, "Does the Soviet Union Have a Global Strategy?" *Renmin Ribao* [People's Daily], May 20, 1981, in Foreign Broadcast Information Service, *Daily Report—China* (hereafter FBIS-China), May 21, 1981, p. C2.

4. Li Dai, "Independence and China's External Relations," *Shijie Zhishi* No. 19 (1981), in FBIS-China, November 19, 1981, p. A4.

5. See, for example, Xinhua News Agency, August 20, 1981, in FBIS-China, August 24, 1981, p. A3, where opposition to the policies pursued by the United States toward "certain Third World countries" is clearly stated.

6. Banning Garrett and Bonnie Glaser, "From Nixon to Reagan: China's Changing Role in American Strategy," in Kenneth A. Oye, Robert J. Lieber, and Donald Rothchild, eds., *Eagle Resurgent? The Reagan Era in American Foreign Policy* (Boston: Little, Brown 1986), p. 283.

7. Xing Shugang, Li Yunhua, and Liu Yingna, "Soviet-American Balance of Power and Its Impact on the World Situation in the 1980s," *Guoji wenti yanjiu* No. 1 (1983), in FBIS-China, April 21, 1983, pp. A1–12.

8. Zong He, "Changes and Developmental Trends in the International Situation," *Shijie Zhishi* No. 11 (1983), in FBIS-China, July 21, 1983, pp. A1–5.

9. See discussion of the May–June 1985 guidance by Generals Zhang Zhen and Li Desheng at a meeting with the editorial board of *Jiefangjun bao* [Liberation Army Daily] reported in *Ta Kung Pao* (Hong Kong), February 16, 1986, in FBIS-China, February 18, 1986, pp. W11–12.

10. Zhou Jirong, "Trend of Changes in World Pattern," *Liaowang Overseas Edition* (Hong Kong), May 13, 1991, in FBIS-China, May 21, 1991, p. 5.

11. Ibid., p. 4.

12. Chen Feng and Chen Xiaogong, "The World Is in the Transition Period of a New Strategic Pattern Replacing the Old," *Jiefangjun bao*, January 4, 1991, in FBIS-China, January 31, 1991, pp. 11–15.

13. For an analysis of Chinese military discussions of the importance of military technology in limited war, see Paul H.B. Godwin, "Chinese Military Strategy Revised: Local and Limited War," *Annals of the American Academy of Political and Social Science* 519 (January 1992):198–200.

14. For an appraisal of this anxiety, see Nicholas D. Kristof, "As China Looks at World Order, It Detects New Struggles Emerging," *New York Times*, April 21, 1992, pp. A1 and A10.

15. *Newsletter*, Embassy of the People's Republic of China, Washington, D.C., No. 18 (June 22, 1992), p. 2.

16. Li Qinggong, "Regional Military Pattern Experiencing Readjustment-Development Trends of (the) World Military Situation (Part 2)," *Jiefangjun bao*, May 15, 1992, in FBIS-China, May 28, 1992, pp. 31–32.

17. Lu Lin, "Political Outlook of the Asian-Pacific Region in the 1990s," *Shehui Kexue* [Social Sciences] No. 3 (March 1991), in Joint Publications Research Service, China (hereafter JPRS-China), July 29, 1991, pp. 1–4.

18. Feng Zhaokui, "Where Is the U.S.-Japanese Security Treaty Going?" *Shijie Zhishi* No. 20 (October 16, 1990), in Joint Publications Research Service, CAR, November 30, 1990, pp. 1–2; and Guo Xiangang, "Long Contemplated Readjustment: U.S. Posture in Asia-Pacific Region," *Shijie Zhishi* No. 4 (February 16, 1992), in FBIS-China, March 24, 1992, pp. 3–5.

19. Zhang Dalin, "Japan's Bill on Cooperation in UN Peacekeeping Operations," *Guoji wenti yanjiu* No. 2 (April 13, 1992), in FBIS-China, May 22, 1992, pp. 4–10.

20. Ibid., p. 6.

21. Ibid., p. 6.

22. Ibid., pp. 6–7.

23. All data except for the 1992 budget are taken from the state budget reports and reflect reported expenditures rather than allocations. The most recent budget report is to be found in Beijing, Xinhua, April 4, 1992, in FBIS-China, supplement, April 10, 1992, pp. 1 and 4.

24. See, for example, Chen Binfu, "An Economic Analysis of the Changes in China's Military Expenditure in the Last Ten Years," *Jingji Yanjiu* No. 6 (June 20, 1990), in FBIS-China, August 6, 1990, pp. 30–35.

25. James Harris et al., "Interpreting Trends in Chinese Defense Spending," in Joint Economic Committee, Congress of the United States, *China's Economic Dilemmas in the 1990s: The Problems of Reforms, Modernization, and Interdependence*, Vol. 2 (Washington, D.C.: U.S. Government Printing Office, 1991), p. 676.

26. Directorate of Intelligence, *The Chinese Economy in 1991* and *1992: Pressure to Revisit Reform Mounts* (Washington, D.C.: Central Intelligence Agency, July 1992), p. 12.

27. Harris et al., "Interpreting Trends in Chinese Defense Spending," pp. 680–681; Directorate of Intelligence, *The Chinese Economy*, p. 12.

28. Richard F. Grimmett, *Conventional Arms Transfers to the Third World, 1984–1991* (Congressional Research Service, Library of Congress, 92-577 F, July 20, 1992), Tables 2F and 2G, pp. CRS-67–68.

29. Directorate of Intelligence, *The Chinese Economy*, pp. 12–13.

30. Tai Ming Cheung, "Loaded Weapons: China on Arms Spree in Former Soviet Union," *Far Eastern Economic Review* 155:35 (September 3, 1992): 21.

31. Lena Sun, "Russia, China Set Closest Ties in Years," *Washington Post*, December 19, 1992, p. 10.

32. Pavel Felgengauer, "Arms Sales: How Much Are We Selling, To Whom, and How Much?: Contradictions Within the Russian Government—The Opinions of the Parties Involved," *Nezavisimaya Gazeta* (Moscow), July 11, 1992, in Joint Publications Research Service, Central Eurasia: Military Affairs, August 26, 1992, pp. 59–65.

33. For example, Chinese Defense Minister Qin Jiwei visited Russia in August 1992, and Admiral Zheng Ming, director of the navy's equipment and technical department, in July 1992.

34. "Only We Can Afford This Ship," *Rossiyskaya Gazeta* (Moscow), August 12, 1992, in Foreign Broadcast Information Service, Central Eurasia, August 13, 1992, p. 13, reports a specific denial of Japanese press reports by an unnamed "Russian Navy Main Staff expert."

35. See Tai Ming Cheung, "Loaded Weapons," for a summary analysis of these reports.

36. Directorate of Intelligence, *The Chinese Economy*, p. ii.

37. Beijing Domestic Service, March 14, 1988, in FBIS-China, March 14, 1988, p. 8.

38. James L. Tyson, "Peking Actively Asserts Its Claims in Strategic South China Sea," *Christian Science Monitor*, March 16, 1988, p. 11; and Agence France Presse (Hong Kong), March 17, 1988, in FBIS-China, March 17, 1988, pp. 6–7.

39. Nayan Chanda et al., "Treacherous Shoals," *Far Eastern Economic Review* 155:32 (August 13, 1992):14–17.

40. Foreign Broadcast Information Service: *Trends*, February 26, 1992, p. 26.

41. Beijing, Xinhua, July 21, 1992, in FBIS-China, July 22, 1992, p. 1.

42. See Tai Ming Cheung, "Fangs of the Dragon: Peking's Naval Build-up Sparks ASEAN Reaction," *Far Eastern Economic Review* 155:32 (August 13, 1992):19–20, for a discussion of China's military capabilities in the region.

43. Julian Baum, "Steel Walls: Taiwan's Naval Modernisation Gathers Pace," *Far Eastern Economic Review* 155:27 (July 9, 1992):9–11.

44. Beijing, Xinhua, July 25, 1992, in FBIS-China, July 27, 1992, p. 3.

45. Baum, "Steel Walls," p. 11.

46. Taipei China News Analysis, September 4, 1992, in FBIS-China, September 4, 1992, p. 54.

47. "France Confirms Sale of Fighter Jets to Taiwan," *Wall Street Journal*, January 8, 1993, p. 10.

48. Jim Mann, "U.S. to Explain Taiwan Arms Deal to China," *Los Angeles Times*, September 3, 1992, p. 2.

49. For a summary of these exchanges, see Julian Baum, "Flags Follow Trade," *Far Eastern Economic Review* 155:37 (September 17, 1992):20–21, and Carl Goldstein, "The Bottom Line," *Far Eastern Economic Review* 155:37 (September 17, 1992):23–24.

50. For a detailed and critical analysis of China's record of missile and nuclear technology proliferation, see Shirley A. Kan, *Chinese Missile and Nuclear Proliferation: Issues for Congress* (Congressional Research Service, Library of Congress, IB92056, June 24, 1992).

51. Richard H. Solomon, assistant secretary for East Asian and Pacific Affairs, "American and Asian Security in an Era of Geoeconomics," address before the Pacific Rim Forum, San Diego, Calif., May 15, 1992, in *U.S. Department of State Dispatch* 3:21 (May 25, 1992):412.

52. Ibid., p. 411.

53. Beijing, Xinhua, July 21, 1992, in FBIS-China, July 22, 1992, p. 1.

54. Presidential Report, *A Strategic Framework for the Asian Pacific Rim: Report to Congress 1992*, prepared by the Office of the Assistant Secretary of Defense for International Security Affairs (East Asia and Pacific Region), p. 13.

55. Ibid., pp. 10–11.

56. Hideya Yamamoto, "Qian Policy Speech Says U.S. 'Seeking Hegemony,'" *Sankei Shimbun* (Tokyo), November 11, 1992, p. 1.

57. Guo Xiangang, "The U.S. Readjusts Its Strategy Toward Asia and the Pacific," *Xiandai Guoji Guanxi* No. 2 (April 13, 1992), in JPRS-China, August 11, 1992, p. 8.

9

Interdependence in China's Foreign Relations

THOMAS W. ROBINSON

Interdependence has been an aspect of human activity since the dawn of civilization. People and institutions have always had to depend on each other to survive or to achieve their goals. So interdependence can hardly be controversial and has for decades been recognized as a fact of international relations and foreign policy,[1] but differences in interpretation or emphasis do arise. Is interdependence sometimes inequitable, so that the "balance of dependence" too heavily favors one partner? To what extent does the spillover of economic interdependence into the political-military and cultural spheres complicate equity calculations as well as engender dangers of overall dependence when gross national power differences are too great? Interdependence is clearly multifaceted, and its assessment is made problematic by differences in the units of calculation and differences between fields. Some fields—for instance, the cultural—are impossible to quantify, and even such traditional fields as the military lack an agreed-on set of measures. How, in the face of these problems, can decision makers make policy on important matters of national security and foreign relations?

There are five types of answers to these questions, each of which applies to China's foreign relations and has at some time or other been recognized by Chinese policy analysts. Most of these stem from economic theory, where the idea of interdependence is most highly developed, but have application to other areas of interdependence—scientific, political, national security, and cultural.

Traditional international trade theory[2] does not refer to "interdependence" but instead concentrates on the idea of mutual advantage. Nations trade only when each gains, and attention centers on comparative specialization, terms of trade, the consequent linking for mutual benefit of internal economies, and the distortions produced by tariffs and other government restrictions. Nations are assumed to be rational and to trade only when their self-interest so dictates. The terms of trade, set by the marketplace, are by definition mutually advantageous, even if internal markets are severely affected and even if specialization leads some countries to remain permanently underdeveloped.

Dependency theory[3] argues that the terms of trade between more- and less-developed nations are by nature unequal in retarding industrial growth in the latter. The supply of raw materials or low-wage goods for industrial countries consigns underdeveloped nations to permanent dependence. Industrial countries ensure the continuation of this relationship by the use of transnational corporations, support of authoritarian governments, undue interference in others' internal affairs, and use of superior power, knowledge, and wealth. This otherwise self-perpetuating system can be meliorated only by deliberate trade concessions to the less-developed nations, artificial increases in raw-materials prices, expanded concessionary capital transfers, and reduced foreign control of the domestic economy through nationalization or other restrictions. Trade must therefore be subordinated as a value to equity and development. In particular, the assumed alliance between "imperialist" Western governments and local authoritarians to keep the people in a servile position must by broken by direct action. This means the end of colonialism and "neo-colonialism." Genuine interdependence is thus impossible until political and economic equality has been attained everywhere.

Developmentalism[4] starts with the same factual base but draws optimistic conclusions. The removal of economic and political barriers will naturally generate industrial growth through the market mechanism. The crucial impediments are internal—traditional attitudes, customs, and institutions, which must be removed for progress. The goal is Western-style capitalism, which should be universally embraced. The important internal prerequisite is political and social stability, best supplied initially by authoritarian governments, which are well equipped to Westernize their societies through free trade, gradual elimination of economic barriers, encouragement of foreign investment, and technology transfer. Export-led growth strategies are the engine of economic modernization. Internationalization of the economy and interdependence thus become synonymous. The Japanese economy between 1868 and 1931 is the best example.

Export-led growth[5] straddles dependency theory and developmentalism by claiming to discover a middle road between political-economic servitude and rapid development. It combines state capitalism, forcible maintenance of very low wages, the unfortunate necessity of authoritarianism, high barriers against manufactured imports, high international economic risk taking, massive acceptance of foreign loans but not always investment (unless highly controlled), artificially low, controlled exchange rates, and aggressive marketing in wide-open Western markets. A deliberately high balance of payments is financed by a continuous flow of new loans and a constant decline of the exchange rate until sufficient sales in developed countries make it possible to repay them. Once a reasonably high gross national product is attained, economic barriers can be lowered, authoritarianism can yield to a more democratic system, and interdependence can be achieved. Interdependence thus becomes a long-term goal rather than a means. The best examples of this orientation are said to be the four Asian "dragons"—South Korea, Taiwan, Hong Kong, and Singapore.

Interdependence[6] sees innate virtue in the notion itself, and not only in economics. Political, cultural, and security interdependence are also both inevitable and good, as is the idea of positive, mutually dependent linkages among them. No conclusions are drawn as to the broader foreign relations effects of interdependence, as problems of dependency would tend to disappear in a world where political and economic boundaries were less and less significant. The best presumed illustration of this orientation is the growth of so-called natural economic regions not coterminous with political boundaries, such as "Greater China" (the Mainland, Hong Kong, and Taiwan).

Chinese Perceptions of Interdependence

At the time of the end of the Cultural Revolution and the death of Mao Zedong in 1976, Chinese discussion of interdependence would have been remarkable, and indeed there was none. China perceived its role on the world stage mostly as strategic, in connection with American-led deterrence of Soviet military expansionism. The central Chinese domestic priority, economic self-sufficiency, remained unchanged. But the return to power of Deng Xiaoping and his reformist associates in 1977 brought a new economic growth strategy based on the notions of release of pent-up economic forces at home and access abroad to the many benefits of the Western capitalist economic system.[7] Along with these important changes gradually emerged an interest in the various ways of viewing interdependence. By the end of the 1980s, Chinese analysts and policy makers were well acquainted with the basic ideas of interdependence, and after a hiatus following the Tiananmen incident of 1989 they viewed them with renewed interest.[8]

Contemporary Chinese attitudes toward interdependence are strongly conditioned by the country's historic relationship to the outside world. During the long dynastic period, Chinese rulers looked on foreigners, their countries, their cultures, and their material attainments as interesting but inferior. This attitude produced the well-known tributary relationship, which by nature lacked essential attributes of interdependence. Only gradually and under Western pressure in the nineteenth and twentieth centuries did this attitude change in the direction of equality in international relations. As China fell increasingly far behind the West in terms of military power and its dynasty declined, it became increasingly dependent on the outside, found itself more and more influenced by foreign ideas and practices, and began to lose its self-respect.[9] Under the circumstances, no positive orientation toward trade, foreigners, cooperative exchanges, and outside investment and technology transfer could be expected to emerge. The natural conclusion was to strengthen the country materially by taking what was necessary from the West, to build a powerful country through China's own efforts, and to shun the nonmaterial aspects of Western societies as inherently evil.

Even under the Nationalist regime this attitude prevailed, and the Communists added only the ideological justification of opposing "neocolonialism," praising self-reliance, and stressing supposed anti-imperialist unity among socialist countries and solidarity between China and the Third World. These were the leitmotifs of Chinese foreign policy during the Mao era, and interdependence could have no currency during that period. With the 1978 Deng-led reforms, however, interdependence was more positively regarded, since those reforms stressed investment, trade, technology transfer, and scientific exchange. It was, however, by no means fully approved. The 1980s campaigns against "spiritual pollution" and "bourgeois liberalization"[10] and in favor of self-reliance all rejected it. As a matter of fact, interdependence was generally viewed as a one-way street, with the West supposed to provide the benefits of interdependence to China without imposing the political, economic, military, and cultural costs. The upshot, for the most part until the mid-1980s, was the adoption of a neocolonialist/dependency approach to interdependence.

The peak of pre-Tiananmen reformism in China also brought a pronounced tilt toward interdependence and its benefits. Now analysts recognized the absolute necessity of constantly keeping the door to the outside wide open, the close connection between internal economic reform and external interdependence, the necessity to join regional and global international economic organizations, and the negative effects of autarky and excessive self-reliance. It was also recognized that interdependence is mutually beneficial—that other nations' development and well-being are inherently desirable and not threatening to China and that nations, through interdependence, can pursue interests in common.[11]

Tiananmen dealt a setback to positive Chinese inclinations toward interdependence, as the regime reverted to extreme emphasis on self-reliance and resistance to Western cultural "pressure." But even then it was recognized that China could no longer isolate itself from the international community. Chinese spokespersons asserted that China had become too important to the world economy as a supplier of raw materials, a locus for Western investment, and a major trading nation for any American-led attempt to punish and isolate it to succeed. Thereupon Chinese pronouncements evolved toward developmentalism by stressing the responsibility of developed nations toward Third World countries such as China. Now the stress was on resolving the debt crisis, reversing the flow of financial resources, eliminating developed countries' trade barriers, and generally raising growth rates. In retrospect, the period of about a year and a half after Tiananmen appears to have been only a temporary interruption of the evolution of Chinese support for interdependence.[12]

Since then, Chinese statements on the subject have become increasingly favorable:

- Interdependence is described as not only a fact but indispensable to China's economic development, such components of it as economic cooperation, capitalist investment in China, exchanges, international cooperation in producing goods and services, and similar cooperation between Chinese and foreign "sister" cities and provinces all being viewed with favor.
- Interdependence is admitted to include the international division of labor, including internationalization of production, economic regionalism, linked growth rates, and parallelism in interest rates set by the capitalist world, and these facets are also supported.
- Interdependence is said to promote peace and security by breaking down the barriers between economics and national security affairs and by promoting diplomatic cooperation and recognition.
- To the Five Principles of Peaceful Coexistence—which have always had an anti-interdependence tinge—are now added the ideas of a New Interna-

tional Economic Order as innately good and the principle of cooperative prosperity.

- North-South relations are viewed in the context of the mutual benefits flowing from the exchange of Chinese resources, investment sites, inexpensive labor, and markets for other countries' capital, technology, and expertise. At the same time, Chinese writers recognize the mutual interpenetration of stabilization of commodity prices and debt repayment in the global South and combating protectionism, lowering interest rates, and pushing up growth rates in the North.
- The post-Tiananmen sanctions are criticized as anti-interdependence. Particularly, deprivation of most-favored-nation status is viewed as leading to exploitation and one-sided benefits.
- There remains the notion that the North owes a debt to the South stemming from the historically based inequity between the two groups of countries. This is manifested in connection with the emerging issue of environmental protection, a set of issues (like all "global issues") inherently interdependent in terms of approach and solution. If developed nations wish to solve such problems, it is argued, they will have to provide developing nations, including China, with funds and technological assistance. Moreover, environmental concerns cannot be allowed to interfere with the inherent right of developing nations to grow as rapidly as possible.[13]

Comparing these notions with the five general approaches to interdependence described earlier, it appears that, whereas Chinese writers and policy spokespersons do not entirely support traditional international trade theory, they have moved much closer to an appreciation of the mutuality of benefits stemming from trade; they are still taken by the dependency argument (the basis of the North-South emphasis), have greatly modified their initial opposition to developmentalism as too capitalist-oriented and too dependent on external political and social influences, have leaned toward the export-led-growth orientation as the success of the South China coast/Hong Kong/Taiwan area has more and more driven the overall Chinese economy, and have come down strongly in favor of interdependence so long as it favors China. In short, there has been a great deal of movement toward understanding and approval of the notion of economic interdependence in the post-Mao reform era. Indeed, the range of views among Chinese writers is at least as wide as can be found in most other countries, including most Western nations, that have been concerned with the question.

The Facts of China's Economic Interdependence

In the current international environment, all nations are interdependent to some degree. As for China, neither isolation nor complete dependence is a workable or desirable policy. What Beijing must do is find a middle ground, maximizing the benefits of interdependence while minimizing the risks. Moreover, its entire economic modernization program rests on its ability to tap the international environment for resources: monetary, technological, and human. Some useful distinctions are nonetheless apparent. First, engagement is not the same as interdependence. China can be part of an international organization or reach out to the international community in some way without necessarily becoming inextricably intertwined with it. It takes advantage of the World Bank and the United Nations for its own purposes without endorsing these institutions' purposes. Second, economic and technological interdependence are not generally symmetrical. Hence, states need not behave in mirror-image fashion toward each other. China and Japan are interdependent in these senses, but to different degrees, and the policies of each toward the other have varied little since long before their interdependence became important. Third, the ultimate test of Chinese interdependence is what happens when China or one of its partners loosens ties. A premise of American policy toward China, for instance, is that if China is enmeshed in a network of international ties it will fear losing them and will avoid unduly angering a major trading partner. It will therefore have a stake in behaving responsibly by international standards. Chinese behavior in the several years after Tiananmen showed that, although the degree of its involvement was less than had been supposed, China was still susceptible to international behavior standards. It modified its foreign economic and diplomatic policies—if not its domestic orientation—in accordance with those standards and slowly worked its way back into general international acceptability.

One measure of Chinese economic interdependence is the substantial growth, in percentage and absolute terms, of its foreign trade. From 1980 to 1989, exports grew from about 27 to 195 billion yuan, while imports grew from 30 to over 200 billion yuan. Following the post-Tiananmen hiatus, this growth resumed, and by 1991 exports were at 375 billion yuan and imports at 333 billion. Another measure is the degree to which China permits foreign investment, including foreign equity participation and foreign management of Chinese plants. China has encouraged the establishment of joint ventures in virtually every industry, some quite large and many foreign-managed. By the end of 1991, direct foreign investment in China totaled $49.6 billion for some twenty-five thousand projects. A third is China's willingness to borrow from foreign commercial and multilateral institutions. Loans give foreigners a say in how the economy is managed and expose China to the vagaries of international financial markets. China has minimized this risk by borrowing within "safe" limits for developing countries and has adeptly managed its external debt. Its debt-to-gross-national-product ratio (16 percent in 1991) is well below the norm for developing countries.

China is not highly interdependent economically if by that term one means exports or imports as a percentage of gross national product. Generally speaking, neither has been much above one-seventh of the total (although both have been rising). If the degree of economic interdependence is defined as the sum of imports and exports as a percentage of gross national product, however, China's "trade dependence" has risen greatly in the last decade, from less than 20 to close to 27 percent (Table 9.1). The comparable figures for other countries in 1991 were about 30 percent for the United States, about 40 percent for Japan, nearly 100 percent for Hong Kong, over 60 percent for Taiwan, about 35 percent for West Germany, and about 60 percent for South Korea. By this definition, then, China was only moderately "trade-dependent," although the degree of such dependence had by the 1990s risen from less than 5 percent historically.[14]

TABLE 9.1   China's Relative Foreign Trade Dependence Since 1976 (billions yuan)

	GNP	Exports	Imports	Exports and Imports	Exports and Imports as % of GNP
1978	358.8	16.76	18.74	35.50	9.89
1979	399.8	21.17	24.29	45.46	11.37
1980	447.0	27.12	29.88	57.00	12.75
1981	477.3	36.76	36.77	73.53	15.41
1982	519.3	41.38	35.75	77.13	14.85
1983	580.9	43.83	42.18	86.01	14.81
1984	696.2	58.05	62.05	120.10	17.25
1985	856.8	80.89	125.78	206.67	24.12
1986	972.6	108.21	149.83	258.04	26.53
1987	1,135.1	147.00	161.42	308.42	27.17
1988	1,401.5	176.76	205.44	382.20	27.27
1989	1,578.9	195.60	219.99	415.59	26.32
1990	1,768.6	293.06	521.23	544.29	32.49
1991	1,975.9	375.04	333.07	708.11	27.90

Sources: China Statistical Yearbook 1989; International Financial Statistics; Zhongguo Jinrong [Chinese Finance]; [China] State Statistical Bureau, *Monthly Bulletin of Statistics*; World Bank, *World Tables; UNCTAD Trade Figures*; International Monetary Fund, *Direction of Trade Statistics Yearbook; China Statistics Monthly*; and *China Economic News.*

Nevertheless, China's imports supply a critical portion of the wherewithal for its industrialization and overall modernization. In contrast, countries at a high level of industrialization produce a larger portion of their modern equipment at home, and hard-currency economies, unlike China's, have less difficulty purchasing needed goods abroad. Therefore, "trade dependence" figures must be modified according to the level of industrial development. Of the many measures of economic modernization, perhaps the most suitable for trade-dependence purposes is the percentage of the population engaged in nonagricultural pursuits. For the United States this figure is more than 98 percent, whereas for China in the early 1990s it was—depending on the definition of "urban"—probably no more than a third. By this measure, China is much more trade-dependent than the United States even though neither nation is near the top of the scale in terms of the percentage of gross national product devoted to trade. Probably China's trade dependence (meaning now the degree to which the country depends on trade to drive economic modernization) is much higher than that of the United States and probably closer to that of South Korea. This is particularly likely in that most of China's growth in the late 1980s and early 1990s occurred in the southern coastal region adjacent to Hong Kong and across the strait from Taiwan, not in the Yangtze (Changjiang) Valley, the Northeast, or the less-developed inland and Northwest provinces, where the slow-growth state-run enterprises are largely located. Some multiplier needs to be attached to trade-dependence figures to take into account the difference in modernization between China and the advanced economies. At the same time, this multiplier is undoubtedly not as high as three to one, which would place China's trade dependence as high as 80 percent. Some composite figure needs to be found that takes into account the fact that China is still a large continental economy that largely produces and consumes its own wealth.

China is linked in both import and export terms with the developed countries of Asia, Europe, and North America but not with the Third World nations of Asia, Africa, and Latin America (Table 9.2). Furthermore, its various regions are differentially interdependent with other nations. The southern coastal provinces, especially Guangdong, Zhejiang, Jiangsu, and Fujian, and some of the coastal cities, especially Guangzhou and increasingly Shanghai, have since 1978 been oriented increasingly toward the international market. Such interdependence spread northward in the later 1980s to encompass Beijing, Tianjin, and Wuhan and by the early 1990s was driving Shandong's economy (thanks to the economic and diplomatic opening to South Korea). Partly as a product of the post-1990 drive to reform state-run industries and the so-called Three-Coasts (the Pacific, the inland Yangzi River, and the inland "coast" of provinces and cities bordering foreign countries) strategy of creating "natural economic regions," economic interdependence has become a feature of large sectors of China.

No figures indicating the degree of such interdependence or its rate of spread are available, but the Chinese press is filled with stories and debates on the efficacy and consequences for China's modernization of the use of trade interdependence as an engine for modernization and for increasing the overall growth rate to near-double-digit levels. This was given additional impetus by Deng Xiaoping's early 1992 "Southern Tour" and the results of the Fourteenth Party Congress later that year, both of which made it clear that trade would continue to be one of the major instruments of further rapid economic modernization (the others being the package of internal economic reforms under the name of the construction of a "socialist market economy" and extension of those reforms to every sector of the internal economy).[15] Thus, the implicit danger of bifurcation of the economy into a modern, foreign-trade-oriented, and interdependent coastal sector and a traditional, internally oriented, and independent inland sector was being addressed directly and, if these various components of the reform program continued to be successful, avoided altogether. The price, however, would be a fully interdependent economy.

Interdependence in Other Areas

China is not merely economically interdependent; it is also interdependent in many other spheres, including science, security, politics, and culture. Chinese scientists have clearly become active participants in the international research community, tapping into the wealth of international scientific literature, attending international conferences, participating in scholarly communications, establishing personal relations with non-Chinese colleagues, and setting up exchange programs in many fields. Both government-to-government and privately funded projects have proliferated to the point that no one can keep track of all that is taking place. During the 1980s, more than seventy thousand Chinese students enrolled in American colleges and universities and probably forty thousand more in other countries. Despite the Tiananmen incident and the reluctance of many students abroad at that time to return home on previous schedules (over a hundred

TABLE 9.2 Direction of China's Foreign Trade Value of Exports/Imports (U.S.$ millions)

	Industrial Countries	Africa	Asia[a]	Europe	Middle East	Western Hemisphere	USSR/CIS and Other Countries
1978	6,094/8,056	533/192	727/450	564/544	661/183	108/458	1,185/1,160
1979	8,708/11,788	603/261	1,044/508	625/747	808/165	229/782	1,353/1,576
1980	12,719/16,561	685/360	1,514/855	773/825	985/357	410/719	1,283/1,484
1981	15,378/16,473	676/375	1,528/796	743/739	1,059/346	506/639	820/923
1982	15,200/14,446	760/261	1,393/1,123	548/661	2,725/272	528/597	707/1,186
1983	15,686/16,330	525/311	1,291/886	539/646	2,742/294	432/1,290	869/1,261
1984	18,202/20,883	543/310	1,552/1,169	507/799	2,435/280	449/888	1,129/1,393
1985	20,617/34,823	421/285	1,493/2,093	754/1,290	1,764/194	501/1,825	1,764/1,901
1986	23,567/35,004	574/254	1,605/2,071	1,034/1,624	2,109/150	363/1,550	2,101/2,530
1987	29,623/35,507	1,230/154	2,121/1,860	1,190/1,393	2,642/279	410/1,161	2,223/2,319
1988	37,127/43,528	1,642/245	2,626/2,677	1,090/1,546	2,089/577	231/1,925	2,748/3,302
1989	42,631/45,806	608/394	3,217/2,803	—	1,410/579	344/2,183	2,866/3,043
1990	51,080/40,249	1,188/357	5,344/5,790	—	1,430/477	640/1,287	2,827/2,159
1991	59,151/50,147	784/376	6,885/7,905	—	1,568/809	567/1,358	2,678/2,516

[a] Hong Kong and Singapore are grouped with the Industrial Countries.

Sources: UN trade statistics; International Financial Statistics; Zhongguo Jinrong [Chinese Finance]; [China] State Statistical Bureau, Monthly Bulletin of Statistics; World Bank, World Tables; UNCTAD Trade Figures; International Monetary Fund, Direction of Trade Statistics Yearbook; China Statistical Yearbook; China Statistics Monthly; and China Economic News.

thousand were estimated to remain in the United States alone in 1992), Beijing continued to send students abroad in large numbers. Given that acquisition of knowledge is the most efficient method of technology transfer and of the introduction of ideas of all sorts into China, this category of interdependence is not only exceedingly important (if impossible to measure quantitatively) but expected to grow.[16]

In the national security realm, China has become interdependent with Asian and globally important nations. Its security has long depended not only on its own efforts but on the structure and processes of Asian and global security as well as on the foreign and national security policies of other nations, especially the United States, other North Atlantic Treaty Organization (NATO) countries, Russia, India, and Japan. During the Cold War, China's security depended on its agility within the American-Chinese-Soviet strategic triangle. Sometimes China played that game well, sometimes not. But its security was not determined by its own efforts alone. With the end of the Cold War in 1989 and the collapse of communism in Eastern Europe and the Soviet Union thereafter, the Soviet security threat declined greatly. China therefore had less need to lean to the American side for security purposes, but it remained security-interdependent not only with the security policies of the remaining superpower, the United States, but also with the rapidly changing structure of power and organization in Asia and elsewhere.[17]

Thus, when the Gulf crisis emerged in late summer 1990 and China found its national security even mildly subverted by a distant Middle East strongman, it looked to interdependence, the principles of the United Nations, and the procedural rules of the Security Council and joined with the other great powers to authorize the use of force against Iraq. In Asia, the Cold War was succeeded by no organized security system; instead, an ad hoc, laissez-faire set of arrangements came into being that bore a structural resemblance to the early-nineteenth-century Concert of Europe. Moreover, large-scale, long-term trends and forces militate in the direction of security interdependence, among them the replacement of bipolarity with multipolarity in Asia and across the globe; the emergence of relative equality in Asia among America, China, Japan, and Russia as great powers and the rapid rise of middle-sized powers (South Korea, Vietnam, Indonesia, Thailand, and India); the revolutions of democratization and marketization; the rise of global issues to foreign policy prominence; the increasing importance of high technology; and even the tendency for Asian states to emphasize domestic matters at the expense of international concerns. Like all other Asian nations, China is subject to these trends and forces. In the middle 1990s, these seemed to favor a cooperative search for new forms of Asian security organization, including the possible creation of somewhat more formal mechanisms for insuring regional security.[18]

China is also politically interdependent. Whether Beijing is able to obtain developmental loans from Europe, Japan, or the United States or from international lending institutions depends on the political attitudes toward China of those nations and the international institutions that they largely control. After Tiananmen, those attitudes soured, resulting in a cutoff or a major slowdown of loans and a sharp decline in investment, trade, technology transfer, and tourism. It was in the hope of reestablishing the flow of such external economic assistance and trade that China in mid-1990 changed its foreign policy orientation to one of co-operation with other countries on many important international issues. Its success in reestablishing contacts with other nations led to its reacceptance as a necessary participant in international life, but further success abroad depends on the continuation of its "good" behavior internationally and nonrepetition of (indeed, repentance for) Tiananmen-like repressions at home. It is for these reasons that China has appeared to bend over backward to appease foreign—especially American—criticism and to refrain, for the while, from the direct use of its newfound and rapidly growing military power in a number of Asian arenas.[19]

Political interdependence means that China is subject to the political transformations associated with economic modernization that are already in advanced stages in South Korea, Taiwan, Thailand, and elsewhere in Asia. Democratization clearly is a necessary (as well as a desirable) resultant of economic development beyond a certain level. With the rise of a new middle class, the devolution of power from the Beijing center to the regions and large cities, the emergence of institutionally based interest-group politics, and the consequent transformation of the Communist Party into an increasingly loose holding corporation for increasingly diverse interests, democratization is becoming more and more likely. And emerging democratization elsewhere in Asia, the continued attraction everywhere of the democratic ideal, and the increasing openness of the country to external influences borne by returning students, visitors, and high-technology communications all make China more susceptible to external political influence.[20] This would not be an example of interdependence, of course, but one of mere dependence were it not for the strong possibility that the Chinese "model" of modernization—economic development first and then, gradually, political democratization after passage through some kind of neo-authoritarian way station—may have some attractiveness for the rest of Asia to the extent that Beijing manages to shrug off its Marxist-Leninist mantle.

Finally, China is culturally interdependent. This too affects Beijing's success in economic development. With its attractive traditional culture, China continues to appeal to many peoples, in Asia and beyond. There is, in effect, an "outflow" of Chinese cultural influences to the rest of the world. This is why, in normal times, large numbers of tourists come to the country and nations such as the United States and Japan take a special interest in the lives of the Chinese people and, other things being equal, try to adopt generally favorable policies toward China. But China has also received a great deal of cultural influence from abroad, particularly in the 1978–1989 and post-1990 open-door periods, via diverse channels that have become impossible to close off. And it has seemed finally to learn—through the failure of the antispiritual-pollution and the antibourgeois-liberation campaigns of the early 1980s, as well as its entire history since 1840—that it is impossible to "cleanse" foreign technology, capital, scientific ideas, and trade of their cultural contents. Thus, China's cultural interdependence has become an admitted fact in the early 1990s and an important factor in the country's economic development and foreign trade.[21] At the same time, it must be noted that China's cultural attractiveness fades away rather rapidly as one moves away from its borders, and in some regions—the Middle East, for instance—its cultural "power" has long been nonexistent and is destined, in all probability, to remain so. There are therefore limits, in this sphere as in all the others, to the degree of its interdependence.

Relations Among Aspects of China's Interdependence and Options for the Future

Once the notion of different arenas of interdependence is introduced, the question arises as to how they interrelate and how each affects China's economic interdependence. The problem is complicated, and perhaps insoluble, for two reasons. First, there is no clear way to measure the interdependence created by the various influences. Even if measures existed there would still be the problem of how to relate one to another. Current equivalents in the trade arena are imports and exports. Perhaps destructive power in the national security realm could be measured, if very roughly, by military budgets (assuming that they accurately reflected a nation's efforts and that exchange rates were themselves accurate—both very dubious assumptions). But scientific, political, and cultural influences are by their nature not measurable, although their influence is real and often pervasive. Second, the above illustrations demonstrate that the various aspects of China's interdependence are themselves interdependent. Economic and security interdependence, for instance, clearly and directly influence each other, and each, in turn, depends on China's political interdependence. And the nature and degree of these interdependences vary from period to period.[22]

Nonetheless, some conclusions may be in order. First, Chinese interdependence in one sphere, say, science, encourages and supports interdependence in other spheres, say, the economy. Once the door is open in one arena, it is easier to open the doors in others and to keep them open. Second, interdependence in one arena can sometimes be converted into or substituted for interdependence in other arenas. It has long been established, for instance, that security and economic interdependence can substitute for each other over a broad spectrum of variables. This has been so in China's case since the 1950s. Its trade during the 1950–1965 period was largely with the Soviet Union and its allies; trade with the United States began in the early 1970s and burgeoned during the era of joint deterrence against Soviet expansionism. Although Beijing was always interested in foreign trade as a component of economic development, it also used trade to buttress its national security. Third, the way is open for China to stress interdependence in areas that seem least harmful to state or party interests. Interestingly, various leaderships in Beijing have considered cultural interdependence much more threatening than security or economic interdependence; the latter are viewed as less harmful and more tolerable. The campaigns against foreign cultural influence have never been accompanied by warnings against "parallel tracks" in American-Chinese national security policies. Nor was there any official movement against increasing trade with China's Western security partners during the anti-Soviet 1970s or 1980s. And there has been no Chinese move during the 1990s to cut back trade with the United States, even though the two countries have experienced many difficulties since 1989 and may even view each other as potential security opponents.[23]

The "bottom line" of China's interdependence is comparatively easy to describe. If trends extant at the beginning of the 1990s continue, China's interdependence will probably increase in most spheres. At the same time, the Beijing leadership will continue, with less and less success, to control the degree of the country's interdependence in all spheres, lest the combination of domestic fluidity and external influence threaten its very capacity to rule. Much, of course, depends on the character of various successor leadership groups exercising power after Deng Xiaoping's demise. In that regard, the composition of the Fourteenth Party Congress leadership appears to be a further step in the direction of expertise and internationalization, hence interdependence, and away from senseless and outmoded ideology.[24] But barring a breakdown of Party rule or the reemergence of late-1980s-style liberal reform groups within the Party (both relatively unlikely), the slow but deliberate movement toward greater interdependence can be expected to continue. The Beijing leadership will continue to try to have it both ways: reaping the benefits of interdependence and avoiding excessive costs. This will not be easy, obviously, since secular trends throughout the globe all point to greater degrees of, and benefits from, interdependence in all spheres, especially the economic. Finally, the disjunction between global trends and Chinese propensities implies that, until there is a post–Communist Party leadership in power in Beijing, China will not modernize[25] as rapidly as it could were it to allow interdependence to exert its full influence over the country.

It is too soon to tell whether China will fall progressively behind in the global drive to modernize or succeed in keeping up. If the regime chooses to try to avoid full interdependence, costs will mount. The country will surely be able to live with such costs, as it has always done, but the toll in terms of lost opportunities and actual burdens will increase. If instead the leadership should come to understand that interdependence—even in the political sphere—is both inevitable and desirable, it could lead the nation into a much brighter future, including the progressive movement of the Chinese Communist Party onto the path of democracy. And if interdependence-induced evolutionary democracy is not the agreed-on end point of Chinese modernization, then that end point may well be a broad popular push to replace the Party by force. In that case, breakdown may be China's future, and both the Chinese people and other nations may be the losers as everyone comes to experience the burden to an interdependent world of a truly dependent China.

Notes

This paper draws liberally from Wendy Frieman and Thomas W. Robinson, "Costs and Benefits of Interdependence: A New Assessment," in Joint Economic Committee, 102nd Congress, *China's Economic Dilemmas in the 1990s: The Problems of Reforms, Modernization, and Interdependence* (Washington, D.C.: U.S. Government Printing Office, 1991), pp. 718–740. In addition to Wendy Frieman, the author thanks Colleen Aylward, Will Eisenbeis, Nicholas Harding, Mehlika Hoodbhoy, Susan McCarthy, Craig Peterson, Tonya Thesing, and Kathleen Walsh for research assistance and Zhiling Lin for helpful commentary and research on Chinese sources.

1. See, for instance, Robert Keohand and Joseph Nye, Jr.'s, now-classic *Transnational Relations and World Politics* (Cambridge: Harvard University Press, 1972) and their *Power and Interdependence: World Politics in Transition* (Boston: Little, Brown, 1977).

200 Thomas W. Robinson

2. The classic work on the topic is Gottfried Haberler, *The Theory of International Trade* (London: William Hodge, 1956).

3. See David A. Baldwin, "Interdependence and Power: A Comparative Analysis," *International Organization*, Spring 1980, pp. 478–506; James A. Caporaso, ed., "Dependence and Dependency in the Global System," *International Organization*, Winter 1978, pp. 1–300; and Tony Smith, "The Underdevelopment of Development Literature: The Case of Dependency Theory," *World Politics*, Winter 1979, pp. 247–288.

4. W. W. Rostow, *Politics and the Stages of Economic Growth* (New York: Cambridge University Press, 1971); Gabriel A. Almond and G. B. Powell, Jr., *Comparative Politics: A Developmental Approach* (Boston: Little, Brown, 1956); and Mancur Olsen, *The Rise and Decline of Nations* (New Haven: Yale University Press, 1982).

5. Anne O. Kruger, "The Effects of Trade Strategies on Growth," *Finance and Development* 20:6–8; William R. Cline, "Can the East Asian Model of Development Be Generalized?" *World Development* 10:81–90; Helen Hughes, ed., *Achieving Industrialization in East Asia* (New York: Cambridge University Press, 1988); Roy Hofheiz, Jr., and Kent E. Calder, *The East Asia Edge* (New York: Basic Books, 1982).

6. Among many sources, see Richard N. Cooper, *The Economics of Interdependence* (New York: McGraw-Hill, 1968); Edward L. Morse, *Modernization and the Transformation of International Relations* (New York: Free Press, 1976); C. Fred Bergsten and Lawrence W. Kraus, eds., "World Politics and International Economics," *International Organization*, Winter 1975, pp. 3–352; Robert Keohane, *After Hegemony: Cooperation and Discord in the World Political Economy* (Princeton, N.J.: Princeton University Press, 1984); Charles B. Kindleberger, *Power and Money* (New York: Basic Books, 1970); Klaus Knorr, *Power and Wealth* (New York: Basic Books, 1973); and John Ruggie, *The Antinomies of Interdependence* (New York: Columbia University Press, 1993).

7. Harry Harding, *China's Second Revolution: Reform After Mao* (Washington, D.C.: Brookings Institution, 1987); and Joint Economic Committee, 99th Congress, *China's Economy Looks Toward the Year 2000*, 2 vols. (Washington, D.C: U.S. Government Printing Office, 1991).

8. Articles on interdependence or containing a discussion of the concept are to be found, beginning in 1988, in *Guoji wenti yanjiu* [International Studies], *Guoji zhangwang* [World Outlook], *Foreign Affairs Journal*, *Guoji zhanlue yanjiu* [International Strategic Studies], and *Xiandai Guoji guanxi* [Contemporary International Relations], all organs of various research institutes in Beijing.

9. Immanuel Hsu, *The Rise of Modern China* (New York: Oxford University Press, 1975), pp. 325–363 and 433–522; and Jonathan Spence, *The Search for Modern China* (New York: W. W. Norton, 1990), pp. 194–268.

10. Thomas Gold, " 'Just in Time!' China Battles Spiritual Pollution on the Eve of 1984," *Asian Survey*, September 1984, pp. 947–974; James Tong, ed., "Party Documents on Anti–Bourgeois Liberalization and Hu Yaobang's Resignation, 1987," *Chinese Law and Government*, Spring, 1988.

11. See, for instance, "Some Questions Concerning the Establishment of a New World Order" and "Partners in Asia-Pacific Economic Cooperation," in *Contemporary International Relations*, July 1991 and February 1992.

12. This comes from a review of the above-mentioned Chinese research institute journals for the period September 1989–December 1990 and the journal *Guoji wenti* [International Affairs] (Shanghai).

13. Review of the above-mentioned Chinese research institute journals for the period January 1991–October 1992.

14. Statistics in the preceding paragraphs were gathered from *International Financial Statistics*; *Zhongguo Jinrong* [Chinese Finance]; [China] State Statistical Bureau, *Monthly Bulletin of Statistics*; World Bank, *World Tables*; UNCTAD *Trade Figures*; International Monetary Fund, *Direction of Trade Statistics Yearbook*; *China Statistical Yearbook*; *China Statistics Monthly*; and *China Economic News*.

15. Foreign Broadcasting Information Service, *Daily Report: China*, for January 1992, and the eight supplements on the Fourteenth Party Congress, October 13–23, 1992.

16. See David M. Lampton, *A Relationship Restored: Trends in U.S.-China Educational Exchanges, 1978–1984* (Washington, D.C.: National Academy Press, 1986); Leo A. Orleans, *Chinese Students in America: Policies, Numbers, and Issues* (Washington, D.C.: National Academy Press, 1988); Leo A. Orleans, "Perspectives of China's Brain Drain," and Mary B. Bullock, "The Effects of Tiananmen on China's International Scientific and Educational Cooperation," both in Joint Economic Committee, 102nd Congress, *China's Economic Dilemmas in the 1990s*, pp. 629–644 and 611–628.

17. Thomas W. Robinson, "Chinese Foreign Policy, From the Forties to the Nineties," in Thomas W. Robinson and David Shambaugh, eds., *Chinese Foreign Policy: Ideas and Interpretations* (Oxford: Oxford University Press, 1993).

18. For further elaboration, see Thomas W. Robinson, "Domestic and International Trends in Asian Security: Implications for American Defense Policy," *Korean Journal of Defense Analysis*, Summer 1992, especially pp. 130–138.

19. Robert G. Sutter, "China in World Affairs: Background, Prospects, and Implications for the United States" (Washington, D.C: Congressional Research Service, 1992); Allen S. Whiting, ed., *China's Foreign Relations*, Annals of the American Academy of Political and Social Science 519 (January 1992); John W. Garver, "China's Foreign Policy: The Diplomacy of Damage Control," *Current History*, September 1991, pp. 241–246.

20. Thomas W. Robinson, ed., *Democracy and Development in East Asia* (Washington, D.C.: American Enterprise Institute Press, 1991); Il Yung Chung, ed., *The Asian-Pacific Community in the Year 2000* (Seoul: Sejong Institute, 1992); William T. Liu and Richard H. Brown, eds., *Modernization in East Asia* (New York: Praeger, 1992).

21. Beverly Hooper, "Chinese Youth: The Nineties Generation," *Current History*, September 1991, pp. 264–269; Zhiling Lin, "Traditional, Modernist, and Party Culture in Contemporary China," in Zhiling Lin and Thomas W. Robinson, eds., *The Chinese and Their Future* (Washington, D.C.: American Enterprise Institute Press, 1993); Deborah Davis and Ezra F. Vogel, eds., *Chinese Society on the Eve of Tiananmen* (Cambridge: Harvard University Press, 1990); Perry Link, Richard Madsen, and Paul G. Pickowicz, eds., *Unofficial China: Popular Culture and Thought in the People's Republic of China* (Boulder, Colo.: Westview Press, 1989).

22. See, in these regards, Thomas W. Robinson, "Military Security and Economic Development in Asia," in Thomas W. Robinson, ed., *Asian Security* (Washington, D.C.: American Enterprise Institute Press, 1993). International relations theorists have, without success, for decades been attempting to quantify their field's central concept—power. One reason they have been unsuccessful is that power is a composite variable, consisting of some elements that are measurable and some that are not. Another reason is that power is situationally relevant. Interdependence shares these qualities.

23. See many of the papers in Ding Xinghao, Zhiling Lin, and Thomas W. Robinson, eds., *New Ideas and Concepts in American-Chinese Relations* (Shanghai and Washington, D.C.: Shanghai Institute of International Relations and American Enterprise Institute, 1993) for ideas about future relations between the two countries.

24. *Beijing Review*, October 26–31, 1992; *China Daily*, October 21, 1992; *Daily Report: China*, October 19, 1992.

25. In Asia, as elsewhere, there has been much discussion concerning the relationship between economic and political modernization. Although there will always be arguments on both sides, trends in China and elsewhere in Asia increasingly point to the necessity for economic development to reach a certain level before political democratization can take hold. See, in this regard, Thomas W. Robinson, "Modernization and Revolution in Post–Cold War Asia," *Problems of Communism*, January-April 1992, pp. 170–179, for specific ideas.

10

Human Rights in Chinese Foreign Relations

JAMES D. SEYMOUR

The human rights issue is the crux of the struggle between the world's two social systems. If we lose the battle on the human rights front, everything will be meaningless to us.

—*Deng Xiaoping*[1]

From the time of the Treaty of Westphalia (1648) until the twentieth century it was generally understood in the West that each state was to enjoy uncompromised sovereignty. This came to mean that a government had absolute authority over the people within its territory (internal sovereignty) and therefore outsiders could not legitimately interfere in a country's domestic affairs (external sovereignty). In the wake of World War II, however, the view came to be widespread that serious human-rights violations in a country were a legitimate subject of transnational concern, both for moral reasons and because an epidemic of human-rights violations, even if "domestic," sometimes posed dangers to the international community. In due course, the United Nations adopted four human-rights agreements that together make up the International Bill of Human Rights. First came the thirty-article Universal Declaration of Human Rights, which was proclaimed in 1948.[2] Though its principles were spelled out in only general terms and did not necessarily have the force of international law, they were "a common standard of achievement for all peoples and all nations" and an implicit limitation on state sovereignty.

The notion of absolute territorial sovereignty came to China relatively late. Historically, there used to be no clear delineation between the Middle Kingdom (*Zhongguo*) and peripheral nations, so there was no concept of external sovereignty. An emperor's sway in the outer realms, usually inhabited by non-Chinese, was limited by the power and authority of local potentates. As for internal sovereignty, although it could be argued that there were no theoretical curbs on an emperor's authority within the Middle Kingdom, it was widely understood that there were limits beyond which a monarch could not go. Still, when it came to human

rights, the mandate of traditional Chinese culture was ambiguous. Rulers persecuted insubordinate officials and dissident intellectuals, but the public reaction
was probably more resignation than approval. Many men who paid a heavy price
for standing up for principle have been treated in China's history books as heroic
rather than as illegitimate.[3]

In the nineteenth century, when China became victimized by foreign powers
(who took their own sovereignty seriously but ignored the rights of the less-developed countries), it embraced the sovereignty concept with a vengeance. Suddenly
the old Confucian notions of imperial propriety were swept away; China was determined to become a centralized empire free of interference by anyone not an
ethnic Chinese. This goal was largely achieved by the Communists in 1949. This
was the year after the adoption of the Universal Declaration, but the Chinese
Communists had not been consulted about that, and they were in any case disinclined to let human-rights considerations interfere with their reach for power and
social revolution. In their view, all governments had virtually unlimited authority
to act within their countries' boundaries; individuals were to have no recourse to
international law.

In the following decades, the international human-rights movement gained
popularity and legal standing. In 1966 the United Nations (with the PRC still ex-
cluded) adopted two detailed covenants on human rights. By 1976 both covenants
had been accepted by enough countries to be considered "in force" at least with
respect to the ratifying countries, though their applicability to nonsignatories
such as China is a moot point of international law. One of the covenants deals
with civil and political rights as they are generally understood in the developed
world (including freedom from government interference in the flow of information and ideas by such means as imprisoning spokespersons for unwelcome view-
points). In these matters, China's leaders take a cultural relativist approach: In applying international human-rights standards, account must be taken of the
diversity of international values, and each government is entitled to make allow-
ances for the nation's historical, social, cultural, and even political realities. It is
complained that the question of civil liberties has been artificially politicized by
the West and "used as a tool to pursue a certain ideology and political model."[4]
The second covenant, on economic, social, and cultural rights, spells out rights
much sought-after in the developing world, including services and material benefits that governments are supposed to provide their citizens. The PRC professes to
take these rights very seriously, its own spotty record notwithstanding.[5]

Although China has not ratified either covenant, since 1980 it has acceded to
nine less controversial human-rights instruments, including the conventions re-
specting the rights of women, children, and refugees and against genocide, racial
discrimination, and torture. In time, numerous old international labor conventions that the Republican government had ratified before 1949 were recognized.[6]
Beginning in 1981, PRC representatives participated in the work of the UN Human Rights Commission in Geneva, where they were particularly active in efforts
concerning the rights of children and migrant workers. China was often less than
forthcoming when it came to reporting on and responding to UN questions
about its own human-rights problems—even when they came under the purview
of instruments the government had signed. Still, these commitments represented

acceptance of the principle that there are internationally protected *individual* human rights. (This was so, for example, in the case of the Convention Against Torture and Other Cruel, Inhuman or Degrading Treatment or Punishments, even though this instrument has had little or no impact on Chinese realities.[7])

China's emphasis, though, has been on *group* rights. In 1986 the General Assembly of the United Nations passed a declaration concerning the right to economic, social, and cultural "development." This step had strong backing from China, which praised it as a "breakthrough" that brought human-rights concepts more in line with the needs of the less affluent countries. Although the right to development is usually viewed as having both individual and collective components, the latter is seen by Beijing as taking precedence over the former. Indeed, many Chinese Communist theorists interpret the right to development as inhering solely in the state, and as such they find it an especially useful concept. PRC scholars concede, however, that the right of development is at too inchoate a theoretical stage to be analyzed as an aspect of international law.[8]

Following the international recognition of the right to development, Beijing appeared to be on the verge of ratifying the two main covenants.[9] But despite some sympathetic attention to them in the Chinese media the matter was shelved after the downfall of Hu Yaobang. Not only were the political winds shifting against liberalism, but many officials doubtless had second thoughts when they discovered how many Chinese laws and practices were at variance with the covenants. The covenants did continue to receive occasional favorable mention in the press (especially by way of pointing out America's human-rights shortcomings) and were given some official recognition in the form of a promise that after Hong Kong's retrocession to China they would continue to be partially applicable to the territory.[10] But otherwise the covenants have in recent years been conspicuously absent from lists of international human-rights agreements about which Beijing is enthusiastic.

Economic, social, and cultural rights are sometimes termed "positive" rights. Whereas civil and political rights generally require simply that governments refrain from taking actions that violate them, positive rights require governments to make provisions for citizens. Of the two kinds of rights, positive rights are the less subject to theoretical controversy. No one objects to the principle that the hungry should be fed. However, there is little international pressure on governments to make good on such rights, and that is how China wants it. Thus, as both practical and theoretical matters, they are more domestic or *citizens'* rights (as distinct from *human* rights) that one possesses by virtue of one's membership in a particular polity (rather than membership in the human race). When it comes to international relief efforts, China gives sovereignty considerations priority over the nutritional rights of starving people and has either opposed or only reluctantly tolerated international efforts to compel local authorities to admit relief missions in such places as Bosnia and Somalia.

The United Nations has also adopted numerous codes. Its Code of Conduct for Law Enforcement has an annex that states: "Law enforcement officials may use force only when strictly necessary and to the extent required for the performance of their duty." Even when it is legitimate to use force, no force going beyond what is necessary to prevent crime or effecting a lawful arrest may be used. "The use of firearms is considered an extreme measure. Every effort should be made to exclude the use of firearms. ... In general, firearms should not be used except when a suspected offender offers armed resistance or otherwise jeopardizes the lives of others and less extreme measures are not sufficient to restrain or apprehend the suspected offender."[11] Such provisions would seem to preclude the Chinese authorities' acting as they did during the 1989 unrest.

The official Chinese view of international human rights has varied somewhat over time and from faction to faction. First, there is what we may call the *ultra-conservative* line, which normally dominates the Public and State Security ministries, according to which the Western and Chinese conceptions are incompatible. A spokesman explained in November 1989:

> As understood by Western scholars, human rights are the innate rights of human beings, or the basic rights and freedoms enjoyed by a person as a human being. They primarily consist of the rights to life, freedom, equality, property, self-defense and happiness, and the right to oppose persecution. These rights are deemed innate, permanent, universal, and inalienable. ... In the context of Marxism, such an interpretation of human rights is unscientific, incorrect, contrived, biased and idealistically metaphysical. ... Human rights, like democracy and freedom, are concrete and class-oriented.[12]

Thus, human rights, according to the ultraconservative line, are subordinate to issues of class and may be suspended by the dictatorship of the proletariat in order to wage domestic or international class struggle. Human rights inhere not so much in individuals as in collectivities, and the state itself is such a collectivity. By no means is it a legitimate function of rights to protect the individual against the state. International scrutiny is justified only in the case of collective rights, where the violations do not simply affect individuals but rather are "large-scale" (such as racism and colonialism). Otherwise, human rights are seen as incompatible with the rights of the state and therefore with effective government. (This is actually a caricature of human-rights theory, which simply holds that unless some slight curbs are put on the state, the rulers' authority will be unlimited, unaccountable, irresponsible, and probably self-serving.)

Even in China, time seems to have passed the ultraconservative view by. Now the dominant line is what we might call *moderate conservative*. The moderate conservatives include many members of the third-generation "Prince" faction, which were once supposed to inherit power after the present leaders leave the scene, and also many former ultraconservatives whose views have evolved. They all now see the need to develop a theory of human rights that speaks a language closer to that of international thinking on the subject. Although rights are no longer related to social class, the emphasis is still placed on *citizens'* rights, and transcendent human rights are hardly recognized at all. This is still contrary to international parlance and stands in contrast to the situation in developed countries, where one has both citizens' rights *and* human rights. The moderate conservatives like to cite Article 51 of the Constitution: "The exercise by citizens ... of their freedoms and rights may not infringe upon the interests of the state, or society and the collective." Thus the state mandates and withholds rights and stipulates duties. Unsurprisingly, of the various human rights, the "right to development" meets with the strongest approval on the part of China's moderate conservatives.

Third, a handful of people generally embrace international thinking on the subject of human rights and in the Chinese context can be called *liberal*. They do have one blind spot in their lack of interest in empowering China's working classes, especially farmers, but they were favorably inclined toward the student demonstrators in 1989. Until that time the liberals had seemed to be gaining headway in official circles, even among some people associated with the internal security apparatus.[13] Unfortunately, in the wake of the massacre by the military, many such government and party supporters of human rights went to prison, and little has been heard from this school since. The liberals have been eclipsed by the moderate conservatives, and there has been a general attempt to debunk internationally recognized human-rights principles. People have been told that historically human rights had been "merely" in the causes of antifeudalism and property rights[14] (both ideas doubtless very appealing to many).

As for where the public has stood on the question of human rights, we can only speculate. In the countryside, where most Chinese live, people would like more say in local politics, but there is little evidence of support for national political liberalization. During the Tiananmen demonstrations, however, it became obvious that international human-rights principles, however poorly understood, found a receptive audience in China's city dwellers, who reject both ultraconservative and moderate conservative lines on this subject.

Foreign Reactions

The June 4 (1989) crackdown saw a tremendous international outpouring of concern, a fact that probably came as quite a shock to Beijing. Although in the 1950s there had been complaints from Taiwan and the United States about repression in China, these were usually so politicized and tied to anticommunist hysteria that they had little credibility or impact. In contrast to the other communist countries, for a long time Beijing enjoyed a free ride when it came to human rights. Even during the Cultural Revolution, when conditions went from bad to worse, the world was largely silent. Indeed, the United States (followed by many other countries) began having diplomatic relations with China during what was probably the greatest period of human-rights violations—a fact not lost on Deng Xiaoping. ("Even I had no rights; why didn't the Americans raise the human rights issue *then*?"[15]) A few years later, the crackdown on the Democracy Wall movement followed immediately upon Deng Xiaoping's upbeat visit to the United States. Cautious requests from Chinese dissidents for sympathy from President Jimmy Carter[16] seemed to go unheeded. With China barely "opened," foreign politicians, diplomats, traders, lawyers, church representatives, travel agents, and academics were reluctant to jeopardize their ability to pursue their professional interests in China by raising human-rights concerns. Even journalists tended to be cautious, at least until near the end of their tours of duty and after winning a few coveted interviews or a trip to one of the many closed parts of the country. It was partly because of this absence of strong reaction to human-rights abuses during the decades leading up to 1989 that China's leaders were taken by surprise by the international reaction to the massacre.

It had been largely left to nongovernmental organizations (NGOs) to blow the whistle on Beijing, and even these were slow to do so. Reasons for neglect ranged from lack of information to fear that Western initiatives would be counterproductive. In the mid-1970s this situation began to change. The first organization to pay serious attention to human-rights violations in China was London-based Amnesty International.[17] Soon Amnesty's worldwide network of local chapters sprang into action to highlight the plight of individual "prisoners of conscience" in China. During the 1980s other organizations (most notably the New York–based Asia Watch, founded in 1985) began publishing exposés about China, now aided by long-silent or newly arrived Chinese exiles.[18] These efforts were given a major boost in 1989, when the international media happened to be on hand (to cover Mikhail Gorbachev's visit) and were able to report firsthand the Tiananmen demonstrations and the Beijing Massacre.[19] Since then, the tendency has been to focus on the capital rather than the provinces, with the notable exception of Asia Watch's 1992 report on Hunan.[20] Reports about China by NGOs used to be tersely dismissed by Beijing as absurd, even though internally they were taken very seriously.[21] Now, however, they are often met not only with official outrage but with lengthy rebuttals. The international human-rights movement is portrayed as disingenuous, and expressions of concern by foreign governments are considered pure hypocrisy. But the human-rights NGOs have become a redoubtable international lobby that has obliged Western governments to take cognizance of the PRC's human-rights problems. Finally, China has had to take note as well.

While it is not the purpose of this chapter to evaluate the human-rights situation in China, we should note at this point the issues that have raised the greatest concern abroad. Repression of political dissent receives the most attention. Also of concern are mistreatment of detainees—unfair trials, wrongful imprisonment, poor prison conditions, and torture. China now claims that in these respects citizens' rights "have been fully protected." However, there is a vast amount of evidence to the contrary. Not only are there many political prisoners, but prison guards, interrogators, and judicial cadres are out of control, and physical mistreatment of prisoners is commonplace. Among those most prone to receive such abuse are workers who attempted to organize independent trade unions, a fact that raises the ire of the international trade union movement. In the United States, at least, five additional issues are considered important: persecution of China's religious groups (notably Christians and Tibetan Buddhists), interference with foreign journalists in China, treatment of overseas Chinese students, restrictions on the right of people to emigrate from the PRC, and the exporting of prison-made products.

As has been noted, the long quiescent international concern about human-rights violations in China suddenly became activated in the wake of June 4.[22] Although a few governments did support Beijing,[23] the overwhelming majority opposed it, though to widely varying degrees. Perhaps the most extreme condemnation came from El Salvador—which was ironic, given the country's own human-rights record. France froze relations with China at all levels, not only cutting back on cultural exchanges but also becoming an immediate haven for refugees from Tiananmen. Other Western governments that took a strong stand were those of Australia, West Germany, Spain, Switzerland, and the Scandinavian countries. Only a few Asian countries followed suit—notably the Philippines, which had looked favorably on the birth of "people power" in China. Many countries in a position to impose economic sanctions did so. Australia cut back on aid and loans. Sweden put aid on hold and banned military shipments to China. Switzerland likewise banned military sales. Norway froze credits and new exports to China. West Germany took steps similar to these and even delayed the signing of already completed financial assistance agreements.

Other governments pursued a middle road. Although disapproving of Beijing's actions, they were ambiguous in their actual responses. Japan, which had been by far the major donor of aid to China and its second largest trading partner after Hong Kong, is an example. Under international pressure, Japan did impose some modest economic sanctions. No new aid projects were launched, and the government restrained Japan's eager bankers from making loans to China. Over Beijing's protest, it granted a visa to the dissident leader Uerkesh Daolet (Wuer Kaixi). But Tokyo believed (or rationalized) that it would be unseemly for Japan to condemn atrocities in China in the light of its own actions in China during World War II.

Some governments, while not condoning the crackdown, took a soft line. This category includes most of the PRC's neighbors, never eager to antagonize the monolith. This was even true of Association of Southeast Asian Nations (ASEAN) countries, with normally liberal Thailand proving no safe haven for Chinese democrats on the run. And there seemed to be a tacit agreement between China and the most repressive Asian governments, such as Burma, that there would be no criticism of each other's behavior. As for the USSR, it had just begun to mend its fences with China. After the bloodbath (which was shown on Soviet television), Gorbachev initially recommended dialogue and later said that an antireform backlash would be "immensely harmful" with respect to relaxing tensions.

As for the United States, although the Bush administration took some steps to register its uneasiness over the Chinese crackdown, it seemed to fail, as the *New York Times* later put it, "to express American outrage."[24] Such outrage was not limited to China's usual critics; even moderate figures who had long sought to promote Sino-American relations were deeply affected by the crackdown.[25] Nonetheless, Washington's initial response was merely to institute some modest sanctions. Specifically announced were suspension of all government-to-government sales, commercial exports of weapons,[26] and exchanges of visits between U.S. and Chinese military leaders. Even these cautious steps gained Washington the disgust of China's leaders, and there was much press criticism of the human-rights situation in the United States. However, the moderate conservatives insisted that the media refrain from besmirching Bush personally, realizing that he was as good a friend as they could have in Washington. The president returned the favor by criticizing only the Chinese *army* (not the leaders who ordered the crackdown) for the June 4 massacre. Believing that trade and other exchanges were the best way to promote democracy in China, Bush was always determined to "maintain the relationship," even though he was obliged by congressional pressure to take further actions against Beijing. Congress, furious about human-rights and other problems in China, insisted on a broad range of sanctions, including suspension of insurance through the Overseas Private Investment Corporation for companies doing business in China, suspension of trade assistance, a freeze on satellite exports, and a halt to sales of most armaments.

Also after the June 4 massacre Washington announced that there would be no high-level Sino-American "exchanges." In reality, numerous unannounced meetings (later officially termed "contacts" rather than exchanges) soon took place, giving rise to charges by human-rights activists that the Bush administration was engaged in deception. Then in 1991 Secretary of State James Baker visited Beijing, and in 1992 President Bush met with Li Peng personally at the United Nations. Although the hope was that "constructive engagement" would be more productive than confrontation, the administration's approach yielded little in the way of an improved human-rights situation. Some dissidents were released from prison, but they might well have been freed anyway for Beijing's own reasons or as a result of more overt foreign pressure from other governments and nongovernmental sources. (However, the PRC is at pains to give the impression that it does not respond to such pressure.) At any rate, in 1992, virtually all the remaining economic sanctions that Western countries and Japan had imposed were lifted, though the specter of sanctions (especially Congress's threat to deny China most-favored-nation treatment) appears to have had an impact.

One area of contention concerns emigration and exiles. The Jackson-Vanik Amendment to the 1974 U.S. Trade Act states that most-favored-nation (moderate-tariff) trading with nonmarket economies is normally to be conditional on a country's human-rights practices, particularly with respect to the right to emigrate. When the law was passed, Congress did not have China in mind. At any rate, the emigration issue is somewhat academic inasmuch as if Beijing were to honor this right (which it does not[27]) only a small portion of would-be emigrants would be accepted as immigrants in other countries. More pressing is the question of Chinese nationals already in the United States. Whereas foreigners in the United States are normally subject to a harsh regimen of visa controls, Chinese students and others have been given extraordinarily hospitable treatment. In 1992 it became American law that Chinese who had been in the United States since April 1990 could apply for permanent residency unless the president certified that it was safe for them to return to China. In the light of the two-month detention of returned student leader Shen Tong in 1992, it appeared unlikely that a president would be able make such a certification.

Beijing's Response

On the surface, China's reaction to such pressures usually seems sharply negative. Regarding Chinese students' being permitted to remain in the United States, for example, a Foreign Ministry spokesperson asserted: "This is a grave step on the part of the U.S. side that seriously contravenes the spirit of the relevant agreements reached by China and the U.S., undermines bilateral exchanges in the fields of education and culture, and obstructs the return of Chinese students. ... The allegation that it is unsafe for them to return to China and that they face political persecution is simply untenable." In general, criticisms of human-rights violations are seen as stemming from "subjective conjecture" and not worth refuting. The United States and Britain are seen as equating China's political stability with suppression of various political views and the happiness of the majority with lack of free expression.[28] "Some Western countries, the United States in particular, always want to use human rights issues to expand their power and attain hegemonic aims. One of their chief means is engaging in 'human rights diplomacy.' ... This kind of diplomacy is more effective and duplicitous than directly dispatching troops."[29] Sometimes there is even a hint of blackmail. Were the pressures for political change to get out of control, one was told, the resulting upheavals might result in China's neighbors' being flooded with tens of millions of refugees. The implication is that it is in the world's interest to support China's leaders' quest for "stability."

Much of the Chinese government's negative reaction to foreign pressure to improve its human-rights record is simply self-serving and power-related. However, the authorities can well argue that some of the international human-rights criticism misses the point of China's situation. For example, complaints concerning birth control, changing employment, changing residence, and property rights tend to be oblivious to China's economic problems. Thus, even some strong foreign proponents of human rights argue that insisting on such rights for the Chinese is so unrealistic that it undermines the general cause. But even if these points were conceded, this would still leave the main case for human rights unanswered.

At any rate, in recent years China's approach to the subject of human rights has not been entirely negative. Deng Xiaoping decided that China had to become more engaged in the subject in order to prevent the issue of human rights from being preempted by the international bourgeoisie. "People have misconceptions. It is as though rights issues are a monopoly of the Western world and only the developed capitalist countries are the redeemers of human rights, whereas the socialist countries disregard and even fear, are hostile toward, and stamp out human rights."[30] Thus, in 1990 the pendulum appeared to be swinging back; indeed, it was decided that, rather than to continue stonewalling, Beijing should go on the human-rights offensive. Chinese think tanks began addressing the subject,[31] and a delegation was sent abroad to investigate the international human-rights policies of other governments. To further the dialogue, Australia and then other countries were permitted to send human-rights missions to China. When the first few of these had seemed to accomplish little, foreign parliamentarians and others attempted in 1992 to make higher-profile protests, including a mini-demonstration in Tiananmen Square. The Australians then sent another mission, which at least elicited the admission from Chinese officials that China held four thousand convicted political prisoners.

There was a considerable outpouring of articles in the Chinese media presenting the government's position on human rights, often stressing the West's own flawed human-rights record in such places as Los Angeles and Northern Ireland. Finally, in 1991 came the publication of an official white paper on human rights.[32] Though this illiberal tract met with opposition from Chinese at home and abroad,[33] it nonetheless signaled the death knell of the ultraconservative line. It did not reject international human-rights principles per se, but it placed major emphasis on the progress China had made in advancing economic, social, and cultural rights. The arguments were considerably overstated, as China is still far behind in terms of some of the rights claimed (in health care, education, and the rights of the handicapped) and there has actually been some backsliding in this area—for example, regarding the right to employment and the right to strike. When the record on civil liberties was recounted, it was difficult to take it all seriously (for example, the assertion that China has no news censorship and no political prisoners[34]). Still, foreign pressures may well have had some impact on official thinking, and the publication of the white paper amounted to an implicit acknowledgment that human rights (however defined) are a legitimate international concern. Indeed, the paper's final section contained a prideful account of how active China had been in international human-rights councils. It was pointed out that China had participated in the drafting of most of the human-rights agreements of recent decades. China, it was argued, had played a constructive role in promoting human rights not only for Palestinians and South Africans but (less convincingly) in Cambodia—where the PRC had actually supported the notorious Khmer Rouge.

In 1992, the State Council issued a second report entitled "Criminal Reform in China." Unlike the white paper on human rights, which had admitted some shortcomings, this report denied that detainees and convicts were treated in any but the most enlightened manner. Great progress was said to have been made in humanizing the handling of prisoners. Conditions, it was maintained, stood in stark contrast to the pre-1949 situation, when torture in prisons, sometimes at the behest of the Americans,[35] was commonplace. However, the report was not very effective in overcoming firsthand reports of widespread physical abuse of prisoners by local authorities and inmate "cell bosses."[36]

It should be borne in mind that China's leaders have long counted on the country's global standing to compensate for its unpopularity at home. At one time the idea that China represented the vanguard of socialism did carry some weight, but it no longer does. With the Cold War ended, the PRC lacks the kind of leverage it once had (casting the swing vote between East and West). When China's human-rights abuses began to receive attention from abroad, the already dubious international legitimacy of the regime was placed in further jeopardy. The publication of the two state papers reflected tacit acknowledgment that China paid a price abroad for the government's human-rights abuses. Beijing had come to understand that the effective conduct of the country's relations with other countries required the reallocation of a significant portion of China's precious diplomatic capital to dealing with the human-rights concerns. For almost two years China even conducted talks with the United States dedicated to these issues, which sometimes resulted in responses, however minimal, on the part of the Chinese. But there appeared to be little benefit in all this for China's leaders, and in 1992 Beijing unilaterally suspended these discussions and refused to accept a list of prisoners on whom the lame-duck Bush administration wanted information. The top leadership even instructed various ministries not to discuss human-rights matters with American officials. Apparently it was decided to deal with the human-rights issue by diverting attention away from civil liberties and toward development rights and rights violations that result from the world's "unreasonable and unjust economic order."[37] But with the election of Bill Clinton, who as a candidate promised to give higher priority to civil liberties in China, Beijing must have understood that the issue would not go away, and the rulers continued to release their critics from prison from time to time in hopes of recouping some of the regime's lost legitimacy.

Many examples might be cited to show the price China pays for this loss. Pressure has been applied by international lending agencies. U.S. law already instructs U.S. representatives in intergovernmental lending organizations, such as the World Bank, to oppose loans to countries guilty of gross violations of human rights unless such assistance will serve basic human needs. In the case of loans to China, immediately after the 1989 massacre the United States did prevent these, though later it only abstained from votes concerning such loans. In the Asian Development Bank (ADB), Washington took a more consistently tough stand. However, by the end of 1992 relations between the Bank and China had been "normalized." Japan (the major voice in the ADB) has been reluctant to use financial muscle to promote human rights in China. In 1991 Premier Kaifu announced a "four-point policy" that would underlie Japan's aid to China, among the operative considerations of which was an improvement in human-rights conditions. Subsequently, human-rights considerations were written into Japan's overseas development assistance laws. It is possible that future administrations in Tokyo or Washington will give human-rights issues high priority. The European Community appears poised to do likewise. All of this should encourage the Chinese to bring their concept of human rights more into line with international thinking.

As it is, the Chinese government even disagrees with outsiders as to what is and is not a human-rights issue. The position is more tenable in some cases than in others. For example, in the case of international commerce in the products of prison labor, the Chinese argue that everyone, including the prisoner, has an obligation to work. Indeed, as long as conditions are humane (which in China they often are not) most prisoners would indeed prefer to work than to sit idly in cells. Assuming that the people are legitimately imprisoned in the first place, it can be argued that requiring a prisoner to work does not in itself amount to a human-rights violation. A dozen American states have prison labor regimes that operate according to principles analogous to those which are supposed to be in effect in China. And the Chinese authorities also have a point when they argue that much of the international objection to prison-made exports derives from economic, not humanitarian, concerns. Indeed, economic considerations probably did underlie America's Smoot-Hawley Act (1930) forbidding prison-made imports. American workers are still unhappy at the prospect of having to compete with virtually unpaid Chinese prison labor. However, in recent years explicit congressional arguments about "forced labor" have been cast largely in human-rights terms. Finally, in 1992, the United States and China signed a memorandum of understanding permitting American diplomats to visit Chinese penal institutions that are suspect.[38] But the Chinese dragged their feet when it came to implementing the agreement, which at any rate did not satisfy congressional critics, who thought the evidentiary threshold was too high and who also wanted international human-rights organizations to have access to Chinese prisons.

As for trade in general, in Beijing's eyes it is a purely economic matter, and the government resents U.S. congressional efforts to make low tariffs contingent on China's passing a human-rights test. Many Americans, both business people and labor unions, have reasons to want to limit Chinese imports. However, the less self-serving arguments for denying most-favored-nation treatment have to do with China's poor human-rights record.[39] During the Bush administration, attempts to limit trade with China had little success because of support on the part of Bush himself for unfettered commerce and the inability of Congress to marshal the two-thirds majority needed to override his veto. In Clinton's 1992 campaign, human rights was the only basis indicated as a reason for denying the PRC most-favored-nation treatment; other problems in U.S.-China relations were to be dealt with by other means. After the election Clinton seemed to place human rights and open markets on an equal footing but sounded unenthusiastic about denying most-favored-nation status.

Another point of disagreement is the extent to which rights may be curbed in the name of citizens' duties. The Universal Declaration of Human Rights allows "such limitations as are determined by law solely for the purpose of securing due recognition and respect for the rights and freedoms of others and of meeting the just requirements of morality, public order and the general welfare in a democratic society" (Article 29), which Beijing often interprets as an unlimited loophole. It is also claimed that there is an internationally recognized principle of law that rights and duties are united. In effect, human rights are subordinated to one's duty to support the national leadership. Totally ignored is the declaration's final article: "Nothing in this Declaration may be interpreted as implying for any State ... any right to engage in any activity ... aimed at the destruction of any of the rights and freedoms set forth herein."

Also at issue is the extent to which a government's institutional structure must conform to an international standard. Although it is obvious that nations have wide latitude in this respect, the Universal Declaration of Human Rights does have some implications for how a government should be structured. In particular, Article 10 requires an independent judiciary. China's moderate conservatives do not dispute this but claim that China already has one. Though there is much evidence to the contrary,[40] one can perhaps infer that China accepts an obligation to meet international standards in this regard.

Sometimes the disagreements over human-rights issues are not so much between China and the rest of the world as within the international community in general. Certainly China is not alone in emphasizing economic rights over civil liberties; this is true for much of the Third World. As an observer at the 1992 Non-Aligned Movement meeting in Jakarta, China enthusiastically supported the consensus that Western countries should not meddle in the human-rights situations in these countries.[41] And other more broad-based intergovernmental organs are often immobilized by the insistence on the part of China and other undemocratic countries that civil liberties violations be winked at.

On some issues, the "First World" is itself divided. One example is birth control and the question of under what circumstances (if any) abortions are to be performed. During the 1980s there were many reports of *obligatory* abortion in China. This generated much more international concern than did the question of *voluntary* abortion, the latter being an issue primarily with the United States (pre-1993) and Catholic countries. Another is the death penalty. It is the position of some governments and some NGOs that capital punishment is incompatible with human rights, and the consensus in the United Nations seems to be moving in that direction. Although Hong Kong no longer imposes the death sentence,[42] executions are common in the PRC for even relatively minor crimes, and at the same time many states in the United States employ the practice. When Washington finally ratified the civil-political covenant in 1992, President Bush did so with the reservation that states could continue to execute juvenile offenders (otherwise outlawed by the covenant). China exploits such differences of opinion in the international community.

Still, human-rights values are deeply held in the West and elsewhere, a fact that China's ultraconservatives appear unable to understand. We may consider them preconditions for honest, efficient government and, indeed, for the liberation of the human spirit, but China's leaders see little sincerity in this. They remember how foreigners used to ignore their own principles of human rights and national sovereignty when it came to their colonies and especially how they trampled on the rights of Chinese. They see human rights as an instrument used selectively by foreigners to pursue other foreign policy objectives. As for the argument that democracy is conducive to international peace and stability, Beijing sees things just the opposite way: China has an international obligation to suppress dissent; chaos and civil war would be a threat to the entire world.[43]

Thus, in a line little changed since the since 1950s, the PRC casts the issue in terms of restoring the international order of sovereign nation-states. National sovereignty, it is claimed, is a precondition for the enjoyment of human rights. Often citing China's history as a "semicolony," the leaders jealously guard the nation's independence. Although some acknowledgment is made of the internationalization of human-rights issues, these "are essentially matters within the domestic jurisdiction of a country." UN declarations are cited to the effect that no state or group of states has the right to intervene directly or indirectly, for any reason, in the internal affairs of any other state and that every state has the duty to refrain from the exploitation and the distortion of human-rights issues as a means of interference in the internal affairs of states. Thus, in the words of the white paper, "China has been firmly opposed to any country making use of the issue of human rights to sell its own values, ideology, political standards and mode of development. ... Using the human rights issue for the political purpose of imposing the ideology of one country on another is no longer a question of human rights, but a manifestation of power politics."[44] The authorities profess to see China's democrats as a group that would sell out the country. For example, Liu Xiaobo was seen as a "traitor" for placing humanism above patriotism and for insisting that China's go-it-alone economic policies had brought nothing but poverty.[45]

The PRC's leaders tend to be highly sensitive about international "interference" in connection with human-rights problems. For example, the annual U.S. State Department human-rights reports have been condemned as "gross violations of the internal affairs and sovereignty of China."[46] A double standard is underscored by Beijing's condemnations of human-rights violations of foreign countries. In mid-1989, when Beijing was criticizing the Israeli practice of holding West Bank prisoners without trial, the practice was widespread in China itself. Beijing has also associated itself with efforts to curb human-rights abuses in Afghanistan, Southern Africa, Panama, and the Israeli-occupied territories (all cases suited to the PRC's more general foreign policy agenda). Much of China's appeal to the Third World has long exploited such positive uses of human-rights diplomacy, although the tactic has been less effective in recent years and has become increasingly difficult to reconcile with China's position regarding sovereignty.

The sovereignty argument has not always been stated in absolute terms, and the thinking on this subject often seems confused. Official Chinese statements stressing this principle nonetheless allow for international intervention in the event of at least some human-rights abuses. Around 1988 the press carried many articles relatively sympathetic to the cause of universal rights. One writer in *People's Daily* even asserted that collective rights should not be stressed at the expense of individual rights.[47] Even after the 1989 crackdown, the newspaper carried a puzzling but still important article discussing various rights for which international concern is legitimate:

> The international law dimension in human rights means that the parts of the constitutions and laws of the various countries concerning human rights issues must conform to, and never violate, that country's international commitment to protect human rights. The various international documents on human rights—which are the basis for international protection of human rights—state that another country's or people's self-determination, development, and permanent sovereignty over natural resources should not be violated; the means of livelihood of a people should not be deprived; their right to life should not be infringed upon or threatened; [and there should be] no racial discrimination, segregation, extermination, serfdom ... , international terrorism, and so on. The violation of any one of the above is an abrogation of international law, and any country has the right to take appropriate action to stop the violation *without constituting interference in the internal affairs of the perpetrating country* [emphasis added]. ... No country can evade its international commitment to respect basic human rights using the excuse of "internal affairs."[48]

This statement appears to allow international action in the cases of a considerable range of human-rights violations.

For the next two years one did not hear any more of such talk. In 1992 there was a revival of the moderately conciliatory line. Addressing the UN Security Council, Premier Li Peng said that the civil liberties and political rights "of all mankind" should be respected, even though he found these less important than questions of national independence and economic development. Although human rights is essentially a domestic matter in which foreigners must not interfere, China stood "ready to engage in discussion and cooperation with other countries on an equal footing and ... on the basis of mutual understanding, mutual respect and seeking consensus while reserving differences." He did appear to undercut somewhat the principle of universal human rights by denying that there was any single criterion or model that could be applied to all countries.[49]

Self-Determination of Peoples

In both of the international human-rights covenants, the very first articles identically assert: "All peoples have the right to self-determination. By virtue of that right they freely determine their political status and freely pursue their economic, social and cultural development. ... The States Parties to the present Covenant ... shall promote the realization of the right of self-determination." Beijing has sometimes been at the forefront of the efforts to implement this provision in other parts of the world but has denied its applicability to the British colony of Hong Kong, Taiwan, or to the non-ethnic-Chinese parts of the PRC. For many years, the double standard proved tenable. More recently, however, with China more of a world player, awkward situations have arisen. For example, in 1992 Beijing decided that it had to resist UN efforts to protect Iraq's ethnic-minority regions for fear that a precedent might be set whereby one day China might find international forces defending, say, the Tibetans against the Chinese. All UN peacekeeping operations, says Beijing, "must be based on respect for the principle of state sovereignty."[50]

Although Beijing has at least an arguable historical claim to most of China's ethnic-minority territories, in the case of Tibet, at least, the claim is subject to challenge. The Chinese now base their territorial claims on the fact that the Mongols and Manchus conquered both China and Tibet. But as for the Mongols, it does not follow from their conquest that China (rather than Mongolia) should inherit Tibet. Actually, the Mongols, like the Manchus after them, treated Tibet as a separate country from China. During the last two periods of ethnic-Chinese rule (the Ming and Republican periods), the present "Tibet Autonomous Region" was in all essential respects independent.[51] The Republican government came to power in 1912 on a wave of anti-Manchu nationalism, and its claim to the other lands the Manchus had conquered was incongruous. In any case, the Republicans were defeated by the Communists before they could gain control of Tibet. In 1951, representatives of Tibet's leader, the Dalai Lama, were forced to sign a "Seventeen-Point Agreement" in which Chinese sovereignty was acknowledged. This agreement was the ultimate "unequal treaty" and for various reasons is of questionable legality. At any rate, the Chinese ignored many of the provisions of the agreement and of related secret understandings (Tibetans were supposed to have their own government, police force, and at least a token army), and the Dalai Lama's government-in-exile considers it no longer binding on Tibet. However, whether a territory is sovereign or part of another country depends at least in part on international acceptance and recognition, and here the advocates of Tibetan independence so far do not have a very compelling case.

For their part, the Communists have not always been consistent in their attitude toward such territories. Although he later became more imperialistic, in the 1930s Mao Zedong promised self-determination for areas which had not clearly and consistently been a part of China. This remained the Communists' line until 1949, when they reversed their position and began insisting that no part of the old Manchu empire was entitled to statehood except for the Mongolian People's Republic (MPR), toward which the Soviets insisted that China renounce any claim. Although today the non-Han areas are called "autonomous," Mao clearly promised a far greater degree of self-government than has generally existed.[52] The MPR case shows that the Chinese Communists can be flexible when they have to be. But when it came to Tibet, the Communists simply subdued it by military force in the 1950s—oblivious to the rights of the people there and to the fact that no ethnic-Chinese government had ever controlled it.

What the international human-rights covenants seem to say is that a "people" of a disputed territory with a plausible argument for sovereignty should decide for itself whether it is to be an independent country or annexed to another country. Although it is not made clear what a "people" is,[53] in 1961 the UN General Assembly declared that the Tibetans met all the requirements for self-determination. Furthermore, Tibetans have suffered egregious violations of their civil liberties. Indeed, vast numbers have been killed, and during the Cultural Revolution nearly all of the Lamist temples were destroyed. These and subsequent human-rights violations generated very strong anti-Chinese sentiment. The government's reaction to the territory's political problems is to keep large numbers of Tibetans in prison.[54]

In terms of cultural preservation, what rights do Tibetans as a people possess? First, as the Chinese began their takeover of Tibet, they guaranteed (in the Seventeen-Point Agreement) to respect "the religious beliefs, customs and habits of the Tibetan People." Furthermore, both international covenants assert the right of peoples (including non-self-governing peoples) to "freely pursue their ... cultural development." Even if the Chinese were to honor such obligations, however, one encounters the problem that Tibetans are in danger of being overwhelmed by Chinese (just as has happened to Mongolians in Inner Mongolia—another much-persecuted minority[55]). Already this is beginning to happen in Amdo and Kham (designated by the Chinese as Qinghai plus parts of Gansu, Sichuan, and Yunnan). Whereas in 1950 Tibetans were the largest ethnic group in Qinghai, they are now outnumbered by Chinese by a ratio of almost three to one.

If one assumes that Tibet is legally part of the PRC, then one runs up against the provision of the Universal Declaration of Human Rights that appears to protect the right of Chinese to move into Tibet. Article 13 states: "Everyone has the right to freedom of movement and residence within the borders of each State." Similar language appears in Article 12 of the International Covenant on Civil and Political Rights. However, in the same article it is added that such rights may be restricted in the interests of "the rights and freedoms of others." The question arises: what "rights and freedoms of others" might override the right of freedom of movement? Perhaps one is contained in Article 27 of the civil/political covenant: "In those States in which ethnic, religious or linguistic minorities exist, persons belonging to such minorities shall not be denied the right, in community with other members of their group, to enjoy their own culture, to profess and practice their own religion, or to use their own language." It could be argued that in a situation such as that in which Tibet finds itself—a nation with a small population adjacent to the world's largest—immigration of Hans is incompatible with the Tibetans' rights to the survival of their culture and nationality. Saving Tibetan culture might even require withholding the one-person-one-vote principle, but this would not be easy to justify.

The general issue of human-rights violations in Tibet has come before the UN Human Rights Commission in Geneva. European countries have provided strong support for resolutions sharply critical of China's record there. One such resolution in 1992 was successfully opposed by the United States, China, and its Third World supporters because it was ambiguous on the self-determination question. Their view, that the integrity of the state took precedence over the rights of national self-determination, prevailed. In spite of such occasional American support, China complains that Western concern for Tibetans' human rights is a cover for imperialistic designs.[56] This view is perhaps understandable, given Britain's historic meddling in Tibet and CIA assistance to Tibetan guerrillas in the 1950s and 1960s.[57] But Washington's position changed during the Nixon administration, and the State Department position now is "The United States ... considers Tibet to be a part of China, with the status of an autonomous region. ... The United States has never taken the position that Tibet is an independent country. ... We are for the self-determination of Tibet, but self-determination is not necessarily equated with independence."[58] Tibetans do have their champions, not only in the U.S. Congress (which has passed resolutions affirming that Tibet is an occupied country) but also in formerly occupied countries such as Lithuania. The independence cause is helped by the fact that Tibetans have a government-in-exile in neighboring India. It is led by the Fourteenth Dalai Lama, who, though widely respected as a Buddhist leader, has not been able to gain recognition as a head of state. The efforts of overseas Tibetans notwithstanding, the cause of Tibetan independence has not made substantial headway.

The question of self-determination for the PRC's other nationalities has been given even less consideration. This is true, for example, in the case of the vast territory that Uygur Turks call Eastern Turkestan and the Chinese call their "New Territories" (Xinjiang). However, there is some sympathy for these and other Muslim nationalities in China on the part of Middle Eastern and newly independent Central Asian countries. Many of the latter share ethnicity with China's minority peoples. Otherwise, there appears to be no present support on the part of foreign governments for such separatism.

The "Peaceful Evolution" Conundrum

If the cause of political reform in China was not dealt a mortal blow in 1989, it may have been dealt one soon thereafter with the demise of Leninism in the former Soviet bloc. The latter development only seemed to confirm the view of China's hard-liners that June 4–type responses are the correct way to deal with dissent. Thus, international events and pressures are sometimes counterproductive when it comes to the issue of liberalization in China. Relations between the PRC and the world have always tended to be a game of realpolitik. But moral issues such as human rights are not quite as marginal as they once were, and since 1989 the human-rights question has changed the landscape of China's international relations from everyone's point of view. China had been in the habit of picking its own foreign policy battles. Inasmuch as most of the countries with whom it had relations were dictatorships, the human-rights issue went unraised by mutual agreement. In the early 1990s China suddenly found that most of the countries it wanted to deal with were democracies, and human rights were on their agenda. Rarely had the Beijing government found itself unavoidably locked in such an unwelcome struggle.

Some of the control had shifted into the hands of foreign countries and NGOs—and of the Chinese people, many of whom eagerly sought to internationalize the human-rights issue. In particular, Chinese students abroad have effectively lobbied their host governments to uphold the cause of human rights in

China. To a considerable extent, therefore, this internationalization has taken place. Political prisoners who have an international reputation (even if only by virtue of having been "adopted" by some local chapter of Amnesty International) often receive less harsh treatment than others. And the persecution of ethnic minorities is apt to arouse concern on the part of their fellows outside of the PRC's boundaries. Ironically, however, internationalization may have the effect of strengthening the hand of the central government. The center's policies regarding the administration of prisons are less inhumane than the practices of the often out-of-control local officials, and "You are embarrassing your country" is apt to be an effective argument in as proud and nationalistic a land as China.

Tiananmen also changed the way foreigners view the PRC as an international actor. Hitherto, they only needed to be concerned with the Chinese government. In that sense, dealing with China was simple. The assumption was that the Chinese "masses" would not generally oppose their government. But now we know that China is a land of many governments and of "cellular totalitarianism."[59] Furthermore, polls taken in the spring of 1989 revealed that the antiestablishment student demonstrators had almost universal support among the populace of the capital. (That was not true in the countryside, but rural China has less relevance to international relations.) Suddenly, everyone from the White House to the Kremlin was confronted with a new situation in which there were at least two Chinas: the official one and the one reflected by the millions of demonstrators. China would never be as simple to deal with as it had been. This has been less a problem for China's neighbors and the Third World in general. Most of these governments cared little about human rights, but not even they could deal with China in quite the same way they had in the past. Few heads of state were eager to be photographed with Premier Li Peng, now notorious as the "Butcher of Beijing."

The issue of human rights in China will be determined by the course of political events there, with international standards and foreign involvement playing a secondary role. It is possible that China will long be led by people who continue to identify their personal political fortunes with that of the nation and will stop at nothing to silence their critics. Under this scenario, the leaders can be expected to refuse to move beyond the Westphalian world order. Either they will be ignorant of the principles the United Nations has advanced or, knowing better, they will choose to manipulate human-rights issues to their own ends. Alternatively, one of those waiting in the wings may emerge as China's leader and turn out to be a democrat and supporter of international human-rights instruments. But even the most enlightened reformers have, at this writing, shown no sign of willingness to bow to domestic and foreign pressures for political liberalization. Certainly human-rights movements in Hong Kong and overseas, which have usually been the main promoters of human rights in China, can only have a limited impact. Other players could have more clout if they were to prove willing to become more involved than they have been in the past. The role of foreign governments depends upon the predilections of whoever happens to be leading each of the various governments, which will change from time to time. For example, although on paper most of the modest U.S. economic sanctions remain in effect, the law allows the president to make exceptions. Given the approach of the Bush administration, this resulted in the laws' having little meaning, but this could change in the Clinton administration (if there is follow-through on campaign rhetoric). And some U.S. laws, such as those protecting foreign students and excluding the products of prison labor, allow little backsliding and may be expected to transcend partisan politics.

Foreign sojourners in China still tend to be very cautious, but a growing minority is now willing to raise human-rights issues. This has even been true of an occasional foreign-owned business. For example, in 1990 Reebok International declared that the company would not operate under martial law conditions, that it encouraged free association among employees and was determined to keep politics out of the workplace.[60] (The government often forces foreign companies to fire political dissidents.) In 1992 there began a drive in the U.S. House of Representatives to enact such trade principles into American law. This would appear to be a much more feasible approach than denying most-favored-nation status altogether, which might primarily hurt the "reformed" sector of the economy unless the status were applied only to state enterprises—an approach promoted by Congress but vetoed by President Bush. If either a good-corporate-citizen or non-most-favored-nation bill were enacted into law, Beijing would surely interpret it as part of a foreign plot to inflict on China the evil of "peaceful evolution" (read: democracy). Thus, in the short run the *threat* of such legislation is more productive than the actual enactment, the long-run effects of which are difficult to gauge.

But unless China largely excludes foreigners again, their subversive influence is bound to continue. China's leaders say they are determined that the country will become more and more "open." If it does, the government will be increasingly confronted with challenges to its human-rights practices. Already, pressures come from many quarters, including some new ones. Former Soviet satellites are pressing Beijing to respect human rights, and those nations whose statehood was restored when the Soviet Union collapsed often sympathize with the national aspirations of the PRC's non-ethnic-Chinese. As for foreign correspondents, wherever they come from they are apt to insist on the rights of their readers to receive unfettered news (which is impossible if journalists are regularly expelled and their Chinese contacts persecuted), and they may also make appeals on behalf of Chinese journalists.[61] International religious movements will press for the rights of China's Buddhists, Muslims, and Christians. Scholars engaged in research will press for academic freedom for themselves and for their Chinese colleagues. Some foreigners will be arrested (for legitimate reasons or otherwise), and this will bring judicial procedures under international scrutiny. International movements (women, labor unionists, gays, and others) are bound to become more interested in the problems of their Chinese counterparts. The only way to prevent this kind of "peaceful evolution" would be to return to the isolation of the 1960s, and no one appears to want that.

Notes

1. These remarks (the authenticity of which remains to be certified) are attributed to Deng in Wang Renzhi, "CPC Takes Offense on HR Issue: CPC Central Committee Document," *Dangdai*

(Hong Kong), July 15, 1992, pp. 39–41, translated in U.S. Foreign Broadcast Information Service, *Daily Report: China* (hereafter FBIS), July 22, 1992, p. 16.

2. The other three components are the International Covenant on Civil and Political Rights, the International Covenant on Economic, Social and Cultural Rights, and the Optional Protocol to the International Covenant on Civil and Political Rights.

3. There is little agreement as to whether human rights are compatible with traditional Chinese culture. For a negative view, see James C. Hsiung, ed., *Human Rights in East Asia: A Cultural Perspective* (New York: Paragon House, 1985), essays by Hsiung (pp. 3–30) and Richard Wilson (pp. 109–198). (The book was critically reviewed by James D. Seymour in *Political Science Quarterly,* Summer 1987.) More thoughtful and balanced discussions are contained in Lydie Koche-Miramond et al., eds., *La Chine et les droits de l'homme* (Paris: L'Harmattan, 1991), especially Part 1, "Chine traditionnelle et droits de l'homme," pp. 11–78, and in He Baogang, "Democratisation: Antidemocratic and Democratic Elements in the Political Culture of China," *Australian Journal of Political Science* 27 (1992):120–136.

4. Ambassador Li Daoyu, remarks to the UN General Assembly's Human Rights Committee, December 2, 1992. United Press International (UPI), December 2, 1992. See also remarks by Ambassador Fan Guoxiang to the Preparatory Committee of the 1993 World Conference on Human Rights, New China News Agency (NCNA) summary in FBIS, September 15, 1992, p. 1.

5. See Ann Kent, "Waiting for Rights: China's Human Rights and China's Constitutions, 1949–1989," *Human Rights Quarterly* 13:2 (May 1991):esp. 193–199.

6. Formally recognized by the PRC in 1984. These conventions, which mostly predate World War II, are listed in Hungda Chiu, "Chinese Attitudes Toward International Law of Human Rights," in Victor C. Falkenheim, ed., *Chinese Politics from Mao to Deng* (New York: Paragon House, 1989), p. 255.

7. China signed the torture convention in 1986 and ratified it in 1988. According to Article 2, authorities have an international obligation to take "effective legislative, administrative, judicial and other measures to prevent acts of torture" in any territory under their jurisdiction. Torture is epidemic in China's prisons, and the central authorities have sent mixed signals as to whether such treatment is condoned. See *Torture in China* (London: Amnesty International, December 1992) and James D. Seymour, "Cadre Accountability to the Law," *Australian Journal of Chinese Affairs,* January 1989, pp. 1–27.

8. Wang Tieya and Wei Min, eds., *Guoji fa* [International Law] (Beijing: Law Press, 1981), cited in Chiu, "Chinese Attitudes," p. 252.

9. *South China Morning Post* (Hong Kong), November 25, 1986, pp. 1–2. See also Shao Jin, "Holding High the Banner of Human Rights—Commemorating the Twentieth Anniversary of the Two Human Rights Covenants …," *Shijie zhishi* [World Knowledge], December 1, 1986, pp. 4–6, U.S. Joint Publications Research Service (JPRS), CAS-87-008, pp. 53–58; and Xu Hong, "Respect Basic Human Rights, Demand Social Progress—Commemorating the Twentieth Anniversary …," *Zhongguo fazhi bao* [China Law News], December 15, 1986, p. 4, JPRS, CAS-87-010, pp. 3–4.

10. Under the terms of the Sino-British Agreement of 1984, citizens of Hong Kong were promised the extension for fifty years of their rights under the two international covenants "as [theretofore] applied to Hong Kong." The latter limitation apparently refers to the absence of democratic rights and of the right of self-determination. Light is shed on the Hong Kong government's view of how the covenants are applied to the territory in the official *Commentary on* [and text of] *the Draft Hong Kong Bill of Rights Ordinance 1990,* March 1990, esp. pp. E32 and E36.

However, even with respect to post-1997 Hong Kong, Beijing apparently intends that the people there will have only those rights granted them by China's leaders. Chapter 3 of the "Basic Law" that is to be imposed on the territory speaks of rights and duties of the "residents." Thus, although the people of Hong Kong are promised rights that other Chinese citizens will not have, the implication is that rights are not basic but granted by law and capable of being withdrawn by law.

11. Resolution 34/169, adopted by the General Assembly on December 17, 1979. The text of this and other international human-rights agreements appear in *Human Rights: A Compilation of In-*

ternational Instruments (New York: United Nations, 1983; UN sales numbers E.83.XIV.1 and C.78.XIV.2 for the English and Chinese versions, respectively).

12. *Guangming ribao,* November 17, 1989, quoted in *Punishment Season: Human Rights in China After Martial Law* (New York: Asia Watch, 1990), p. 7.

13. See, for example, Yu Haocheng, "Baowei renquan shi renlei jinbu de zhengyi shiye" [Just Progress for Humanity Requires That Human Rights Be Protected], *Shijie zhishi* [World Knowledge], December 1, 1988, esp. p. 3. Yu worked for the Masses Publishing House, under the Ministry of Public Security. In this essay he insisted that the notion that human rights is a purely internal matter was untenable.

14. Pi Jianlong, "On the Form and Nature of Bourgeois Human Rights," *Guangming ribao,* November 6, 1989, p. 3, FBIS, November 21, 1989, pp. 30–31. (It almost seemed as though the people assigned to write articles debunking human rights did not have their hearts in it.)

15. Quoted by Wang Renzhi in *Dangdai,* July 15, 1992, pp. 39–41, JPRS, July 22, 1992, p. 15. On the tendency of the international community to ignore human-rights violations in China, see Roberta Cohen, *People's Republic of China: The Human Rights Exception* (n.p.: Parliamentary Human Rights Group, n.d.). An article based on this report appeared in *Human Rights Quarterly* 9:4 (November 1987).

16. Gong Min (pseud.), "Letter to President Carter," translated in James D. Seymour, ed., *The Fifth Modernization: China's Human Rights Movement, 1978–1979* (Stanfordville, N.Y: Earl Coleman, 1980), pp. 227–239.

17. See *Political Imprisonment in the People's Republic of China: An Amnesty International Report* (London, 1978). This was followed by its *China—Violations of Human Rights: Prisoners of Conscience & the Death Penalty in the People's Republic of China* (London, 1984).

18. Other organizations have included Human Rights in China (New York), Lawyers' Committee for Human Rights (New York), LawAsia (Manila), and Tibet Information Network (London). The "long-silent" description does not apply to exiled Tibetans, who have always been vocal on the subject of human-rights conditions in their homeland.

19. See *Turmoil at Tiananmen: A Study of U.S. Press Coverage of the Beijing Spring of 1989* (Cambridge, Mass.: John F. Kennedy School of Government, Harvard University, 1992).

20. Tang Boqiao, *Anthems of Defeat: Crackdown in Hunan Province, 1989–1992* (New York: Asia Watch, 1992).

21. In the mid-1980s, Amnesty International's reports were dismissed as "utterly groundless" (FBIS, October 9, 1985, p. A1); "We have ... no political prisoners" (*Beijing Review,* August 25, 1986, p. 15). More recently, Chinese Ambassador to the U.K. Ma Yuzhen stated: "Frankly, the Chinese people have no illusion at all about Amnesty International. We have given up any hope of developing any understanding with them because they are so biased towards China" (BBC, May 20, 1992). For evidence of the concern aroused by such reports, see the internal 1983 memorandum "Avoid Giving Amnesty International Pretexts," *Xuanchuan dongtai,* no. 8, trans. in *Chinese Law and Government,* Winter 1991–1992, p. 51.

22. For more on the subject, see James D. Seymour, "The International Reaction to the Crackdown in China," *China Information* (Leiden), April 1990, pp. 1–14.

23. This of course included the hard-line communist states. Romania's ruler (Nicolae Ceaucescu) praised the Chinese leaders for their actions, as did East Germany's (both soon out of power). North Korea's leaders were quick to express support for the crackdown, and in November Kim Il Sung apparently visited Beijing. Bulgaria supported the crackdown and opposed outside interference in China's internal affairs. Cuban authorities said that the action of the military against "counterrevolutionaries" was justified. Probably the only noncommunist government explicitly to support Beijing was Iran, which claimed that Zhao Ziyang had been an unwitting participant in an American plot, having become a victim of the U.S. conspiracy because of his reformist views, flexibility, and leniency.

24. *New York Times,* editorial, August 4, 1992.

25. See, for example, the article by the former ambassador to the PRC Winston Lord, "China and America: Beyond the Big Chill," *Foreign Affairs* 68:4 (Fall 1989):1–26. For one scholar's balanced account of these matters, see Robert S. Ross, "National Security, Domestic Politics, and Human Rights: The Bush Administration and China," in Kenneth Oye, Robert Lieber, and Donald Rothchild, eds., *Eagle in a New World: American Grand Strategy in the Post–Cold War World* (New York: Harper Collins, 1992).

26. Four "foreign military sales" deals were suspended, involving an avionics upgrade for Chinese F-8 aircraft, equipment for munitions production, antisubmarine torpedoes, and artillery-locating radars. In December 1992 (just before Bush left office) it was announced that these sales would be allowed but there would be no follow-up support and there were no plans for additional sales. Japan Economic Newswire, December 22, 1992.

27. On efforts to curb "illegal emigration," see NCNA dispatch of September 2, 1991, FBIS, September 5, 1991, pp. 37–38.

28. Quoting (respectively) UPI, October 14, 1992, and NCNA, November 25, 1992, FBIS, November 25, 1992, p. 1.

29. Gu Zhaoji and Zhang Jun, "The Answer to the Human Rights Question Is Doubtful and Disputable," *Xuexi yu yanjiu* [Study and Research (journal of the Beijing Municipal CPC Committee)], November 5, 1990, pp. 18–21, JPRS, CAR-91-007, p. 5.

30. Gu and Zhang, "The Answer to the Human Rights Question," p. 3.

31. For some of the findings, see *Waiguo wenti yanjiu* [Studies in Foreign Affairs], no. 2 (March 15, 1990):esp. 16–25, 51–59, 66–75, and 82–84.

32. On the high-level behind-the-scenes background of the white paper, see "Confidential Document on Study of the Human Rights Issue," *Dangdai* (Hong Kong), no. 15, June 15, 1992, pp. 67–70, FBIS, June 23, 1992, pp. 32–36. This document, prepared by the CCP Central Propaganda Department, reflects the ultraconservative line (whereas the white paper itself takes the moderate conservative one). Thus, individual human rights are absolutely a domestic matter, and it is appropriate for the United Nations to "care about" only certain "large-scale" violations. The white paper was largely researched and written under the direction of a Central Party School assistant professor named Dong Yunhu (who thereby won China's top academic prize). It was issued by the State Council and translated as "Human Rights in China" in both *Beijing Review,* November 4, 1991, pp. 8–45, and FBIS, supplement, November 21, 1991, pp. 1–29. Cited hereafter as "White Paper," with pagination referring to the FBIS version.

33. Opposition to the white paper was especially pronounced on college campuses. See "Statement on the Human Rights Issue in China," which appeared as a poster at Beijing University. *Ming Bao,* November 16, 1991, p. 6, FBIS, November 18, 1991. Exiled dissidents dismissed it as "all lies."

34. "White Paper," pp. 6 and 13.

35. "Criminal Reform in China," FBIS, August 11, 1992, p. 14. (The complete text occupies pp. 13–23.) For critiques, see "China: Political Prisoners Abused in Liaoning Province as Official Whitewash of Labor Reform System Continues" (Asia Watch, September 1992) and "China's Laogai: Comments on 'Criminal Reform in China'" (Laogai Research Foundation, September 1992).

36. Aside from the various reports of Amnesty International and Asia Watch, see Harry Hongda Wu, *Laogai—The Chinese Gulag* (Boulder, Colo.: Westview Press, 1992).

37. Li Daoyu, discussing plans for the 1993 World Conference on Human Rights in Vienna. UPI, December 2, 1992. "The conference should not only reaffirm that the right to development is an inalienable human right, but introduce effective measures for the realization of this right." Li did not mention civil liberties.

38. *New York Times,* August 8, 1992, p. 3. China's prison exports in 1988 are believed to have been worth $100 million. *Dangdai,* August 15, 1992, pp. 27–29, FBIS, September 11, 1992, p. 27, citing *China Law Yearbook, 1988.*

39. An article on most-favored-nation status and related subjects coauthored by a former congressman is almost entirely devoted to the human-rights aspect of the problem, with only two

short paragraphs on the issues of trade imbalance, nuclear proliferation, and weapons sales. Robert F. Drinan and Teresa T. Kuo, "The 1991 Battle for Human Rights in China," *Human Rights Quarterly* 14:1 (February 1992):21–42. For the arguments against withholding most-favored-nation status, see *The Cost of Removing MFN from China* (Washington, D.C.: United States–China Business Council, 1990). For views of Chinese exiles, see "Opinion Divided: Conditional or Unconditional MFN?" *Human Rights Tribune* (published by the New York–based organization Human Rights in China) 2:3 (June 1991):13–14.

40. For example, the journalist Zhang Weiguo says that while in prison he was told that, whatever the evidence in his case might be, "it will be up to the leaders at a higher level to determine the nature of your case." Comments Zhang: "The top government leaders proclaim judicial independence at press conferences, but my impression is to the contrary. … In the real world of adjudication, there still exists an authority higher than the law." "Text of Shanghai Dissident Zhang Weiguo Letter to Wan Li," *Baixing*, August 16, 1991, pp. 5–9, JPRS, CAR-91-074, December 31, 1991, pp. 30–31.

41. NCNA, September 6, 1992, FBIS, September 8, 1992, p. 4; NCNA, September 19, 1992, FBIS, September 23, 1992, p. 5. A thoughtful commentary is Sidney Jones, "Who Will Empower the Powerless?" *Human Rights Tribune* 3:3 (Fall 1992):4–7.

42. No executions have been carried out in Hong Kong in recent history. The legislature has voted in favor of abolishing capital punishment de jure, but this has not yet been fully carried out.

43. Gu and Zhang, "The Answer to the Human Rights Question," p. 5.

44. "White Paper," pp. 28–29.

45. Gu and Zhang, "The Answer to the Human Rights Question," p. 6.

46. *Hongkong Standard*, February 28, 1990, p. 7, FBIS, pp. 28–29.

47. *Renmin ribao*, December 3, 1988, p. 4.

48. Fu Xuezhe, "The Principle of Noninterference in the Internal Affairs of Other Countries on the Question of Human Rights—Also Commenting on the Illegality of the United States and Other Countries Interfering in China's Internal Affairs," *People's Daily*, December 8, 1989, p. 7, FBIS, December 12, 1989, p. 4. Earlier, Wang and Wei had also taken the view that certain serious, state-sanctioned human-rights violations could legitimately be dealt with internationally. Their list of such rights included terrorism, racial discrimination, genocide, slavery, and inhumane treatment of refugees. Chiu, "Chinese Attitudes," p. 253.

49. Text released by PRC Mission to the UN, January 31, 1992.

50. UN delegate Cheng Jinye, as paraphrased by NCNA, November 13, 1992, FBIS, November 16, 1992, p. 1.

51. During these periods, and even during the non-Chinese dynasties, the reality was that Tibet's rulers were chosen by Tibetans. In the Tang period, all of the ethnic Tibetan territories, including Amdo and Kham, were independent from China. This amounts to a large portion of the present PRC. (For Beijing's position on the Tibet question, see the State Council's "Tibet—Its Ownership and Human Rights Situation," translated in *Beijing Review*, September 28, 1992, pp. 10–43, and in FBIS, October 9, 1992, supplement, pp. 1–23.)

52. Mao said that Korea and Taiwan could be independent if they wished. The Mongols would "automatically become a part of the Chinese federation, at their own will. The Mohammedan and Tibetan peoples, likewise, will form autonomous republics attached to the China federation." Edgar Snow, *Red Star over China* (New York: Grove Press, 1961), p. 96.

53. The term "people" would seem to have some ethnic implications but does not apply when ethnic groups are historically intermingled with others. Thus, a "people" must have some territorial integrity before it has a right to independence. In the UN's official Chinese translation of the covenants (*Human Rights*), "peoples" is translated not as *minzu* (nationality) but as *renmin*, which might be translated "public" and has no ethnic implications. For its part, Beijing views all PRC citizens as belonging to the same *renmin*, no subset of which is entitled to self-determination.

54. An excellent account of these matters is *Defying the Dragon: China and Human Rights in Tibet* (Manila: LawAsia/London: Tibet Information Network, 1991).

55. See "Crackdown in Inner Mongolia" and "Continuing Crackdown in Inner Mongolia" (New York: Asia Watch, 1991 and 1992).

56. See Sun Zhengda, "Xizang wenti yu Meiguo de 'renquan waijiao'" [American "Human Rights Diplomacy" and the Problem of Tibet], in *Waiguo wenti, no. 2* (March 15, 1990):76–81.

57. On the CIA's activities, see A. Tom Grunfeld, *The Making of Modern Tibet* (Armonk, N.Y.: M. E. Sharpe, 1987), especially pp. 149–153. Regarding Britain's role, delegate Zhang Yishan declared to the UN's Third Committee that there are no human-rights problems in Tibet and added: "I'd like to tell the British delegate: Those things that could not be achieved in colonial times can never be achieved today." NCNA, November 25, 1992, FBIS, November 25, 1992, p. 1.

58. Testimony by L. Desaix Anderson, principal deputy assistant secretary of state, before the Senate Foreign Relations Committee on July 28, 1992. (The last sentence was in response to a question.)

59. This term is suggested by Harry Harding in "The Evolution of Chinese Politics, 1949–1989," in Raymond H. Myers, ed., *The Republic of China and the People's Republic of China: Two Societies in Opposition* (Stanford, Calif.: Hoover Institution Press, 1991), p. 338.

60. International League for Human Rights, *Getting Down to Business: The Human Rights Responsibilities of China's Investors and Trade Partners* (New York, 1992). Also still useful is the League's 1991 report *Business as Usual ... ? The International Response to Human Rights Violations in China.*

61. Though the government has a narrow view of a foreign correspondent's role, it was perhaps understandable that, in 1992, three writers were expelled for helping dissident Shen Tong hold a press conference. But on many other occasions correspondents have been harassed or expelled for having engaged in unarguably legitimate journalistic activities. On the rules that govern journalists, see Nicholas D. Kristof, "China Imposes Tighter Curbs on Foreign Reporters," *New York Times,* January 21, 1990, sec. 1, p. 5. For an example of foreign journalists' efforts on behalf of their Chinese counterparts, see *China Report* (New York: Committee to Protect Journalists, forthcoming).

11

China and the Multilateral Economic Institutions

WILLIAM R. FEENEY

For nearly a decade and a half, China has pursued a long-term economic development strategy based upon greatly expanded domestic market incentives, foreign loans, credits, investment, and trade largely within the framework of the world capitalist economic system. A critical component of its efforts to build a prosperous modern economy has been the adoption of an inclusive participatory approach to the global economic system in order to gain access to foreign capital and expertise and the longer-term economic benefits of Ricardo's international trade theory of comparative advantage.[1] China's current accommodative development strategy stands in marked contrast both to the combative system-transforming posture it adopted shortly after the 1949 Communist Revolution and to the self-righteous system-reforming approach of the 1970s based upon principles of a Third World–oriented New International Economic Order (NIEO).[2]

An especially important aspect of China's integration into the global economic system has been its membership and active participation in a number of multilateral economic institutions.[3] Beginning in 1978, China acknowledged the need for external development assistance by shifting its status from aid giver to aid recipient within the framework of the United Nations Development Program (UNDP). Subsequent revisions in China's long-standing policy of self-reliance opened the way for significantly higher levels of foreign trade and acceptance of foreign investment, loans, and credits from both bilateral and multilateral sources. One important outgrowth of this so-called open door policy in 1980 was China's formal entry into the World Bank Group (WBG)—the International Monetary Fund (IMF), the International Bank for Reconstruction and Development (IBRD) or World Bank, and its affiliated agencies the International Development Association (IDA) and the International Finance Corporation (IFC). In 1983 China was granted observer status in the General Agreement on Tariffs and Trade (GATT), and in 1986 it formally applied for full GATT membership and joined the Asian Development Bank (ADB). This chapter will focus upon China's participation in these institutions—the nature and consequences of its relationships with them, the impact of the June 1989 Tiananmen Square incident on those ties, current is-

TABLE 11.1   UNDP Country Program in China, 1978–1992

Country Program	No. Projects[a]	Funding Sources (U.S.$ millions)		
		UNDP	PRC/Other	Total
Ad hoc initial program (1978–1981)	27	$ 15.0	$ 12.5	$ 27.5
UNDP-CPI (1982–1985)	150+	66.0	15.0	81.0
UNDP-CP2 (1986–1990)	200+	135.9	27.2	163.1
UNDP-CP3 (1991–1995)	200+	141.8	22.5	164.3
Estimated totals (1978–1992)	450+[a]	273.6[b]	63.7[b]	337.3[b]

[a] These figures are approximations, since many projects overlap from one country-program period to another.

[b]These are estimated dollar totals as of the end of 1992, with CP-3 spending based upon an annual pro-rated increment for the 1991–1992 period.

Source: United Nations Development Program, *UNDP in China* (New York: UNDP, September 1989), pp. 5–6; United Nations Development Program, *UNDP Advisory Note on the Third Country Programme for the People's Republic of China (1991–1995)* (Beijing: UNDP, January 1990), pp. 2, 4; and UN Document, DP/CP/CPR/3, *Third Country Programme for China,* March 22, 1991, pp. 1, 25.

sues in these relations, and their implications for both China and the global community.

China and the United Nations Development Program

China's relationship with the United Nations Development Program (UNDP) began soon after the PRC delegation was seated in the world body in 1971. In November 1972 China began to take part in UNDP pledging conferences, and over the next several years it participated in a number of UNDP-supported programs in Asia and Africa. In 1974 China made token contributions in nonconvertible renminbi to the organization. The following January it agreed to serve on the UNDP Governing Council, but over the next four years it steadfastly refused any UNDP assistance despite its technical eligibility.[4] During this time China regarded UNDP assistance policies as ill-conceived and wrongly restricted to certain types of technical objectives rather than a broadly based NIEO-type program spanning the entire development spectrum. In November 1978 it unexpectedly acknowledged its need for modernization and requested UNDP assistance, which was approved by the UNDP Governing Council despite displeasure from some Third World states and the former Soviet Union and its erstwhile allies. Much of this concern derived from intensified competition for available UNDP resources and later what seemed to be artificially deflated and self-serving per capita income statistics used by China to justify larger aid allotments.

China has done well in its relationship with the UNDP (see Table 11.1). In 1978 it paid the UN U.S.$27.1 million in regular dues and token contributions and received nothing in UNDP assistance. Though the planning deadline for the UNDP's 1977–1981 aid disbursement cycle had passed, it lobbied successfully for a U.S.$15 million grant for the last three years of the cycle, which was combined with U.S.$12.5 million from other funding sources to finance 27 specific projects prior to the next regular UNDP resource allotment period. In the wake of Beijing's determined efforts to justify a broad range of technical assistance projects, China's first country program received some U.S.$66 million (an increase of 340 percent), which was added to U.S.$15 million from other sources to pay for more than 150 projects. China enjoyed a more than 100 percent increase in UNDP assistance, to U.S.$135.9 million, during its second country program (1986–1990), which when supplemented by other revenues made a total of U.S.$163.1 million available to fund over 200 projects. Finally, during its third country program (1991–1995) it will receive about the same level of UNDP resources and an overall total of U.S.$164.3 million to finance over 200 more projects.

Since 1979 the UNDP-China partnership has expanded dramatically. By 1992 China had received some U.S.$273.6 million to fund more than 400 projects, becoming the largest single recipient of UNDP assistance. Many of these endeavors are regarded as precursors to more extensive projects undertaken by such major institutions as the ADB and the IBRD/IDA. Through cooperative planning and cost sharing, the UNDP has been able to mobilize and multiply resources not only from the multilateral economic institutions but also from the PRC government, other governments and international agencies, and private sources. More specifically, the UNDP China program has emphasized specialized training, preinvestment surveys, technology transfer, and highly beneficial small-scale projects in energy development, agriculture, fishing, forestry, industry, environment, information processing, and rural development.[5] Two particularly useful UNDP programs have been TOKEN (Transfer of Knowledge through Expatriate Nationals), which brings back overseas Chinese specialists for two- to eight-week consultancies, and STAR (Senior Technical Advisers' Recruitment) for similar visits by non-Chinese experts.

The events of June 1989 had little perceptible impact on the UNDP China program. The midterm review carried out in March–April 1988 had resulted in a modest expansion of activities.[6] The immediate impact of the Tiananmen Square incident was the evacuation of most UNDP program officers and staff from Beijing and formal efforts to ensure the safety of UNDP personnel. The UNDP office in Beijing, established in September 1979, remained open, and within two weeks the full staff had returned. Thereafter, there was a review of all UNDP projects in the pipeline to determine their continued desirability and feasibility from the perspective of the host government and the altered programmatic context. Though one small project jointly funded at U.S.$3–400,000 by the UNDP and the Ford Foundation was suspended, no projects were canceled.

Since the advent of the UNDP China relationship, organization officials have believed that the program would provide important support for the Chinese leadership's modernization commitment. Though the events of June 1989 prompted the leadership to reemphasize state ownership and central planning and control, raising some questions about the role that the UNDP third country program would play in China's reform-oriented Eighth Five-Year Plan (1991–1995), developments culminating in the Fourteenth Congress of the Chinese Communist Party (CCP) in October 1992 strongly suggested that reformist modernization policies were back in favor. Thus, it appears likely that the UNDP's China program will be limited only by available resources and will continue to play an important seeding function in China's modernization.

China and the World Bank Group

China's relationship with the WBG has also experienced profound changes over time. Between the 1949 Communist Revolution and its 1971 seating in the UN, China disparaged the WBG as "citadels of international capitalism." In 1979, as part of its new modernization strategy, China suspended its criticism and called for a restoration to its rightful place in the WBG. Strenuous efforts during 1979–1980 ultimately led to China's formal entry into the IMF on April 17, 1980, and the World Bank, the IDA, and the IFC on May 15, 1980.[7] An important prerequisite for effective WBG assistance to China was a thorough study and analysis of the Chinese economy. In an intensive year-long review, a thirty-member World Bank team produced a three-volume report concluding that future Chinese growth would depend upon specific economic priority decisions, substantial sectoral infrastructure investments, and an emphasis on manufactured exports to the world market. But because import-financing requirements would exceed earnings from exports, direct investment, and net transfers, China would need to borrow foreign funds at a rate commensurate with its desired growth.[8] This report was followed by an analysis of development issues and options, a series of sector studies that pinpointed problem areas and impediments, and a lengthy list of recommendations and specific projects to overcome these developmental barriers.[9]

Membership in the IMF proved to be eminently beneficial to China during the 1980s. The major functions of the IMF for member states are to facilitate the balanced growth of international trade, promote foreign exchange stability and orderly exchange relations, overcome temporary balance-of-payments problems by providing supplemental credits as needed, and encourage overall international monetary cooperation. On several occasions after 1980, China experienced temporary bouts of currency inflation and sharp domestic budgetary and foreign trade deficits and turned to the IMF for credit and advisory assistance (see Table 11.2). In December 1980 and January 1981 it made its first IMF drawings from the reserve tranche (or segment) in the combined amount of SDR368.1 million (U.S.$478 million).[10] The following March China utilized its second tier or first credit tranche in the amount of SDR450 million (U.S.$550 million) as well as a loan of SDR309.5 million (U.S.$365 million) from the IMF Trust Fund.[11] In return, it pledged to readjust its modernization strategy, eliminate its budget deficit, control the growth of its money supply, curb inflationary pressures, and reduce its foreign trade deficit. During its first year of IMF membership, China borrowed nearly U.S.$1.4 billion and implemented an ambitious economic stabilization program. In May 1983 it announced that it would repay its first credit tranche drawing early, and at the end of 1984 it did so.

In mid-1984 China's balance-of-payments position again deteriorated, a situation aggravated a year later by a 60 percent surge in imports and sharply lower oil export earnings. In response, China tightened its financial policies and economic management, raised interest rates, and devalued the renmimbi to cut imports and

TABLE 11.2 China's IMF Drawings, 1980–1992 (SDR millions; U.S.$ millions in parentheses)

Date of Inception	Source/Amount	Terms
December 1980	Reserve tranche/SDR218.1[a] (U.S.$278)	Interest-free; no service fee; indefinite repayment (repaid)
January 1981	Reserve tranche/SDR150 (U.S.$200)	Same as above (repaid)
March 2, 1981/December 31, 1981	First credit tranche/SDR450 (U.S.$550)	6.4% interest; 0.5% service fee; 3–5-yr. repayment (repaid 1984)
March 31, 1981/March 30, 1991	Trust Fund/SDR309.5 (U.S.$365)	0.5% interest; 10-yr. repayment (repaid 1991)
November 12, 1986/November 11, 1987	First credit tranche/SDR597.7 (U.S.$717)	5.97% interest; 0.25% service fee; 3–5 yr. repayment (repaid 1992)[b]
Total 1980–1992	SDR1,725.3 (U.S.$2,110)	

[a]The SDR (special drawing right) is the composite value of a weighted basket of five national currencies and varies over time against individual national currencies. It is an artifical international reserve unit and can be used to settle accounts among central banks. The advantage over individual national currencies is its greater relative stability. Since August 1983 the SDR interest rate has been determined weekly by reference to a combined market interest rate that is the weighted average of interest rates on specified short-term obligations in the money markets of the same five countries whose currencies are included in the SDR valuation basket.

[b] The 1986–1987 first credit tranche drawing was repaid in the amount of SDR74.72 million in 1989–1990, SDR298.86 million in 1990–1991, and SDR224.15 million in 1991–1992.

Sources: Friedrick W. Wu, "External Borrowing and Foreign Aid in Post-Mao China's International Economic Policy: Data and Observations," *Columbia Journal of World Business* 19 (Fall 1984):57; International Monetary Fund, *Annual Report 1981* (Washington, D.C.: IMF, 1981), pp. 83, 103–104, 120; International Monetary Fund, *Annual Report 1984* (Washington, D.C.: IMF, 1984), p. 113; International Monetary Fund, *Annual Report 1987* (Washington, D.C.: IMF, 1987), pp. 79, 152, 162; International Monetary Fund, *Annual Report 1990* (Washington, D.C.: IMF, 1990), p. 77; International Monetary Fund, *Annual Report 1991* (Washington, D.C.: IMF, 1991), p. 90; and International Monetary Fund, *Annual Report 1992* (Washington, D.C.: IMF, 1992), p. 101.

boost exports. Recommendations made by a 1986 IMF consultative mission were important in helping China to formulate these decisions.[12] In the meantime it was able to negotiate a standby arrangement in the first credit tranche for up to SDR597.7 million (U.S.$717 million) to cushion the impact of retrenchment. During these several negotiation sessions with the IMF, it became clear that China was highly sensitive to any action by an external agency that suggested imposed specific conditionality, but China did express readiness to consider and implement the IMF's recommendations at least in part.[13]

Largely because of its learning experiences in the early years of IMF membership, China was prepared to cope with the economic crisis of 1988–1989, which involved excessive money supply expansion, double-digit inflation, a rising budget deficit, a deteriorating trade balance, and escalating foreign debt but a modest rise in foreign exchange reserves.[14] To deal with this situation, it adopted a three-year austerity program in September 1988 with IMF support. Though the Tiananmen Square incident temporarily aggravated the economic situation, a general turnaround was under way by mid-1990. Thereafter, the growth in the money supply was cut substantially; inflation dropped to less than 3 percent in 1991 but turned up in 1992; the trade situation turned positive in the amount of U.S.$8.7 billion in 1990 and U.S.$8.1 billion in 1992, and foreign exchange reserves leaped to U.S.$29 billion in 1990 and to U.S.$42 billion at the end of 1991, the sixth-largest in the world.[15]

Though it would be unfair to attribute China's solid economic recovery since 1990, especially in its foreign trade balance and foreign exchange reserves, in any significant degree to the IMF, responsible Chinese government personnel have gained an expanded understanding of budgetary and foreign exchange and trade enhancement tools available to them as a consequence of IMF membership. Indeed, a mutually productive and cooperative relationship has emerged that has focused on regular consultation and professional interaction; extensive training for Chinese personnel in statistical data collection, methodology, and accounting procedures; formal lectures, joint seminars, colloquia, and seminars; informal discussions; a full-scale technical assistance program since 1985; and, perhaps most important, an increasing understanding and acceptance by the Chinese of the vagaries of budget development and projection, the role of the money supply, the variable nature of business and trade cycles, and the verities of the international merchandise and foreign exchange markets. In short, IMF membership has greatly aided China in managing its new status as a major trading nation and reaping the significant economic dividends of its increasingly important role in the global economy.

China has also enjoyed a highly beneficial and productive relationship with the World Bank and its IDA and IFC affiliates. The primary purpose of the 160-member World Bank and the 142-member IDA has been to promote economic development and structural reform in the less-developed countries (LDCs) by long-term financing of development projects and programs through borrowing on the international bond market, retained earnings, and loan repayments. IBRD loans and IDA credits support a wide variety of projects in thirteen sectoral categories.[16] World Bank loan capital is raised by member subscriptions, borrowing in the world capital markets, retained earnings, and loan repayments. IDA credits are derived mostly from member subscriptions, periodic replenishments by the developed member-states, and net IBRD earnings transfers. IDA resources have been replenished eight times to date, with the most recent agreement (1991–1993) in the amount of SDR11.7 billion.[17] The principal mandate of the 147-member IFC is to foster economic growth by promoting private-sector investment in its member LDCs. To do so, it provides both equity investment capital through a paid-in capital base, international bond issues, and retained earnings and a full array of technical assistance and advisory services.

China has been singularly successful in securing World Bank financial assistance to implement its open-door modernization policy. Between 1981 and 1992 it received over U.S.$13.3 billion in loans and credits for some 109 projects, with IBRD loans accounting for U.S.$7.46 billion, or 56 percent of the total World Bank commitment to China, and IDA credits contributing U.S.$5.85 billion, or 44 percent of the total (see Table 11.3). Between 1982–1983 and 1987–1988, World Bank assistance to China rose each year, achieving an annual high of nearly U.S.$1.7 billion. In 1988–1989 China's borrowing fell off to almost U.S.$1.35 billion, and in 1989–1990 it plunged to less than half that amount as a result of the suspension of World Bank project approvals prompted by the Tiananmen Square incident.

That incident had significant short-range consequences but few discernible long-term repercussions for China in terms of its World Bank relationship. Initially, much of the Bank resident mission staff was evacuated from Beijing for about ten days to ensure members' personal safety. In the meantime, under intense international pressure especially from the Bush administration, World Bank officials deferred discussions on seven pending loans and credits totaling some U.S.$786 million, with 44 projects worth U.S.$7.1 billion in the pipeline. During the annual economic summit meeting in Paris in mid-July, the Group of Seven (G-7) leaders formally endorsed postponement of new World Bank loans to China. This action had a similar deferment impact on the third round of Japan's bilateral assistance program for China, worth U.S.$5.8 billion, and future project and technical assistance loans from the Asian Development Bank and the international banking community.

Beginning in December 1989, the U.S. position on the World Bank lending freeze was subjected to numerous pressures. First, the Bush administration responded to calls by the U.S. business community by lifting the ban on lending to China by the Export-Import Bank. Second, despite strong opposition from some of its members, the U.S. Congress expressed its sense that the United States under Section 701(f) of the International Financial Institutions Act should oppose loans to countries engaging in a pattern of human-rights violations unless the loans were directed to programs that served the basic human needs of citizens of those countries. In February 1990, after martial law had been lifted in Beijing and under increasing pressure from the G-7 nations and World Bank officials (who had a vested bureaucratic interest in unclogging the administrative pipeline), the Bush administration announced that the United States was prepared to support renewed World Bank loans to China on a case-by-case basis for so-called basic human needs projects.[18] This policy modification, along with the May 1990 extension of China's most-favored-nation trade status for another year, suggested that the Bush administration was trying to use economic incentives to bolster moder-

TABLE 11.3 World Bank Annual and Cumulative Lending to China, 1981–1992 (U.S.$ millions)

	IBRD		IDA		Annual Totals		Cumulative Totals		Cumulative Numerical Ranking[a]
	No.	Amount	No.	Amount	No.	Amount	No.	Amount	
1980–1981	1	$ 100.0	0	$ 100.0	1	$200.0	1	$200.0	70/125
1981–1982	0	0.0	1	60.0	1	60.0	2	260.0	63/125
1982–1983	5	463.1	1	150.4	6	613.5	8	873.5	28/128
1983–1984	5	616.0	5	423.5	10	1,039.5	18	1,913.0	18/132
1984–1985	7	659.6	5	442.3	12	1,101.9	30	3,014.9	14/136
1985–1986	7	687.0	4	450.0	11	1,137.0	41	4,151.9	11/136
1986–1987	8	867.4	3	556.2	11	1,423.6	52	5,575.5	8/137
1987–1988	10	1,053.7	4	639.9	15	1,693.6	68	7,269.1	6/137
1988–1989	7	833.4	5	515.0	12	1,348.4	78	8,617.5	6/137
1989–1990	0	0.0	5	590.0	5	590.0	83	9,207.5	6/139
1990–1991	6	601.5	4	977.8	10	1,579.3	93	10,786.8	6/142
1991–1992	8	1,577.7	8	948.6	16	2,526.3	109	13,313.1	5/160
Total	64	$ 7,459.4	45	$5,853.7	109	$ 13,313.1			

[a]China's ranking as a cumulative borrower compared with total World Bank membership.

Sources: World Bank, *Annual Report 1981*, pp. 120, 188; *Annual Report 1982*, pp. 118, 184; *Annual Report 1983*, pp. 126, 218; *Annual Report 1984*, pp. 139, 210; *Annual Report 1985*, pp. 145, 166; *Annual Report 1986*, pp. 137, 158; *Annual Report 1987*, pp. 139, 160; *Annual Report 1988*, pp. 131, 152; *Annual Report 1989*, pp. 158, 178; *Annual Report 1990*, pp. 156, 178; *Annual Report 1991*, pp. 161, 182; *Annual Report 1992*, p. 176.

ate elements within the Chinese leadership to resume economic liberalization policies and to temper human-rights abuses. But domestic U.S. political realities in the form of a strong "sustain indignation" school in Congress that cut across party and ideological lines and the risk of a public backlash precluded any early end to the U.S. basic-human-needs loan policy for China.

What constituted a basic-human-needs project was never clearly defined. In May 1990, to the dismay of congressional critics, the Bush administration supported an IDA afforestation project, which suggested informal definitional elasticity.[19] At the Houston G-7 summit in July 1990, a joint statement promised to explore other World Bank loans that would "contribute to reforms of the Chinese economy," including those for environmental concerns.[20] Iraq's military takeover of Kuwait in August and a number of conciliatory human-rights gestures by China further defused congressional and public opposition. By November 1990 the World Bank, with the acquiescence of the Bush administration, had approved eight basic-human-needs projects (one financed by the IBRD and seven by the IDA) worth U.S.$793.2 million.

In December 1990, soon after China had abstained (rather than use its veto) on a UN Security Council vote that authorized the use of force to expel Iraq from Kuwait, all remaining objections to unrestricted World Bank loans to China disappeared.[21] Though the Bush administration persisted for a time in maintaining the basic-human-needs fiction, the policy was soon abandoned, and the rate of World Bank lending to China accelerated to record levels due largely to the number of projects delayed in the pipeline. From a 1990–1991 level of U.S.$1,579.3 million, which was somewhat above the average annual amount during the pre-Tiananmen period from 1986–1987 to 1988–1990, about U.S.$1,488.5 million, the volume of lending soared in 1991–1992 to an all-time high of U.S.$2,526.3 million. In 1992, China was the fifth-largest combined IBRD/IDA borrower (ninth largest in IBRD loans and third largest in IDA credits) (see Table 11.4). The most important project funding categories have been agricultural and rural development (U.S.$3.45 billion), transportation (U.S.$2.87 billion), energy (U.S.$1.25 billion), and education (U.S.$1.11 billion).

China's relationship with the International Finance Corporation has been far less extensive than with the other WBG agencies. For the first few years of its World Bank membership, China, though technically eligible even as a socialist country, chose not to seek IFC funds for private or mixed enterprises. However, in 1985 China requested and obtained a U.S.$18.2 million IFC commitment to finance the Guangzhou Peugeot Automobile Company Ltd., a joint French-Chinese motor vehicle production venture. In 1987 the IFC approved two additional China-related investments: a U.S.$5 million commitment to the China Bicycles Company, Ltd., to expand production to 1 million bicycles annually, 85 percent for export, and a U.S.$3 million mixed-equity commitment to J.F. China Investment Company, Ltd., of Hong Kong, a project sponsored by the Jardine Fleming investment company of Hong Kong to finance small and medium-sized joint ventures in China. In 1989 the IFC made two commitments to China, the first in the amount of U.S.$15 million (subsequently reduced to U.S.$12.5 million) to the Crown (China) Electronics Company, Ltd., a joint Sino-Japanese venture to manufacture audio and visual consumer electronic products for export, and the sec-

TABLE 11.4 Summary of Cumulative IBRD Loans and IDA Credits to Ten Largest Borrowers as of June 30, 1992 (U.S.$ millions)

	IBRD Loans				IDA Credits				Combined Lending		
Country	No.	Amount	% Total	Country	No.	Amount	% Total	Country	No.	Amount	% Total
1. Mexico	136	$ 20,734.6	9.50	1. India	186	$18,916.6	26.62	1. India	333	$ 39,515.8	13.67
2. India	147	20,599.2	9.44	2. Bangladesh	136	5,961.3	8.39	2. Mexico	136	20,734.6	7.17
3. Brazil	194	19,734.6	9.04	3. China	45	5,853.7	8.24	3. Brazil	194	19,734.6	6.82
4. Indonesia	169	18,054.3	8.27	4. Pakistan	87	3,630.2	5.11	4. Indonesia	215	18,986.1	6.56
5. Turkey	107	11,399.4	5.22	5. Tanzania	75	2,156.1	3.03	5. China	109	13,313.1	4.60
6. Philippines	125	8,014.6	3.67	6. Kenya	58	2,023.4	2.85	6. Turkey	117	11,577.9	4.00
7. Republic of Korea	100	7,624.0	3.49	7. Ghana	59	1,775.5	2.50	7. Pakistan	163	8,413.4	2.91
8. Colombia	131	7,538.6	3.45	8. Sri Lanka	58	1,751.9	2.47	8. Philippines	129	8,238.8	2.85
9. China	64	7,459.4	3.42	9. Uganda	44	1,630.7	2.29	9. Republic of Korea	106	7,734.8	2.67
10. Nigeria	84	6,248.2	2.86	10. Ethiopia	48	1,414.8	1.99	10. Colombia	131	7,558.1	2.61
Total[a]	3,414	$218,209.9	100.00		2,218	$71,065.0	100.00		5,632	$289,274.9	100.00

[a] Cumulative totals for all member states.

Source: World Bank, *Annual Report 1991* (Washington, D.C.: IBRD, 1991), pp. 182–185; *Annual Report 1992* (Washington, D.C.: IBRD, 1992), pp. 176–177.

ond in the amount of U.S.$3 million (a U.S.$2 million loan and U.S.$1 million in equity) to the Shenzhen-Chronar Solar Energy Company, Ltd., to establish a factory to manufacture amorphous silicon photovoltaic panels principally for export. Prior to the Tiananmen Square incident, total IFC commitments to China amounted to U.S.$44.27 million (Table 11.5).

After Tiananmen Square, further expansion of the China-IFC relationship was completely blocked until 1992 for several reasons. First, the U.S. policy freezing World Bank loans to China extended to IFC commitments, which were unaffected by any mitigating private-sector basic-human-needs criteria. Second, China's policy commitment to economic liberalization and reform and the role of private venture capital in that process became a contentious issue within the Chinese Communist Party hierarchy. Finally, private investor confidence both within and outside China was adversely affected, dampening the potential for IFC initiatives. Ultimately, China did signal its reformist intentions in February 1990 by signing the Convention on the Settlement of Investment States and Nationals of Other States and by its adherence two months later to the convention that established the Multilateral Investment Guarantee Agency (MIGA).[22] In addition to contracting for several MIGA projects, China invited the staff of the Foreign Investment Advisory Services (FIAS), a joint MIGA-IFC component, to conduct diagnostic studies on the investment climate in China, including obstacles to foreign direct investment.[23] In 1992 the IFC extended a second loan of U.S.$12.5 million and took a U.S.$2.5 million equity position to build a new plant for China Bicycles Company, Ltd., increasing its capacity from 1.2 million to about 2.5 million bicycles per year. In addition, the IFC exercised its preemptive rights to subscribe to the capital increase of Guangzhou Peugeot Automobile Company, Ltd., to expand production capacity.[24] Though the volume of IFC projects has been limited, the recent increase in support for freer markets, especially as a result of the Fourteenth Congress of the CCP, and the decline in the state sector of the economy suggest that this may change.[25]

Since 1980 China has derived a broad range of benefits from WBG membership: (1) the preparation and dissemination of a large number of detailed studies about virtually every aspect of the Chinese economy by highly skilled IMF and World Bank analysts; (2) periodic balance-of-payments and budgetary deficit assistance through the IMF; (3) access to a large pool of lending capital at either favorable or zero interest rates to expand domestic production and productivity in a broad array of primary and finished products for domestic consumption and foreign trade and to finance a large number of costly infrastructure projects necessary for rapid modernization; (4) assistance to a large number of training and research institutions; and (5) extensive training and educational opportunities in the form of fellowships and scholarships, courses, seminars, workshops, conferences, study tours, and materials in virtually every aspect of international economic activity for mid- and top-level Chinese career functionaries at IMF and IBRD staff headquarters, the staff missions in Beijing, and, through the IMF Institute, the World Bank Economic Development Institute (EDI), programs sponsored by the UN Department of Technical Cooperation for Development (UN/DTCD), and training sessions in other LDCs under the UNDP Regional Program for Asia and the Pacific.[26]

TABLE 11.5 IFC Commitments to China, 1986–1992 (U.S.$ millions)

Enterprise/Sector	FY of Commitment	Original Commitment[a]	Investments Held for IFC		
			Loans[a]	Equity[a]	Total[a]
Guangzhou Peugeot Automobile Company, Ltd./ automotive and accessories	FY 1985–1992	$18.23/19.5	$12.19/10.3	$3.23/4.5	$15.41/14.9
China Bicycles Company, Ltd./ general manufacturing	FY 1988–1992	5.00/19.9	3.33/15.0	0.00/2.4	3.33/17.4
J.F. China Investment Company, Ltd./ development financing	FY 1988	3.04/3.0	3.00/3.0	0.04[b]	3.04/3.0
Crown (China) Electronics Company, Ltd./ general manufacturing	FY 1989	15.00/15.0	15.00/12.5	–	15.00/12.5
Shenzhen-Chronar Solar Energy Company, Ltd./ general manufacturing	FY 1989	3.00/1.0	–	1.00/1.0	1.00/1.0
Total China		$44.27/58.4	$33.52/40.8	$4.27/7.9	$37.78/48.8
Total All Members			$7,718.0	$999.3	$8,717.3

[a]The first figure is the amount as of the end of FY 1989; the second figure is the amount as of the end of FY 1992. Commitments include funds to be provided by the IFC for its own account, funds to be provided by participants through the purchase of an interest in IFC's investment, and funds to be provided by other financial institutions in association with IFC. Original commitments are composed of disbursed and undisbursed balances. The undisbursed portion is revalued at current exchange rates; the disbursed portion represents the cost of the commitment at the time of disbursement. Loans held for the IFC are revalued at current exchange rates. Amounts shown in the second columns are for currently outstanding commitments, not of cancellations.

[b]Less than $50,000.

Sources: International Finance Corporation, *Annual Report 1991* (Washington, D.C.: IFC, 1991), pp. 83, 88, 92; International Finance Corporation, *Annual Report 1992* (Washington, D.C.: IFC, 1992), pp. 99, 104, 120.

The importance of China's WBG connection for domestic policy cannot be overestimated. Not only have World Bank analyses had a deep and far-reaching impact on the economic decisions of the Chinese political leadership, but WBG participation has prompted the creation of an extensive government bureaucracy to manage that relationship. World Bank research findings and recommendations have played an important role in the formulation and implementation of China's five-year plans, and IBRD- and IDA-funded projects have become an integral part of that planning cycle. However, it is probably the educational and socialization function of WBG training and personal interaction that will have the most profound and enduring impact on the thinking, understanding, and policy proclivities of China's present and future economic and financial bureaucratic elite. Any protracted rupture in that symbiotic relationship comparable to the immediate post-Tiananmen period would have profoundly negative consequences for the pace of China's continued economic progress and development.

In a broader sense, China's WBG connection has helped to transform it from a hortatory self-abnegating champion of the Third World to a more activist self-serving advocate for its own modernization. From its WBG entry in 1980 until the Tiananmen Square episode, China's WBG participation was an important hallmark of its political maturity and commitment to the existing global economic order, befitting a worthy and honorable international creditor, producer, and customer. For that commitment China was handsomely rewarded in the form of heavy external funding for infrastructural expansion, significantly higher levels of foreign investment, extensive infusions of technical expertise and assistance, and an explosion in foreign trade and export earnings. As China's economic stake in WBG membership grew in the form of access to external credits, foreign investment, and markets and the attendant foreign exchange earnings and reserves, the WBG freeze after Tiananmen Square came as a sudden jolt to China's sensibilities, expectations, and pocketbook and forced it to make some grudging human-rights concessions. But it was the WBG G-7 elite that ultimately made most of the concessions, and within a decent interval of less than eighteen months it was business as usual with essentially symbolic Chinese kowtows. Indeed, China skillfully played upon G-7 fears of hard-line permanency in the world's largest marketplace to induce a change in WBG policy. All the while, China, which has long identified with the Third World and the Group of Twenty-Four (the LDC lobby in the WBG) but has never become a formal member of the group or assumed a Third World advocacy role within the WBG, has staked an ever-increasing claim on WBG resources. Its size and needs have meant far greater LDC competition for a limited pool of ordinary capital loan resources and especially concessional IDA credits. Although the Tiananmen Square freeze temporarily redirected such resources to other LDC recipients, China has successfully reasserted its claim to even more than its traditional share of the WBG pie. Somewhat less clear at this point is whether China has irrevocably embarked upon the reformist road. What is very clear is that it has had its modernization wheels well greased by the WBG. Although this development may provoke an unwelcome dose of Third World envy and some small bones of human-rights crow in China's craw, the voracious Chinese appetite for capital to finance growth and modernization is certainly being appeased with increasing WBG largesse.

China and the Asian Development Bank

On March 20, 1986, China became the forty-seventh member of the ADB. Deng Xiaoping had expressed an interest in joining the ADB as early as February 1979, and in February 1983 China officially had applied for membership on the condition that Taiwan be expelled.[27] The United States insisted that Taipei had been a founding member of the organization in 1966 and on joining the Bank had emphasized that it represented only the Taiwan area. Furthermore, the ouster of Taiwanese representatives from China's UN seat was unconnected to the ADB situation (the latter having no linkage to the United Nations), and there was no reason for the ADB to treat Taipei's as the only Chinese seat. Most members at the time—including the United States and Japan which together held just over 27 percent of the votes—opposed Taiwan's ouster. Though China would become one of the Bank's largest borrowers, it pledged to subscribe to about 7 percent of the ADB's capital. Retention of Taiwan as a capital provider and guarantor for about 1.2 percent of the Bank's capital added to the PRC capital subscription would expand the ADB's capital stock to the benefit of all borrowing member-states. Finally, and most important, not only did the ADB Charter stipulate that a member could be expelled only for defaulting on a loan (which did not apply to Taiwan) but such action would have increased Taiwan's diplomatic isolation and encouraged the island's independence movement.

Up to 1985, Taiwan had reacted negatively to the PRC membership application, arguing that there were no valid grounds for its expulsion from the Bank. After the 1985 PRC-ADB memorandum of understanding, Taiwan announced its "three-noes" policy—no acceptance of the "Taipei, China" designation, no withdrawal from the Bank, and no participation in ADB meetings. Although Taiwan did attend several technical meetings that did not involve official names and flags, it had no representatives at the 1986 and 1987 annual ADB meetings.[28] In January 1988 Republic of China (ROC) President Chiang Ching-kuo died, and his successor, Lee Teng-hui, ended Taiwan's self-imposed ADB exile by sending a delegation to the April 1988 ADB board of governors meetings in Manila. However, the Taiwanese registered their objections by covering their country's nameplate with an "Under Protest" sign, presenting a written statement alluding to the ADB Charter for the official country designation and disavowing acceptance of the "blatantly unfair designation," and using the ROC designation in their final report to the Bank on Taiwan's financial and economic development.[29] In May 1989, for the first time in twenty years, Taiwan sent an official delegation to Beijing to attend the twenty-second ADB annual meetings. Thus, it would seem that just one month before the Tiananmen Square incident Taipei had essentially accepted its new status but only after both sides had made significant concessions.[30]

From 1986 until the Tiananmen Square incident, the ADB provided China with seven loans valued at U.S.$416 million, twenty-two technical assistance projects in the amount of U.S.$8.42 million, and a U.S.$3 million private-sector investment equity line to the Shanghai SITCO Enterprise Co., Ltd. Bank lending to China increased each year up to 1989, when China was scheduled to receive some U.S.$500 million in new loans. As a result of the 1989 Tiananmen upheaval, however, U.S.$422.5 million in fully negotiated loans for five projects and a variety of technical assistance projects were put on hold.[31] ADB officials pressed for a resumption of lending, but because the United States did not agree to a basic-human-needs exemption for ordinary capital loans and China had chosen not to seek concessional credit through the Asian Development Fund (ADF—comparable to the IDA), ADB lending to China was not resumed until November 1990. In the interim, China's share of ADB loans was allocated to other developing member countries, increasing the average loan size by some 50 percent.

By the end of November 1990 a large backlog of ADB loans and technical assistance projects for China was finally unblocked with the change in U.S. policy. Over the next twenty-five months the Bank approved no fewer than sixteen project loans worth some U.S.$1,449.3 million. During the latter period the number of ADB loans was more than double the number extended for the 1986–1989 period, and their value exceeded that of the earlier period by U.S.$1,072.8 million. There was a similar jump in the numbers and values of technical assistance projects. The Bank approved sixty-seven technical assistance projects worth U.S.$29.97 million compared with twenty-two projects valued at U.S.$8.42 million for the earlier period. Finally, the Asian Finance and Investment Corporation (AFIC) made two private-sector commitments to China worth U.S.$14.3 million in contrast to one project for U.S.$3 million previously.

During its relatively brief membership in the Asian Development Bank, China has been able to replicate its WBG benefits on a more modest regional scale. From 1986 to 1992 it gleaned some U.S.$1.92 billion in loans (including private-sector operations) and U.S.$38.4 million in technical assistance project preparatory and advisory and operational grants, for a total of more than U.S.$1.96 billion (see Table 11.6). In 1993 it is scheduled to receive ADB loans worth an additional U.S.$1,670 million.[32] As the largest and most populous Bank member, China has quickly established itself as an important borrower (ninth-largest of the thirty-one regional borrower members) and has been able to use the Bank to accelerate its development pace as well as boost its regional visibility and prestige. ADB participation has also set an important political precedent by formalizing an organizational relationship with Taiwan and providing a useful framework for burgeoning mainland-Taiwan trade. Since the ADB dual-membership breakthrough, similar arrangements with comparable formal participation by Taiwan and Hong Kong have been devised for the Pacific Economic Cooperation Conference (PECC), where Taiwan is designated "Chinese Taipei," and the Asia-Pacific Economic Cooperation (APEC) conference, in which Taiwan is referred to as "Taipei, China."[33] Though reluctant to lend additional formal organizational legitimacy to Taiwan as a separate entity, China is also sensitive to the possibility of the collapse of the Uruguay round of GATT trade talks and the need for an inclusive regional trade organization within the framework of the world trade system.[34]

China and the GATT

On July 14, 1986 China formally applied to rejoin the GATT. The GATT is an international trade regime that encourages its 110 members to trade on the most favorable terms available by developing rules ensuring reciprocity, nondiscrimination, and transparency in each member's trade regime and by providing an in-

241

TABLE 11.6 ADB Annual and Cumulative Lending to China, 1986–1992, as of December 31, 1992 (U.S.$ millions)

	No. Loans	Loan Amount	No. Technical Assistance Projects[a]	Amount	No. Private Sector Operations	Amount	Total Lending Amount
1986	0	$ 0.0	1	$ 0.075	0	$ 0.0	$ 0.075
1987	2	133.3	5	1.402	0	0.0	134.702
1988	4	282.9	10	3.359	1	3.0	289.259
1989	1	39.7	6	3.585	0	0.0	43.285
1990	1	50.0	4	1.777	0	0.0	51.777
1991	6	496.3	30	14.426	2	14.3	252.026
1992	9	903.0	33	13.767	0	0.0	916.767
Total	23	$1,905.2	89[a]	$38.391[a]	3	$17.3	$1,960.891

[a]Of this total, 64 technical assistance projects were exclusively ADB-funded in the amount of U.S.$23.748 million; 21 projects were funded by the Japan Special Fund (JSF) in the amount of U.S.$12.875 million; 1 project was supported by the French government for U.S.$0.60 million; 2 projects were financed by the UNDP in the amount of U.S.$0.75 million; and 1 project was jointly supported by the JSF and the UNDP in the amount of U.S.$0.83 million.

Sources: Asian Development Bank, *Loan Technical Assistance and Private Sector Approvals No. 92/1* (January 1992), pp. 1, 22–23, 60; Asian Development Bank, *Annual Report 1991* (Manila: ADB, 1992), pp. 81–82; and Asian Development Bank, Board of Governors, *Annual Report 1992* (Manila: ADB, May 4–6, 1993), pp. 68, 173, 196–197.

stitutional framework for periodic multilateral trade negotiations. China's decision was a logical outgrowth of its growing involvement in the world economic system but one marked by long ambivalence and controversy.[35] In April 1948 the ROC had been one of the twenty-three original founding GATT members, but the Nationalist government had quit the organization in May 1950 after it had fled to Taiwan and the Communist government had come to power on the mainland. Though the PRC government frequently asserted that it was the sole legal government of all of China, implying that it had a right to reverse the withdrawal decision, Beijing regarded the GATT as a rich-man's club and chose not to participate even after its UN seating in 1971. Nevertheless, it closely monitored GATT activities and remained in indirect contact with GATT officials in Geneva through the United Nations Conference on Trade and Development (UNCTAD).[36]

GATT membership would have both advantages and disadvantages for China. On the positive side, China would be able to increase its trade volume (some 85 percent of which is with GATT members) and the ensuing gains (earnings) by winning most-favored nation status (whereby the lowest prevailing tariff between any two GATT members is automatically extended to all other members) and preferential export market access to the industrialized member-states under the Generalized System of Preferences (GSP). GATT membership also would enable China to avoid the annual U.S. congressional threat to revoke its conditional most-favored-nation status and to qualify for a wide range of special GSP tariff rates.[37] China would also belong to a formal organization that coordinates international economic policies and activities of member-states and provides rules, procedures, and protection against unfair trade practices, discrimination, and other trade disputes. Third, the GATT would be a useful source of information on world and member economic and trade policy that could help China with its own policy agenda, including reform.[38] Finally, the GATT would be a valuable mechanism for promoting and legitimating China's reformist policies, providing trade and investment assurances to the international business and banking communities, and validating its major trade status within the global trading system.

On the negative side, GATT membership would require China to liberalize its trade policies by reducing tariffs and nontariff barriers, decentralizing trade decisions, phasing out import licensing, expanding market access through competitive bidding, and limiting import substitution. China would need to end its own trade discrimination practices by eliminating export subsidies and dumping (i.e., pricing exports at less than their true costs). It would have to stop treating important aspects of its trade regime as *neibu* (internal or secret) and begin full disclosure of its trade policies, rules, and regulations, its production and trade target levels, its pricing practices, its state foreign trade organizations' balances and operating rules, its foreign trade plan and priorities, and a broad variety of market and trade data and statistics. Finally, it would have to restructure its artificial two-tiered renminbi exchange rate (which subsidizes exports), loosen accessibility to foreign exchange, and revise the special economic zones to ensure a unified national trade regime. Though China could invoke developing country status under Article 18 and Part 4 of the GATT and avoid many of the more onerous aspects of membership (e.g., infant industry protection, balance-of-payments-motivated import restrictions, and government development subsidies), its overall control and flexibility in managing its economy and foreign trade regime would be diminished.[39]

Between its WBG entry in 1980 and the granting of permanent GATT observer status in November 1984, China increasingly took part in GATT-sponsored meetings and activities.[40] Despite some limited reform, its foreign trade regime remained subject to broad official administrative controls, central planning, and arbitrary and *neibu* criteria, rules, and procedures. Specifically, from 70 to 80 percent of China's exports were part of the government's foreign trade plan; most imports were governed by a command plan or a priority system; state foreign trading organizations continued to play an important intermediary trade role; 30 percent of imports were covered by licensing requirements; government subsidies distorted export pricing and raised the possibility of dumping; tariffs, surcharges, and an array of administrative nontariff barriers discriminated against imports; an administered artificially low renminbi exchange rate discouraged imports and advantaged exports; and the use of foreign exchange was subject to government regulation.[41]

China's GATT accession process involves three distinct phases: (1) examination of China's foreign trade regime by other GATT signatories; (2) the drafting of a protocol outlining China's rights and obligations within the GATT; and (3) negotiations over China's specific tariff concessions. To initiate the process in February 1987, China submitted a detailed memorandum describing the nature and functioning of its domestic economy and foreign trade regime. A China Working Group (CWG) was established the following May and convened in July to examine this document and begin negotiations on an accession protocol. In a series of six meetings prior to April 1989, the CWG requested and received answers to over twelve hundred related questions and examined China's foreign trade regime in depth.[42] A major obstacle in this period was whether China would be admitted as a less-developed country rather than as a nonmarket economy. LDC status would permit China to maintain tariffs and quotas to protect infant domestic industries and reverse balance-of-payments problems, whereas nonmarket economy status would allow other GATT members to retain their quotas and nontariff barriers against a flood of cheap and often state-subsidized imports.[43]

The Tiananmen Square incident postponed the scheduled July 1989 CWG meeting, and a large number of additional questions were presented to China in December. During the ensuing post-Tiananmen hiatus (the ninth CWG session was held in September 1990), China responded in writing to some eight hundred additional questions, and in October 1991 it submitted a detailed report on its trade regime, including a substantial number of reforms either implemented or under way.[44] Significant headway was apparent during the tenth session of the CWG in February 1992, and it was generally agreed that China was making a sincere effort to implement a broad range of reforms to meet membership qualifications. Indeed, the end of that meeting concluded a five-year survey by the CWG of China's economic system and foreign trade regime.

The eleventh CWG meeting, held later in 1992, marked the beginning of the last two phases of China's GATT application: the drafting of precise language for an accession protocol and the negotiation of specific tariff concessions. The process was advanced by a twelfth CWG meeting in December that drew up a list of specific issues to be negotiated, but it was only at the thirteenth CWG meeting in March 1993 that hard bargaining began.[45] The most significant hurdle that China must overcome is to assuage concerns of the contracting parties, particularly the United States, regarding five explicit and three implicit issues. The former include the incorporation into the protocol of (1) a unitary national trade policy in which imports receive the same treatment at every entry point, (2) full transparency for all regulations, requirements, and quotas, (3) elimination of nontariff barriers, (4) a commitment to move to a full market economy, and (5) temporary safeguards against Chinese export surges.[46] Though bargaining over the explicit issues is likely to be difficult and protracted, it is the implicit issues that will play the critical behind-the-scenes role in determining the success of the negotiations. These issues are (1) the increasing imbalance in U.S.-China trade in favor of China, (2) the potential loss of the leverage over China that annual most-favored-nation hearings now confer on the United States, and (3) Taiwan's entry into the GATT.

The growing U.S.-China trade imbalance (U.S.$1.5 billion in 1989, U.S.$12.8 billion in 1991, and U.S.$18.2 billion in 1992) increasingly put pressure on the Bush administration to force China to ease its trade restrictions against U.S. exports. In August 1992 the United States threatened China with punitive 100 percent tariff increases on exports worth U.S.$3.9 billion if no agreement could be reached by October 10.[47] That pressure intensified as a result of candidate Bill Clinton's charges that President Bush was unwilling to demand trade and human-rights concessions from China in exchange for its continued access to the U.S. market. With more than one-third of its foreign trade with the United States, China gave in at the last minute and agreed to phase out most trade barriers, import quotas, and licensing requirements and institute transparency over a two-year period (i.e., by fall 1994). Though the Clinton administration has subsequently modified its public rhetoric, the United States has maintained its negotiation pressure with emphasis on Chinese flexibility on all outstanding issues.

The second implicit issue is the potential loss of political and economic leverage over China enjoyed by the United States as a result of the requirement of the Jackson-Vanik Amendment calling for annual most-favored-nation status recertification for communist countries. The GATT requires that contracting parties grant one another unconditional most-favored-nation status. However, the United States has sought to preserve a loophole under Article 35 that permits members to circumvent that requirement on the basis of internal constraints (the Jackson-Vanik Amendment).[48] Thus, the Clinton administration would be able to maintain leverage over China regarding domestic human-rights repression, intimidation directed at Hong Kong, Macao, and Taiwan, and increased sales of Chinese weapons and military technology to Third World buyers. Though the administration has softened its policy toward China, the pressure of various foreign and domestic problems it makes unlikely that Washington will be willing to squander much political capital on China's expeditious entry into the GATT. For these reasons it is probable that negotiations will not be successfully concluded until sometime in 1994.

A third implicit issue has been the question of GATT membership for Taiwan, which submitted its formal application on January 1, 1990, and its trade regime memorandum a year later. Taiwan had been granted observer status in 1965 but had been ousted after the PRC government assumed China's UN seat in 1971. At the time of its application it had been the world's thirteenth largest trading entity, with a 1989 total trade worth U.S.$118.5 billion and the second-largest foreign exchange reserves, worth U.S.$75 billion. Despite the fact that Taiwan had applied not as the Republic of China but rather under Article 33 as "The Customs Territory of Taiwan, Penghu, Kinmen, and Matsu" (the main ROC islands), China reacted angrily to the possible erosion of its territorial claims and accused Taiwan of seeking to gain the recognition of "two Chinas."[49] Its preference would be to join the GATT and then sponsor Taiwan for GATT membership as a customs territory, much as Britain had in 1986 sponsored Hong Kong. Taiwan would prefer prior accession in order to diminish Taipei's current political isolation and give it greater status and leverage in defining its political and commercial relationship with Beijing.[50]

The decision by the Bush administration in July 1991 to support Taiwan's GATT membership and the establishment of a Taiwan Working Group on September 29, 1992, just days before the October 10 deadline, suggested that the United States would use this issue to extract concessions from China on explicit issues. Although it would appear that there is an international consensus in favor of letting China enter the GATT before Taiwan, it is still possible that a mutually acceptable arrangement might be worked out to permit the simultaneous GATT accession of China and Chinese Taipei under an APEC formula.[51] In any event, resolution of the China-Taiwan GATT membership question will be of great importance in institutionalizing the future political and economic roles of both entities in the world economic system and in casting the China reunification question within a framework of vital mutual economic interests.

Conclusions and Prognosis

China's affiliations with multilateral economic institutions have proved beneficial in a variety of ways. Membership in these institutions has enabled China to draw upon valuable foreign professional economic expertise to analyze the strengths and weaknesses of the Chinese economy, jointly draft a long-range development blueprint, and provide broad and diversified training for large numbers of Chinese experts and officials. It has enabled China to tap a huge pool of lending capital and to garner billions of dollars in grants, loans, and concessionary rate credits to cope with temporary monetary and trade imbalances and to finance an ambitious array of essential but costly infrastructural, developmental, and production projects. It has provided a vital economic structural framework within which dialogue, interaction, bargaining, and negotiation can take place. It has brought China's bureaucratic, technical, and emerging entrepreneurial elite into close personal and professional contact with foreign experts that has served not only to sensitize Chinese cadres to the psychological, methodological, and policy requisites of successful economic development but also to advance and consolidate vested career interests. It has conferred a large measure of international legitimacy and acceptance upon China's political leadership and its economic modernization goals, helping to inspire international business, banker, and investor confidence and provide added assurances for direct foreign investment, trade arrangements, and commercial lending. Finally, because the institutional arrangements include Taiwan, it may eventually be useful in resolving the question of Chinese unification.

The Tiananmen Square incident had a direct and at least initially deleterious impact upon this participation. It led to a temporary suspension of lending to China in the billions of dollars, and, though China remained active in these institutions, its fall from financial grace had a sobering (though publicly tempered) impact on the Chinese leadership. Faced with a serious impediment to its modernization drive, the latter made a major effort to have the economic sanctions removed and to alleviate the resulting adverse economic fallout, isolation, and loss of status. The institutions' continuing private contacts with Chinese personnel provided all parties with useful information and a communications channel that eventually could be activated to help in restoring a more normal working relationship. Until the Gulf War, China suffered a substantial loss of leverage over its situation in that the end of the Cold War had eliminated the utility of its Soviet card and much of the Third World had come to regard it as a major self-serving competitor for multilateral-institutional resources. The need for its active or at least benign support in the UN Security Council on the Persian Gulf issue during the closing months of 1990 led directly to a full restoration of its borrower status. The utility of that status as well as an improved economy contributed in no small way to the revival of reformist fortunes prior to the Fourteenth CCP Congress.

For China to continue to reap the benefits of membership in these multilateral institutions, adequate funding resources must remain available to borrower member-states at a time of ever-increasing demand. Although China has not been a major IMF aid recipient, the agency has aided China through some difficult times. In recent years IMF guidelines have helped China to cut back on unrestrained spending and borrowing, improve its balance of payments, generating significant trade surpluses, avoid being squeezed by escalating debt-service ratios, and create an enviable stockpile of over U.S.$43 billion in foreign exchange reserves. IBRD loans to China not only have been restored but can now be made at higher levels because China has ample matching project funds and global market interest rates have declined precipitously. IDA credits have also been resumed and should continue to be forthcoming, since the replenishment level for 1991–1993 is only slightly lower than for the previous period. However, because of the influx of new member-states from the old Soviet bloc, the worsening plight of many Third World countries, especially in Africa and Latin America, and the uncertain prospects of the current (1994–1996) replenishment negotiations, China's future access to concessionary IDA credits could be adversely affected. At the same time, ADB project loans should continue to be ample for China, with the added dividend of potential expansion of PRC-Taiwan investment and commercial ties. Finally, limited but level funding for China should continue through the UNDP and the IFC.

Further benefits will also depend on the level of commitment of China's leadership to participation in the global economic system and to a regime that at the minimum avoids future Tiananmen-type excesses and human-rights abuses and at best opts for greater liberalization and accountability. Though these issues and the question of China's long-term political succession have not been resolved, the current Chinese leaders are well-aware of the interlinkage among these issues. The predication of China's development strategy on the open-door principle with participation in multilateral economic institutions represents a rejection of the orthodox Maoist statist and autarkic development model and acceptance of the classical Smith-Ricardian approach. That decision, now well over a decade old, was a calculated gamble to improve the odds for achieving rapid modernization. The Tiananmen trauma and the collapse of communist regimes in Eastern Europe and the Soviet Union have raised the stakes enormously. For China's leadership, participation in the multilateral economic institutions has been an important hedge in China's shift to a market economy. By relying on capitalist-style competition to unleash traditional Chinese entrepreneurial dynamism supplemented by multilateral-institional and other foreign capital resources and technical assistance, the leadership has sought to upgrade the economy not only within a continuing authoritarian political framework but also in order to preserve it.

Finally, by opting to participate in the GATT China has cast its lot with global economic multilateralism with its rewards of greatly expanded export earnings and its costs of an accelerated dismantling of the socialist command economy and import regime. Should the Uruguay round of GATT trade talks succeed, China could expect to share in the resulting global trade gains, and the political successors to the current leadership might entertain the option of greater future political liberalization perhaps along the lines of some of the Four Asian Tigers (Taiwan and South Korea). However, in recent years there has been a surge in global economic bilateralism and regionalism that could threaten China with a possible rise in protectionism, exclusion from many of its newly developed and highly lucrative world markets, or the possible strictures of a Japanese-Taiwanese dominated regional trading bloc. In this event the Chinese leadership could be faced with adverse economic consequences at a time of heightened popular material expectations and the attendant possibility of renewed domestic instability and regime reaction. Although China no doubt will continue to operate as a self-serving Group of One both within and outside the multilateral economic institutions, the key question is the long-term unforeseen political consequences and ramifications for China of its economic choices.

Notes

1. The basis of Ricardo's theory is that any two nations will benefit if each one specializes in producing and exporting goods that it makes comparatively cheaply and acquires as imports goods that it could produce only at higher cost. Recent works on China's open-door policy include Kevin B. Bucknall, *China and the Open Door Policy* (Sydney: Allen & Unwin, 1989); Nicholas R. Lardy, *Foreign Trade and Economic Reform in China, 1978–1990* (Cambridge: Cambridge University Press, 1992); and Robert Kleinberg, *China's "Opening" to the Outside World: The Experiment with Foreign Capitalism* (Boulder, Colo.: Westview Press, 1990).

2. See Samuel S. Kim, "Post-Mao China's Development Model in Global Perspective," in Neville Maxwell and Bruce McFarlane, eds., *China's Changed Road to Development* (Oxford: Pergamon Press, 1984), pp. 214–215.

3. See my chapters "Chinese Policy in Multilateral Financial Institutions," in Samuel S. Kim, ed., *China and the World: Chinese Foreign Policy in the Post-Mao Era* (Boulder, Colo.: Westview

Press, 1984), chap. 11; "Chinese Policy in Multilateral Economic Institutions," in Samuel S. Kim, ed., *China and the World: New Directions in Chinese Foreign Relations*, 2nd ed. (Boulder, Colo.: Westview Press, 1989), chap. 10; and "China's Relations with Multilateral Economic Institutions," in U.S. Congress, Joint Economic Committee, *China's Economic Dilemmas in the 1990s: The Problems of Reforms, Modernization, and Interdependence*, 102nd Cong., 1st sess. Vol. 2 (April 1991), pp. 795–816; and especially Harold K. Jacobson and Michel Oksenberg, *China's Participation in the IMF, the World Bank, and GATT: Toward a Global Economic Order* (Ann Arbor: University of Michigan Press, 1990).

4. For a survey of this early relationship see Samuel S. Kim, *China, the United Nations, and World Order* (Princeton, N.J.: Princeton University Press, 1979), pp. 318–328.

5. For details of the UNDP China program, see United Nations Development Program, *UNDP in China* (New York: UNDP, September 1989).

6. A sixth program (economic reform and policy research) with fourteen new projects worth U.S.$16 million was appended to the five already in place (food production and agricultural productivity, consumer goods and services, energy and conservation, human resources, and infrastructure), and six new agricultural projects valued at U.S.$8.6 million were added to the existing agriculture program. See United Nations Development Program, *UNDP Advisory Note on the Third Country Programme for the People's Republic of China (1991–1995)* (Beijing: UNDP, January 1990), p. 4.

7. For a survey of this process, see Jacobson and Oksenberg, *China's Participation in the IMF, the World Bank, and GATT*, chap. 3.

8. See World Bank, *China: Socialist Economic Development*, 3 vols. (Washington, D.C.: IBRD, 1983).

9. See World Bank, *China: Long-Term Development Issues and Options* (Baltimore and London: Johns Hopkins University Press, 1985). For a recent listing of World Bank publications, see Jacobson and Oksenberg, *China's Participation in the IMF, the World Bank, and GATT*, pp. 176–179, and World Bank, *Development Profile: People's Republic of China* (Washington, D.C.: IBRD, 1991), pp. 33–34.

10. A country's IMF quota is divided into four credit tranches, each equal to 25 percent of the total. Easiest access is to the reserve tranche, which is the hard-currency member contribution payable in special drawing rights (SDRs) interest-free for an indefinite period to deal with balance-of-payments difficulties. With an initial IMF quota of SDR1.2 billion, China's reserve tranche amounted to SDR300 million. In December 1980 China's quota was raised to SDR1.8 billion and the reserve tranche to SDR450 million.

11. This source is a now-defunct account capitalized by a 1976 IMF gold sale from early member quotas to boost resources for current member borrowing.

12. China increased interest rates but not by as much as the IMF wanted. Similarly, the renminbi was devalued by 15.8 percent against major currencies rather than the nearly 30 percent recommended by the IMF. Jacobson and Oksenberg, *China's Participation in the IMF, the World Bank, and GATT*, p. 125.

13. Ibid.

14. From 1987 to 1989 China's money supply grew at double-digit averages; inflation reached 18.5 percent overall and almost 30 percent in some urban areas; the budget deficit rose by 40 percent to a record U.S.$6.7 billion; the trade deficit more than doubled to U.S.$7.7 billion; foreign exchange reserves dropped by U.S.$0.5 billion to U.S.$17 billion; and the foreign debt jumped by one-third to U.S.$41.3 billion. In contrast, foreign exchange reserves went from U.S.$15.2 billion in December 1987 to U.S.$17.5 billion a year later to U.S.$13.6 billion in July 1989. See Lee Zinser, "The Performance of China's Economy," in Joint Economic Committee, *China's Economic Dilemmas in the 1990s*, Vol. 1 (April 1991), pp. 103–105, 107, 116; and Erin McGuire Endean, "China's Foreign Commercial Relations," in Joint Economic Committee, *China's Economic Dilemmas in the 1990s*, Vol. 2 (April 1991), pp. 748, 762.

15. See United States Central Intelligence Agency, Directorate of Intelligence, *The Chinese Economy in 1991 and 1992: Pressure to Revisit Reforms Mounts* (Washington, D.C.: CIA, 1992), pp. 4–5. For an IMF review of China's reforms since 1978, see International Monetary Fund, *China: Economic Reform and Macroeconomic Management*, Occasional Paper No. 76 (Washington, D.C.: IMF, January 1991).

16. These sectors include agriculture and rural development; development finance; education; energy (oil, gas, coal, and power); industry; nonproject government programs; population, health, and nutrition; public-sector management; small-scale enterprises; technical assistance; telecommunication; urban development; and water supply and sewerage. IBRD loans are for fifteen to twenty years with a five-year grace period and charge current market interest rates; IDA credits are for thirty-five to forty years with a ten-year grace period and no interest.

17. World Bank, *Annual Report 1991* (Washington, D.C.: IBRD, 1991), p. 77.

18. For a survey of these developments, see U.S. Congress, House, Subcommittee on International Development, Finance, Trade and Monetary Policy, Committee on Banking, Finance and Urban Affairs, *World Bank Lending to the People's Republic of China*, 101st Cong., 2nd sess., May 8, 1990, pp. 40–45.

19. The administration's rationale for the loan was that planting trees in fifteen provinces would generate significant part-time employment for poor rural farm families, increase peasant wood supplies, and confer environmental benefits through increased forest cover and soil erosion control. As an offset the administration blocked a second loan of U.S.$150 million for roads and waterways in Jiangsu province. See Clyde H. Farnsworth, "China Gets One Loan, but Another Is Put Off," *New York Times* (hereafter cited as *NYT*), May 30, 1990, pp. C1, C2; and Susumu Awanohara, "No More Favours," *Far Eastern Economic Review* (hereafter cited as *FEER*) 148 (June 7, 1990):56–57. Key legislators warned that if both loans went forward, administration aid requests including funding for the replenishment could be held up.

20. See "The Houston Two-Step," *FEER* 149 (July 19, 1990):57.

21. On November 30, 1990, the day after China's Security Council abstention vote, President Bush met with Chinese Foreign Minister Qian Qichen for the first time since the Tiananmen Square incident. On December 4, 1990, the World Bank approved its first clearcut non-basic-human-needs project in the form of a U.S.$50 million IBRD loan and a U.S.$64.3 million IDA credit for a rural industrial technology project. See Stephen Labaton, "World Bank to Lend $114.3 million to China," *NYT*, December 5, 1990, p. A5. The controversial Jiangsu transportation project blocked in May 1990 was approved the following May in the amount of U.S.$153.6 million.

22. MIGA was organized in April 1988 as the fourth agency of the WBG and is designed to encourage and guarantee private investment against various noncommercial risks in the Third World, advise developing member governments on the design and implementation of policies, programs, and procedures related to foreign investment, and sponsor a dialogue between host governments and the international business community on investment issues. See World Bank, *Annual Report 1990* (Washington, D.C.: IBRD, 1990), pp. 102–103; and Multilateral Investment Guarantee Agency, *Annual Report 1990* (Washington, D.C.: IBRD, 1990).

23. See International Finance Corporation, *1992 Annual Report* (Washington, D.C.: IFC, 1992), pp. 39–43.

24. Ibid., p. 41.

25. The state industrial sector declined from 78 percent to 53 percent between 1981 and 1991 and is projected to drop to 27 percent by the year 2000. The private sector, in contrast, has grown from 1 percent to 11 percent and is likely to account for 25 percent by 2000. The balance of the production mix is generated by cooperatives. Nicholas D. Kristof, "Chinese Communism's Secret Aim: Capitalism," *NYT*, October 19, 1992, pp. A1, A4. See also Nicholas D. Kristof, "Chinese Shake Up Top Party Group; Free Market Gains," *NYT*, October 20, 1992, pp. A1, A6.

26. China is the only country to have its own EDI program. Approximately one-quarter of the EDI budget is devoted to training Chinese personnel. See United Nations Development Program,

UNDP in China; and Jacobson and Oksenberg, *China's Participation in the IMF, the World Bank, and GATT,* pp. 109, 122, 124, 140–143, 151–152.

27. China had expressed its interest in joining the ADB in 1982, and in June 1983, four months after its application for formal ADB membership, it agreed to Taiwan's presence as a Bank member under the designation "Taipei, China." The November 1985 memorandum of understanding between China and the ADB also provided that the Taiwan authorities would use that designation in all ADB documents, papers, materials, statistics, and other publications; that it would be the responsibility of the ADB to ensure consistency in this regard; and that Taipei, China, would belong to the same voting group. See Peter Kien-Hong Yu, "On Taipei's Rejoining the Asian Development Bank (ADB) Subsequent to Beijing's Entry: One Country, Two Seats?" *Asian Affairs; An American Review* 17 (Spring 1990):4–5; and David S. Chou, "The ROC's Membership Problems in International Organization," *Asian Outlook* (Taipei) 26 (May–June 1991):23–24.

28. Taiwan also donated U.S.$2 million between 1983 and 1986 to preserve its symbolic Bank presence. Yu, "On Taipei's Rejoining the Asian Development Bank," p. 8.

29. Ibid., p. 10.

30. At the 1989 Beijing ADB meeting, members of the ROC delegation stood when PRC President Yang Shangkun entered the conference room for the opening ceremonies and again when the PRC national anthem was played. For its part Beijing agreed to preserve Taiwan's voting rights, seat the ROC delegation next to Thailand at Bank meetings, list Taipei separately in ADB publications rather than under the PRC as in IMF and World Bank materials and refrain from flying the PRC flag at ADB headquarters in Manila. Ibid., pp. 10–11.

31. See Philip Bowring, "Market Developer," *FEER* 148 (May 17, 1990):71.

32. Asian Development Bank, *Country Program Notes (1993–1996)* (Manila: ADB, March 1993), p. 55.

33. Taiwan began to participate in annual meetings of the Pacific Economic Cooperation Conference (PECC), a seventeen-member trans-Pacific economic consultative organization, in May 1988, with the designation "Chinese Taipei." In 1991 China along with Taiwan and Hong Kong joined the fifteen-member Asia-Pacific Economic Cooperation (APEC) conference, which focuses upon trade questions and economic cooperation. See Yu, "On Taipei's Rejoining the Asian Development Bank," p. 11; and CIA, *The Chinese Economy in 1991* and *1992,* p. 34, n. 9.

34. "Minister on Sino-U.S. Trade, GATT Accession," Foreign Broadcast Information Service, *Daily Report—China* (hereafter cited as FBIS-China), February 20, 1992, p. 3.

35. For a review, see Robert E. Herzstein, "China and the GATT: Legal and Policy Issues Raised by China's Participation in the General Agreement on Tariffs and Trade," *Law and Policy in International Business* 18 (1986):371–415; Penelope Hartland-Thunberg, "China's Modernization: A Challenge for the GATT," *Washington Quarterly* 10 (Spring 1987):81–97; J.E.D. McDonnell, "China's Move to Rejoin the GATT System: An Epic Transition," *World Economy* (London) 10 (September 1987):331–350; Paul D. McKenzie, "China's Application to the GATT: State Trading and the Problem of Market Access," *Journal of World Trade* 24 (October 1990):133–150; Jacobson and Oksenberg, *China's Participation in the IMF, the World Bank, and GATT,* pp. 62–63; chap. 4, pp. 126–127; and James V. Feinerman, "The Quest for GATT Membership," *The China Business Review* 19 (May–June 1992): 24–27.

36. Jacobson and Oksenberg, *China's Participation in the IMF, the World Bank, and GATT,* p. 63.

37. As a GATT contracting party, China would be able to eliminate more than ninety bilateral trade arrangements with its trading partners that are susceptible to periodic conditionality or unilateral termination. See Feinerman, "The Quest for GATT Membership," pp. 24–25.

38. Ibid., p. 25. For a comprehensive listing of benefits, see Jacobson and Oksenberg, *China's Participation in the IMF, the World Bank, and GATT,* pp. 92–93.

39. Feeney, "China's Relations with Multilateral Economic Institutions," p. 812.

40. In April 1980 China resumed its seat on the UN Interim Commission for the International Trade Organization, which appoints the GATT secretariat. In July 1981, as a major textile exporter, it was granted observer status at a GATT meeting to renew the Multifibre Arrangement, which sets

the rules for the textile trade. In November 1982 China was granted full observer status at sessions of the GATT contracting parties at the ministerial level. Finally, it applied for membership in GATT's Multifibre Arrangement in December 1983 and was accepted in January 1984. Such membership would provide China with access to markets in industrialized countries for its growing textile sector as well as experience with GATT procedures. Jacobson and Oksenberg, *China's Participation in the IMF, the World Bank, and GATT*, pp. 83–84.

41. Ibid., p. 87; Herzstein, "China and the GATT," pp. 374–375; and McKenzie, "China's Application to the GATT," pp. 135–140.

42. Jacobson and Oksenberg, *China's Participation in the IMF, the World Bank, and GATT*, pp. 94–96. Especially helpful was a detailed 1986 World Bank study. See World Bank, *China: External Trade and Capital* (Washington, D.C.: IBRD, 1988). The three-month delay in setting up the working group was due to differences over China's accession status. China contended that it was resuming its GATT membership rather than joining as a new contracting party. In the end the matter was tabled for the negotiating process.

43. Endean, "China's Foreign Commercial Relations," p. 748, n. 6.

44. See "To Enhance GATT Bid," FBIS-China, November 12, 1991, p. 46; "Commentator on Increasing Trade Transparency," FBIS-China, December 24, 1991, pp. 26–27; and "Efforts on Reforms in Effort to Join GATT," FBIS-China, January 27, 1992, p. 9.

45. In 1991 China had abolished subsidies for state trading firms and narrowed the margin between the official and the quasi-market renminbi exchange rate. It had further agreed to remove sixteen product categories from a list of fifty-three (nearly one-third) subject to import licensing, with a two-thirds cut promised in two to three years; to abolish all import regulatory duties by April 1; to adopt a floating renminbi exchange rate over time; to formulate a foreign trade law and an antidumping law; to lower gradually the general tariff level beyond the 225 tariffs thus far reduced; and to increase the transparency of the trade regime. At the start of 1993 China unilaterally reduced its tariff levels on 3,371 import items, but the average remaining tariff on a range of 6,000 products continued to be a high 42.5 percent. See "Foreign Trade Official on GATT Membership," FBIS-China, March 2, 1992, pp. 2–3; "Import Reform Measures to Aid GATT Accession," FBIS-China, April 13, 1992, p. 48; Feinerman, "'Significant Progress' Expected in GATT Bid," FBIS-China, February 1, 1993, p. 35; "The Quest for GATT Membership," p. 25; and Lincoln Kaye, "Slow Boat for China," *FEER* 156 (March 11, 1993):57.

46. Kaye, "Slow Boat for China," p. 56.

47. See "301 Clock Ticks On," *China Business Review* 19 (May-June 1992):27.

48. Kaye, "Slow Boat for China," p. 57.

49. Frances Williams and Jonathan Moore, "Who Goes First?" *FEER* 147 (February 1, 1990):36–37.

50. Julian Baum, "Waiting for the Call," *FEER* 155 (March 12, 1992):48; and Carl Goldstein and Julian Baum, "Outside GATT's Door," *FEER* 156 (October 22, 1992):58. For Taiwan, which conducts some 90 percent of its trade with members of the GATT, membership would not be without cost. Taiwan would be required to end its discriminatory trade restrictions in the form of high tariffs on or exclusions of Japanese exports and the ban on direct commercial ties with China and to reform its domestic agricultural base.

51. During 1991 and 1992 officials from Beijing and Taipei conducted a rhetorical fencing contest over the appropriate order of GATT accession. Reports have suggested that China agreed to that arrangement during Secretary of State James Baker's visit to Beijing in November 1991 but soon after reneged publicly (although not privately). "Reviews on Support for Taiwan," FBIS-China, December 12, 1991, p. 2; and "'Internal Document' on Simultaneous GATT Entry," FBIS-China, April 7, 1992, pp. 1–2.

PART FOUR

Prospects

12

The Future of Chinese Foreign Policy

ALLEN S. WHITING

Forecasting is difficult enough in the natural sciences, whether one is attempting near- or long-term projections in climate, earthquakes, or the atmosphere. The many variables to be considered and the partial theories and data allow for a wide variety of scenarios, depending on the individual expert's intuitive imagination as well as the complexity of the particular computer model. Forecasting in the social sciences is rendered even more problematic because of the human variable. Individuals' specific behavior in singular circumstances is not wholly predictable. Decision making is rarely completely rational. Governments, as collective decision-making bodies, are susceptible to a host of human impulses and motivations, and in addition to this their decisions are subject to imperfect implementation.

The consequent sense of uncertainty in forecasting foreign policy in general is heightened for the People's Republic of China in particular by major variables, both domestic and foreign. We do not know how long the present regime will endure in its present guise. As the last remaining major communist system, it faces a serious challenge in trying to maintain political control by the Communist Party while moving toward a decentralized market economy driven by private capital. Moreover, the erosion of Marxism–Leninism–Mao Zedong Thought as a guiding ideology leaves a vacuum of values to condition behavior on the basis of belief in the collective good rather than in the pursuit of individual gain. Finally, the question of what type of leader will succeed Deng Xiaoping may not be wholly determined for several years after his demise. The possible confluence of institutional and ideological crisis could radically transform or even overturn the existing order.

This potential crisis may be alleviated or exacerbated, depending on the composition of the ruling group in the balance of this decade. The regime's survival of its first leadership transition following the death of Mao as the founding father in 1976 required a palace coup and two years of political struggle resulting in the ascendancy of Deng Xiaoping. In the absence of rule by law and any agreed-upon constitutional procedure for leadership succession, Deng's departure from politics is likely to trigger another struggle among individuals and factions for control. Policy at home and abroad inevitably becomes involved, partly as a matter of belief and partly as a weapon, in such struggle.

The political outcome of leadership succession is critical, given the institutional and ideological challenge facing a regime with more than one billion people growing by fifteen million yearly. Economic conditions vary widely from the booming coastal areas to the impoverished inner regions. The Han or Chinese majority faces resentful, if not at present rebellious, Tibetan, Muslim, and Mongol minorities along its far-flung borders. Meanwhile a restive urban intellectual elite bitterly recalls the brutal military repression of student demonstrations in 1989 and looks to the West as a political role model.

Last but not least, the external environment challenges the post-Deng leadership as well as our forecasting of that environment. China's economic growth and modernization are to a large extent dependent on the world economy for trade and technology. Yet the world economy has major areas of uncertainty. Growth rates in the industrial world stagnated in the early 1990s. Trade imbalances prompted rising protectionist sentiment. Potential economic blocs in Europe and North America threatened the expansion of free trade nurtured under the General Agreement on Tariffs and Trade (GATT). A worst-case combination of recession and protectionism could paralyze Chinese export growth while domestic demands for employment and higher living standards continued to climb.

Beijing's foreign policy agenda is also burdened by territorial security problems, albeit not to the extent of earlier decades when both superpowers were perceived as military threats. The end of Sino-American confrontation in 1972 and the dissolution of the Soviet Union in 1991 eliminated the military siege mentality induced by confrontational relations with Moscow and Washington in the 1960s. But a political siege mentality arose as domestic stability became threatened by the influence of the West both as role model and as advocate of human rights. These two aspects are defined by assertive nationalists in Beijing as interference in internal affairs that is subversively motivated and to be resisted as potentially fatal to Communist rule.

In addition, territorial integrity on China's terms remains as a long-standing goal. Taiwan is still outside Beijing's control. Neighboring regimes contest Beijing's claim to islands and underwater resources in the East China and South China Seas. A long-standing border dispute with India and lesser disputes over portions of the borders with Vietnam and the former Soviet Union have yet to be formally resolved. Resolution of these questions involves economic as well as political-military considerations. Beijing's choice of posture, compromising or confrontational, will influence its access to foreign investment, trade, and technology, and this in turn will affect economic growth and modernization.

Framing our forecast of foreign policy prospects within these internal and external variables at the outset is important for maintaining an appropriate modesty in our claims for it. Probable projections have persuasive logic, but alternative scenarios are sufficiently likely to deserve attention. For the sake of simplicity, I will address two variants of possible post-Deng leadership: reform-internationalist (RI) and reform-nationalist (RN). Both approaches are committed to major change toward a market economy based primarily on private capital, although they may differ in the pace and extent of such change. RI leadership makes international interdependence the point of departure in foreign policy, while its RN counterpart takes China's sense of identity as the defining factor. These are not polar opposites but rather differing degrees of willingness to compromise territorial claims and domestic politics for the sake of accommodating international pressures. In focusing on these two types of regime, I will give only brief attention to a third situation, namely, prolonged leadership instability arising from a deadlock between the two approaches and I will omit altogether any such radical change of regime as occurred in Eastern Europe and the Soviet Union. Although prolonged instability and radical change are possible, their likelihood seems sufficiently remote and the consequences sufficiently unforeseeable to be omitted from our purview.

With respect to the key external variable, I assume that the international economy will for a time remain similar to today's with regard to rates of growth and patterns of trade and investment. In part this is justified by the constant monitoring of that economy and close consultation among its primary participants so as to minimize the likelihood of sudden change, much less a collapse such as occurred in the Great Depression of the 1930s. In part, however, the competing global scenarios within which different projections of China's role and economic relations might be made are too varied and complex to include here. Nevertheless, it is important to note that this assumption is subject to error with far-reaching consequences for China's future economic growth and political stability.

Domestic Politics and Foreign Policy

The People's Republic has pursued so constant a foreign policy since 1981 as to make credible the continuation of that basic policy through the rest of this century. The premise that peaceful relations in the region are necessary for China's top priority of economic modernization has paid handsome dividends with little or no sacrifice of national interests. Annual growth rates of roughly 9 percent have benefited an ever-widening geographic and demographic portion of the society, albeit with wide variations between sectors. Sensitive to the political reaction of interior regions growing more slowly than coastal areas, in June 1992 Beijing named the hub city of Wuhan one of 28 inland centers open to foreign investment with special tax benefits.[1] Rapidly expanding border trade in Yunnan, Xinjiang, Inner Mongolia, and the Northeast spurs local economic growth. With 167 "open ports on the 22,000-kilometer border," this trade jumped from $1.1 billion in 1990 to more than $2 billion in 1991 and was expected to double again in 1992.[2]

Deng's open-door policy, accompanied by major economic reforms, generated a revolution of rising expectations in the early 1980s, but by 1988 soaring inflation, rampant corruption, and reform problems had frustrated expectations, especially in the urban sectors. Severe economic retrenchment and brutal political repression in 1989–1990 restored stability on both fronts. Economic growth continued, most markedly in rural areas adjacent to large cities and along the coast from Guangzhou in the south to Dalian in the north. As a result, a powerful coalition of vested interests—bureaucratic and private, central and regional, industrial and agricultural—supports the status quo and opposes any significant reversal of policy.

This impressive record would seem to ensure its continuation, regardless of who succeeds Deng, but certain factors caution against this assumption. First and foremost, our continued reference to Deng underscores his importance as first among equals. Despite the proliferation of various constituencies in domestic and foreign policy, the perceived power of a single leader has remained important. This is not because of any unique need for charisma or an unquestioning acceptance of personal dictatorship such as can be found in some Third World countries. Instead it flows from the traditional Chinese role of a leader-figure at the pinnacle of power, in more recent times accompanied by a chain of loyal and ambitious followers who form a hierarchical authority structure extending through the party and government. Traditional court politics around an emperor expand to become political and bureaucratic factionalism throughout the vast administrative system, down to the provincial and municipal levels. Under these circumstances, anyone perceived as dominant is accepted by various segments below as the key person in decision making. But because this individual is not vested with truly autocratic authority—Deng has lacked any official position in his final years—opposition tends to coalesce around a rival figure in the hope of challenging and eventually replacing the existing leadership faction. Although Mao filled the traditional role as supreme decision maker, Deng has had to cope with recalcitrant colleagues by coalition building and compromise.

As is acutely pointed out by David Bachman, none of the apparent contenders for succession command Deng's power and prestige.[3] Therefore they will be forced to move even farther from the traditional pattern toward some form of collective decision making. Transition to this new pattern of politics will take time and, in the absence of institutional or legal guidelines, entail personal conflict. The process may be prolonged, complicating responses to foreign developments and limiting the consideration of policy options. The result may range from inopportune passivity to ill-considered action.

A second reason for focusing on the impact of domestic politics on foreign policy lies in the nature of Deng's economic revolution and the opposition it aroused from a small but vocal, highly placed minority in the Party. That opposition shrewdly and perhaps sincerely based its public attack on an assertive nationalism. Antiforeign impulses have a long history derived from what Chinese term "a century of shame and humiliation." From the Opium War of 1839–1842 to the proclamation of "New China" by Mao Zedong in 1949, the determination to triumph over foreign political, economic, and military domination drove the foreign policy of both Nationalists and Communists.

Dependence on the Soviet Union in 1949 was necessitated by opposition from the United States and justified by the common communist ideology, but despite its obvious benefits to China's economic reconstruction and military modernization Mao personally led a campaign ten years later to reduce that dependency, proclaiming "self-reliance first, foreign aid second." His Great Proletarian Cultural Revolution of 1966–1976 inveighed against dependency to the point of refusing foreign relief assistance after a devastating earthquake in 1976 killed two hundred thousand persons in Tangshan. It had already become clear to many of

Mao's colleagues, including Deng, however, that the exclusion of foreign loans and investment doomed China to permanent economic backwardness and military vulnerability. With his ascendancy established by December 1978, Deng proceeded to transform the domestic economy and to make external economic ties the basis of industrial growth. Self-reliance remained a referent but clearly took second place to dependence on foreign trade and technology together with foreign loans, grants, and investment.

With economic dependence came political costs and risks. The costs included compromise on the pursuit of territorial objectives opposed by key foreign powers. Beijing could exercise force against Vietnam over the Paracel and Spratly Islands in the South China Sea with relative impunity in 1974 and 1988, respectively; Hanoi contributed nothing to China's economy. It could not, however, use the same means to challenge Japan over the Diaoyu (Senkaku) Islands in the East China Sea; Tokyo was too important a market and a source of technology, loans, and investment. Likewise, Beijing could fulminate against Taipei's growing tolerance of an opposition party pressing for Taiwanese self-determination, but it could not use force to reunite the island with the mainland; Washington's reaction in economic if not in political-military terms would have been too severe.

The political risks were less immediate but no less galling to Deng's more conservative and ideologically inclined colleagues. Their media campaigns against "spiritual pollution" and "bourgeois liberalization" linked the influx of Western business methods, capital, and tourism to the outflow of Chinese delegations and students abroad, with an allegedly consequent growing demand for greater political participation. After the 1989 Beijing massacre these ideological campaigns gained fresh impetus from the Western condemnation of military suppression and the economic sanctions imposed. Those responsible for media management and political indoctrination alleged a systematic American plot to overthrow socialism everywhere, including China. This plot ostensibly utilized all aspects of human exchange, economic as well as intellectual and cultural. The coincident collapse of communism in Eastern Europe and subsequently in the Soviet Union further fueled this argument. In its most fundamental sense, this campaign challenged Deng's open-door policy in terms of China's identity as well as Communist control.

Given this recent past, it is necessary to project two different tendencies in future Chinese policy, depending on whether a mainstream reform-internationalist or an opposition reform-nationalist leadership emerges. The odds strongly favor an RI regime for the aforementioned reasons. In addition, the opposition to Deng was led by his original revolutionary contemporaries, most of whom he has physically outlasted. Their incapacitation or death prompted many of their followers to hedge their bets by supporting Deng's policy. In January 1992 his sudden burst of political activity on behalf of his program provided a powerful bandwagon stimulus for the open door and faster economic reform, and this won endorsement at the Fourteenth Party Congress in October.

As a final consideration, although neither side had a comprehensive ideology to replace Marxism–Leninism–Mao Zedong Thought, Deng's pure pragmatism proved profitable, and his opposition could not promise anything better. His simple homilies "To get rich is good" and "It makes no difference whether the cat is white or black so long as it catches mice" ostensibly defined "socialism with Chinese characteristics." By comparison, his opponents' strident call for "patriotism" rang hollow to a more worldly wise and sophisticated successor generation.

But while the open door cannot be shut on the basis of gain versus loss, the associated issue of human rights can provide leverage for a determined nationalist pressure on an internationalist posture. Should this coincide with a crisis involving territorial integrity, perhaps over Taiwan, the continuity of policy might be interrupted. The importance of human rights for domestic politics affecting foreign policy depends on the specific situation. For example, Tibet is not a contentious political issue for most Chinese. The region is remote, uninviting, and relatively inaccessible. Its proponents speak for a national minority of little concern to the Han population at large. Finally, its location involves national security. Its disputed border provoked a brief war with India in 1962, and India continues to host a virtual Tibetan government in exile. On these various counts, foreign efforts on behalf of imprisoned or repressed Tibetans will arouse united resistance in China. Domestic politics do not pertain, even though Tibet recurringly arises as a minor foreign relations problem.[4]

However, if the regime continues to imprison dissident intellectuals, journalists, and students or a post-Deng regime again forcibly suppresses demonstrations for political freedom, Western reactions may equal or surpass those of 1989–1991. Here domestic politics will have a more serious impact on foreign policy in general and Sino-American relations in particular. An RI regime will be pressured to make domestic practices emulate those in the West, but its RN opponents will exploit any such concession as subjecting China to foreign control. A heated debate at the highest levels will reverberate in significant sectors of the urban populace. The outcome may well depend on the quality of leadership and the balance of power, independent of objective policy considerations at the time.

A more volatile situation would arise were Taiwanese independence to appear imminent. The interests at stake are formidable. They include the realization of final victory in a civil war waged intermittently between Communists and Nationalists since 1927 and the removal of the Republic of China as a political competitor in the international arena. Taiwan is an immensely profitable economic asset whose foreign exchange reserves in mid-1992 stood at $86.6 billion, first in the world and double that of the PRC.[5] To sum up these varied interests under the rubric of territorial integrity understates both the real and the emotional factors at play, but the term does pinpoint the ultimate sensitivity of Taiwan in terms of Chinese nationalism. The fact that Washington prevented Beijing from taking Taiwan during 1950–1979 and subsequently contributed to the continued separation of the island further heightens this sensitivity.

In October 1991 a small, recently formed opposition group on Taiwan—the Democratic Progressive Party (DPP)—adopted a platform plank to "found a Republic of Taiwan with independent sovereignty." PRC President Yang Shangkun publicly warned, "We will absolutely not sit by and watch any act of separating Taiwan from China."[6] This strengthened Yang's earlier caveat, "Those who play with fire will be burned." *Renmin ribao* reiterated, "The Chinese Government will not stand idly by and remain indifferent."[7] These specific formulations echoed identically worded warnings uttered in September 1950 and September 1962 aimed at deterring American military advances in Korea and Indian advances in the Himalayas, respectively. Ignoring China's threats resulted in war both times. In 1991, however, no military action occurred in the Taiwan Strait, and the DPP was roundly defeated in the subsequent election. Nevertheless, the authoritatively uttered threats underscored Beijing's serious, if exaggerated, perception of the situation and foreshadowed future possibilities.

Here domestic politics could determine the choice between face-saving passivity and face-risking action. An RI regime would recognize that in addition to the military difficulty of blockading or invading Taiwan, the political reactions in Washington, Tokyo, and the European Community would jeopardize economic growth. Some formula would be sought to accommodate the new situation without overtly acknowledging defeat in this long-held objective. An RN regime would be more likely to argue that military force, threatened or exercised, might collapse resistance on the island before external assistance could intervene. Beijing would hope that, as after Tiananmen, the world community would eventually accept the fait accompli. Prolonged stalemate between opposing tendencies in a post-Deng succession crisis could work in favor of a minority nationalist faction. The emotional component in the argument for unification at any cost, heightened by foreign involvement, would be difficult to refute for a leadership with less than commanding authority. This in turn could result in a reversal of Beijing's foreign relations on a broad front, depending on how the situation evolved on Taiwan.

The foregoing contingency is possible but unlikely. In addition to favoring an RI regime, the odds favor the continuation of Taiwan's present status at least through this decade. The situation is profitable for Taiwanese investment and trade with the mainland while remaining relatively free of tension. By 1992 that investment totaled $3 billion, almost half of which occurred in 1991, while "indirect" trade exceeded $5 billion.[8] In addition, Beijing's oft-repeated threat to use force against independence inhibits support for the Taiwan-oriented opposition party. The status quo is also profitable for the mainland, given the growing flow of capital and tourism from Taiwan. Thus combining the two probability estimates on domestic politics in both Beijing and Taiwan is reassuring, although it is no guarantee that the long-quiescent separation of "two Chinas" will remain so. Considering this remote contingency serves to illustrate the duality of uncertain variables in all foreign policy relationships involving the politics in Beijing and another regime.

The Broader Foreign Policy Agenda

A formidable array of foreign policy issues and problems will confront the post-Deng leadership, whatever its composition. Two basic frames of reference will condition its approach to this agenda. The first, Chinese economic development, we have already addressed. The second is Beijing's global assessment or image of immediate and near-term international relations.

Since the collapse of the Soviet Union, Chinese scholars and publicists have advanced various analyses of the international system. They differ over the extent to which it is unipolar or multipolar and the prospects of change in either direction. More particularly, they advance alternative assessments of American hegemony and the degree of challenge to it by Japan and Western Europe. Although the implications for policy are never addressed in publicly available materials, they are recognized internally and at higher levels.

For example, American power may be seen either as a central threat if unchecked or as a declining weight offset by a rising Japan. The first case would pose simple alternative responses of confrontation or cooperation. The second would add a third possibility of playing on Japanese-American tensions to woo Tokyo as an offset to Washington. This third possibility characterized much of Beijing's posture after Tiananmen, Tokyo's response to that event being milder than Washington's and its lifting of sanctions much earlier. Meanwhile, the image of American hegemony grew with the Gulf War.[9] President Bush's sudden announcement of the sale of 150 F-16 fighters to Taiwan in 1992 enhanced the sense of threat to China's national interest in reunification in addition to violating the laboriously negotiated 1984 agreement with Beijing on arms sales to the island. This weakened Deng's argument for Bush as the best defender of Beijing on the American scene. More important, it strengthened the case for changing the short-run tactic of exploiting Japanese-American tensions by playing Tokyo off against Washington into a long-term triangular strategy.

Basic to any such strategy is the world view of the leadership. A perception of American hegemony might exaggerate the need to raise tension in the Taiwan Strait so as to confront Washington directly and deter it from further involvement. A multipolar assessment would encourage taking advantage of Tokyo-Washington problems to alter the balance of power in East Asia. An RI regime holding the first world view would try to avoid confrontation for the sake of economic growth, but its ability to do so would depend on the strength of RN opposition to concession on so sensitive an issue as Taiwan. Alternatively, an RI regime's choice of alignment with Tokyo in a multipolar world might be opposed by RN rejection of the past aggressor, Japan, as a political partner in the power game.

Japan's importance as an economic partner contrasts with its past role as aggressor and conflicts with its potential as a rival leader in East Asia. Its place in Chinese foreign policy may vary radically depending on the world view and priorities of the post-Deng leadership. This may determine the posture to be adopted toward contention with Japan over ownership and exploitation of the continental shelf under the East China Sea as well as the Diaoyu (Senkaku) Islands. A further consideration is the linkage between this dispute and contention with Vietnam and other Southeast Asian nations over the Spratly Islands and South China Sea underwater resources. This linkage became explicit in February 1992 with passage by the National People's Congress of legislation specifying the two disputed areas, among others, as falling within China's territorial sovereignty, to be defended by force if necessary. Thus contention, passivity, or compromise in one situation could set a precedent for the other.

An additional factor is China's growing military capability. The acquisition of aerial refueling technology in the early 1990s significantly increased the range of fighter planes from the mainland and Hainan Island. The purchase of advanced fighters from Russia further increased the potential projection of military power. Combined People's Liberation Army (PLA) air and naval exercises in the South

China Sea demonstrated Beijing's ability to use force to defend its claims. Meanwhile it proposed cooperation in resources exploration and exploitation in both disputed areas, simultaneously proclaiming Chinese ownership and declaring that this question could be postponed for later negotiation.

A readiness to act unilaterally while proposing multilateral solutions surfaced in May 1992 when Beijing contracted with an American oil company to explore in an area of the Gulf of Tonkin of which Hanoi claimed ownership.[10] Vietnamese protests proved unavailing, the Chinese steadfastly asserting sovereignty over the particular area. The issue was more symbolic than substantive so long as the actual value of the seabed resources remained undetermined. However, whether here or elsewhere in the South China Sea, discoveries of exploitable oil and natural gas will eventually prove useful for the domestic economies and foreign exchange earnings of all the contenders as energy demand increases relative to supply in East Asia.

Beijing's posture will depend on the central focus of its leadership and the assessment of economic versus political priorities. Japan and the Association of Southeast Asian Nations (ASEAN) are China's principal partners in any regional effort to solve common problems. They also are important sources of trade and investment. In 1992 both the Japanese Self-Defense Agency in its annual white paper and ASEAN in its July conclave expressed concern over conflict potential in the South China Sea. An RI leadership would try to maneuver as Deng did between abandoning territorial claims and pursuing them by military means. An RN regime would be more willing to countenance the political and economic fallout from militant confrontation in the South China Sea and perhaps hope that this would persuade Japan to give in. For the next few years the more moderate posture is likely to prevail, assuming that the leadership is stable. Beyond that, however, the chances will increase for an assertive nationalism to take unilateral action as the capability to do so increases. On balance, the chances of this more militant course are still less than even because of its negative impact on foreign economic relations.

In Southeast Asia, the Cambodian problem is likely to persist. The financial and human requirements for the United Nations establishment of a viable elected government in a peaceful country are daunting. Hanoi and Bangkok will compete for influence in the country. Beijing will be loath to abandon the patron-client role it has played through divers means and various factions since Cambodia's postwar establishment in 1955. Factionalism has been endemic since 1975, and it was only after the Vietnamese withdrawal of troops in 1989 that the intervening and competing outside powers—Russia, China, and the United States— cooperated in seeking an end to hostilities. Cambodia has no strategic or economic value for Beijing, but the compulsive game of power politics and the historic competition between Vietnam and China are likely to perpetuate Chinese involvement there. The Khmer Rouge as the strongest faction enjoyed Beijing's support until 1990. Then the aftermath of Tiananmen and the convergence of Russian, Vietnamese, and American interest in a UN-supervised settlement persuaded Beijing to change course. Basically, however, the Chinese role will probably combine competition with cooperation.[11] To accommodate ASEAN and its own UN role, an RI regime would allow the Khmer Rouge to fade away as its depleting arms reserves forced compliance with the cease-fire or participation in UN-sponsored elections. An RN regime would tend to be more assertive in preserving a Chinese interest to be served by Khmer Rouge intransigence.

Myanmar (Burma) presents another situation in which Chinese influence has grown incrementally through military help to a brutally repressive regime, although here help came through open weapons sales rather than indirectly. These transactions had their own logic in Beijing's policy of generating foreign exchange through weapon transfers regardless of the ideological or strategic consequences for other states. Missile sales in the Middle East raised opposition in Washington, but Myanmar's conventional arms purchases evoked little comment in the West. Locally, however, they caused concern in India and Thailand, which faced tens of thousands of Muslim refugees seeking refuge across their borders. More generally, ASEAN opposed support for the Yanggon (Rangoon) junta, whose slaying or imprisonment of dissidents and persecution of Muslims ran against the rising tide of pluralism in the region.

This situation raised a broader question concerning Beijing's willingness to abide by international norms that entail some national sacrifice, in this case the earnings from weapon sales. The regime argued logically that similar sales worldwide by the United States, Britain, France, and Russia required constraints on all and not just on China. Finally, after considerable pressure, Beijing agreed to stop missile transfers to the Middle East and pledged not to provide nuclear weapons technology or knowledge to other countries. Yet serious doubts remained as to implementation of this pledge, initially with respect to Pakistan and subsequently with respect to Iran.

Pakistan's geopolitical situation has attracted China's support since the early 1960s.[12] It was a useful counterweight against India, perceived both as a neighboring threat and as a client of the Soviet Union. In addition, the proximity of Kashmir to the disputed Sino-Indian border area took on strategic importance with a nearby road from Xinjiang through western Tibet serving essential military logistical needs. The Moscow–New Delhi link disappeared with the fall of the USSR, removing a key component of Beijing's concern over India, but the nuclear balance in the subcontinent remained of interest. New Delhi's denial of seeking this capability seemed contingent if not actually misleading. Reciprocally, Pakistan's similar denial served to avoid an open nuclear arms race while preserving the option for a rapid response should India's posture change. In this triangular game Chinese interests could be served by reinforcing the "nonnuclear" nuclear balance in the subcontinent by covertly helping Pakistan to keep its options open.

Whereas the collapse of the Soviet Union freed Beijing of competition with Moscow in third countries, it also denied New Delhi its principal patron. As a result, Sino-Indian military relations improved, at least symbolically. In July 1992 the Indian defense minister visited Beijing, where he agreed to the visit to India of a Chinese warship in the near future.[13] Then in October China reportedly agreed in principle to reduce its troop strength along the disputed border.[14] Yet despite these tokens of détente, renewed efforts at resolving the long-standing border dispute achieved little beyond limited confidence-building measures. Domestic politics in New Delhi mirrored those in Beijing. Each side refused to compromise beyond allowing the status quo to continue without its formal legitimation through signed agreements. Potential rival power aspirations won widespread comment with reports of Chinese interest in purchasing an aircraft carrier from Russia or Ukraine. Although no deal had been closed by the year's end, this possible extension of Beijing's naval presence in the Indian Ocean could foreshadow a conventional arms race that would be destabilizing for the entire region.

The mixture of nationalistic issues in Tibet and the disputed border with international power issues in the subcontinent complicate Chinese compliance with global arms control agreements. Beijing had refused to sign the Nuclear Non-Proliferation Treaty (NPT) for nearly twenty years while claiming that it would not spread nuclear capabilities abroad. It finally announced its readiness to join the NPT regime in December 1991 as a response to the Japanese prime minister's visit that summer and Secretary of State Baker's visit that fall. If fully implemented, this would weaken the Sino-Pakistan alignment. Moving toward a more neutral stance on Kashmir also distanced China from Pakistan. A breakthrough on the Sino-Indian border dispute would further erode the strategic triangle. In this conciliatory context, an RI and RN consensus could be readily reached on policy toward both subcontinent powers. However, the border breakthrough has eluded successive regimes in New Delhi and Beijing for more than thirty years, and resolution will not come easily in either capital. Meanwhile, Washington intelligence analysis claims that Beijing continues to assist Pakistan's missile program, contrary to explicit promises made to Baker in November 1991 that no such deliveries would be made in violation of the 1987 Missile Technology Control Regime.[15]

Still another dimension of national interest could adversely affect Sino-Pakistan relations should Islamic fundamentalism be perceived as a serious threat to Chinese rule over Muslim minorities in Xinjiang. An officially admitted instance of armed dissidence there in 1990 probably did not justify Beijing's label of "counterrevolutionary rebellion."[16] Nevertheless, while the Soviet Union still ruled adjacent Central Asian Muslim peoples it set a worrisome precedent for what might develop now that the former Soviet republics are independent states. The image of sovereignty for Kazakhs, Kyrgyz, Uzbeks, and Tajiks could prove inspiring for the non-Han peoples in Xinjiang, dissatisfied with second-class citizenship manifest in economic as well as political discrimination. Alternatively, civil strife in these areas could trigger a refugee exodus across the mountainous border.

Beijing's 1990 accusations of subversion's being masked by demands for religious freedom or "separatism" came within a broader claim that "foreign forces" were plotting a so-called East Turkestan Republic in Xinjiang. Although this charge allegedly involved a shadowy exile figure in Turkey, ample opportunity exists to smuggle arms and explosives through neighboring states with large Muslim populations, including Pakistan. Such activity would not be sponsored by the various governments, all of which are anxious to avoid provoking China, but their ability to control it, given the long frontier, is doubtful.

The charge of promotion from abroad of an East Turkestan Republic (ETR) has a historic precedent, in addition to the nineteenth-century Muslim revolts, within memory of the Chinese leadership. In 1944–1949 nearly half of Xinjiang fell under ETR rule in a revolt that was aided by Moscow through support of ethnic kinsmen across the border. The rebel regime disappeared with the Communist takeover, most of its leadership reportedly being killed in an airplane accident en route to Beijing. Again in 1962 Beijing accused Moscow of seeking to detach Xinjiang when more than eighty thousand Uygurs and other Muslims fled across the Soviet border to escape the economic hardships following collapse of the Great Leap Forward. Because their departure was facilitated by Soviet visas, Beijing closed Moscow's consulates in the region. Later the 1966–1976 Cultural Revolution had a serious impact on Xinjiang, targeting mosques as it did temples in Tibet and further alienating the local populace.

The linkage between domestic security and foreign relations has mixed results in Xinjiang. On the economic front, cross-border trade has soared with the need of the new republics for consumer goods in plentiful supply from China. Completion of the transcontinental railroad, planned in the early 1950s but suspended on the Chinese side as Sino-Soviet differences mounted, facilitates larger exchanges with Kazakhstan and beyond. At the same time, trade and travel open up expanded opportunity for political interaction between similar peoples on the two sides of the border that cannot be monitored, much less controlled, by Chinese authorities. This tendency is not necessarily disruptive of stability, but it has that potential. Given past history, it is likely to be so viewed in Beijing.[17] RN advocates will seek greater vigilance with tighter minority management and border control, RI proponents greater security through faster economic improvement in the border areas.

Ironically, the larger relationship with Russia, a traditional threat, is the least troublesome of those within our purview. It is true that the collapse of communism and its replacement by democratic pluralism struck at confidence in Beijing. The failure of a restorationist conservative coup against then-President Mikhail Gorbachev in August 1991 genuinely rocked the Chinese leadership, triggering renewed debate between radical and conservative reformists. Nevertheless, the mainstream group under Deng quickly recovered its composure, insisting that it was the failure of economic reform and not ideological impotence that had doomed the Soviet Union. Therefore China had to accelerate economic growth and not worry about political indoctrination as a means of Communist survival.

On the positive side, the collapse of the USSR ended any possible military threat from the north for years to come. Instead, Russia became a possible source of advanced military weapons systems newly available to China because of its burgeoning foreign exchange reserves and Moscow's pressing economic need. Although only an initial deal for 24 Su-27s appeared firm by late 1992, it was reported that negotiations were under way for additional fighter jets together with bombers, helicopters, and interceptors.[18] Much of the PLA's equipment had originally come from the Soviet Union or was based on Soviet design, so the more recent systems were readily compatible, as were their spare parts. This totally reverses the security situation that Beijing confronted from 1960 onward. Instead of facing possible attack by Moscow, Beijing can once again acquire a stronger military capability from the former Soviet Union as it did in the 1950s, albeit at a considerably lower level than in the earlier period.

As a by-product of Moscow's loss of superpower status, Beijing no longer had to compete for influence in Pyongyang. It became free to establish diplomatic relations with Seoul, where mutual economic interests offer a rapid increase in trade and investment, and did so in 1992. North Korea could no longer extract economic and military aid by playing off Moscow against Beijing. Now it had to seek better relations with Tokyo, Washington, and even Seoul to attract investments and trade. The possibility that deliberate or inadvertent North Korean actions would trigger war on the peninsula almost totally faded away, relieving Beijing of that worst-case worry.

In this new context, unprecedented regional cooperation appeared possible, at least for discussion. The most far-reaching but probably least feasible proposal envisaged a Tumen River project with adjoining special economic zones established by North Korea, China, and Russia. Funding would come from South Korea, Japan, and international agencies. The vast complex of harbor and land facilities would rival Shanghai and Hong Kong as a focal point of industry and transportation on the Sea of Japan. This point in turn would serve the participating countries and Mongolia both locally and as a launching pad for Euro-Asian exchange along the trans-Siberian railroad. The economic costs are believed to exceed $10 billion, and three of the five participants have no ready funds to contribute. The engineering obstacles will require perhaps twenty years for full completion. Political problems remain, with Russia and Japan at loggerheads over the southern Kurile Islands, held by Moscow and claimed by Tokyo. As a result, there is still no peace treaty between the two governments, and Japan refuses large-scale contributions to the Russian economy. In addition, Korea remains divided, with heavily armed forces facing one another across the Demilitarized Zone. Repeated efforts at defusing this confrontation with a summit meeting between the two heads of state have failed, although some progress has been made at lower levels.

On balance, therefore, the Tumen River project is far from realization. However the $850,000 committed by the United Nations Development Program (UNDP) in 1991 succeeded in bringing the participants to the table for a series of planning meetings at successively higher levels of discourse, winning a subsequent UNDP pledge of $3.1 million in 1992. Beijing and Tokyo may improve their mutual perception through this approach, perhaps facilitating cooperation in more feasible regional endeavors. Each will eye the other warily and test for intent every step of the way, especially on the Chinese side. Their competition in the Korean peninsula and Southeast Asia will remain paramount even as cooperation is under way. But over time such positive interaction can strengthen the internationalist position in Beijing and weaken that of the assertive nationalist faction.

The dilution of political tension with economic gain characterizes an important development in China–Hong Kong–Taiwan relations. The massive infusion of Hong Kong capital in Guangdong province and of Taiwan capital in Fujian province together with the consequent growth of industry and trade encourages the vision of a "Greater China."[19] Three-way trade reached $70 billion in 1991 and three-way investment $36.4 billion.[20] An estimated three million workers in sixteen thousand Hong Kong–owned factories produce almost $11 billion worth of exports from Guangdong. Therefore strong local interest in continued growth inhibits pressure from Beijing for political conformity.

Despite these impressive economic gains from the status quo, however, developments in late 1992 and early 1993 eroded confidence in Beijing's ability to balance such gains against political costs. Provocations from the new Hong Kong governor combined with angry denunciations from Beijing to create a mini-crisis. The governor proposed a modest increase in democratization of the colony but did so publicly without prior consultation with the Chinese. They responded by implying that they might simply scrap the 1984 Sino-British agreement on Hong Kong after its takeover by the PRC in 1997.[21] The Hong Kong stock market fell 7 percent in the following days. Meanwhile the Hong Kong government announced that it would spend $1.2 billion to prepare the site for a new airport even though Beijing had refused to approve the financing. The Chinese responded that it would "not accept any unilateral action taken without consultation with and approval by the Chinese side ... the future special administrative region government [in 1997] will not be responsible for any consequences therefrom."[22] A storm of attacks in the local Chinese Communist press and from mainland media failed to budge the governor. Thereupon Beijing escalated its pressure by threatening that as of June 30, 1997, all contracts "signed or ratified by the Hong Kong Government" would become invalid.[23] The market plunged further, dropping a total of 23 percent in three weeks.

Beijing apparently counted on financial pressures' forcing the governor's hand, and local businessmen reacted accordingly. For his part, the governor relied on his support from Prime Minister John Major to stand firm. Each side seemed to accept a collision course in a classic game of "chicken." Each side also appeared to be defining its identity by taking a strong stand. *Renmin Ribao* pointedly recalled Hong Kong's imperialist origins in a staunchly nationalistic warning:

> We would like to tell those people whose minds are still residing in times more than 100 years ago: Do not entertain any illusions about another run of "Eight-Power Allied Forces" to bully the Chinese people. ... Today's Chinese Government is not the Qing Dynasty Government and today's Chinese people are no longer the "sick man of East Asia." Whoever has a wrong concept of time, and of whom they are dealing with, and tries to force history backward, will surely have lifted a rock only to drop it on his own foot.[24]

Living up to the 1984 Sino-British agreement on Hong Kong after its takeover in 1997 seems doubtful in light of Beijing's continued complaints and challenges to increased democratization in the colony. Yet flagrantly breaking the agreement would sharply reduce investor confidence and slow the growth that has made Guangdong the richest province in China. Likewise, militant threats against Taiwan for unwonted political activity there would cause concern among the investors responsible for a major sector of employment and profits along the coast. Together, Hong Kong and Taiwan pose the sharpest point of political tension between RI and RN views because they fuse the economic gains of modernization and the political costs of Communist and nationalist compromise.

Conclusion

This overview of the actual and potential issues confronting Chinese decision makers in foreign policy is not exhaustive. With more than 150 countries and important though more distant issues in the Middle East, Europe, Africa, and Latin

America, the leadership's aspiration to play at the highest level of world politics goes well beyond our necessarily brief span of attention. In addition, there are the transnational problems of atmospheric warming, air and sea pollution, drugs, terrorism, and disease control, all of which entail foreign policy to some extent. They also link foreign policy with domestic politics to an even greater degree than much of the agenda reviewed above.[25]

Yet these issues lack the cutting edge of politics and national interest, and they are less pressing in their demand for immediate decisions that involve political or economic costs. They can be addressed incrementally in multilateral fora attended by technocrats and specialists relatively uninvolved in factional struggles at higher levels. More than twenty years after entering the United Nations, Beijing's demonstrated willingness and ability to advance these common causes as part of the international community will not change in any appreciable way regardless of the post-Deng regime's composition. The importance of remedying these global problems is increasingly appreciated by a leadership facing the consequences of economic modernization in a population of 1.2 billion. But China's development will receive first priority, leaving the consequences and the costs of addressing them to others.

For the issues at the leading edge of politics, however, forecasting must be more qualified. On the positive side, the gradual erosion of assertive nationalism in favor of reformist internationalism has been a steady trend with only brief interruptions since 1978. The open-door policy has benefited so wide a sector of Chinese society as to prevail repeatedly in public discourse between advocates and critics. It also has involved so large a sector of the bureaucracy as to socialize an entire new generation of technocrats. Their personal experience contrasts vividly with the years of Cultural Revolution, precluding any return to xenophobic isolation.

On the negative side, the absence of an all-powerful leader leaves foreign policy open to greater contention than when Mao launched his attack against "Khrushchev revisionism" in 1959 or, to a lesser degree, when Deng accepted American diplomatic recognition without halting arms sales to Taiwan in 1978. While Deng's authority was far less than Mao's, he still commanded greater power and support than any of his successors can hope for. Although the context of foreign policy decisions has become less threatening on the traditional front of security against attack, it is more threatening on the domestic front of maintaining Communist Party control. At the same time, economic priorities have increased China's vulnerability to foreign pressures and sanctions on issues of greater nationalistic sensitivity. This linkage between domestic and foreign policy came most sharply to the fore after June 4, 1989. It could arise again through the challenge of dissident demonstrations, Taiwanese independence, or territorial disputes.

Desperate times can evoke desperate acts. In 1989 a sense of desperation prompted the ruling elite to order military measures against the populace of Beijing. A similar sequence of domestically stimulated siege mentality and extremist measures cannot be ruled out in the future. In 1992 Beijing's words, albeit without any assertive actions, suggested a renewed siege mentality in response to foreign provocations. The American sale of F-16s to Taiwan prompted a parallel French sale of Mirage fighters to the island republic, both actions being fiercely denounced by Beijing. An American cabinet official visited Taiwan, the first such representative from Washington since the termination of official ties in 1979, evoking another protest. Meanwhile the aforementioned imbroglio begun by the Hong Kong governor's democratization proposals and airport developments proceeded apace.

Amid this concatenation of external events, Deng Xiaoping's domestic priority was to secure a successor Party leadership that would ensure implementation of his economic reforms. Under the circumstances, an assertive nationalistic stance may have been tactically necessary to avoid further attacks by his conservative opposition. Alternatively, this assertive stance may have represented Deng's own views.[26] In any event, the verbal flare-up and its repercussions abroad demonstrated the precarious balance between economic pragmatism and political nationalism in Beijing's handling of foreign relations.

Yet while acknowledging this precarious balance, the weight of probability lies with a moderate Chinese foreign policy posture that aims at managing confrontation so as to maximize access to markets, capital, and technology that will advance the economy. This is further driven by Deng Xiaoping's defining the survival of Communist rule as dependent on ever-improved living conditions. In one sense China could stand alone. Its resources, human and material, could sustain survival at a bare minimum level for quite a while without foreign involvement. The ability of the people to endure incredible hardship was dramatically proven in the Great Leap Forward catastrophe of 1958–1962, when more than 20 million died of famine. But to remain viable as the last surviving Communist giant Beijing must do far better than meet minimum need, and for this it must manage foreign relations on the basis of what it calls "an independent policy of peace." This is so well known to all participants in the policy process that change under any but the most extreme circumstances is unlikely.

Beijing will not become a benign power as a result. Tough bargaining remains standard practice. No formal compromise of pronounced principles is tolerable. China's central role in regional politics will be assumed and at times asserted. As the largest non–status quo power in the world, it will insist on not being taken for granted. At the same time, the flexibility and prudence that have characterized policy under Deng are likely to prevail under his successors, assuming that they constitute a stable leadership. They will misperceive and miscalculate, as do all governments, but with less frequency and lower costs at home and abroad than was true under Mao.

This is the most that can be expected in the coming years, but it is sufficient to offer East Asia the possibility of political stability and economic growth second to none in the world and unprecedented in its recent history. Beyond this decade, much larger questions arise concerning the role and responsibility of a country with the economic and military power proportionate to its size. In the interim, however, the interactions of China with the international system should prove a mutually advantageous learning experience that may provide a more positive prospect for the longer-term future.

Notes

1. *Far Eastern Economic Review* (hereafter *FEER*), vol. 155, No. 46 (November 19, 1992), pp. 66–67.

2. Zou Dedong, "Rapid Development in China's Border Trade," *Liaowang Overseas Edition,* October 5, 1992, in Foreign Broadcast Information Service, *Daily Report—China* (hereafter FBIS-China), October 30, 1992, pp. 20–23.

3. David Bachman, "The Limits to Leadership," in *The Future of China,* Analysis, National Bureau of Asian Research, vol. 3, No. 3 (August 1992), pp. 23–35.

4. For Beijing's response to Western, especially American, pressures, see its lengthy white paper "Tibet—Its Ownership and Human Rights Situation," *Beijing Review* No. 39 (September 28–October 4, 1992):10–43.

5. *The Economist,* vol. 155, No. 33 (August 22, 1992), p. 88.

6. Beijing live television relay of rally commemorating the eightieth anniversary of the 1911 revolution, in FBIS-China, October 15, 1991, p. 35.

7. *Renmin Ribao,* October 15, 1991, in *New York Times,* October 16, 1991.

8. David M. Lampton et al., *The Emergence of "Greater China": Implications for the United States,* National Committee China Policy Series, No. 5 (October 1992), p. 1. One plausible calculation of the actual Taiwan-mainland trade passing indirectly through Hong Kong estimated that the 1992 total could reach $14 billion; Andrew B. Brick, "The Emergence of Greater China: The Diaspora Ascendant," Heritage Foundation Lectures, No. 411, p. 10.

9. Robert G. Sutter, *China in World Affairs—Background, Prospects, and Implications for the United States,* Congressional Research Service, October 1, 1992, pp. 10–11.

10. For fuller coverage of this situation see *FEER,* vol. 155, No. 32 (August 13, 1992), pp. 14–21.

11. In late 1992 Beijing abstained on the Security Council resolution imposing trade sanctions in areas of Cambodia controlled by the Khmer Rouge and moving ahead toward free elections in 1993, with or without the Khmer Rouge; it had supported the fourteen previous resolutions on a Cambodian settlement. *New York Times,* November 30, 1992. See also *FEER,* vol. 155, No. 46 (November 19, 1992), p. 13, for the Chinese tactics at talks in Beijing in early November.

12. For a more complete analysis, see John Garver, "China and South Asia," in Allen S. Whiting, ed., *China's Foreign Relations,* Annals of the American Academy of Political and Social Science, 519 (January 1992):67–85.

13. *FEER,* vol. 155, No. 45 (November 12, 1992), p. 29.

14. *FEER,* vol. 155, No. 46 (November 19, 1992), p. 8.

15. *New York Times,* December 5, 1992.

16. According to well-informed Uyghur sources in Alma-Ata, the incident involved several dozen youths, lightly armed, in a badly executed attack on local officials. Interviews by the author, October 1990. For unconfirmed reports of racial riots in October 1992 occurring in Urumqi and other cities, see *South China Morning Post,* December 11, 1992, in FBIS-China, December 11, 1992, pp. 28–29.

17. Beijing reportedly sent an urgent message to Xinjiang officials in October 1992 warning against "domestic and foreign enemies" working with "separatists in Xinjiang," including "Moslem religious leaders" and infiltrators posing as tourists. FBIS-China, December 11, 1992, pp. 28–29.

18. *FEER,* vol. 155, No. 35 (September 3, 1992), p. 21; *New York Times,* October 18, 1992.

19. PRC sources claim that Hong Kong and Macao investors put $4 billion into the Pearl River Delta in 1991 alone; Lampton, et al., *The Emergence of "Greater China,"* p. 1.

20. Information from Hong Kong Trade Development Council, ibid.

21. For the full account of these developments, see *FEER,* vol. 155, Nos. 43, 47, and 48 (November 5 and 26, 1992, December 3, 1992).

22. Xinhua Domestic Service, November 19, 1992, in FBIS-China, November 20, 1992, p. 57.

23. *New York Times,* November 31, 1992.

272 Allen S. Whiting

24. Tong Xing, "Commentary on Hong Kong," *Renmin Ribao*, November 20, 1992, in FBIS-China, November 20, 1992, pp. 55–56.

25. On linkages between domestic politics and economic modernization, on the one hand, and foreign relations, on the other, see China's environmental problems and policies in *FEER*, vol. 155, No. 42 (October 29, 1992), pp. 42–44.

26. "An authoritative source" in Beijing quoted an anonymous "senior CPC figure" believed to be Deng to the effect that "we should not follow others in saying that the Cold War has ended. ... The Cold War between the West and the Third World has just started. Moreover there are great economic pressures." *Wen Wei Po*, November 19, 1992, in FBIS-China, November 19, 1992, p. 2.

Bibliography

This bibliography has grown out of our teaching and research experience in the field of Chinese foreign policy. The basic aim is to familiarize students with the range and type of materials now available for exploring in greater depth the various issues of Chinese foreign relations covered in this volume, with emphasis on post-Mao developments. Journal articles are included only where published books and monographs are spotty. With a few notable exceptions, the selection favors the more recent publications.

The PRC publications listed below are available in major research libraries in the United States. Subscriptions to such periodicals as *Beijing Review, Guoji wenti yanjiu, Liaowang, Renmin ribao* (overseas edition), and *Qiushi* can be obtained through China Books and Periodicals, Inc., which has retail centers in Chicago, New York, and San Francisco. Foreign Broadcast Information Service, *Daily Report—China* (FBIS-China) is the most useful and widely consulted reference in English; it is available in paper and microfiche versions and includes English translations of important PRC newspaper and journal articles and monitored radio broadcasts on both domestic and international issues.

Non-PRC English-language sources are arranged topically, approximating somewhat the organization of the book. Major newspapers and journals of particular value for the study of Chinese foreign policy include *American Asian Review, Asian Affairs, Asian Wall Street Journal* (Hong Kong), *Asian Perspective* (Seoul), *Asian Survey, Australian Journal of Chinese Affairs, China Business Review, China Information* (Leiden), *China Quarterly* (London), *Chinese Law and Government, Christian Science Monitor, Far Eastern Economic Review* (Hong Kong), *Foreign Affairs, Foreign Policy, International Affairs* (London), *International Organization, International Security, International Studies Quarterly, Issues & Studies* (Taipei), *Japan Times Weekly* (Tokyo), *Journal of Contemporary China, Journal of Northeast Asian Studies, New York Times, Orbis, Pacific Affairs* (Vancouver), *Pacific Review* (Oxford), *Political Science Quarterly, South China Morning Post* (Hong Kong), *World Policy Journal,* and *World Politics.*

PRC Publications

Beijing Review. (Weekly in English; March 4, 1958–; *Peking Review* before January 1, 1979.)

Changes and Development in China (1949–1989). Beijing: Beijing Review Press, 1989.

Che Muqi. *Beijing Turmoil: More Than Meets the Eye.* Beijing: Foreign Languages Press, 1990.

Chen Shicai. *Guoji fayuan toushi* [A Perspective on the International Court of Justice]. Beijing: Zhongguo youyi chuban gongsi, 1984.

Chen Zhongjing. *Problems in International Strategy.* Hong Kong: Man Hai Language Publication, 1989.

Chi Baotai. *Foreign Investment in China: Questions and Answers.* Beijing: Foreign Languages Press, 1986.

China Daily (English, 1982–).

China for Peace. Beijing: New World Press, 1985.

China's Foreign Economic Legislation. Vol. 1. Beijing: Foreign Languages Press, 1982.

China's Foreign Economic Legislation. Vol. 2. Beijing: Foreign Languages Press, 1986.

China's Foreign Relations: A Chronology of Events (1949–1988). Beijing: Foreign Languages Press, 1989.

Deng Xiaoping. *Deng Xiaoping wenxuan, 1975–1982* [The Selected Works of Deng Xiaoping, 1975–1982]. Beijing: Renmin chubanshe, 1983.

————. *Jianshe you Zhongguo tese de shehui zhuyi* [Building Socialism with Chinese Characteristics]. Beijing: Renmin chubanshe, 1987.

————. *Fundamental Issues in Present-Day China*. Beijing: Foreign Languages Press, 1985.

Deng Zhenglai, ed. *Wang Tieya wenxuan* [Selected Works of Wang Tieya]. Beijing: Zhongguo zhengfa daxue chubanshe, 1993.

Du Xichuan and Zhang Lingyuan. *China's Legal System: A General Survey*. Beijing: New World Press, 1990.

Fang, Percy Jucheng, and Lucy Guinong Fang. *Zhou Enlai—A Profile*. Beijing: Foreign Languages Press, 1987.

Faxue yanjiu [Legal Research]. (Bimonthly, April 1979–; edited by the Institute of Law, Chinese Academy of Social Sciences, Beijing.)

Guofang xiandaihua [National Defense Modernization]. Beijing: Kexue puji chubanshe, 1983.

Guoji heping nian: Xueshu taolunhui ziliao huibian [The International Year of Peace: An Anthology of Materials from an Academic Symposium]. Beijing: Shehui kexue wenxian chubanshe, 1986.

Guoji wenti yanjiu [Journal of International Studies]. (Quarterly, July 1981–; edited by the Institute of International Relations, Beijing.)

Guoji xingshi nianjian [Yearbook of International Affairs]. Shanghai: Zhongguo da baikequanshu chubanshe. (Annual, 1982–; edited by the Shanghai Institute for International Studies.)

Hongqi [Red Flag]. (Semimonthly; June 1958–June 1988; the official organ of the Central Committee of the Chinese Communist Party.)

Hu Yaobang. *For Friendship and Cooperation*. Beijing: Foreign Languages Press, 1985.

Huan Xiang, ed. *Dangdai shijie zhengzhi jingji jiben wenti* [Basic Problems of Contemporary World Political Economy]. Beijing: Shijie zhishi chubanshe, 1989.

Information Office of the State Council. "Human Rights in China." *Beijing Review* 34:44 (November 4, 1991):8–45; also in FBIS-China, supplement, November 31, 1991, pp. 1–29.

————. "Tibet—Its Ownership and Human Rights Situation," in FBIS-China, supplement, October 9, 1992, pp. 1–23.

Lan Mingliang. *Guoji zuzhi gaikuang* [A Survey of International Organizations]. Beijing: Falu chubanshe, 1983.

Legislative Affairs Commission of the Standing Committee of the National People's Congress of the People's Republic of China, comp. *The Laws of the People's Republic of China 1979–1982*. Vol. 1. Beijing: Foreign Languages Press, 1987.

————. *The Laws of the People's Republic of China 1983–1986*. Vol. 2. Beijing: Foreign Languages Press, 1987.

Li Chengrui. *A Study of China's Population*. Beijing: Foreign Languages Press, 1992.

Liang Yuntong et al. *Meiguo heping yanbian zhanlue* [America's Peaceful Evolution Strategy]. N.p.: Jilin renmin chubanshe, 1992.

Liu Ding, ed. *Guoji jingjifa* [International Economic Law]. Beijing: Zhongguo renmin daxue chubanshe, 1984.

Liu Guoguang et al., comp. *China's Economy in 2000*. Beijing: New World Press, 1987.

Liu Haishan and Li Mei. *Caijun yu guojifa* [Disarmament and International Law]. Chengdu: Sichuan renmin chubanshe, 1990.

Liu Xiao. *Chu shi Sulian ba nian* [Eight Years as Ambassador to the Soviet Union]. Beijing: Zhonggong ziliao chubanshe, 1986.

Lu Yi et al., eds. *Qiuji: Yige shijiexing de xuanze* [Global Citizenship: A Worldwide Choice]. Shanghai: Baijia chubanshe, 1989.

Ma Hong. *New Strategy for China's Economy.* Beijing: Foreign Languages Press, 1983.

_____ , ed. *Modern China's Economy and Management.* Beijing: Foreign Languages Press, 1990.

Ma Yin, ed. *China's Minority Nationalities.* Beijing: Foreign Languages Press, 1989.

Major Documents of the People's Republic of China (December 1978–November 1989). Beijing: Foreign Languages Press, 1991.

Mao Zedong. *Mao Zedong sixiang wansui* [Long Live Mao Zedong's Thought]. N.p.: 1967.

_____ . *Mao Zedong sixiang wansui* [Long Live Mao Zedong's Thought]. N.p.: August 1969.

_____ . *Selected Works of Mao Tse-tung.* Vols. 1–4. Peking: Foreign Languages Press, 1961, 1965.

_____ . *Selected Works of Mao Tsetung.* Vol. 5. Peking: Foreign Languages Press, 1977.

_____ . *Mao Zedong xuanji* [Selected Works of Mao Zedong] (the first four volumes in Chinese published as one volume). Beijing: Renmin chubanshe, 1969.

Ni Shixiong, Feng Shaolei, and Jin Yingzhong. *Shiji fengyun de chan'er—Dangdai guoji guanxi lilun* [An Unstable Offspring of the Century—Contemporary International Relations Theory]. Zhejiang: Zhejiang renmin chubanshe, 1989.

Nie Rongzhen. *Nie Rongzhen huiyilu* [Memoirs of Nie Rongzhen]. Beijing: Jiefangjun chubanshe, 1984.

Pan Guang, ed. *Dangdai guoji weiji yanjiu* [Research on Contemporary International Crises]. Beijing: Zhongguo shehui kexue chubanshe, 1989.

Peng Dehuai. *Memoirs of a Chinese Marshall—The autobiographical notes of Peng Dehuai (1898–1974).* Trans. Zheng Longpu. Beijing: Foreign Languages Press, 1984.

Qin Xuanren, ed. *Guoji jingji maoyi guanxi—lilun he shijian* [International Economic Trade Relations—Theory and Practice]. Beijing: Zhongguo duiwai fanyi chuban gongsi, 1985.

Qiushi [Seeking Truth]. (July 1, 1988–; the successor to *Hongqi*; the official journal of the Central Committee Party School.)

Qu Geping. *Zhongguo huanjing wenti ji duice* [China's Environmental Problems and Policies]. Beijing: Zhongguo huanjing kexue chubanshe, 1989.

_____ . *Zhongguo de huanjing guanli* [China's Management of the Environment]. Beijing: Zhongguo huanjing kexue chubanshe, 1989.

Renmin ribao [People's Daily]. (June 15, 1948–; the official organ of the Central Committee of the Chinese Communist Party.)

Renmin ribao suoyin [Index to People's Daily]. (Monthly; 1951–.)

Shijie zhishi [World Knowledge]. (Semimonthly; September 1934–.)

Shijie zhishi nianjian [World Knowledge Yearbook]. (Annual, 1952–1966, 1982–.)

Social Sciences in China. (Quarterly in English; 1980–; edited by the Chinese Academy of Social Sciences.)

Song Yimin. *On China's Concept of Security.* Geneva: United Nations Institute for Disarmament Research, 1986. (United Nations Publication Sales No. GV.E.86.0.1.)

Sun Haichen, comp. and trans. *The Wiles of War: 36 Military Stratagems from Ancient China.* Beijing: Foreign Languages Press, 1991.

Wang Huijiang and Li Boxi. *China Toward the Year 2000.* Beijing: New World Press, 1989.

Wang Shengzhu, ed. *Guoji guanxi shi* [The History of International Relations]. Vol. 1. Wuhan: Wuhan daxue chubanshe, 1983.

_____ . *Guoji guanxi shi* [The History of International Relations]. Vol. 2. Wuhan: Wuhan daxue chubanshe, 1983.

Wang Tieya, ed. *Guojifa* [International Law]. Shijiazhuang: Falu chubanshe, 1981.

Wei Min et al., eds. *Guojifa gailun* [An Introduction to International Law]. Beijing: Guangming ribao chubanshe, 1986.

Wu Xiuquan. *Eight Years in the Ministry of Foreign Affairs.* Beijing: New World Press, 1985.

Xiandai quoji guanxi [Contemporary International Relations]. (Irregular, October 1981–; edited by the Institute of Contemporary International Relations, Beijing.)

Xiao Guangwu and Zong Yue, eds. *Dangdai shijie zhengzhi jingji yu guoji guanxi* [Contemporary World Political Economy and International Relations]. Beijing: Zhongguo zhanwang chushe, 1990.

Xue Mouhong and Pei Jianzhang, eds. *Dangdai Zhongguo waijiao* [Contemporary Chinese Foreign Relations]. Beijing: Zhongguo shehui kexue chubanshe, 1987. (An official history of Chinese foreign relations covering the period 1949–1986 prepared by the PRC Foreign Ministry.)

Zhao Lihai. *Lianheguo xianzhang de xiugai wenti* [The Problems of the United Nations Charter Review]. Beijing: Beijing daxue chubanshe, 1981.

————. *Haiyangfa de xin fazhan* [The New Development of the Law of the Sea]. Beijing: Beijing daxue chubanshe, 1981.

Zheng Duanmu, ed. *Guojifa* [International Law]. Beijing: Beijing daxue chubanshe, 1989.

Zhong Wenxian, comp. *Mao Zedong: Biography, Assessment, Reminiscences.* Beijing: Foreign Languages Press, 1986.

Zhongguo baike nianjian [Chinese Encyclopedic Yearbook]. Beijing: Zhongguo dabaikequanshu. (Annual, 1980–; edited by the Chinese Encyclopedia Publisher.)

Zhongguo fazhi bao [China Legal Journal]. (Three times a week since August 1980; daily since July 1, 1986.)

Zhongguo guojifa niankan [Chinese Yearbook of International Law]. Beijing: Zhongguo duiwai fanyi chuban gongsi. (Annual, 1982–; edited by the China International Law Society.)

Zhongguo waijiao gailan [Survey of Chinese Foreign Relations]. Beijing: Shijie zhishi chubanshe. (Annual, 1987–; edited by the Editorial Office of Diplomatic History, PRC Ministry of Foreign Affairs.)

Zhou Zhonghai. *Guoji haiyang fa* [International Law of the Sea]. Beijing: Zhongguo zhengfa daxue chubanshe, 1987.

Non-PRC Publications in English

The Study of Chinese Foreign Policy and International Relations

Bobrow, Davis. "Old Dragons in New Models." *World Politics* 19:2 (January 1967):306–319.

Breslauer, George W., and Philip E. Tetlock, eds. *Learning in U.S. and Soviet Foreign Policy.* Boulder, Colo.: Westview Press, 1991.

Callahan, Patrick, Linda P. Brady, and Margaret G. Herman. *Describing Foreign Policy Behavior.* Beverly Hills, Calif.: Sage Publications, 1982.

Dial, Roger L., ed. *Advancing and Contending Approaches to the Study of Chinese Foreign Policy.* Halifax, Nova Scotia: Centre for Foreign Policy Studies, Dalhousie University, 1974.

Ferguson, Yale H., and Richard W. Mansbach. *The Elusive Quest: Theory and International Politics.* Columbia: University of South Carolina Press, 1988.

George, Alexander L. *Bridging the Gap: Theory and Practice in Foreign Policy.* Washington, D.C.: United States Institute of Peace Press, 1993.

Harding, Harry. "The Study of Chinese Politics: Toward a Third Generation of Scholarship." *World Politics* 36:2 (January 1984):284–307.

————. "International Studies in China." *China Exchange News* 20:3–4 (Fall/Winter 1992):2–6.

Hermann, Charles F., Charles W. Kegley, Jr., and James N. Rosenau, eds. *New Directions in the Study of Foreign Policy.* Boston: Allen & Unwin, 1987.

Holsti, K. J., et al. *Why Nations Realign: Foreign Policy Restructuring in the Postwar World.* London: Allen & Unwin, 1982.

Jensen, Lloyd. *Explaining Foreign Policy.* Englewood Cliffs, N.J.: Prentice-Hall, 1982.

Kapur, Harish, ed. *As China Sees the World: Perceptions of Chinese Scholars.* London: Frances Pinter, 1987.

Kubalkova, Vendulka, and Albert Cruickshank. *Marxism and International Relations.* New York: Oxford University Press, 1989.

Kim, Samuel S. "China's Place in World Politics." *Problems of Communism* 31:2 (March–April 1982):63–70.

———. "Advancing the American Study of Chinese Foreign Policy." *China Exchange News* 20:3–4 (Fall/Winter 1992):18–23.

Korany, Bahgat, et al. *How Foreign Policy Decisions Are Made in the Third World.* Boulder, Colo.: Westview Press, 1986.

McGowan, Pat, and Charles W. Kegley, Jr., eds. *Foreign Policy and the Modern World-System.* Beverly Hills, Calif.: Sage Publications, 1983.

Murray, Douglas P. *International Relations Research and Training in the People's Republic of China: A special report of the Northeast Asia–United States Forum on International Policy.* Stanford, Calif.: Stanford University, 1982.

Ng-Quinn, Michael. "The Analytic Study of Chinese Foreign Policy." *International Studies Quarterly* 27 (June 1983):203–224.

Robinson, Thomas, and David Shambaugh, eds. *Chinese Foreign Policy: Theory and Practice.* New York: Oxford University Press, 1993.

Rosenau, James N. *Turbulence in World Politics: A Theory of Change and Continuity.* Princeton, N.J.: Princeton University Press, 1990.

Rozman, Gilbert. "China's Soviet Watchers in the 1980s: A New Era in Scholarship." *World Politics* 37:3 (July 1985):435–474.

Schurmann, Franz. *The Logic of World Power: An Inquiry into the Origins, Currents, and Contradictions of World Politics.* New York: Pantheon Books, 1974.

Shambaugh, David. "China's National Security Research Bureaucracy." *China Quarterly* No. 110 (June 1987):276–304.

———. "New Sources and Research Opportunities in the Study of China's Foreign Relations and National Security." *China Exchange News* 20:3–4 (Fall/Winter 1992):24–27.

———, and Wang Jisi. "Research on International Studies in the People's Republic of China." *PS* 17:4 (Fall 1984):758–764.

Shih, Chih-yu. *The Spirit of Chinese Foreign Policy: A Psychological View.* London: Macmillan, 1990.

Snyder, Jack. "Richness, Rigor, and Relevance in the Study of Soviet Foreign Policy." *International Security* 9:3 (Winter 1984–1985):89–108.

Walker, Stephen, ed. *Role Theory and Foreign Policy Analysis.* Durham, N.C.: Duke University Press, 1987.

Whiting, Allen S. "Chinese Foreign Policy: A Workshop Report." *SSRC Items* 31 (March–June 1977):1–3.

Wu, Friedrich W. "Explanatory Approaches to Chinese Foreign Policy: A Critique of the Western Literature." *Studies in Comparative Communism* 13 (Spring 1980):41–62.

Yahuda, Michael, ed. *New Directions in the Social Sciences and Humanities in China.* New York: St. Martin's Press, 1986.

Zhuralov, V. "Chinese Studies of International Relations (Late 1970s and Early 1980s)." *Far Eastern Affairs* (Moscow) No. 2 (1984):134–142.

The Weight of the Past

Banno, Masataka. *China and the West 1858–1861: The Origins of the Tsungli Yamen.* Cambridge, Mass.: Harvard University Press, 1964.

Crammer-Byng, John. "The Chinese View of Their Place in the World: An Historical Perspective." *China Quarterly* No. 53 (January–March 1973):67–79.

Duara, Prasenjit. "De-Constructing the Chinese Nations." *Australian Journal of Chinese Affairs* 30 (July 1993):1–26.

Fairbank, John K. "China's Foreign Policy in Historical Perspective." *Foreign Affairs* 47:3 (April 1969):449–463.

————— , ed. *The Chinese World Order: Traditional China's Foreign Relations.* Cambridge, Mass.: Harvard University Press, 1968.

Feuerwerker, Albert. "Chinese History and the Foreign Relations of Contemporary China." *Annals of the American Academy of Political and Social Science* 402 (July 1972):1–14.

Fitzgerald, C. P. *The Chinese View of Their Place in the World.* London: Oxford University Press, 1965.

Franke, Wolfgang. *China and the West.* Trans. R. A. Wilson. New York: Harper Torchbooks, 1967.

Ho, Ping-Ti. "The Chinese Civilization: A Search for the Roots of Longevity." *Journal of Asian Studies* 35 (August 1976):547–554.

Hsu, Cho-yun. "Applying Confucian Ethics to International Relations." *Ethics & International Affairs* 5 (1991):15–31.

Hsü, Immanuel C.Y. *China's Entrance into the Family of Nations: The Diplomatic Phase 1858–1880.* Cambridge, Mass.: Harvard University Press, 1960.

Hunt, Michael H. "Chinese Foreign Relations in Historical Perspective," in Harry Harding, ed., *China's Foreign Relations in the 1980s.* New Haven: Yale University Press, 1984, pp. 1–42.

Jenner, W.J.F. *The Tyranny of History: The Roots of China's Crisis.* New York: Penguin Books, 1992.

Kierman, Frank A., and John K. Fairbank, eds. *Chinese Ways in Warfare.* Cambridge, Mass.: Harvard University Press, 1974.

Mancall, Mark. *China at the Center: 300 Years of Foreign Policy.* New York: Free Press, 1984.

Reardon-Anderson, James. *Yenan and the Great Powers: The Origins of Chinese Communist Foreign Policy, 1944–1946.* New York: Columbia University Press, 1980.

Rossabi, Morris, ed. *China Among Equals: The Middle Kingdom and Its Neighbors.* Berkeley: University of California Press, 1983.

Schwartz, Benjamin I. *The World of Thought in Ancient China.* Cambridge, Mass.: Harvard University Press, 1985.

Shih, Chih-yu. *The Spirit of Chinese Foreign Policy: A Psychological View.* London: Macmillan, 1990.

Spence, Jonathan D. *To Change China: Western Advisers in China, 1620–1960.* New York: Penguin Books, 1980.

Teng, Ssu-yu, and John K. Fairbank. *China's Response to the West: A Documentary Survey, 1839–1923.* Cambridge, Mass.: Harvard University Press, 1954.

Walker, Richard L. *The Multi-State System of Ancient China.* Hamden: Shoe String Press, 1953.

Wright, Arthur. "Struggle v. Harmony: Symbols of Competing Values in Modern China." *World Politics* 6:1 (October 1953):31–44.

Zhang Yongjin. *China in the International System, 1918–20: The Middle Kingdom at the Periphery.* New York: St. Martin's Press, 1991.

General Works: Contemporary Developments

Camilleri, Joseph. *Chinese Foreign Policy: The Maoist Era and Its Aftermath.* Seattle: University of Washington Press, 1980.

Dreyer, June T., ed. *Chinese Defense and Foreign Policy.* New York: Paragon House, 1989.

Garver, John W. *Foreign Relations of the People's Republic of China.* Englewood Cliffs, N.J.: Prentice-Hall, 1993.

Gittings, John. *China Changes Face.* Oxford: Oxford University Press, 1989.

Hao, Yufan, and Guocang Huan, eds. *The Chinese View of the World.* New York: Pantheon Books, 1989.

Harding, Harry, ed. *Chinese Foreign Relations in the 1980s.* New Haven, Conn.: Yale University Press, 1984.

Hsiung, James C., ed. *Beyond China's Independent Foreign Policy.* New York: Praeger, 1985.

Kapur, Harish, ed. *The End of an Isolation: China After Mao.* Boston: Martinus Nijhoff, 1985.

Macchiarola, Frank J., and Robert B. Oxnam, eds. *The China Challenge.* New York: Academy of Political Science, 1991.

Robinson, Thomas, and David Shambaugh, eds. *Chinese Foreign Policy: Theory and Practice.* New York: Oxford University Press, 1993.

Segal, Gerald, ed. *Chinese Politics and Foreign Policy Reform.* London: Kegan Paul International, 1990.

Sutter, Robert G. *Chinese Foreign Policy: Developments After Mao.* New York: Praeger, 1986.

Whiting, Allen S., ed. *Chinese Foreign Relations.* Annals of the American Academy of Political and Social Science 519 (January 1992).

Yahuda, Michael. *China's Role in World Affairs.* New York: St. Martin's Press, 1978.

———— . *Towards the End of Isolationism: China's Foreign Policy After Mao.* New York: St. Martin's Press, 1983.

Competing Determinants and Explanations

Adomeit, Hannes, and Robert Boardman, eds. *Foreign Policy Making in Communist Countries.* New York: Praeger, 1979.

Armstrong, J. D. *Revolutionary Diplomacy: Chinese Foreign Policy and the United Front Doctrine.* Berkeley: University of California Press, 1977.

Bialer, Seweryn, ed. *The Domestic Context of Soviet Foreign Policy.* Boulder, Colo.: Westview Press, 1981.

Brugger, Bill, and David Kelly. *Chinese Marxism in the Post-Mao Era.* Stanford, Calif.: Stanford University Press, 1990.

Chan, Steve. "Rationality, Bureaucratic Politics, and Belief System: Explaining the Chinese Policy Debate, 1964–66." *Journal of Peace Research* 16 (1979):333–347.

———— . "Chinese Conflict Calculus and Behavior: Assessment from a Perspective of Conflict Management." *World Politics* 30:3 (April 1978):391–410.

Dial, Roger L., ed. *Advancing and Contending Approaches to the Study of Chinese Foreign Policy.* Halifax, Nova Scotia: Centre for Foreign Policy Studies, Dalhousie University, 1974.

Dittmer, Lowell. *Sino-Soviet Normalization and Its International Implications, 1945–1990.* Seattle: University of Washington Press, 1992.

East, Maurice A., Stephen A. Salmore, and Charles F. Hermann, eds. *Why Nations Act: Theoretical Perspectives for Comparative Foreign Policy Studies.* Beverly Hills, Calif.: Sage Publications, 1978.

Fingar, Thomas, ed. *China's Quest for Independence: Policy Evolution in the 1970s.* Boulder, Colo.: Westview Press, 1980.

Gittings, John. *The World and China, 1922–1972.* New York: Harper & Row, 1974.

Gottlieb, Thomas M. *Chinese Foreign Policy Factionalism and the Origins of the Strategic Triangle.* R-1902-NA. Santa Monica: RAND Corporation, 1977.

Kim, Samuel S. *The Maoist Image of World Order.* Princeton, N.J.: Center of International Studies, Princeton University, 1977.

Lieberthal, Kenneth. *The Foreign Policy Debate in Peking as Seen Through Allegorical Articles.* P-5768. Santa Monica: RAND Corporation, 1977.

Liao, Kuang-sheng. "Linkage Politics in China: Internal Mobilization and Articulated External Hostility in the Cultural Revolution 1967–1969." *World Politics* 28:4 (July 1976):590–610.

Ng-Quinn, Michael. "Effects of Bipolarity on Chinese Foreign Policy." *Survey* 26 (Spring 1982):102–130.

O'Leary, Greg. *The Shaping of Chinese Foreign Policy.* New York: St. Martin's Press, 1980.

Onate, Andres D. "The Conflict Interactions of the People's Republic of China, 1950–1970." *Journal of Conflict Resolution* 18:4 (December 1974):578–594.

Pollack, Jonathan D. *China's Potential as a World Power*. P-6524. Santa Monica: RAND Corporation, 1980.

Schram, Stuart, ed. *Chairman Mao Talks to the People*. New York: Pantheon, 1974.

Schurmann, Franz. *The Logic of World Power*. New York: Pantheon, 1974.

Shih, Chih-yu. *China's Just World: The Morality of Chinese Foreign Policy*. Boulder, Colo.: Lynne Rienner, 1993.

Solinger, Dorothy, ed. *Three Visions of Chinese Socialism*. Boulder, Colo.: Westview Press, 1984.

Waltz, Kenneth N. *Theory of International Politics*. Reading, Mass.: Addison-Wesley, 1979.

Whiting, Allen S. *Chinese Domestic Politics and Foreign Policy in the 1970s*. Ann Arbor, Mich.: Center for Chinese Studies, 1979.

Zhao Quansheng. "Domestic Factors of Chinese Foreign Policy: From Vertical to Horizontal Authoritarianism." *Annals of the American Academy of Political and Social Science* 519 (January 1992):158–178.

The Decision-making Process

Axelrod, Robert, ed. *Structure of Decision: The Cognitive Maps of Political Elites*. Princeton, N.J.: Princeton University Press, 1976.

Barnett, A. Doak. *The Making of Foreign Policy in China*. Boulder, Colo.: Westview Press, 1985.

Bobrow, Davis B., Steve Chan, and John A. Kringen, *Understanding Foreign Policy Decisions: The Chinese Case*. New York: Free Press, 1979.

_____ . "Understanding How Others Treat Crises: A Multimethod Approach." *International Studies Quarterly* 21 (March 1977):199–223.

Chang, Jaw-ling Joanne. *United States–China Normalization: An Evaluation of Foreign Policy Decision Making*. Baltimore, Md.: Occasional Papers/Reprint Series in Contemporary Asian Studies, 1986.

Cohen, Raymond. *Negotiating Across Cultures*. Washington, D.C.: United States Institute of Peace Press, 1991.

Gurtov, Melvin, and Byong-Moo Hwang. *China Under Threat: The Politics of Strategy and Diplomacy*. Baltimore, Md.: Johns Hopkins University Press, 1980.

Jacobson, Harold K., and Michel Oksenberg. *China's Participation in the IMF, the World Bank, and GATT*. Ann Arbor: University of Michigan Press, 1990.

Li Fan. "The Question of Interests in the Chinese Policy Making Process." *China Quarterly* No. 109 (March 1987):64–71.

Lieberthal, Kenneth, and Michel Oksenberg. *Policy Making in China: Leaders, Structures, and Processes*. Princeton, N.J.: Princeton University Press, 1988.

Sylvan, Donald A., and Steve Chan, eds. *Foreign Policy Decision Making: Perception, Cognition, and Artificial Intelligence*. New York: Praeger, 1984.

Tretiak, Daniel. "Who Makes Chinese Foreign Policy Today (Late 1980)?" *Australian Journal of Chinese Affairs* No. 5 (1981):137–157.

Vertzberger, Yaacov. *Misperceptions in Foreign Policymaking: The Sino-Indian Conflict 1959–1962*. Boulder, Colo.: Westview Press, 1984.

Whiting, Allen S. *China Crosses the Yalu: The Decision to Enter the Korean War*. New York: Macmillan, 1960.

_____ . "New Light on Mao: Quemoy 1958: Mao's Miscalculations." *China Quarterly* No. 62 (June 1975):263–270.

Diplomatic and Negotiating Style

Chang, Jaw-ling Joanne. "Negotiation of the 17 August 1982 U.S.-PRC Arms Communiqué: Beijing's Negotiating Tactics." *China Quarterly* No. 125 (March 1991):33–54.

Hsu, Kai-yu. *Chou En-Lai: China's Gray Eminence*. Garden City, N.Y.: Doubleday, 1968.

Kapp, Robert A., ed. *Communicating with China.* Chicago: Intercultural Press, 1983.

Keith, Ronald C. *The Diplomacy of Zhou Enlai.* London: Macmillan, 1989.

Kim, Samuel S. "Behavioural Dimensions of Chinese Multilateral Diplomacy." *China Quarterly* No. 72 (December 1977):713–742.

Lall, Arthur. *How Communist China Negotiates.* New York: Columbia University Press, 1968.

Pye, Lucian. "Mao Tse-tung's Leadership Style." *Political Science Quarterly* 91:2 (Summer 1976):219–235.

_____ . *Chinese Commercial Negotiating Style.* Cambridge, Mass.: Oelgeschlager, Gunn & Hain, 1982.

Solomon, Richard H. *Chinese Negotiating Behavior: A Briefing Analysis.* Santa Monica: RAND Corporation, 1985.

Tung, Shih-Chung. *The Policy of China in the Third United Nations Conference on the Law of the Sea.* Geneva: Graduate Institute of International Studies, 1981.

Wilson, Dick. *Zhou Enlai: A Biography.* New York: Viking, 1984.

Young, Kenneth T. *Negotiating with the Chinese Communists: The U.S. Experience.* New York: McGraw-Hill, 1966.

Zhai Qiang. "China and the Geneva Conference of 1954." *China Quarterly* No. 129 (March 1992):103–122.

China and the Soviet Union/Russia

Boris, Oleg B. *Sino-Soviet Relations, 1945–1973: A Brief History.* Moscow: Progress Publishers, 1975.

Borisov, O. B., and B. T. Koloskov, *Soviet- Chinese Relations 1945–1980.* Moscow: Mysl Publishers, 3d supplemental ed., 1980.

Chang, Gordon H. *Friends and Enemies: The United States, China, and the Soviet Union, 1948–1972.* Stanford, Calif.: Stanford University Press, 1990.

Dittmer, Lowell. *Sino-Soviet Normalization and Its International Implications, 1945–1990.* Seattle: University of Washington Press, 1992.

Ellison, Herbert J., ed. *The Sino–Soviet Conflict: A Global Perspective.* Seattle: University of Washington Press, 1982.

Garver, John W. *Chinese-Soviet Relations, 1937–1945: The Diplomacy of Chinese Nationalism.* New York: Oxford University Press, 1988.

Gittings, John. *Survey of the Sino-Soviet Dispute 1963–1967.* London: Oxford University Press, 1968.

Goldstein, Joshua S., and John R. Freeman. *Three-Way Street: Strategic Reciprocity in World Politics.* Chicago: University of Chicago Press, 1990.

Hamrin, Carol Lee. "China Reassesses the Superpowers." *Pacific Affairs* 56:2 (Summer 1983):209–231.

Hart, Thomas G. *Sino-Soviet Relations: Re-examining the Prospects for Normalization.* Brookfield, Vt.: Gower, 1987.

Jones, Peter, and Sian Kevill, comp. *China and the Soviet Union, 1949–84.* Essex: Longman Group, 1985.

Kim, Ilpyong, ed. *The Strategic Triangle: China, the United States, and the Soviet Union.* New York: Paragon House, 1987.

Medvedev, Roy A. *China and the Superpowers.* Trans. Harold Shukman. Oxford: Basil Blackwell, 1986.

Pollack, Jonathan. *The Sino-Soviet Rivalry and Chinese Security Debate.* R-2907-AF. Santa Monica: RAND Corporation, 1982.

Rozman, Gilbert. "Moscow's China-Watchers in the Post-Mao Era: The Response to a Changing China." *China Quarterly* No. 94 (June 1983):231–236.

_____ . *The Chinese Debate About Soviet Socialism, 1978–1985.* Princeton, N.J.: Princeton University Press, 1987.

_____ . *A Mirror for Socialism: Soviet Criticisms of China*. Princeton, N.J.: Princeton University Press, 1985.

Wich, Richard. *Sino-Soviet Crisis Politics: A Study of Political Change and Communication*. Cambridge, Mass.: Harvard University Press, 1980.

Yin, John. *Sino-Soviet Dialogue on the Problem of War*. The Hague: Martinus Nijhoff, 1971.

Zagoria, Donald S. *The Sino-Soviet Conflict 1956–1961*. Princeton, N.J.: Princeton University Press, 1962.

_____ . *Vietnam Triangle: Moscow/Peking/Hanoi*. New York: Pegasus, 1967.

China and the United States

Atlantic Council of the United States and National Committee on United States–China Relations. *United States and China Relations at a Crossroads*. Washington, D.C.: Atlantic Council of the United States, 1993.

Barnett, A. Doak. *U.S. Arms Sales: The China-Taiwan Tangle*. Washington, D.C.: Brookings Institution, 1982.

Brzezinski, Zbigniew. *Power and Principle*. New York: Farrar, Straus, Giroux, 1983.

Carter, Jimmy. *Keeping Faith: Memoirs of a President*. New York: Bantam Books, 1982.

Chang, Gordon H. *Friends and Enemies: The United States, China, and the Soviet Union, 1948–1972*. Stanford, Calif.: Stanford University Press, 1990.

Fairbank, John K. *The United States and China*. Cambridge, Mass.: Harvard University Press, 4th ed., 1979.

Goldstein, Joshua S., and John R. Freeman. *Three-Way Street: Strategic Reciprocity in World Politics*. Chicago: University of Chicago Press, 1990.

Hamrin, Carol Lee. "China Reassesses the Superpowers." *Pacific Affairs* 56:2 (Summer 1983):209–231.

Harding, Harry. *A Fragile Relationship: The United States and China Since 1972*. Washington, D.C.: Brookings Institution, 1992.

Harding, Harry, and Yuan Ming, eds. *Sino-American Relations, 1945–1955*: A Joint Reassessment of a Critical Decade. Wilmington, Del.: Scholarly Resources, 1989.

Hsiao, Gene T., and Michael Witunski, eds. *Sino-American Normalization and Its Policy Implications*. New York: Praeger, 1983.

Hunt, Michael H. *The Making of a Special Relationship: The United States and China to 1914*. New York: Columbia University Press, 1983.

Hunt, Michael, et al. *Mutual Images in U.S.-China Relations*. Occasional Paper No. 32. Washington, D.C.: Wilson Center, June 1988.

Johnson, U. Alexis, George R. Packard, and Alfred D. Wilhelm, Jr., eds. *China Policy for the Next Decade: Report of the Atlantic Council's Committee on China Policy*. Boston: Oelgeschlager, Gunn & Hain, 1984.

Kim, Ilpyong, ed. *The Strategic Triangle: China, the United States, and the Soviet Union*. New York: Paragon House, 1987.

Kissinger, Henry A. *White House Years*. Boston: Little, Brown, 1979.

_____ . *Years of Upheaval*. Boston: Little, Brown, 1982.

Lampton, David M. *A Relationship Restored: Trends in U.S.-China Educational Exchanges 1978–1984*. Washington, D.C.: National Academy Press, 1986.

Oksenberg, Michel. "A Decade of Sino-American Relations," *Foreign Affairs* 61 (Fall 1982):175–195.

Oksenberg, Michel, and Robert B. Oxnam, eds. *Dragon and Eagle: United States–China Relations: Past and Future*. New York: Basic Books, 1978.

Schaller, Michael. *The United States and China in the Twentieth Century*. New York: Oxford University Press, 2nd ed., 1990.

Segal, Gerald. *The Great Power Triangle*. London: Macmillan, 1982.

Shambaugh, David. *Beautiful Imperialist: China Perceives America, 1972–1990.* Princeton, N.J.: Princeton University Press, 1991.

―――― . "China's America Watchers." *Problems of Communism* 37 (May-August 1988):71–94.

Solomon, Richard H., ed. *The China Factor: Sino-American Relations and the Global Scene.* Englewood Cliffs, N.J.: Prentice-Hall, 1981.

Starr, John Bryan, ed. *The Future of U.S.–China Relations.* New York: New York University Press, 1981.

Sutter, Robert G. *China-Watch: Sino-American Reconciliation.* Baltimore: Johns Hopkins University Press, 1978.

Tucker, Nancy Bernkopf. *Patterns in the Dust: Chinese-American Relations and the Recognition Controversy, 1949–1950.* New York: Columbia University Press, 1983.

Whiting, Allen S. "Sino-American Relations: The Decade Ahead." *Orbis* 26 (Fall 1982):697–719.

China and Japan

China and Japan: History, Trends, and Prospects. China Quarterly No. 124 (December 1990).

Hellmann, Donald C., ed. *China and Japan: A New Balance of Power.* Lexington, Mass.: Lexington Books, 1976.

Hsiung, James C., and Steven I. Levine, eds. *China's Bitter Victory: The War with Japan 1937–1945.* Armonk, N.Y.: M. E. Sharpe, 1992.

Lee, Chae-Jin. *Japan Faces China: Political Economic Relations in the Postwar Era.* Baltimore, Md.: Johns Hopkins University Press, 1976.

―――― . *China and Japan: New Economic Diplomacy.* Stanford, Calif.: Hoover Institution Press, 1984.

Ono, Shuichi. *Sino-Japanese Economic Relationships: Trade, Direct Investment, and Future Strategy.* Washington, D.C.: World Bank, 1992.

Radtke, Kurt Werner. *China's Relations with Japan, 1945–83: The Role of Liao Chengzhi.* Manchester: Manchester University Press, 1990.

Taylor, Robert. *The Sino-Japanese Axis: A New Force in Asia?* London: Athlone Press, 1985.

―――― . *China, Japan, and the European Community.* London: Athlone Press, 1990.

Tow, William T. "Sino-Japanese Security Cooperation: Evolution and Prospects." *Pacific Affairs* 56 (Spring 1983):51–83.

Wang, Qingxin Ken. "Recent Japanese Economic Diplomacy in China." *Asian Survey* 33:6 (June 1993):625–641.

Whiting, Allen S. *China Eyes Japan.* Berkeley: University of California Press, 1989.

―――― . "China and Japan: Politics Versus Economics." *Annals of the American Academy of Political and Social Science* 519 (January 1992):39–51.

China and Europe

Bailes, Alyson J. "China and Eastern Europe: A Judgment on the Socialist Community." *Pacific Review* 3:3 (1990):222–242.

Biberaj, Elez. *Albania and China: A Study of an Unequal Alliance.* Boulder, Colo.: Westview Press, 1986.

Boardman, Robert. *Britain and the People's Republic of China 1949–1974.* New York: Macmillan, 1976.

Jain, Jagdish P. *China in World Politics: A Study of Sino-British Relations, 1949–1975.* New Delhi: Radiant Press, 1976.

Kapur, Harish. *China and the European Economic Community: The New Connection.* Boston: Martinus Nijhoff, 1986.

―――― . *Distant Neighbours: China and Europe.* London: Pinter 1990.

Shambaugh, David. "China and Europe." *Annals of the American Academy of Political and Social Science* 519 (January 1992):101–114.

Shaw, Yu-ming, ed. *China and Europe in the Twentieth Century.* Taipei: Institute of International Relations, 1986.

Stuart, Douglas T. "Prospects for Sino-European Security Cooperation." *Orbis* 26 (Fall 1982):721–747.

Stuart, Douglas T., and William T. Tow. "China's Military Modernization: The Western Arms Connection." *China Quarterly* No. 90 (June 1982):253–271.

Taylor, Robert. *China, Japan, and the European Community.* London: Athlone Press, 1990.

Tow, William T., and Douglas T. Stuart. "China's Military Turns to the West." *International Affairs* 57 (Spring 1981):286–300.

China and the Third World

Abidi, A.H.H. *China, Iran, and the Persian Gulf.* Atlantic Highlands, N.J.: Humanities Press, 1982.

Adel, Daljit Sen. *China and Her Neighbours.* New Delhi: Deep and Deep, 1984.

Bartke, Wolfgang. *China's Economic Aid to Developing and Socialist Countries.* New Providence, N.J.: K. G. Saur, 1989.

Behbehani, Hashim S.H. *China's Foreign Policy in the Arab World, 1955–75.* London: Kegan Paul International, 1981.

Calabrese, John. *China's Changing Relations with the Middle East.* London and New York: Garland, 1991.

———— . "Peaceful or Dangerous Collaborators? China's Relations with the Gulf Countries." *Pacific Affairs* 65:4 (Winter 1992–93):471–485.

Chang, Pao-min. *Kampuchea Between China and Vietnam.* Singapore: Singapore University Press, 1985.

———— . *The Sino-Vietnamese Territorial Dispute.* New York: Praeger, 1986.

Chen, King C., ed. *China and the Three Worlds.* White Plains, N.Y.: M. E. Sharpe, 1979.

Copper, John F. *China's Foreign Aid: An Instrument of Peking's Foreign Policy.* Lexington, Mass.: Lexington Books, 1976.

Garver, John W. "China and South Asia." *Annals of the American Academy of Political and Social Science* 519 (January 1992):67–85.

Harris, Lillian Craig. *China's Foreign Policy Toward the Third World.* New York: Praeger, 1985.

Harris, Lillian, and Robert Worden, eds. *China and the Third World: Champion or Challenger?* Dover, Mass.: Auburn House, 1986.

Harris, Nigel. *The End of the Third World: Newly Industrializing Countries and the Decline of an Ideology.* London: I. B. Taurius, 1986.

Horvath, Janos. *Chinese Technology Transfer to the Third World: A Grants Economy Analysis.* New York: Praeger, 1976.

Johnson, Cecil. *Communist China and Latin America.* New York: Columbia University Press, 1970.

Kim, Samuel S. *The Third World in Chinese World Policy.* Princeton, N.J.: Center of International Studies, Princeton University, 1989.

Krasner, Stephen D. *Structural Conflict: The Third World Against Global Liberalism.* Berkeley: University of California Press, 1985.

Larkin, Bruce D. *China and Africa 1949–1970.* Berkeley: University of California Press, 1971.

Lawson, Eugene K. *The Sino-Vietnamese Conflict.* New York: Praeger, 1984.

Lin, Teh-chang. "Foreign Aid: A Theoretical Framework for Analyzing Communist China's Foreign Policy." *Issues & Studies* 27:5 (May 1991):78–102.

Martin, Edwin W. *Southeast Asia and China: The End of Containment.* Boulder, Colo.: Westview Press, 1977.

Mortimer, Robert A. *The Third World Coalition in International Politics.* Boulder, Colo.: Westview Press, 2nd ed., 1984.

Neuhauser, Charles. *Third World Politics: China and the Afro-Asian People's Solidarity Organization, 1957–1967.* Cambridge, Mass.: Harvard University Press, 1968.

Ogunsanwo, Alaba. *China's Policy in Africa, 1958–1971.* New York: Cambridge University Press, 1979.

Ross, Robert S. *The Indochina Tangle: China's Vietnam Policy, 1975–1979.* New York: Columbia University Press, 1988.

———. "China and Post-Cambodia Southeast Asia: Coping with Success." *Annals of the American Academy of Political and Social Science* 519 (January 1992):52–66.

Rubinstein, Alvin, ed. *Soviet and Chinese Influence in the Third World.* New York: Praeger, 1975.

Schichor, Yitzhak. *The Middle East in China's Foreign Policy, 1949–1977.* New York: Cambridge University Press, 1979.

———. "China and the Middle East Since Tiananmen." *Annals of the American Academy of Political and Social Science* 519 (January 1992):86–100.

Segal, Gerald. "China and Africa." *Annals of the American Academy of Political and Social Science* 519 (January 1992):115–126.

Simon, Sheldon W. *The Broken Triangle: Peking, Djakarta, and the PKI.* Baltimore, Md.: Johns Hopkins University Press, 1969.

Singham, A. W. *The Non-Aligned Movement in World Politics.* Westport, Conn.: Whirlwind Books, 1978.

Snow, Philip. *The Star Raft: China's Encounter with Africa.* Ithaca, N.Y.: Cornell University Press, 1988.

South Commission. *The Challenge to the South.* New York: Oxford University Press, 1990.

Taylor, Jay. *China and Southeast Asia: Peking's Relations with Revolutionary Movements.* New York: Praeger, 2nd ed., 1976.

Van Ness, Peter. *Revolution and Chinese Foreign Policy: Peking's Support for Wars of National Liberation.* Berkeley: University of California Press, 1971.

Vertzberger, Yaacov. *The Enduring Entente: Sino-Pakistani Relations, 1960–1980.* New York: Praeger, 1983.

———. *Misperceptions in Foreign Policymaking: The Sino-Indian Conflict 1959–1962.* Boulder, Colo.: Westview Press, 1984.

———. *China's Southwestern Strategy: Encirclement and Counterencirclement.* Westport, Conn.: Greenwood, 1985.

Wang, Chien-hsun. "Peking's Latin American Policy in the 1980s." *Issues & Studies* 27:5 (May 1991):103–118.

Military and Strategic Policy

Adelman, Jonathan R., and Chih-yu Shih. *Symbolic War: The Chinese Use of Force, 1840–1980.* Taipei: Institute of International Relations, 1993.

Bitzinger, Richard A. "Arms to Go: Chinese Arms Sales to the Third World." *International Security* 17:2 (Fall 1992):84–111.

Chan, Steve. "Chinese Conflict Calculus and Behavior: Assessment from a Perspective of Conflict Management." *World Politics* 30:3 (April 1978):391–410.

Chen, King C. *China's War with Vietnam, 1979.* Stanford, Calif.: Hoover Institution Press, 1987.

Chen, Min. *The Strategic Triangle and Regional Conflicts: Lessons from the Indochina Wars.* Boulder, Colo.: Lynne Rienner, 1992.

Dellios, Rosita. *Modern Chinese Defense Strategy: Present Developments, Future Directions.* New York: St. Martin's Press, 1990.

Dittmer, Lowell. "The Strategic Triangle: An Elementary Game Theoretical Analysis." *World Politics* 33:4 (July 1981):485–515.

Dreyer, June T. *China's Military Power in the 1980s.* Washington, D.C.: China Council of the Asia Society, 1982.

Folta, Paul Humes. *From Swords to Plowshares? Defense Industry Reform in the PRC*. Boulder, Colo.: Westview Press, 1992.

Garrett, Banning, and Bonnie Glaser. *War and Peace: The Views from Moscow and Beijing*. Berkeley: University of California Institute of International Studies, 1984.

Grimmett, Richard F. *Conventional Arms Transfers to the Third World, 1984–1991*. Washington, D.C.: Congressional Research Service, Library of Congress, 92-577 F, July 20, 1992.

Godwin, Paul H.B., ed. *The Chinese Defense Establishment: Continuity and Change*. Boulder, Colo.: Westview Press, 1983.

Griffith, Samuel B., trans. *Sun Tzu: The Art of War*. New York: Oxford University Press, 1963.

Gurtov, Melvin, and Byong-moo Hwang. *China Under Threat: The Politics of Strategy and Diplomacy*. Baltimore, Md.: Johns Hopkins University Press, 1980.

Hood, Steven J. *Dragons Entangled: Indochina and the China-Vietnam War*. Armonk, N.Y.: M. E. Sharpe, 1992.

Jencks, Harlan W. *From Muskets to Missiles: Politics and Professionalism in the Chinese Army, 1945–1981*. Boulder, Colo.: Westview Press, 1982.

Joffe, Ellis. *The Chinese Army After Mao*. Cambridge, Mass.: Harvard University Press, 1987.

Johnston, Alastair I. *China and Arms Control*. Ottawa: Canadian Centre for Arms Control and Disarmament, 1986.

Kan, Shirley A. *Chinese Missile and Nuclear Proliferation: Issues for Congress*. Washington, D.C.: Congressional Research Service, Library of Congress, 1B92056, June 24, 1992.

Kierman, Frank A., and John K. Fairbank, eds. *Chinese Ways in Warfare*. Cambridge, Mass.: Harvard University Press, 1974.

Lewis, John Wilson, and Xue Litai. *China Builds the Bomb*. Stanford, Calif.: Stanford University Press, 1988.

Lewis, John W., Hua Di, and Xue Litai. "Beijing's Defense Establishment: Solving the Arms-Export Enigma." *International Security* 15:4 (Spring 1991):87–109.

Lin, Chong-pin. *China's Nuclear Weapons Strategy*. Lexington, Mass.: Lexington Books, 1988.

Lo, Chi-Kin. *China's Policy Towards Territorial Disputes: The Case of the South China Sea Islands*. London: Routledge, 1989.

Nelson, Harvey W. *Power and Insecurity: Beijing, Moscow, and Washington, 1949–1988*. Boulder, Colo.: Lynne Rienner, 1989.

Pollack, Jonathan D. *Security, Strategy, and the Logic of Chinese Foreign Policy*. Berkeley: University of California Institute of East Asian Studies, 1981.

Ryan, Mark A. *Chinese Attitudes Towards Nuclear Weapons: China and the United States During the Korean War*. Armonk, N.Y.: M. E. Sharpe, 1989.

Sawyer, Ralph D., trans. *The Seven Military Classics of Ancient China*. Boulder, Colo.: Westview Press, 1993.

Schichor, Yitzhak. *East Wind over Arabia*. Berkeley: University of California Institute of East Asian Studies, 1989.

Segal, Gerald. *Defending China*. New York: Oxford University Press, 1985.

Segal, Gerald, and William T. Tow, eds. *Chinese Defense Policy*. Urbana: University of Illinois Press, 1984.

Stockholm International Peace Research Institute (SIPRI). *SIPRI Yearbook 1992: World Armaments and Disarmament*. New York: Oxford University Press, 1992. (Annual.)

Stolper, Thomas. *China, Taiwan, and the Offshore Islands*. Armonk, N.Y.: M. E. Sharpe, 1985.

Tien, Chen-Ya. *Chinese Military Theory: Ancient and Modern*. London: Mosaic Press, 1992.

Whiting, Allen S. *China Crosses the Yalu: The Decision to Enter the Korean War*. New York: Macmillan, 1960.

———. *The Chinese Calculus of Deterrence: India and Indochina*. Ann Arbor: University of Michigan Press, 1975.

———. "The Use of Force in Foreign Policy by the People's Republic of China." *Annals of the American Academy of Political and Social Science* 402 (July 1972):55–66.

Wortzel, Larry M., ed. *China's Military Modernization: International Implications.* Westport, Conn.: Greenwood Press, 1988.

Yin, John. *Sino-Soviet Dialogue on the Problem of War.* The Hague: Martinus Nijhoff, 1971.

China and the Global Political Economy

Amin, Samir. *The Future of Maoism.* New York: Monthly Review Press, 1983.

Barnett, A. Doak. *China's Economy in Global Perspective.* Washington, D.C.: Brookings Institution, 1981.

Brahm, Laurence J. *Foreign Exchange Controls and Strategies for the People's Republic of China.* Hong Kong: Longman Group, 1990.

Crane, George T. *The Political Economy of China's Special Economic Zones.* Armonk, N.Y.: M. E. Sharpe, 1990.

Gray, Jack, and Gordon White, eds. *China's New Development Strategy.* New York: Academic Press, 1982.

Grub, Phillip Donald, and Jian Hai Lin. *Foreign Direct Investment in China.* New York: Quorum Books, 1991.

Hooke, A. W., ed. *The Fund and China in the International Monetary System.* Washington, D.C.: International Monetary Fund, 1983.

Hsiao, Gene T. *The Foreign Trade of China: Policy, Law, and Practice.* Berkeley: University of California Press, 1977.

Hsu, John. *China's Foreign Trade Reforms: Impact on Growth and Stability.* Cambridge: Cambridge University Press, 1989.

International Monetary Fund. *World Economic Outlook.* Washington, D.C.: IMF, May 1983. (Annual.)

_____. *Direction of Trade Statistics Yearbook 1992.* Washington, D.C.: IMF, 1992.

Khan, Zafar Shah. *Patterns of Direct Foreign Investment in China.* Washington, D.C.: World Bank, 1991.

Kleinberg, Robert. *China's "Opening" to the Outside World: The Experiment with Foreign Capitalism.* Boulder, Colo.: Westview Press, 1990.

Lardy, Nicholas. *Foreign Trade and Economic Reform in China, 1978–1990.* Cambridge: Cambridge University Press, 1992.

Lim, Edwin, et al. *China: Long-Term Development Issues and Options.* Baltimore, Md.: Johns Hopkins University Press for the World Bank, 1985.

Lin Teh-chang. "Foreign Aid: A Theoretical Framework for Analyzing Communist China's Foreign Policy." *Issues & Studies* 27:5 (May 1991):78–102.

Maxwell, Neville, and Bruce McFarlane, eds. *China's Changed Road to Development.* Oxford: Pergamon Press, 1984.

McDonnell, J.E.D. "China's Move to Rejoin the GATT." *World Economy* 10:3 (September 1987):331–350.

Organization for Economic Cooperation and Development. *The Aid Programme of China.* Paris: OECD, March 1987.

Pearson, Margaret M. *Joint Ventures in the People's Republic of China.* Princeton, N.J.: Princeton University Press, 1991.

Reynolds, Paul D. *China's International Banking and Financial System.* New York: Praeger, 1982.

Sheahan, John. *Alternative International Economic Strategies and Their Relevance for China.* Washington, D.C.: World Bank, 1986.

Teng, Weizao, and N. T. Wang, eds. *Transnational Corporations and China's Open Door Policy.* Lexington, Mass.: Lexington Books, 1988.

United Nations. *World Investment Report 1992: Transnational Corporations as Engines of Growth.* New York: United Nations, 1992.

UN Centre on Transnational Corporations. *Foreign Direct Investment in the People's Republic of China.* New York: United Nations, 1988.

U.S. Congress, Joint Economic Committee. *China's Economic Dilemmas in the 1990s: The Problems of Reforms, Modernization, and Interdependence.* 2 vols. Washington, D.C.: U.S. Government Printing Office, 1991.

Wang, Hong. *China's Exports Since 1979.* New York: St. Martin's Press, 1993.

Wang, N. T. *China's Modernization and Transnational Corporations.* Lexington, Mass.: Lexington Books, 1984.

World Bank. *China Between Plan and Market.* Washington, D.C.: World Bank, 1991.

————. *China: Reform and the Role of the Plan in the 1990s.* Washington, D.C.: World Bank, 1992.

————. *World Development Report 1993.* New York: Oxford University Press, 1993. (Annual.)

Yeats, Alexander J. *China's Foreign Trade and Comparative Advantage: Prospects, Problems, and Policy Implications.* Washington, D.C.: World Bank, 1991.

Chinese and Global Human Rights

Aird, John S. *Slaughter of the Innocents: Coercive Birth Control in China.* Washington, D.C.: American Enterprise Institute Press, 1990.

Amnesty International. *China: The Massacre of June 1989 and Its Aftermath.* New York: Amnesty International, April 1990.

————. *China: Punishment Without Crime.* New York: Amnesty International, September 1991.

————. *China: Continued Patterns of Human Rights Violations in China.* New York: Amnesty International, May 1992.

————. *China: Torture in China.* New York: Amnesty International, December 1992.

————. *China: Update on Torture.* New York: Amnesty International, March 1993.

————. *Amnesty International Report 1993.* New York: Amnesty International, 1993. (Annual.)

Asia Watch. *Punishment Season: Human Rights in China After Martial Law.* New York: Asia Watch, 1990.

————. *Freedom of Religion in China.* New York: Asia Watch, January 1992.

————. *Anthems of Defeat: Crackdown in Hunan Province, 1989–1992.* New York: Asia Watch, 1992.

————. *Continuing Religious Repression in China.* New York: Asia Watch, June 1993.

Cheng, Chester J. *Documents of Dissent: Chinese Political Thought Since Mao.* Stanford, Calif.: Hoover Institution Press, 1980.

Chiu, Hungdah. "Chinese Attitudes Toward International Law of Human Rights," in Victor Falkenheim, ed., *Chinese Politics from Mao to Deng.* New York: Paragon House, 1989, pp. 237–270.

Cohen, Roberta. "People's Republic of China: The Human Rights Exception." *Human Rights Quarterly* 9:4 (November 1987):447–549.

Copper, John F., Franz Michael, and Yuan-li Wu. *Human Rights in Post-Mao China.* Boulder, Colo.: Westview Press, 1985.

Donnelly, Jack. *Universal Human Rights in Theory and Practice.* Ithaca, N.Y.: Cornell University Press, 1989.

Drinan, Robert F., and Teresa T. Kuo. "The 1991 Battle for Human Rights in China." *Human Rights Quarterly* 14:1 (February 1992):21–42.

Edwards, R. Randle, Louis Henkin, and Andrew J. Nathan. *Human Rights in Contemporary China.* New York: Columbia University Press, 1986.

Falk, Richard. *Human Rights and State Sovereignty.* New York: Holmes & Meier, 1981.

Forsythe, David P. *The Internationalization of Human Rights.* Lexington, Mass.: Lexington Books, 1991.

————, ed. *Human Rights and Development: International Views.* New York: St. Martin's Press, 1989.

Gastil, Raymond D., ed. *Freedom in the World: Political Rights and Civil Liberties 1983–1984.* Westport, Conn.: Greenwood Press, 1984, esp. Part 3.

Goldman, Merle. "Human Rights in the People's Republic of China." *Dædalus* 112:4 (1983):111–138.

Grunfeld, A. Tom. *The Making of Modern Tibet.* London: Oxford University Press, 1987.

Han Minzhu, ed. *Cries for Democracy: Writings and Speeches from the 1989 Chinese Democracy Movement.* Princeton, N.J.: Princeton University Press, 1990.

Hsiung, James C., ed. *Human Rights in East Asia: A Cultural Perspective.* New York: Paragon House, 1985.

Human Rights Watch. *The Human Rights Watch Global Report on Prisons.* New York: Human Rights Watch, 1993.

International Campaign for Tibet. *Forbidden Freedoms: Beijing's Control of Religion in Tibet.* Washington, D.C.: International Campaign for Tibet, 1990.

Kent, Ann. *Between Freedom and Subsistence: China and Human Rights.* New York: Oxford University Press, 1993.

———. "Waiting for Rights: China's Human Rights and China's Constitutions, 1949–1989," *Human Rights Quarterly* 13:2 (May 1991):193–199.

Lee, Jae Jin. *China's Korean Minority: The Politics of Ethnic Education.* Boulder, Colo.: Westview Press, 1986.

Liu Binyan. *China's Crisis, China's Hope.* Cambridge, Mass.: Harvard University Press, 1990.

Nathan, Andrew J. *Chinese Democracy.* New York: Columbia University Press, 1985.

———. *China's Crisis: Dilemmas of Reform and Prospects for Democracy.* New York: Columbia University Press, 1991.

Rummel, R. J. *China's Bloody Century: Genocide and Mass Murder Since 1990.* New Brunswick, N.J.: Transaction Publishers, 1991.

Seymour, James D., ed. *China: The Fifth Modernization, China's Human Rights Movement, 1978–1979.* Stanfordville, N.Y.: Coleman Enterprises, 1980.

———. "Human Rights and the Law in the People's Republic of China," in Victor Falkenheim, ed., *Chinese Politics from Mao to Deng.* New York: Paragon House, 1989, pp. 271–297.

———. "The Rights of Ethnic Minorities in China: Lessons of the Soviet Demise." *American Asian Review* 11:2 (Summer 1993):44–56.

United States Department of State. *Country Reports on Human Rights Practices for 1992.* Washington, D.C.: U.S. Government Printing Office, 1993. (Annual.)

United Nations. *Human Rights: Status of International Instruments.* New York: United Nations, 1987.

United Nations Development Program. *Human Development Report 1993.* New York: Oxford University Press, 1993. (Annual.)

Van Ness, Peter. "Human Rights and International Relations in East Asia." *Ethics and International Politics* (July 1992):43–52.

Van Walt van Praag, Michael C. *The Status of Tibet: History, Rights, and Prospects in International Law.* Boulder, Colo.: Westview Press, 1987.

Vincent, R. J. *Human Rights and International Relations.* New York: Cambridge University Press, 1986.

Wu, Hongda Harry. *Laogai: The Chinese Gulag.* Boulder, Colo.: Westview Press, 1992.

Wu, Yuan-li, et al. *Human Rights in the People's Republic of China.* Boulder, Colo.: Westview Press, 1988.

Science and Technology

Bauer, E. E. *China Takes Off: Technology Transfer and Modernization.* Seattle: University of Washington Press, 1986.

China's Scientific and Technological Modernization: Domestic and International Implications. Occasional Paper No. 11. Washington, D.C.: Wilson Center, 1982.

Gelber, Harry. *Technology, Defense, and External Relations in China, 1975–78.* Boulder, Colo.: Westview Press, 1979.

Haas, Ernst B., Mary Pat Williams, and Don Babai. *Scientists and World Order: The Uses of Technical Knowledge in International Organizations.* Berkeley: University of California Press, 1977.

Leibo, Steven A. *Transferring Technology to China.* Berkeley: University of California Institute of East Asian Studies, 1985.

Liu Jing-tong. *On Introducing Technology to China.* New York: China-International Business Series, Columbia University, 1983.

Orleans, Leo. *Science in Contemporary China.* Stanford, Calif.: Stanford University Press, 1981.

Ostron, Benjamin C. *Conquering Resources: The Growth and Development of the PLA's Science and Technology Commission for National Defense.* Armonk, N.Y.: M. E. Sharpe, 1991.

Ridley, Charles P. *China's Scientific Policies: Implications for International Cooperation.* Washington, D.C.: American Enterprise Institute for Public Policy Research, 1976.

Saich, Tony. *China's Science Policy in the 80s.* Manchester: University of Manchester Press, 1989.

Simon, Denis Fred, and Merle Goldman, eds. *Science and Technology in Post-Mao China.* Cambridge, Mass.: Harvard University Press, 1989.

Suttmeier, Richard P. *Science, Technology, and China's Drive for Modernization.* Stanford, Calif.: Hoover Institution Press, 1980.

U.S. Congress, Office of Technology Assessment. *Technology Transfer to China.* Washington, D.C.: Office of Technology Assessment, 1987.

Environmental Issues

Conly, Shanti R., and Sharon L. Camp. *China's Family Planning Program: Challenging the Myths.* Country Study Series No. 1. Washington, D.C.: Population Crisis Committee, 1992.

Hao, Yufan. "Environmental Protection in Chinese Foreign Policy." *Journal of Northeast Asian Studies* 11:3 (Fall 1992):25–46.

He Bochuan. *China on the Edge: The Crisis of Ecology and Development.* San Francisco: China Books and Periodicals, 1991.

Glaeser, Bernhard, ed. *Learning from China?* London: Allen & Unwin, 1987.

Goldstone, Jack A. "Imminent Political Conflict Arising from China's Environmental Crises." *Occasional Paper Series of the Project on Environmental Change and Acute Conflict* No. 2 (December 1992):41–58.

Jhaveri, Nayna. "The Three Gorges Debacle." *Ecologist* 18:2 (1988):56–63.

Luk, Shiu-hung, and Joseph Whitney, eds. *Megaproject: A Case Study of China's Three Gorges Project.* Armonk, N.Y.: M. E. Sharpe, 1992.

Ostrom, Elinor. *Governing the Commons: The Evolution of Institutions for Collective Action.* New York: Cambridge University Press, 1990.

Robinson, Thomas W., ed. *The Foreign Relations of China's Environmental Policy.* Washington, D.C.: American Enterprise Institute Press, August 1992.

Ross, Lester. *Environmental Policy in China.* Bloomington: Indiana University Press, 1988.

Ross, Lester, and Mitchell A. Silk. *Environmental Law and Policy in the People's Republic of China.* New York: Quorum Books, 1987.

Ryle, Martin. *Ecology and Socialism.* London: Radius, 1988.

Smil, Vaclav. *China's Environmental Crisis: An Inquiry into the Limits of National Development.* Armonk, N.Y.: M. E. Sharpe, 1993.

———. "Environmental Change as a Source of Conflict and Economic Losses in China." *Occasional Paper Series of the Project on Environmental Change and Acute Conflict* No. 2 (December 1992):5–39.

Woodard, Kim. *The International Energy Relations of China.* Stanford, Calif.: Stanford University Press, 1980.

World Bank. *Environment and Development.* Washington, D.C.: World Bank, 1984.

_____ . *The World Bank and the Environment: First Annual Report Fiscal 1990*. Washington, D.C.: World Bank, 1990.

_____ . *World Development Report 1992*: Development and the Environment. New York: Oxford University Press, 1992.

World Commission on Environment and Development. *Our Common Future*. New York: Oxford University Press, 1987.

World Resources Institute. *World Resources 1990–91*. New York: Oxford University Press, 1990.

Worldwatch Institute. *State of the World 1993*. New York: W. W. Norton, 1993. (Annual.)

Young, Oran R. *International Cooperation: Building Regimes for Natural Resources and the Environment*. Ithaca, N.Y.: Cornell University Press, 1989.

National Identity and "Greater China"

Bloom, William. *Personal Identity, National Identity, and International Relations*. New York: Cambridge University Press, 1990.

Chan, Steve, and Cal Clark. *Flexibility, Foresight, and Fortune in Taiwan's Development: Navigating Between Scylla and Charybdis*. London: Routledge, 1992.

Chang, Parris H., and Martin H. Lasater. *If PRC Crosses the Taiwan Strait: The International Response*. Lanham, Md.: University Press of America, 1992.

Cheng, Tun-jen, and Stephan Haggard, eds. *Political Change in Taiwan*. Boulder, Colo.: Lynne Rienner, 1992.

Chien, Frederick F. "A View from Taipei." *Foreign Affairs* 70:5 (Winter 1991–1992):93–103.

Chiu, Hungdah, Y. C. Jao, and Yuan-li Wu. *The Future of Hong Kong: Toward 1997 and Beyond*. Westport, Conn.: Greenwood Press, 1987.

Clough, Ralph N. *Reaching Across the Taiwan Strait*. Boulder, Colo.: Westview Press, 1993.

Cushman, Jennifer, and Wang Gungwu, eds. *Changing Identities of the Southeast Asian Chinese Since World War II*. Hong Kong: Hong Kong University Press, 1988.

Dittmer, Lowell, and Samuel Kim, eds. *China's Quest for National Identity*. Ithaca, N.Y.: Cornell University Press, 1993.

Gellner, Ernest. *Nations and Nationalism*. Ithaca, N.Y.: Cornell University Press, 1983.

Gladney, Dru C. *Muslim Chinese: Ethnic Nationalism in the People's Republic*. Cambridge, Mass.: Council on East Asian Studies, Harvard East Asian Monograph No. 149, 1991.

Grunfeld, A. Tom. *The Making of Modern Tibet*. Armonk, N.Y.: M. E. Sharpe, 1987.

Haggard, Stephan. *Pathways from the Periphery: The Politics of Growth in the Newly Industrializing Countries*. Ithaca, N.Y.: Cornell University Press, 1990.

Harding, Harry. *China and Northeast Asia: The Political Dimension*. New York: Asia Society, 1988.

Hartland-Thunberg, Penelope. *China, Hong Kong, Taiwan, and the World Trading System*. New York: St. Martin's Press, 1991.

Heberer, Thomas. *China and Its National Minorities: Autonomy or Assimilation*. Armonk, N.Y.: M. E. Sharpe, 1989.

Lin, Zhiling, and Thomas W. Robinson, eds. *The Chinese and Their Future: Beijing, Taipei, and Hong Kong*. Washington, D.C.: American Enterprise Institute Press, 1992.

Long, Simon. *Taiwan: China's Last Frontier*. New York: St. Martin's Press, 1991.

Morley, James W., ed. *Driven by Growth: Political Change in the Asia-Pacific Region*. Armonk, N.Y.: M. E. Sharpe, 1993.

Myers, Raymond H., ed. *The Republic of China and the People's Republic of China: Two Societies in Opposition*. Stanford, Calif.: Hoover Institution Press, 1991.

Oborne, Michael West, and Nicolas Fourt. *Pacific Basin Economic Cooperation*. Paris: OECD, 1983.

Pye, Lucian W. "How China's Nationalism Was Shanghaied." *Australian Journal of Chinese Affairs* 29 (January 1993):107–133.

Simon, Denis Fred, and Michael Y.M. Kau, eds. *Taiwan: Beyond the Economic Miracle*. Armonk, N.Y.: M. E. Sharpe, 1992.

Sung, Yun-Wing. *The China–Hong Kong Connection: The Key to China's Open-Door Policy.* New York: Cambridge University Press, 1991.

Sutter, Robert, ed. *Taiwan's Role in World Affairs.* Boulder, Colo.: Westview Press, 1994.

Tien, Hung-mao. *The Great Transition: Political and Social Change in the Republic of China.* Stanford, Calif.: Hoover Institution Press, 1989.

Van Walt van Praag, Michael C. *The Status of Tibet: History, Rights, and Prospects in International Law.* Boulder, Colo.: Westview Press, 1987.

Vogel, Ezra F. *The Four Little Dragons: The Spread of Industrialization in East Asia.* Cambridge, Mass.: Harvard University Press, 1991.

Wang Gungwu. *China and the Chinese Overseas.* Singapore: Times Academic Press, 1991.

———. *The Chineseness of China: Selected Essays.* Oxford: Oxford University Press, 1992.

Yee, Herbert S. "China and the Pacific Community Concept." *The World Today* (February 1983), pp. 68–74.

International Law and International Organizations

Bartke, Wolfgang. *The Agreements of the People's Republic of China with Foreign Countries 1949–1990.* München: Institute of Asian Affairs Hamburg, 2nd and enl. ed., 1992.

Chai, Trong R. "Chinese Policy Toward the Third World and the Superpowers in the UN General Assembly 1971–1977: A Voting Analysis." *International Organization* 33 (Summer 1979):391–403.

Chan, Gerald. *China and International Organizations: Participation in Non-Governmental Organizations Since 1971.* New York: Oxford University Press, 1989.

Chang, Luke T. *China's Boundary Treaties and Frontier Disputes.* Dobbs Ferry, N.Y.: Oceana, 1982.

Chiu, Hungdah. *Agreements of the People's Republic of China: A Calendar of Events 1966–1980.* New York: Praeger, 1981.

———. "Chinese Attitudes Toward International Law of Human Rights," in Victor Falkenheim, ed., *Chinese Politics from Mao to Deng.* New York: Paragon House, 1989, pp. 237–270.

———. "Chinese Attitudes Toward International Law in the Post-Mao Era, 1978–1987." *International Lawyer* 21:4 (Fall 1987):1127–1166.

Chiu, Hungdah, and Shao-chuan Leng, eds. *Law in Chinese Foreign Policy: Communist China and Selected Problems of International Law.* Dobbs Ferry, N.Y.: Oceana, 1972.

Chu, Yun-han, ed. *The Role of Taiwan in International Economic Organizations.* Taipei: Institute for National Policy Research, 1990.

Cohen, Jerome Alan, ed. *China's Practice of International Law: Some Case Studies.* Cambridge, Mass.: Harvard University Press, 1972.

Cohen, Jerome Alan, and Hungdah Chiu. *People's China and International Law: A Documentary Study,* 2 vols. Princeton, N.J.: Princeton University Press, 1974.

Feinerman, James V. "The Quest for GATT Membership." *China Business Review* 19 (May-June 1992):24–27.

Franck, Thomas M. *The Power of Legitimacy Among Nations.* New York: Oxford University Press, 1990.

Greenfield, Jeanette. *China and the Law of the Sea, Air, and Environment.* Germantown, Md.: Sijthoff & Noordhoff, 1979.

———. *China's Practice in the Law of the Sea.* Oxford: Clarendon Press, 1992.

Hartland-Thunberg, Penelope. "China's Modernization: A Challenge for the GATT." *Washington Quarterly* 10 (Spring 1987):81–97.

Herzstein, Robert E. "China and the GATT: Legal and Policy Issues Raised by China's Participation in the General Agreement on Tariffs and Trade." *Law and Policy in International Business* 18 (1986):371–415.

Hooke, A. W., ed. *The Fund and China in the International Monetary System.* Washington, D.C.: International Monetary Fund, 1983.

Hsiung, James C. *Law and Policy in China's Foreign Relations: A Study of Attitudes and Practice.* New York: Columbia University Press, 1972.

International Monetary Fund. *China: Economic Reform and Macroeconomic Management.* Occasional Paper No. 76. Washington, D.C.: IMF, January 1991.

Jacobson, Harold K., and Michel Oksenberg. *China's Participation in the IMF, the World Bank, and GATT.* Ann Arbor: University of Michigan Press, 1990.

Johnston, Douglas M., and Hungdah Chiu. *Agreements of the People's Republic of China 1949–1967: A Calendar.* Cambridge, Mass.: Harvard University Press, 1968.

Kenworthy, James L. *Guide to the Laws, Regulations, and Policies of the People's Republic of China on Foreign Trade and Investments.* New York: William S. Hein, 1990.

Kim, Samuel S. *China, the United Nations, and World Order.* Princeton, N.J.: Princeton University Press, 1979.

————— . "The People's Republic of China and the Charter-Based International Legal Order." *American Journal of International Law* 62 (April 1978):317–349.

————— . "Whither Post-Mao Chinese Global Policy?" *International Organization* 35 (Summer 1981):433 –465.

————— . "The Development of International Law in Post-Mao China: Change and Continuity." *Journal of Chinese Law* 1:2 (Fall 1987):117 –160.

————— . "Reviving International Law in China's Foreign Relations," in June T. Dreyer, ed., *Chinese Defense and Foreign Policy.* New York: Paragon House, 1989, pp. 87–131.

————— . "International Organizations in Chinese Foreign Policy." *Annals of the American Academy of Political and Social Science* 519 (January 1992):140–157.

Lichtenstein, Natalie G. "The People's Republic of China and Revision of the United Nations Charter." *Harvard International Law Journal* 18 (Summer 1977):629–647.

————— . "China's Participation in International Organizations." *China Business Review* 6 (May – June 1979):28–36.

McDonnell, J.E.D. "China's Move to Rejoin the GATT System: An Epic Transition." *World Economy* 10 (September 1987):331–350.

McKenzie, Paul D. "China's Application to the GATT: State Trading and the Problem of Market Access." *Journal of World Trade* 24 (October 1990):133–150.

Moser, Michael, ed. *Foreign Trade, Investment, and the Law in the People's Republic of China.* New York: Oxford University Press, 1987.

Oldham, John R., ed. *China's Legal Development.* Armonk, N.Y.: M. E. Sharpe, 1986.

Rajan, M. S., V. S. Mani, and C.S.R. Murthy, eds. *The Nonaligned and the United Nations.* New York: Oceana, 1987.

Salem, David. *The People's Republic of China, International Law, and Arms Control.* Baltimore, Md.: Occasional Papers/Reprint Series in Contemporary Asian Studies, 1983.

Scott, Gary L. *Chinese Treaties: The Post-Revolutionary Restoration of International Law and Order.* Dobbs Ferry, N.Y.: Oceana, 1975.

Shinobu, Takashi. "China's Bilateral Treaties, 1973–82: A Quantitative Study." *International Studies Quarterly* 31:4 (December 1987):439–456.

Tzou, Byron N. *China and International Law: The Boundary Disputes.* New York: Praeger, 1990.

United Nations Development Program. *UNDP in China.* New York: UNDP, September 1989.

Van Walt van Praag, Michael C. *The Status of Tibet: History, Rights, and Prospects in International Law.* Boulder, Colo.: Westview Press, 1987.

Weng, Byron S.J. *Peking's UN Policy: Continuity and Change.* New York: Praeger, 1972.

Yuan, Paul C. "The United Nations Convention on the Law of the Sea from a Chinese Perspective," *Texas International Law Journal* 19:2 (1984):415–433.

The Future of China and World Order

Bachman, David. "The Limits to Leadership." *NBR Analysis* 3:3 (August 1992):23–35.

Camilleri, Joseph, and Jim Falk. *The End of Sovereignty? The Politics of a Shrinking and Fragmenting World.* Aldershot, England: Edward Elgar, 1992.

"China in Transformation," *Dædalus* 122 (Spring 1993).

Garver, John W. "China and the New World Order," in William A. Joseph, ed., *China Briefing, 1992.* Boulder, Colo.: Westview Press, 1993, pp. 55–80.

Hamrin, Carol Lee. *China and the Challenge of the Future: Changing Political Patterns.* Boulder, Colo.: Westview Press, 1990.

Hsiung, James C., and Samuel S. Kim, eds. *China in the Global Community.* New York: Praeger, 1980.

Jacobson, Harold K., and Michel Oksenberg. *China's Participation in the IMF, the World Bank, and GATT.* Ann Arbor: University of Michigan Press, 1990.

Jervis, Robert. "The Future of World Politics: Will It Resemble the Past?" *International Security* 16:3 (Winter 1991–1992):39–45.

Kennedy, Paul. *Preparing for the Twentieth-First Century.* New York: Random House, 1993.

Kim, Samuel S. *China In and Out of the Changing World Order.* Princeton, N.J.: Center of International Studies, Princeton University, 1991.

Lampton, David M., and Catherine H. Keyser, eds. *China's Global Presence: Economics, Politics, and Security.* Washington, D.C.: American Enterprise Institute Press, 1988.

Lardy, Nicholas R. "China's Growing Economic Role in Asia." *NBR Analysis* 3:3 (August 1992):5–12.

Lieberthal, Kenneth. "China in the Year 2000: Politics and International Security." *NBR Analysis* 3:3 (August 1992):13–22.

Mackay, Louis. *China, a Power for Peace?* London: Merlin Press, 1986.

Miller, Lynn H. *Global Order: Values and Power in International Politics.* Boulder, Colo.: Westview Press, 2nd ed., 1990.

Oksenberg, Michel. "China Joins the World: Prospects and Implications." *Issues in Science and Technology* 1:3 (Spring 1985):113-127.

Oksenberg, Michel, and Kenneth Lieberthal. "Forecasting China's Future." *National Interest* No. 5 (Fall 1986):18–27.

Sutter, Robert. "China's View of the 'New World Order': Possible Implications for Sino-U.S. Relations." *CRS Report for Congress* (September 11, 1991).

Tung, Shih-Chung. *The Policy of China in the Third United Nations Conference on the Law of the Sea.* Geneva: Graduate Institute of International Studies, 1981.

Wang, Jianwei, and Zhimin Lin. "Chinese Perceptions in the Post–Cold War Era." *Asian Survey* 32:10 (October 1992):902–917.

Whiting, Allen S. *China's Future.* New York: McGraw-Hill, 1977.

———. "China and the Superpowers: Toward the Year 2000." *Dædalus* 109 (Fall 1980):97–113.

Woodruff, John. *China in Search of Its Future.* Seattle: University of Washington Press, 1989.

About the Book

As the postwar international system continues its dramatic transformation, the fundamental question of what role China will play is becoming increasingly central. In this thoroughly revised and updated edition of *China and the World,* the contributors focus on the developments of the post-Tiananmen years, addressing the issues raised by China's expanding and increasingly complex relationships with a rapidly changing global environment. They consider such questions as: What is the principal challenge of post-Tiananmen foreign policy? How will China cope with the call for a more peaceful, equitable, democratic, and ecological world order? How has the nexus between China and the world changed in this transition period, and why? What are the implications for China's future and for the future of the rest of the world?

Combining a broad theoretical framework with specific case studies, this text tackles themes that have long puzzled Westerners. Seeking the often elusive sources of Chinese foreign policy, the contributors assess the relative influences of domestic and foreign factors in shaping policy goals. They also examine the changes and continuities that have characterized Chinese foreign relations over the years, identifying the patterns underlying China's interactions with the major global actors and its policies on specific international issues. Special attention is paid to the word/deed (and at times word/word) disjuncture in Chinese foreign relations, with several chapters probing the discrepancies between rhetoric and reality, policy pronouncements and policy performance, and intent and outcome. In addition, there is a new chapter focused specifically on the vitally important human-rights component of China's foreign policy. The concluding chapter identifies and explores China's foreign policy options for the last decade of the century.

About the Editor
and Contributors

Samuel S. Kim (Ph.D., Columbia), formerly a Fulbright professor at the Foreign Affairs Institute, Beijing, China (1985–1986), and a professor at Princeton University (1986–1993), is Senior Research Scholar at the East Asian Institute of Columbia University. He is the author or editor of over a dozen books on Chinese foreign policy and world order studies. His articles have appeared in leading professional journals on China and international relations, including *American Journal of International Law, China Quarterly, International Interactions, International Organization, Journal of Chinese Law, Journal of Peace Research, World Politics,* and *World Policy Journal.*

David Bachman (Ph.D., Stanford) is an associate professor at the Henry M. Jackson School of International Studies, University of Washington. He is the author of *Chen Yun and the Chinese Political System; Bureaucracy, Economy, and Leadership in China: The Institutional Origins of the Great Leap Forward;* and *Yan Jiaqi and China's Struggle for Democracy* (coeditor and cotranslator with Yang Dali). His articles have appeared in *Asian Survey, Current History, Fletcher Forum of World Affairs, Issues & Studies, Pacific Affairs,* and *World Politics.*

Lowell Dittmer (Ph.D., Chicago) is professor of political science at the University of California, Berkeley. He is the author of several books including *China's Continous Revolution: The Post-Revolutionary Epoch, 1949–1981,* and *Sino-Soviet Normalization and Its International Implications, 1945–1990.* His articles have appeared in *American Political Science Review, China Quarterly, Problems of Communism,* and *World Politics.*

William R. Feeney (Ph.D., SAIS, Johns Hopkins) is a professor of political science at Southern Illinois University at Edwardsville. He is coeditor, with William T. Tow, of *U.S. Foreign Policy and Asian-Pacific Security* and is a contributor to anthologies. He has published articles in *Asian Affairs, Current History, Korea and World Affairs, Asian Thought & Society, Asian Survey,* and *Current Scene.*

Edward Friedman (Ph.D., Harvard) is professor of political science at the University of Wisconsin, Madison. He is the editor of *The Politics of Democratization: Vicissitudes and Universals in the East Asian Experience* and coauthor of *Chinese Village, Socialist State.* He has served as a consultant on China for the United Nations and as a staff member of the Foreign Affairs Committee of the U.S. House of Representatives.

Paul H.B. Godwin (Ph.D., Minnesota) is professor of national security policy at the National War College. He is coauthor of *The Making of a Model Citizen in Communist China,* editor of and contributor to *The Chinese Defense Establishment: Continuity and Change in the 1980s,* and a contributor to various anthologies. His articles have appeared in *Comparative Politics, Problems* *of Communism, Comparative Communism, Contemporary China,* and *China Quarterly.* He was a visiting professor in the fall of 1987 at the Chinese People's Liberation Army National Defense University in Beijing, China.

Donald W. Klein (Ph.D., Columbia) is professor of political science at Tufts University. He is co-author of *Biographic Dictionary of Chinese Communism, 1921–1965* and *Rebels and Bureaucrats: China's December 9ers* and is a frequent contributor to anthologies and learned journals. He is an editorial board member of *China Quarterly, Asian Survey,* and *Pacific Affairs.*

Steven I. Levine (Ph.D., Harvard), currently visiting professor of political science at the University of Michigan, is Senior Research Associate at Boulder Run Research in Hillsborough, N.C. He is the author of *Anvil of Victory: The Communist Revolution in Manchuria, 1945–1948* and coeditor of *China's Bitter Victory: The War with Japan, 1937–1945* (with James C. Hsiung) and has contributed numerous articles to conference volumes and to such journals as *Political Science Quarterly, Asian Survey, International Journal,* and *Problems of Communism.* He is currently collaborating with Andrew Nathan on a book on Chinese foreign policy.

Thomas W. Robinson (Ph.D., Columbia) is president of American Asian Research Enterprises, Arlington, Va., adjunct professor of national security at Georgetown University, and course chairperson (China) at the Foreign Service Institute, Department of State. Formerly director of the Asian Studies Program at the American Enterprise Institute, Washington, D.C., he is the author, editor, or coeditor of *Chinese Foreign Policy: Ideas and Interpretations; The Chinese and Their Future: Beijing, Hong Kong, and Taipei; Democracy and Development in East Asia: South Korea, Taiwan, and the Philippines; New Ideas and Concepts in Sino-American Relations; The Foreign Relations of China's Environmental Policy; Forecasting in International Relations;* and *The Cultural Revolution in China.* His articles and chapters on Chinese politics and foreign relations have appeared in over fifty other books and journals. He is currently writing books on Chinese foreign policy, Asian security, Lin Biao's biography, and Russia in post–Cold War Asia, as well as a television series on China.

James D. Seymour (Ph.D., Columbia) is Senior Research Scholar at Columbia University's East Asian Institute. His books include *China: The Politics of Revolutionary Reintegration; The Fifth Modernization: China's Human Rights Movement, 1978–1979;* and *China's Satellite Parties.* He is also the author of many journal and reference-volume articles about China and about human rights and is currently working on a book about recent Tibetan politics.

Allen S. Whiting (Ph.D., Columbia) was director of the Office of Research and Analysis, Far East, in the U.S. Department of State (1962–1966) and deputy consul general, Hong Kong (1966–1968), and is currently a professor of political science at the University of Arizona. He has produced many books, including *China Crosses the Yalu, The Chinese Calculus of Deterrence, Siberian Development and East Asia, China Eyes Japan,* and *China's Foreign Relations* (ed.), and has contributed numerous articles to leading professional journals on China and international relations.

Index